NORTHWEST
GARDENER'S HANDBOOK

First published in 2014 by Cool Springs Press, an imprint of Quarto Publishing Group USA Inc.,
400 First Avenue North, Suite 400, Minneapolis, MN 55401

Cool Springs Press titles are also available at discounts in bulk quantity for industrial or sales-
promotional use. For details write to Special Sales Manager at Quarto Publishing Group USA Inc.,
400 First Avenue North, Suite 400, Minneapolis, MN 55401 USA. To find out more about our books,
visit us online at www.coolspringspress.com.

Library of Congress Cataloging-in-Publication Data

Mulvihill, Susan.
  Northwest gardener's handbook : your complete guide : select, plan, plant, maintain, problem-solve :
Oregon, Washington, northern California, British Columbia / Susan Mulvihill and Pat Munts.
    pages cm
  ISBN 978-1-59186-606-0 (sc)
  1. Gardening--Northwest, Pacific--Handbooks, manuals, etc. I. Munts, Pat, 1951- II. Title.

SB453.2.A19M85 2015
635.09795--dc23

2014025524

Acquisitions Editor: Billie Brownell
Design Manager: Cindy Samargia Laun
Layout: Sara Anglin
Zone maps: Bill Kersey

Printed in China
10 9 8 7 6 5 4 3 2 1

NORTHWEST
GARDENER'S HANDBOOK

OREGON, WASHINGTON, NORTHERN CALIFORNIA, BRITISH COLUMBIA

YOUR COMPLETE GUIDE
SELECT · PLAN · PLANT · MAINTAIN · PROBLEM-SOLVE

PAT MUNTS & SUSAN MULVIHILL

Cool
Springs
Press
Home and Garden Experts™

MINNEAPOLIS, MINNESOTA

ACKNOWLEDGMENTS

A book is not written by one person sitting in front of a computer with a pile of books. This one is no exception.

Thank you, Susan Mulvihill, for jumping from a text consultant into the co-authorship when I figured out that fighting a very treatable case of breast cancer and writing a book at the same time was impossible.

Thank you to friends Linda Bartholomew and Janice Sather, who served as text consultants and offered much appreciated encouragement. Thank you to Carol Newcomb of Northland Rosarium for your rose expertise. Many thanks to my husband, Steven, for keeping the clothes washed, dinners cooked, and the house cleaned through this process. I'm grateful to our daughter Lisa Howell for her GIS skills for modifying the maps in Chapter 1 and to our niece Annie Thomas for editing much of the text.

Lastly, to the many family, friends and fellow Spokane County Master Gardeners who offered encouragement and advice to both of us. It makes all the effort worth it.

—Pat Munts

***

I owe a debt of thanks to many special people who made the *Northwest Gardener's Handbook* possible.

Thank you, Pat, for your confidence in my writing abilities. Writing nearly 300 plant descriptions was a monumental task but you never seemed to doubt I could do it. This project gave us valuable time with each other as we pulled it all together. I am in awe of your diverse horticultural knowledge.

A huge thank-you goes to my wonderful husband, Bill. I could not have done this without your support, encouragement and freshly-sharpened pencils always at the ready to edit my prose. Thanks, honey, for literally keeping the home fires burning and the meals coming while I was locked away in my office this winter.

I received a lot of encouraging words from my family, dear friends and my many Master Gardener colleagues, including offers of assistance if and when I needed it. That's what kept me going—thank you!

Pat and I are grateful for the opportunity to write this book, our first. Thank you to Billie Brownell, Tracy Stanley, and the folks at Cool Springs Press and Quarto Publishing Group for guiding us through the process so this book could become a reality.

—Susan Mulvihill

CONTENTS

FEATURED PLANTS

WELCOME TO GARDENING

in the Northwest

The Northwest is a gardener's paradise. While many people from outside the region think it just rains all the time here, most of them don't realize that all that rain helps create some of the most innovative gardens anywhere. They also don't realize that the biggest challenge faced by most gardeners here is actually the dry summers on both sides of the Cascades, and that the region is made up of myriad climates.

Gardeners in the Northwest are passionate about their gardens. Cutting-edge gardening is almost a competitive sport in some places. In Portland, Seattle, and Vancouver, B.C., gardeners push the boundaries of conventional gardening by growing green roofs, creating outdoor living spaces, planting edible landscapes, and using native plants. They practice sustainable gardening and landscape methods to conserve water, provide habitat for wildlife, protect beneficial and pollinator insects, and recycle materials of all sorts into their garden designs.

Furthermore, many people in our region strongly support community gardens, urban agriculture, and sustainable urban infrastructure that use plants and landscapes to mitigate storm water, provide energy-saving shade, and clean the air. Many gardeners in our region are also very generous in sharing their knowledge with beginning gardeners or those new to the region. After all, the Master Gardener™ programs, which now provide gardeners across North America with research-based information, started in Seattle in 1973.

While there are a lot of exceptional gardeners in the region, each one of them had to start learning somewhere. We all picked up a packet of seed for the first time and tried to grow something. Sometimes we succeeded, sometimes we failed, but we kept trying. We all realized, at some point, that gardening is just a series of experiments. So even though this book is aimed at a more experienced gardener, regardless of whether you are just discovering the difference between a hosta and a hoe or you're a more experienced gardener who knows the difference between *Hamamelis virginiana* and *Hydrangea paniculata*, this book is a good reference for your library.

We hope you will use this book to learn about sustainable gardening practices that will save you time, effort, and money, and learn to build a garden that respects the soil, water, air, and wildlife that share your space. The plants featured here were selected for their reliability, proven hardiness, and ease of care in a wide range of environments. Many native plants or their cultivars suitable for home gardens were included in these plant profiles. To help you expand your knowledge base, the resource and bibliography lists at the end of this book will put you in touch with more in-depth information and experts who can fine-tune your knowledge of your area's microclimates and gardening style.

WEST SIDE, EAST SIDE

How you go about doing your gardening in this paradise depends on which side of the Cascade Mountains you live on. The Cascades, which run through the center of the region from southern British Columbia south into northern California, divide the Northwest into two distinct climatological regions. West of the summit of the Cascades, the climate is heavily influenced by marine air off the Pacific Ocean. Summers are cool and dry, and winters are mild and wet. East of the summit, the climate is still influenced by Pacific weather systems, but without the cooling effect of the ocean. Summers are much warmer and drier, and winters are cold and snowy. Occasionally in the winter, arctic air masses flow over the Rocky Mountains from the east and drive temperatures to well below 0 degrees Fahrenheit. A plant that flourishes in Seattle might freeze to death in Spokane or fry in the heat in the Tri-Cities, so it's important to understand your region's climate before choosing plants.

In the U.S., the area west of the summit of the Cascade Mountains is commonly referred to as the Pacific Northwest, which reflects the moderating effect of the marine climate. The area east of the summit is known as the Inland Northwest and reflects the drier, more extreme conditions found there. In British Columbia, the Cascade Mountains

Weather systems off the Pacific Ocean collide with mountain ranges, creating rain forests on the west slopes and rain shadows on the east slopes. Winter storm at Cape Lookout State Park on the Oregon coast.

The Hoh River Valley on the west flanks of the Olympic Mountains in the Olympic National Park is considered a temperate rain forest where sword ferns, red cedar, and Douglas fir thrive.

merge into the Coast Range and divide the marine-influenced coastal southwestern British Columbia and Vancouver Island from the colder and drier interior southern British Columbia. As a result, because of the major differences in climate and growing conditions in the eastern and western parts of the region, we will use the terms "west of the Cascades" or "east of the Cascades" throughout this book to refer to differences in growing conditions or gardening methods.

THE NORTHWEST'S CLIMATE: RAIN FORESTS AND RAIN SHADOWS

The climate in the Northwest is driven by two things: the weather systems that sweep in off the Pacific Ocean, and the mountain ranges they collide with. The three mountain ranges run north to south and are stacked eastward in succession.

The storms first encounter the Oregon Coast Range, Olympic Mountains, and Vancouver Island

Ranges, parallel to the coast from northern California north through Oregon, Washington, and onto Vancouver Island. They next run into the Cascade Mountains that run north to south from southern British Columbia down the middle of Washington and Oregon where the Cascades merge with the Klamath Mountains in northern California. Lastly, the storms encounter the northern Rocky Mountains along the eastern borders of British Columbia, Washington, and Oregon. The Rockies are the boundary of the marine-influenced Northwest and the continental climate.

As the weather systems develop over the eastern Pacific, they pick up moisture from the relatively warm ocean water. The prevailing winds then carry these warm, moist systems ashore, where the increasing elevation of the mountains forces the storms up and over; this process is called "orographic lifting." As they rise, the systems cool and the moisture condenses and falls as rain or snow on the western slopes of the mountains. Past the mountain summits, the weather systems are much drier and the eastern slopes receive much less rainfall. These areas are in the rain shadow of the mountains.

Winter rainfall totals along the Oregon Coast Range and Olympic Mountains are impressive. On the western slopes of the Olympics in the Hoh and

The floor of Northwest rain forests are often covered with ferns that thrive in the moist soil and shade of tall trees. Maidenhair fern in the Olympic National Park.

Quinault river valleys, annual precipitation ranges from 140 to 170 inches a year—so much rain that the Hoh River valley in Washington is considered a temperate rain forest. Farther south in the Oregon Coast Range, along the Oregon and Northern California coasts, annual precipitation rates range from 150 to nearly 170 inches a year. The area around Crescent City, California, is wet enough to support the giant redwood trees, some of which tower to over 200 feet tall. On Vancouver Island, rainfall averages 128 inches at Tofino on the coast and 112.2 inches at Gold River to the north.

Once the systems are over the Oregon Coast Range, the Olympics, and the Vancouver Island Ranges, they descend into the Willamette Valley, Puget Sound Basin, and Strait of Georgia and pick up more moisture but don't drop as much rain. These regions immediately east of the coastal mountains from southern Oregon north to Vancouver, Victoria, and along the Georgia Strait in British Columbia receive an average of 35 to 40 inches of rain a year. An interesting exception to this average is on the northeast tip of the Olympic Mountains around Sequim, Port Townsend, Victoria, the southern San Juan Islands, and the southernmost Gulf Islands in British Columbia, where the intense rain shadow of the Olympics holds annual precipitation to 17 to 20 inches a year.

The weather systems then begin to ascend again as they encounter the much taller Cascade Mountains. The western slopes of the Cascades commonly receive 100 to 150 inches of rain a year, much of which falls as snow in the high elevations. The accumulated snow pack then melts during the summer and provides power generation, irrigation, and drinking water for a large portion of the region.

The weather systems lose most of the rest of their moisture as they cross the Cascades, so they are very dry when they descend into the rain shadow of the eastern slopes. Consequently, rainfall amounts are in the single digits through central Oregon and Washington and on up into the British Columbia Okanagan Valley. Wenatchee, Washington, gets 8.85 inches; Bend and Klamath Falls, Oregon, get 16.77 and 11.94 inches respectively, while Kelowna, B.C., gets 13.6 inches annually.

Vantage, Washington, where I-90 crosses the Columbia River, gets 8 eight inches of rain annually and is considered a desert. It is the rain shadow of the Cascades, 130 miles east of Seattle.

On the east side of the Washington Cascades, weather systems again pick up moisture as the topography slowly rises from an altitude of 407 feet in Kennewick to 2,300 feet in Spokane. Rainfall amounts increase as the weather systems move east and rise dramatically upon encountering the northern Rockies and the central Idaho mountains. Rainfall in the valleys of northeast Washington averages 20 to 30 inches annually, with higher amounts in the mountains.

East of the Cascades in Oregon, the topography is very different. The region is a high desert plateau with an elevation between 3,000 to 5,000 feet, punctuated by several small mountain ranges with peaks over 9,000 feet. The high, uneven topography forces weather systems to drop varying amounts of rain depending on elevation across all of central and eastern Oregon.

In southwestern British Columbia and Vancouver Island west of the Cascades, the Vancouver Island Ranges and the British Columbia Coast Range and Cascades rise quickly from sea level to over 7,000 feet. Weather systems can easily dump between 100 to 150 inches of rain on the steep slopes. Once over the crest of the mountains, weather systems encounter the high Interior Plateau and a series of north-to-south mountain ranges all the way to the Rocky Mountains. The plateau immediately east of the Cascades is in the rain shadow of the mountains and receives less than 20 inches of rain annually. The mountain ranges further to the east create a very uneven terrain of high mountain ranges and deep, narrow river valleys with equally uneven rainfall amounts.

SO, WHAT CAN GARDENERS EXPECT FOR WEATHER?

Gardeners along the Pacific Coast, from Crescent City in California to the Straits of Juan de Fuca in Washington and coastal Vancouver Island, can expect cool summers with regular morning fog close to the coastline. Summer temperatures are generally in the 60s to 70s Fahrenheit, which makes it difficult for warm-season vegetable crops to produce fruit unless they are in a greenhouse.

Winters are wet and cool with only occasional frosts. Exposed gardens will need wind breaks to prevent the desiccation of plants from strong, steady winds off the ocean. Gardens very close to the ocean are likely to be affected by salt spray, so gardeners will have to select salt-tolerant plants.

The Puget Sound Basin and Willamette Valley are known for a mild, Mediterranean climate characterized by warm, dry summers and cool, wet winters. Summers are usually dry from July into September and October. Mornings can be cloudy but the sun usually burns off the clouds by midday. Summer temperatures average in the 60s, 70s, and 80s Fahrenheit, with an occasional heat wave in the 90s Fahrenheit. Between November and March, the weather is generally rainy, overcast, and often foggy. Winter temperatures average in the 40s and 50s Fahrenheit with an occasional blast of cold, snowy weather. Temperatures close to the shore on Puget Sound are generally cooler than the surrounding area but rise quickly away from the water.

Southern Oregon and the northern California border counties of Del Norte, Modoc, and Siskiyou are bounded by Eugene on the north, Klamath Falls on the east, and the Pacific coast to Crescent City on the west. Most of the region is mountainous, with the Siskiyou Mountains on the west and the Klamath Mountains on the east. Most gardeners in this region live along the coast or in the Rogue River Valley. The lower-elevation interior valleys around Medford and Grants Pass are cool and wet in the winter and hot and very dry in the summer. Winter temperatures are in the 40s Fahrenheit, while summer temperatures are commonly in the 90s. On the coast, winter temperatures are in the 40s to 50s Fahrenheit and in the 60s to 70s in the summer. Summers are dry, but low morning clouds and fog are common and keep the humidity high which benefits the nearby redwood forests. The higher elevations of the Siskiyou and Klamath mountains receive heavy snow in the winter.

Gardeners in central and eastern Oregon are blessed with short but warm, dry summers, cool falls, and wet, often snowy, winters and springs. The region is in the rain shadow of the Cascades, so rainfall across much of the region is less than

The Palouse region of eastern Washington is a series of rolling hills that produces most of the state's dryland wheat crop. Here, south of Spokane, the Palouse is giving way to pine forests as rainfall amounts increase as the elevation rises.

15 inches. The growing season is around ninety days, and frost can occur any month of the year. Winter temperatures average in the 20s to 40s Fahrenheit depending on the elevation; they can dip well below zero when an occasional continental arctic air mass sneaks over the Rockies from the northeast. Summer temperatures average in the 70s and 80s Fahrenheit depending, again, on elevation. Night temperatures during the summer are quite cool, making it difficult to grow warm-season vegetables without greenhouse protection.

Washington's Columbia Basin and Palouse regions are bounded by the Cascades on the west, the Columbia River on the south, the Idaho border on the east, and the Okanogan Highlands to the north. The region is at a much lower elevation than eastern Oregon and is impacted by the Cascades' rain shadow. Summers in the western part of the region along the Columbia River are hot and dry—some small areas are considered desert with fewer than 9 inches of rain a year. Winters around the Tri-Cities (Richland, Pasco, and Kennewick) are cool and wet, with temperatures in the 30s to 40 Fahrenheit. In the Palouse region to the east, summers aren't quite as warm and winters are colder with more rain and snow.

The elevation in eastern Washington rises slowly from 407 feet at Kennewick on the Columbia River to around 2,300 feet at Spokane in the northeast. As the topography rises, so do rainfall totals; 9.23 inches in Kennewick to 16.13 in Spokane. Interestingly, the Spokane area is at the topographic point where weather systems really start rising to go over the Rockies. As a result, rainfall in the Spokane area varies from 16 to 17 inches west of the city to 20 inches at the Idaho state line 35 miles away.

The Okanogan Highlands and northeast Washington mountains stretch from the Cascades on the west to the Idaho border on the east, the Columbia and Spokane rivers to the south, and the British Columbia border on the north. The region is quite mountainous with deep, north-to-south valleys. Summer temperatures in the Omak, Columbia, Colville, and Pend Oreille valleys are in the 80s Fahrenheit but cool down significantly at

night. As a result, many people use temporary greenhouses to grow vegetable crops. At higher elevations, summer temperatures are much cooler and frosts can occur year-round. Winters are cold and snowy with temperatures averaging in the teens to low 30s. The western part of the region is in the rain shadow of the Cascades so rainfall amounts are light but increase as elevations rise to the east.

In British Columbia, gardens on the eastern side of Vancouver Island and southwestern British Columbia mainland around Vancouver are strongly influenced by the rain shadow of the Vancouver Island Ranges and the Olympic Mountains so the summers are cool and dry with sun after the morning fog burns off. The region is divided by the Strait of Juan de Fuca and the Georgia Strait, which funnel cold Pacific Ocean water through the heart of the region and provide a cooling influence. Summer temperatures average in the 60s and 70s Fahrenheit. Winters are cloudy and cool with temperatures in the 40s. Snow storms are infrequent and snow doesn't stay on the ground for long.

In southwestern British Columbia along the Fraser River valley away from the marine influence of the straits and the rain shadows of the mountains, summers are slightly warmer while winters are cooler and wetter. In areas east of Vancouver around Abbotsford, Chilliwack, and Hope, summer temperatures average in the 70s Fahrenheit. January temperatures average in the 40s. Rainfall totals vary widely depending on how close to the mountains you are. Abbotsford on the west averages 60 inches, while Hope on the east averages 80 inches.

Cold air draining down the Fraser River valley from interior British Columbia during the winter can have a strong influence on the area's climate. Arctic blasts of strong winds, snow, and ice can take temperatures well into the teens and lower, killing plants that aren't hardy enough. Heavy, wet snow can break branches. Fortunately, these conditions happen infrequently.

The Cascade Mountains grade into the Coast Mountains just north of the Washington-British Columbia border and divide coastal southwestern

AVERAGE ANNUAL RAINFALL AND SUMMER AND WINTER TEMPERATURES FOR SELECTED NORTHWEST CITIES

CITY	ELEVATION (FEET)	AUGUST AVERAGE TEMPERATURE (F)	JANUARY AVERAGE TEMPERATURE (F)	ANNUAL RAINFALL (INCHES)
WASHINGTON				
Bellingham	149	74	43.7	35.39
Sequim	184	71.8	44.4	16.21
Seattle	60	74.6	47.1	37.92
Aberdeen	10	69.8	45.8	83.20
Wenatchee	800	87	34.6	8.85
Kennewick	407	87	36.7	9.23
Spokane	235.3	82.7	33	16.13
OREGON				
Portland	159	78.9	44.8	42.51
Eugene	390	81.6	46.1	38.16
Newport	122	64.8	50.1	67.76
Medford	1,457	87.9	46.1	20.39
Bend	3,660	81.9	41	11.86
La Grande	275.5	86	38.1	20.24
Klamath Falls	4,092	83.1	39.8	11.9
CALIFORNIA				
Crescent City	44	67.2	54.1	70.77
BRITISH COLUMBIA				
Cranbrook	3,084	78.8	28.6	15.2
Kelowna	1129	81.7	33.4	13.6
Fernie	3,314	76	28	34
Saltspring Island	0	72	42	41
Vancouver	501	72	44	57.3
Victoria	75	68	45	24

British Columbia from southern interior B.C. This region stretches from the east slopes of the Cascades in the Okanagan Valley to the crest of the Rocky Mountains north of western Montana. Like the U.S. Okanogan Highlands and northeast Washington, the region is mountainous and cut by deep north-to-south running river valleys. Elevations are quite variable and have an impact on rainfall amounts across the region. Areas in the rain shadow of the Cascades in the Okanagan Valley average around 13 inches while Cranbrook to the east gets 15.2 inches, and Fernie near the continental divide gets 34 inches.

In the Okanagan Valley with elevations between 900 and 1,100 feet summers are short but warm. In fact, the valley is the warmest place in Canada and brings in many people from the Canadian prairies during the summer. Summer temperatures average in the 80s Fahrenheit while winter temperatures are into the 30s. Snow is the norm in the region starting in late October through late April. Growing seasons are short, making greenhouse protection necessary for tender vegetables.

East of the Okanagan Valley, the region is mountainous and bisected by deep valleys carved out by glaciers. Summers on the valley floors are cool and short with frost possible nearly every month. Warm season vegetable crops need greenhouse protection to mature while ornamental plants need to be hardy. Summer temperatures average in the 70s Fahrenheit while winter temperatures average in the 20s. At times, Arctic air funnels down these valleys during the winter creating occasional very cold conditions. Many of the valleys contain large, narrow lakes that help modify temperatures close to the shoreline, especially in the summer, creating microclimates that can support less hardy plants.

Throughout this book, particularly in the plant profiles, we will be talking about plants and their differing water needs. Our terms in the plant profiles are low, medium, and high, with a brief description of any additional important watering advice. We will also talk about drought-tolerant plants. To translate these words into the equivalent of inches of water in a given timeframe is not possible with any semblance of accuracy. When we use the term "drought tolerant" or "low water" it refers to the fact that the plant can tolerate longer periods of dryness than other plants. Drought tolerant doesn't always mean native either; lots of native plants need moist soils. Soil types and cultural factors like soil organic matter content, presence of competing plants, and mulches to retain soil moisture will also have an effect on how much water a plant needs. Finally, even low water requirement or drought-tolerant plants are going to need regular watering for their first couple of years to become established. It will take some experimentation on your part, in your own garden's conditions, to define these terms.

MICROCLIMATES

While these large-scale regional weather patterns will give you a general idea of what to expect, the actual precipitation, temperature and winds in your garden may vary. Called "microclimates," these very localized climate conditions can have subtle differences in rainfall, temperature, and airflow distinct from other areas nearby. Even in a single garden, there can be several microclimates depending on the drainage of cold or warm air, the orientation of your garden to the sun, and subtleties of the slope of the land. Cold air will flow downhill or pool behind a hedge or fence, creating a cold pocket where tomatoes can freeze while the rest of the garden is fine. Open areas can be windy, making it necessary to water more there than in a shady corner behind the garage. Tall trees can create shade that cools plants, while beds backed by a south-facing concrete wall will stay warmer because of the stored heat.

Gardens near large lakes, rivers, the ocean, or the Puget Sound will have a more moderate and often slightly warmer climate than that of a garden just a few hundred yards inland. Water stores a lot of heat and gives it up slowly to the atmosphere, modifying the surrounding air mass. Areas close to water may even be a hardiness zone higher than the surrounding area, so plants can be grown that would not survive away from the shore.

PLANT HARDINESS ZONES

Plant hardiness is a measure of how tolerant a particular plant is to cold winter temperatures. Some plants can tolerate winter temperatures well below zero, while others will succumb to temperatures that just touch the freezing mark. The U.S. Department of Agriculture Hardiness Zone Map breaks the entire region into zones based on the average winter low temperature. Each zone represents a change of 10 degrees, divided into "A" and "B" zones of 5 degrees each. The USDA has issued a newer map using new digital mapping technology to vastly improve the detail and accuracy of the previous map.

The Canadian plant hardiness zones were developed by Agriculture Canada and the Canadian Forest Service and are based on a broader range of climatic variables, including maximum temperatures and the length of the frost-free period as well as average winter minimum temperatures. The most recent map was created in 2000 using 30 years of data from 1961 to 1990. This system uses basically the same zone designations and temperature ranges as the USDA hardiness map, only converted into Celsius. In areas that have reliable, deep snow cover, particularly in southern interior British Columbia, the snow acts as an insulating blanket that can protect marginally hardy plants from cold damage.

USDA COLD-HARDINESS ZONES FOR THE NORTHWEST

Southern British Columbia

Washington

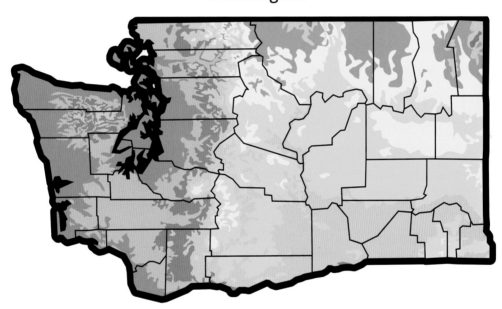

ZONE	Average Annual Minimum Temperature (°F)	ZONE	Average Annual Minimum Temperature (°F)	ZONE	Average Annual Minimum Temperature (°F)
2B	-40 to -45	5B	-10 to -15	8B	20 to 15
3A	-35 to -40	6A	-5 to -10	9A	25 to 20
3B	-30 to -35	6B	0 to -5		
4A	-25 to -30	7A	5 to 0		
4B	-20 to -25	7B	10 to 5		
5A	-15 to -20	8A	15 to 10		

USDA Plant Hardiness Zone Map, 2012. Agricultural Research Service, U.S. Department of Agriculture. Accessed from http://planthardiness.ars.usda.gov.

USDA COLD-HARDINESS ZONES OF THE NORTHWEST

Oregon

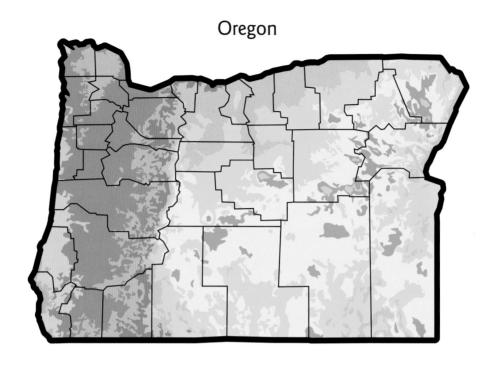

Northern California

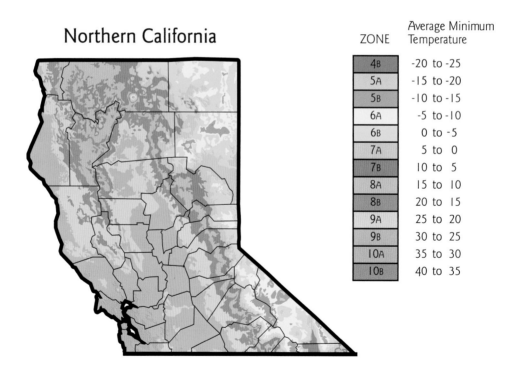

ZONE	Average Minimum Temperature
4B	-20 to -25
5A	-15 to -20
5B	-10 to -15
6A	-5 to -10
6B	0 to -5
7A	5 to 0
7B	10 to 5
8A	15 to 10
8B	20 to 15
9A	25 to 20
9B	30 to 25
10A	35 to 30
10B	40 to 35

USDA Plant Hardiness Zone Map, 2012. Agricultural Research Service, U.S. Department of Agriculture. Accessed from http://planthardiness.ars.usda.gov.

MEDIAN DATE OF FIRST 32-DEGREE F. TEMPERATURE IN AUTUMN

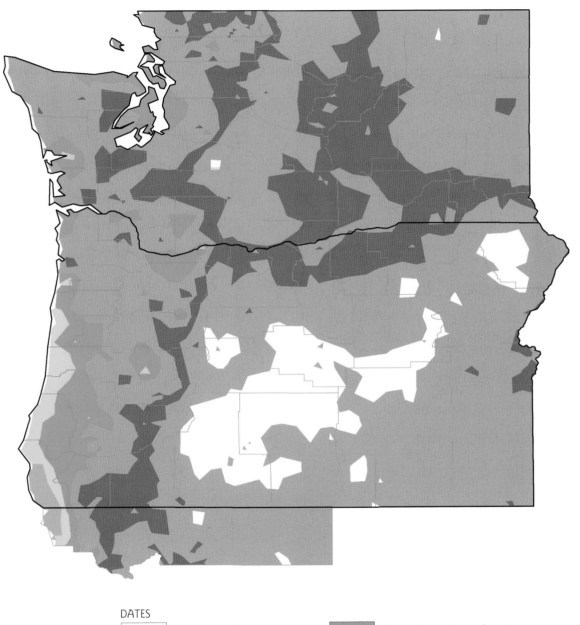

DATES

August 1 – August 31

September 1 – September 30

October 1 – October 15

October 16 – October 31

November 1 – November 15

November 16 – November 30

December 1 – December 31

Based on information from NOAA National Climate Data Center

MEDIAN DATE OF LAST 32-DEGREE F. TEMPERATURE IN SPRING

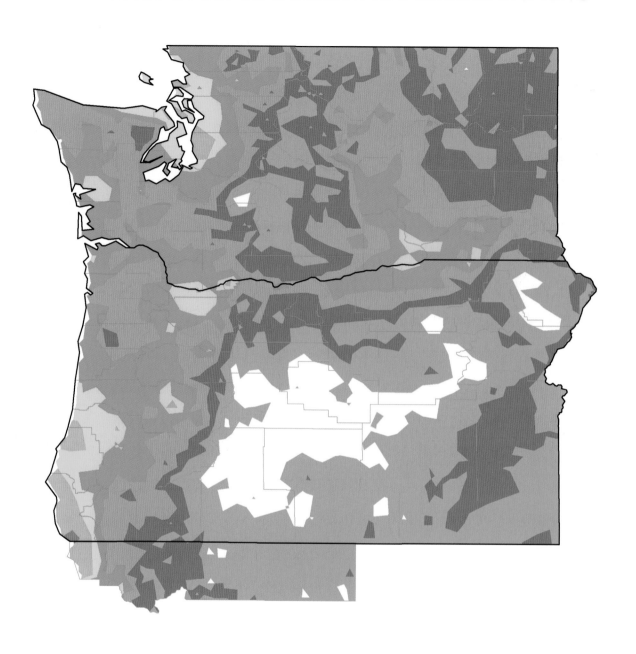

DATES

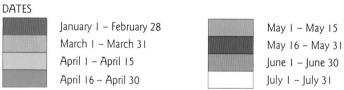

January 1 – February 28

March 1 – March 31

April 1 – April 15

April 16 – April 30

May 1 – May 15

May 16 – May 31

June 1 – June 30

July 1 – July 31

Based on information from NOAA National Climate Data Center

Snow insulates plants against cold temperatures and drying winter winds.

Hardiness zone information appears as a temperature range or zone designation on plant tags, or as a note in catalog listings. Hardiness zones represent the average winter temperature but they don't represent those unusual cold blasts of winter air that go well below the average. When this happens, even hardy plants can freeze.

Many adventurous gardeners in the region play the "zonal denial" game and deliberately put in plants that are hardy to one or two zones above their actual conditions, just to say they tried. This works fine if we get a warmer-than-usual winter but can be a disaster if it gets really cold. If you want to play this game, that's fine; just don't bet the whole garden on achieving bragging rights.

FIRE AND ICE: THE NORTHWEST'S SOILS

The soils in the Northwest and southern British Columbia are quite variable and represent the region's complex geologic history. The region's topography is made up of sedimentary and volcanic rocks created by the collision of the continental North American and oceanic Pacific plates. As the region's mountain ranges were bent and folded upward, volcanic eruptions exploded through cracks in the plates to form the tall volcanic cones we know today as Mt. Rainier, Mt. Hood, the Three Sisters, the Garibaldi Volcanic Belt in B.C., and a dozen other peaks in the Cascades. These volcanic eruptions created thick layers of fine ash throughout the western U.S. and southern British Columbia, forming the major component of the region's soils. Fluid basalt lava flowed from huge fissures in the earth in central Washington, spreading across the Columbia Basin and down the Columbia River Gorge and leaving behind massive cliffs of basalt. Volcanic activity is still ongoing in the region. In 1981, Mount St. Helens exploded and dropped ash several inches thick across eastern Washington. Several other volcanic Cascade peaks, including Mt. Rainier and the Three Sisters in Oregon, have shown signs of life.

During the last Ice Age, continental ice sheets and glaciers covered all of British Columbia, much of northern Washington, and the high mountain ranges to the south. As they retreated, they left behind huge amounts of gravelly glacial outwash that filled many of the valleys and low areas. In eastern Washington, a series of 40 enormous outwash floods scoured much of the Columbia Basin as the glacier retreated 12,000 to 15,000 years ago. The floods were the result of repeated ice dam failures near Sandpoint, Idaho, that drained ancient Lake Missoula and filled much of western Montana. They scoured off topsoil across the Basin and sent it, along with enormous quantities of outwash gravels, down the Columbia Gorge, into the Willamette Valley, and eventually far into the Pacific Ocean.

GETTING GOOD GARDENING INFORMATION

Let's face it, there is a lot of gardening information out there. Some of it is very useful, but a lot of it hasn't been tested for accuracy. Sorting out the good advice from the mediocre or downright inaccurate takes time and effort.

The best source for localized gardening information is the Master Gardener program. In the U.S., the programs are supported by the Extension Services of the University of California, Oregon State University, and Washington State University, respectively. In British Columbia, the Master Gardener program operates in several communities through the Master Gardeners Association of British Columbia. The Master Gardener programs provide educational opportunities and research-based information tempered by the local experience of specially trained volunteers. Most of the programs offer classes and publications, and some even have plant clinics where you can take samples of insects and plants for identification. Many of their publications are available online through each program's publication services, often as free downloads.

Beyond the Master Gardener and Extension Service programs, look at botanical garden, plant society, and gardening association websites to find local information and specialized gardening education opportunities. Websites for many of these programs and organizations are listed in the Resources section at the end of this book.

Regional gardening books and magazines that focus on the Northwest are better sources of localized information than those written for a national audience. Many national gardening books and magazines have lots of great information that will work in a broad environment, but not necessarily in the Northwest. Read them with the knowledge that you will probably have to adapt their growing ideas and plant suggestions for your conditions.

Plant and seed catalogs can also be a great source of information about plants and their growing requirements. A good catalog will list the hardiness zones for each plant along with specific growing information, such as its mature size and its water, light, and soil requirements. The catalogs should provide clear return and guarantee policies. Avoid catalogs that tell you a particular plant will "grow anywhere." A note of caution: Mail-order plants are usually small and may come bare root in order to keep the shipping costs down. Expect to pay a fair price for good plants; a catalog that offers cut-rate prices will likely deliver cut-rate plants.

Last, but not least, make friends with the staff at local nurseries and garden centers. Many of these people have gardened for years in your area. They are very familiar with the local microclimates and which plants will thrive. They are also a great source of information on new plant introductions and gardening trends, and may even order that special plant you can't live without.

Mountainous interior southern British Columbia is cut by deep north-to-south valleys often filled with beautiful lakes. Christina Lake B.C.

SUSTAINABLE LANDSCAPING & GARDENING

Just what is "sustainable landscaping and gardening?" These words get bantered around quite often in conversations among Western gardeners. However, they can mean many different things to different people. To some, it means using a minimum amount of water in the garden or not using chemicals to control bugs. Others think of the concept as a way to introduce more native plants into a garden and rip out the lawn entirely. Others think of it as providing a way to bring birds, animals, beneficial insects, and bees back into their garden.

In reality, sustainable gardening and landscaping includes all these things. A sustainable landscape is one that is designed, laid out, and maintained in such a way as to respect the natural environment and minimize the use of water, fertilizers, chemicals, labor, and maintenance while still providing spaces for the kids to play, growing your own food, entertaining and relaxing with friends and family, or displaying your prized rose collection.

This can be a huge mindset change for many gardeners. Our historic tradition of gardening was to impose our ideas of what a garden should look like on whatever land we encountered. If we wanted a green lawn in a desert, we planted it and then used copious amounts of scarce water resources to keep it that way. Under this old philosophy, we thought we had the right to control the land around us even when those ideas ignored the reality of the environment. In the process, we created high-maintenance gardens that used more resources than necessary and took a lot of time and money to maintain. Fortunately, times have changed. We are realizing now that by working with the existing natural environment, using a minimum of resources, and planning smartly, we can still create beautiful gardens.

PLANNING A SUSTAINABLE, LOW-MAINTENANCE LANDSCAPE

Creating a sustainable landscape is a process that, by necessity, is very individualistic. Each garden will have its own set of microclimates, soils, existing native plant communities, land forms, and sun and wind exposure that must be taken into account in the planning process. Each gardener will have certain expectations of the landscape: a place for the kids to play, an outdoor sitting space, a garden that looks good without a lot of upkeep, or a showcase of botanical delights. The challenge is to blend all of the ideas and existing conditions.

The planning process begins with good research. As you read this book and continue your research in other books, on websites, and through visits with local experts, challenge yourself to think beyond just a layout of beds and plants that looks great on paper. Consult with your area's Master Gardener program to learn what grows best in your area and get insights into the microclimates and soils you might encounter.

Begin by taking an inventory of the existing conditions on your property. What trees, shrubs, rocks, slopes, or views could you incorporate into your plan? What are the current soil conditions and sun and shade patterns? Are there potential problem areas like steep slopes or perennial wet patches? Where does the irrigation and storm water runoff go? What street traffic, structures or other intrusions do you want to screen off?

Now ask yourself what you want out of this garden. What types of activities do you want to do in the landscape? What kind of features do you need to do them? Do you really need all the lawn you are currently watering or would a small patch for playing and relaxing be sufficient? Could the lawn be replaced completely by groundcovers? Can you use alternatives to lawns altogether? How much money and work do you really want to put into this garden? Can you redesign your irrigation system and install water-efficient heads and a new high-tech timer?

The next step is to create a drawing of your site with its major features and structures. Note existing plantings you want to keep and where you want new plantings. What structures do you want to keep? What view beyond the property line do you want to frame or hide? Where are there major shaded or sunlit areas? With existing features identified, what other features and plantings do you want to add to the garden? Where do you want sitting and play areas or the vegetable garden?

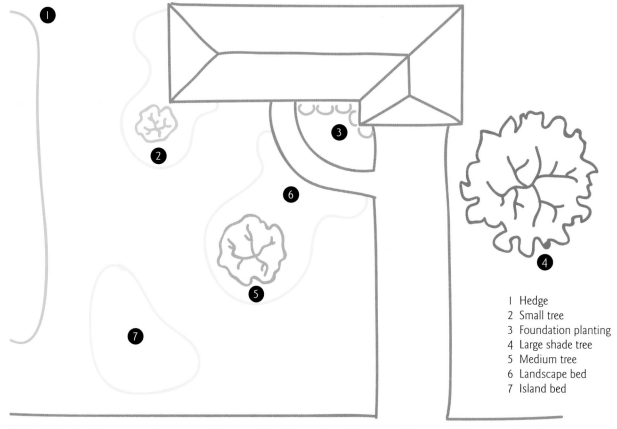

To begin the planning process, draw a map of your yard. Include major existing trees, hedges, and plants as well as the house, decks, walkways, and driveways.

1 Hedge
2 Small tree
3 Foundation planting
4 Large shade tree
5 Medium tree
6 Landscape bed
7 Island bed

If this task is daunting, consult with a local landscape designer or landscape architect to help work through your ideas and concepts and to see the full potential of your property. Their experience and design sense can open new possibilities and even save you from an expensive mistake.

WHAT IS YOUR SOIL LIKE?

Every sustainable garden project begins with understanding the soil. It is, after all, what your plants will live in. Healthy soil will mean healthy plants that need less care and fewer pesticides and are more resilient to drought, pests, diseases, and weather extremes.

As was discussed in the previous chapter, the complex geology of the Northwest has resulted in a complex mix of soils around the region. Soil is made up of fine particles of clay, silt, and sand created by the erosion of rocks by wind, water, ice, and chemical reactions. The particles can mix in an infinite number of soil types that have different characteristics.

Clay soils tend to be heavy and dense with a very fine texture. Wet clays feel sticky to the touch. The very small particle size creates many tiny spaces that can hold a lot of water and air, while the surface area of the particles can hold nutrients and minerals. The downside is that clay soils don't drain excess water away easily, don't dry out quickly, and stay colder later into the spring.

Silt particles are sized between clays and sand and form a lighter, less dense soil. They feel slippery when wet. Silts hold a lot of nutrients which makes them very good for growing plants. They don't hold as much water as clay.

Sand particles are larger and coarser than clay and silt. Think of the sand you find at the beach: A handful of sand will easily run through your fingers.

It forms a very loose soil that drains quickly, making it necessary to irrigate more frequently. Sand also doesn't hold nutrients very well, thus making it necessary to fertilize more often.

Organic matter is the last component of a soil and the most important when it comes to improving soil quality. Created by the decay of plants, soil organisms and other organic detritus, it is an important source of nutrients and acts like a sponge to hold water in the soil. The addition of organic matter in the form of compost, manure, and cover crops will lighten clay and silt soils and help sandy soils retain moisture and nutrients.

Whether you are rehabilitating an old landscape or starting with bare ground, the best way to determine the condition of your soil is through a soil test. A soil test will tell you your soil type, the amount of nitrogen, phosphorus, and potassium currently in your soil, its pH level and its organic matter content. This information gives you a baseline to make decisions about how much and what type of soil amendments and fertilizer to add and whether your soil is acidic or alkaline. In the Northwest, soils west of the Cascades tend to be more acidic than those to the east.

Soil tests can be done using kits purchased at local garden centers or by sending them to a soil testing laboratory near you. Do-it-yourself kits are not as accurate as a lab test, but they can give you a general idea of your soil conditions. Laboratory tests are much more precise and many of them will give you recommendations of what nutrients and quantities are needed. Another advantage of laboratory tests is that they can also measure micronutrients such as iron (Fe), copper (Cu), and boron (B) that are important for plant health. They can also tell you what the levels of toxic elements such as arsenic (As), lead (Pb), and cadmium (Cd) are and if they are within acceptable levels. This is critical when deciding where you will plant vegetable and fruit crops or where your kids might spend a lot of time digging in the dirt. Don't despair if a soil test comes back showing levels of higher-than-threshold toxic minerals; it's easy to lay down a non-porous barrier fabric and then build raised box beds filled with good soil on top of it. See Garden Know-How on page 45 for instructions regarding how to take a soil sample.

If you find you need large quantities of soil or organic matter for your garden projects, it's best to purchase it in bulk from a reputable local soil supplier. They can offer you a wide range of mixes and deliver it to your driveway if you don't own a truck. Some soil companies will even have nutrient level information available for their compost mixes. Good quality commercial compost will be dark with no discernable woody material and have a rich, earthy smell. Good keywords to search the Internet for are "soil suppliers," "compost suppliers," or "landscape materials" in your local area. If possible, visit the company you choose to see exactly what you are getting. There are no standardized definitions of soil mixes.

MANAGING WATER

Water is a precious commodity in the Northwest and British Columbia, even in the rainy parts. Much of our summer irrigation water comes from mountain snow packs laid down by the previous winter's storms. As the population of the Northwest grows and droughts become more common due to climate change, this resource is becoming less reliable. Many municipal governments have enacted water use regulations that limit how much and when you can water residential landscapes, or have increased fees for heavy water users. These limitations will only increase over time. Before you start a large landscape project, check with your local water board about restrictions and costs. Some water suppliers may even have rebate or cost-share programs that can help you create a new irrigation system or re-engineer an old one.

Most landscapes in the region, even the drought-tolerant ones, will need some summer irrigation to look their best. This makes having an efficient sprinkler system a must. In recent years, new irrigation technology developments have created good alternatives to the old traditional systems that threw massive quantities of water everywhere, hoping that enough drops would land in the right place. Drip and micro-spray heads can deliver water right to the plants at or below the soil surface, which reduces loss from evaporation created by throwing water high into the air. These systems are commonly available and relatively inexpensive to purchase and install, even for a tool-challenged do-it-yourself gardener.

Irrigation timers have become more sophisticated, making it possible to set watering times more precisely. Some technologies are even using soil or air moisture sensors to determine run times. The development of satellite-based sensors has even made it possible to set an irrigation timer's run times according to real-time weather data pulled down from orbiting weather satellites. Talk to local sprinkler designers and equipment suppliers to help you retrofit an old system or design a new system.

You don't have to make a huge expenditure for a new irrigation system, however, to be more efficient. Just making sure your existing system is as efficient as possible goes a long way toward reducing wasted water. Periodically check your system during the watering season for broken or plugged heads, leaky joints, or places where plants have blocked spray from other plants. If you don't have a sprinkler system, invest in some soaker hoses and lay them amongst the plants so that the water is applied right to the root zones. Set them on battery or solar-powered electronic timers so you don't even have to remember to turn on the water. There are also lots of different, inexpensive kits available on the market to make simple drip watering systems for deck containers, garden boxes, and that odd corner of the garden that the sprinklers miss.

Captured rain is another source of moisture that can be channeled into irrigation. Rather than letting rain and sprinkler water run down the street into storm drains, design your landscape to channel excess water into swales or catchment devices. Swales in low spots or at the bottom of slopes will allow runoff water to percolate into the ground naturally and make the perfect place to incorporate plants that like a little more moisture. Rain gutters can channel rainwater from the roof into barrels or storage tanks that can then be used to water gardens using low-pressure drip irrigation systems.

Roofs on houses, sheds, and other structures can be planted with low-growing sedums, saxifrage, grasses, prairie flowers, and even moss. This structure-based garden style is called a green roof. The plants slow the flow of rain and storm water and allow it to drain slowly into storm systems or water catchment systems. Green roofs can also insulate interior spaces and moderate indoor temperatures, thus saving heating and cooling energy. Designing and installing a green roof requires some architectural expertise to build the structure so that it can sustain the weight of the plants, the soil mix, and water and keep the space under it dry.

Throughout this book, particularly in the plant profiles, we will be talking about plants and their differing water needs. Our terms are low, medium, and high. We will also talk about drought-tolerant plants. To translate these words into the equivalent of inches of water in a given time frame is not possible with any semblance of accuracy. When we use the term "drought tolerant" or "low water" it refers to the fact that the plant can tolerate longer periods of dryness than other plants. Drought tolerant doesn't always mean native either; lots of native plants need moist soils. Soil types and cultural factors like soil organic matter content, presence of competing plants, and mulches to retain soil moisture will also have an effect on how much water a plant needs. Last, even low-water requirement or drought-tolerant plants are going to need regular watering for their first couple of years to become established. It will take some experimentation on *your* part, in *your* own conditions, to define these terms.

USING THE RIGHT PLANT IN THE RIGHT PLACE

One of easiest ways to create a sustainable garden is to use well-adapted plants in places where their needs are met without the use of additional inputs or resources: In other words, the right plant in the right place. Selecting plants that thrive in your particular conditions and the time and inclination you have to care for them will go a long way toward having a sustainable—as well as beautiful—garden.

There are several additional elements that must be considered when picking the right plants for in your garden. The amount of shade or sun your garden receives will affect your plant choices; some plants do well in shade while others thrive in full sun. If plants are grown in the wrong light, they will either become thin and leggy or burn up in the heat. Ironically, the cloudiness often found west of the Cascades can protect normally shade-tolerant plants enough so that rhododendrons, hostas, and hydrangeas can thrive in full sun. If some of your planting spaces are on a southern and/or western exposure backed by stone or concrete walls, choose plants that can handle the extra heat. Be aware of the growth habits of your plant choices and choose plants that will grow together well. It's frustrating when one shrub grows so quickly or so large that it crowds out its neighbors or takes a lot of pruning to keep in check.

Persistent, drying winds are common in open areas of the region, especially in the summer. These winds can dry out plants very quickly when summer humidity levels are low. Often, plants with small, thick, hairy leaves will stand up to the wind better than those with large, thin leaves. In the warmer parts of the region, even well-watered plants can succumb very quickly to a hot, dry wind. If you live in such an area, ask about wind tolerance when buying plants or consult with your local Master Gardeners.

USING NATIVE PLANTS AND THEIR ALLIES

Native plants are the unsung heroes of sustainable landscapes. After all, they have been living in the natural environment around your garden for eons. They have adapted to the yearly cycles of rain, temperature fluctuation, insect attack, and soil fertility levels and still look good through it all. Because they are already highly adapted to an area, they need far less care and fewer resources.

Start your planning process by inventorying the existing native plants on your site that could be included in your final design. That clump of vine maple or manzanita just might be the perfect centerpiece for the garden. Incorporating native plants also ties your garden into the surrounding landscape and gives it a more settled look, as if it had always been part of the landscape. Finally, the root systems of established native shrubs, trees, and grasses will hold soil in place, reducing the potential of erosion, especially along shorelines and steep slopes.

Native plants aren't always easy to find in the nurseries, but supplies are becoming more available as interest in sustainable landscaping, wildlife habitat development, and restoration increases. A number of native plants have been hybridized into very familiar garden plants. For example, our native ninebark shrub (*Physocarpus opulifolius*) has been hybridized into a series of cultivars with dark purple ('Diablo'), coppery ('Coppertina'), and gold ('Dart's Gold') leaves. A number of the plants in this book's plant guide are native plants or their cultivars that are commonly found in nurseries throughout our region.

Plants that may not be native but grow in similar circumstances in other parts of the world may also be a good choice for a garden. Because much of the coastal Northwest, Northern California and British Columbia are considered Mediterranean climates, plants native to that region and other areas with cool, wet winters and hot, dry summers can be very useful in a sustainable garden.

PLANTING FOR POLLINATORS, BENEFICIAL INSECTS AND WILDLIFE

A sustainable garden also takes into account the pollinator and beneficial insects, indigenous birds, mammals and reptiles that share your space. These animals were part of the landscape long before us and we have a lot to learn about their role in a healthy ecosystem.

Fragmentation of habitats—especially in urban areas where native groundcovers, shrubs and trees have been removed by development—has led to significant declines in wildlife populations. By including native species along with your non-native

Deer are a common interloper in urban and rural gardens. The best way to keep them out of your prized but delectable plants is with a 7-foot-tall fence. A young buck samples sunflower seed set out for the squirrels as Dusty the cat looks on.

plants, you will encourage wildlife to return to your garden. They will in turn provide you with natural pest control and pollination services as well an endless source of entertainment with their antics. That said, some wildlife—like deer, elk, moose, skunks, squirrels, and raccoons—can become a nuisance with their foraging; see Garden Know-How, page 45, for methods of controlling them.

Plant in vertical layers so that shorter grasses and groundcovers grade in height into taller shrubs and then trees, creating a vertically layered landscape. This provides wildlife with a variety of spaces to gather food, build nests, hide from predators, and get out of the weather.

The first layer can be low-growing grasses, annuals, and perennials with patches of bare earth that grade in height into taller perennials and small deciduous and evergreen shrubs. These layers provide seeds and berries for food, grasses for nest-building, and open spaces for predators to hunt in. These lower layers then grade in height

into medium-height shrubs and trees, followed by taller trees. Twiggy, dense evergreen and deciduous shrubs in this layer provide much of the nesting space and shelter for song birds. The tallest layer of shrubs and trees protects the lower layers from the elements and provides perching and nesting sites for predators like owls and hawks and cavity nesters like downy woodpeckers and flickers.

Last, water is a critical element of a good habitat. All critters need a source of clean water for drinking and bathing. There are many ways to provide a steady source by simply harnessing existing features in your garden. Water can be provided in shallow pools or depressions filled by a sprinkler, drip line, or small waterfall. Shallow containers can be placed under drippy faucets or at downspouts to catch otherwise wasted runoff. Insects, including butterflies and bees, need muddy patches of earth or flat pans filled with gravel and water where they can alight and sip but not fall in and drown.

To develop a wildlife-friendly garden, create layers of low, medium and tall-growing plants to provide wildlife places to feed, nest, hide, and sleep. Source: Washington Department of Fish and Wildlife.

There are dozens of native pollinators in the Northwest besides the familiar honey bee. Solitary mason or blue orchard bees lay eggs in tight spaces like these cardboard tubes placed in a protective shelter and then plug the hole with mud.

Pollinator and beneficial insects rely on a wide variety of plants that bloom in succession throughout the growing season for food. Planting flowers that bloom in succession from early spring through fall will provide a moving feast of pollen (a source of protein) and nectar (a source of carbohydrates and sugars). The chart on page 237 has a list of nectar and pollen plants preferred by pollinator and beneficial insects.

The honey bee is not the only pollinator insect in the garden. There are actually hundreds, if not thousands, of native solitary bees (such as the orchard mason bee), as well as leafcutter bees, bumblebees, wasps, butterflies, moths, flies, and even birds that provide the same service. All of the

pollinators are important in our home gardens but they are also vitally important to the Northwest's commercial tree fruit, berry, vegetable, and forage crop production.

Beneficial insects need access to other insects for food and breeding; they often eat a wide variety of other insects. They are particularly valuable to the gardener when they go after pests that attack our favorite plants. To encourage them to hang around, plant out-of-the-way corners of the garden with plants that attract their preferred insects. This creates a reservoir of food for the beneficial insects so they are present when the population of undesirable insects increases. Check page 237 for a list of plants that draw pollinator and beneficial insects.

INTEGRATED PEST MANAGMENT

There was a time when the appearance of an insect or disease on a favorite flower would send a gardener to the shed for a can of kills-everything-in-the-garden spray to dispatch the intruder. Fortunately, times have changed. We no longer look to insecticides and fungicides as the only way to manage pests and diseases in the garden.

Integrated pest management (IPM)has replaced the old philosophies and, in the process, changed how we look at pest management in general. According to the Statewide Integrated Pest Management Program at the University of California at Davis:

> Integrated pest management (IPM), is an ecosystem-based strategy that focuses on long-term prevention of pests or their damage through a combination of techniques such as biological control, habitat manipulation, modification of cultural practices, and use of resistant varieties. Pesticides are used only after monitoring indicates they are needed according to established guidelines, and treatments are made with the goal of removing only the target organism. Pest control materials are selected and applied in a manner that minimizes risks to human health, beneficial and nontarget organisms, and the environment.

There are four steps in a good IPM program: 1) Preventing or reducing potential problems before they start; 2) using cultural practices to reduce the numbers of pest insects to an acceptable threshold; 3) using beneficial insects to biologically control pest insects; 4) if none of the previous steps work, applying the most benign chemicals possible to control the problem.

As the old saying goes, "An ounce of prevention is worth a pound of cure." IPM begins with preventing pests from gaining a foothold in the first place. Keep your garden clean. Rake up fallen leaves and old fruit so there are fewer places for insects and their eggs to hide over the winter. Thin and prune overgrown plants so there is good air circulation and leaves can dry off quickly. Quiet, moist pockets of air around plants are often a perfect breeding place for mold, fungus, and bugs.

Make sure the right plant is in the right place so it thrives. Select plants that are resistant to disease. Struggling plants send out chemical signals that attract insects and are more prone to disease. For example, the popular eastern dogwood (*Cornus florida*) is very susceptible to dogwood anthracnose, a fungal disease that causes a tree's leaves to yellow, making it difficult to carry out photosynthesis. There is no cure for it and most trees die unless they are sprayed frequently with expensive fungicides. Instead, plant the Kousa dogwood (*C. kousa*) that is much less susceptible to the disease but just as pretty.

The second step is to use ordinary gardening techniques or cultural practices to deter problems. Water plants properly so they remain healthy. Too much or too little water puts plants under stress and opens them to disease and insects. European birch trees, for example, planted in the middle of a lawn and watered with a sprinkler set only to reach the shallow grass roots won't get enough water to their deeper roots. The tree then releases a stress signal that attracts the European birch borer, which then attacks the tree.

Too little or, more often, too much fertilizer also stresses plants. Overfertilization generates quick growth in plants at the expense of good root development, which weakens them over time. That dark green sod you fertilize five or more times a year is growing so fast that it can't establish a deep root system. Without a good root system, the sod is easily affected by drought, which opens it up to weed, bug, and disease issues.

Mow lawns to the right height so they shade the ground, which prevents weed germination and helps retain moisture in the roots. Water your lawn for longer periods of time, but space out the waterings so they are less frequent. To check how deep the water is going, dig down into the roots after a watering to see if they are damp. If not, increase your watering time.

The insect world has had biological control for as long as there have been food chains. We have only recently begun taking advantage of the natural instincts of predator and prey and using them to our benefit. The appearance of a few aphids on your plants is an opportunity to watch beneficial insects like ladybug larvae, braconid wasps, and lacewing larvae (a.k.a. "aphid lions") move in and gobble up the aphids.

Using biological control methods does take a certain amount of patience and tolerance on your part, though. It often takes two to three weeks for the population of predator insects to grow to sufficient numbers to have an impact; meanwhile, the problem insects chew holes in everything. When the predators do knock down the bad bugs, they don't eliminate them completely. There will always be a few around.

There are times when it may become necessary to bring out the organic or conventional chemicals to address a problem. Often, deciding when that should be depends on your tolerance for the damage

This red currant leaf is infested with aphids that have blistered the leaf from the underside. The lady beetle and its larvae will seek out the aphids and devour them, an example of biological control by insects.

the pest has caused and the effectiveness of the other methods already discussed. If you can stand a certain amount of damage on a plant, then you aren't as likely to haul out the spray as someone who can't tolerate the same level. This is called the "tolerance threshold" and it can be different for every person and situation. Someone raising roses for an important rose show will want fewer signs of damage than someone who just wants to be able to smell them.

In the fruit-growing regions of the Northwest, the wider community agricultural tolerance for pests that affect fruit crops will have an impact on how home gardeners need to manage fruit trees. In many apple-growing areas, there is little tolerance of unkempt backyard apple trees because they harbor unchecked populations of codling moth, apple maggot, and other insects that can get into the commercial orchard. Another example is the noxious weed laws in each state or province, which can mandate the control of certain weeds that can seriously impact the economic, environmental, and aesthetic values of the land.

In general, IPM methodologies dictate that you should start with the most benign chemical that has the lowest long-term effect on the environment and other plants, animals, and people as possible. Selecting the right chemical for the job means getting an accurate identification of the problem first. Take damage samples to your local Master Gardener's office for identification and recommendations of approved chemicals and other practices for your area. Use the Internet carefully to research pesticide information; there are a lot of sites with information that is inaccurate or written for other parts of the country. Each state and province sets its own rules on the use of both organic and conventional pesticides, and you are required to follow those regulations.

Chemicals are generally divided into two classes: Organic and conventional. Organic pesticides are derived from naturally occurring botanical and mineral-based substances (such as plant oils and extracts) and minerals (such as sulfur, mineral oils, phosphorus, and potassium). Synthetic chemicals, on the other hand, are man-

Weeds in patio blocks can be very difficult to pull by hand. For a nonchemical way to control individual weeds in a patio, sidewalk, or driveway, you can use horticultural vinegar, boiling water, or a propane torch.

made chemicals synthesized from other chemicals.

So which is better? It depends on the problem you are treating and the results you want. Organic insecticides can be very effective while organic herbicides have a mixed range of effectiveness. On the other hand, some synthetic chemicals are very effective and leave little to no residual after the application is made.

Are organic pesticides safer than synthetic pesticides? Not necessarily. There are organic pesticides that are just as dangerous to humans, animals, and the environment as synthetics. Horticultural vinegar, which is used as an organic herbicide, is 20 percent acetic acid—compared to household vinegar at five percent acetic acid. Horticultural vinegar can easily burn your skin as well as burn down the weeds.

There are a lot of homemade chemical recipes available, especially on the Internet, that purport to treat pest issues. *Use them with caution.* Most of these folk remedies have not been scientifically tested for their reliability or efficacy. While many people use them because they seem cheaper than commercial pesticides and easy to make from household ingredients, they don't have a predictable track record.

USE CHEMICALS SAFELY AND LEGALLY

Anytime you use an organic or conventional pesticide, always read the label on the container first and follow the directions carefully. The label is the law in each state or province on how the chemical is to be used, how much is to be applied, under what conditions it can be used and how it must be disposed of. The label will also have first aid information on how to handle accidental poisoning and spills.

Using sustainable gardening methods can be a big shift of perspective for some people. It will take time for the full impact of efforts to conserve water, use fewer chemicals, and choose plants that fit your environment to become apparent in the world around us. If the shift to sustainable gardening seems daunting, take small steps as you learn new methods and new plants. Even little steps will add up to a healthier environment if enough people take them.

GARDEN
KNOW-HOW

Becoming a good gardener takes time and a lot of trial and error with a heavy emphasis on the error. Each gardener will have their own methods and ways of doing things. This chapter describes a wide range of topics and methods with the idea that this is a starting place for you to then adapt the ideas to your garden's environment and your abilities.

MAKING AND USING COMPOST

Making your own compost at home is easy and it's the most sustainable way to handle yard waste. The composting process uses bacteria that are already present in the environment to break down the plant material into plant nutrients and organic matter or humus that adds texture to the soil and increases the soil's water-holding capacity.

Almost any fresh or dried plant-based material can go into a compost pile: Lawn clippings *without herbicides*, leaves, *weeds without seeds*, kitchen vegetable scraps, and manure (horse, cow, llama, rabbit, and chicken). Shredded pine and fir needles and fine wood chips from pruning can be used sparingly in the mix but they will take much longer to break down. It is a myth that conifer needles can markedly acidify the soil.

Avoid using seedy weeds, bones and meat scraps, dairy products, eggs (although crushed shells are okay) and dog, cat, and pig manure (and cat litter). Meat and dairy scraps can draw rats, mice, raccoons, skunks, and even coyotes to the pile. Dog, cat, and pig manures and cat litter can carry diseases that are transmittable to humans.

Shredding materials either with a lawn mower or a shredder prior to building a pile helps break

Build a compost pile by mixing equal parts brown, dried material with fresh green material. Shred material with a lawn mower or shredder and build a pile approximately 3 feet tall, wide, and deep.

Keep an eye out for earthworms in your lawn soil. These wriggly little creatures are a sure sign of healthy soil, because they process decaying matter and create waste, or "castings," that add to the nutrients your lawn uses to make its own food. They will not proliferate in an unhealthy soil base, and a lack of earthworms is oftentimes the "canary in the coal mine" of your lawn's health.

the materials into finer pieces, which allows the bacteria more surface area to work on. Green and brown materials should be mixed in equal parts to prevent the development of anaerobic bacteria that can make a pile smelly. If this does occur, add more brown material to your pile. As you build a pile, moisten it to the consistency of a wrung-out sponge.

The ideal size for a compost pile is 3 × 3 × 3 feet, which allows the bacteria enough mass to work. Piles can be contained in any structure that can hold them together and allows air to reach all sides of the pile. Wooden pallets that are often available for free are a good low-budget option. Circles of fence wire, squares of scrap timber, or lumber are easy to construct out of readily available salvaged materials. Last, there are a number of commercial compost systems available if you want something fancy or the compost pile needs to be in a more visible space.

Once a pile is created and properly moistened, the metabolism of the bacteria heats up the center of the pile to 140 to 170 degrees Fahrenheit. The pile will stay at that temperature for several days before falling as the bacteria consume the readily available food. Temperatures can be measured with long compost thermometers available at garden centers. At these temperatures, most weed seeds will be

destroyed. If you want compost in a matter of weeks, the pile will have to be turned to re-establish the bacterial action once the temperature drops. If you like to conserve *your* energy, a static pile can be created and then left alone for several months to break down.

A pile should always smell earthy. If it starts to get stinky, there is too much green material in the pile and the anaerobic bacteria have taken over. To correct this problem, break the pile up and add more brown material. It is not necessary to add commercial compost activators as nature provides more than enough bacteria on its own. During the Northwest's traditionally dry summers, compost piles will periodically need extra water to keep them working. In the winter, west of the Cascades, piles should be covered with a tarp to reduce nutrients leaching from the pile.

PREPARING YOUR LANDSCAPE FOR WILDFIRE

In much of the Northwest, wildfires are a constant threat during the dry summers and can occur in both rural and urban environments. "Firewise planning" involves using landscape design and maintenance methods to create three zones of defense around structures that will slow the movement of a fire. The key word here is "slow"—there is no such thing as a fireproof structure. If a fire is big enough, it will burn everything in its path.

Zone 1 is the area within 30 feet of your house and outbuildings. In this zone, the goal is to keep a fire on the ground and out of the treetops. All landscaping plants should be low-growing and fire resistant. A list of fire-resistant plants is at the end of this section. Keep foundation areas around the house clear of any flammable materials. Use stone, gravel, or other non-flammable mulches instead of bark. Install wide concrete or graveled paths around the house to create a break in the fuel supply that might slow a fire down.

Maintenance in this zone includes keeping lawns well watered and properly mowed. Install fire-resistant composite or metal roofing and clear gutters and roofs of leaves and conifer needles before

Cleared or defensible space around this house saved it from a wildfire.

fire season starts. Remove flammable clutter and stack firewood away from structures. Close off spaces under decks and eaves so sparks don't blow in.

Zone 2 is the area 30 to 60 feet from the house. Continue to plant fire-resistant plants whenever possible. Thin trees so their branches aren't touching the neighboring trees and thin out any dense, twiggy shrubs. Limb up trees 12 feet above the ground to prevent fire from climbing into the tree. Plant low-growing native grasses like Idaho fescue in this area, and keep it mowed.

Zone 3 is 60 to 100 feet from the house. Thin out dense stands of trees, especially dead ones, and limb up lower branches. Clear trees and brush away from your driveway so you have a safe escape route.

If you live in a wooded neighborhood, consider gathering your neighbors together to create a Firewise Community and work together to create a fire-resistant landscape around the houses. Most local conservation districts and state and provincial forestry and natural resource agencies can help you implement a Firewise Community and may even have money, crews, and equipment to do some of the clearing. More information is available at www.firewise.org.

DEALING WITH CRITTERS

Deer are often the most common problem for many rural and urban gardeners. These beautiful creatures seem to know just when the tulips are ready to bloom, the hostas are at their best, and your carrots are their sweetest. Deer are browsers that nibble on a wide variety of annuals, perennials, shrubs, and trees. They are more likely to show up in midsummer as forage plants in the wild begin to dry out and your well-watered garden looks like a five-star restaurant. In the winter, they will browse on twigs and eat some shrubs to the ground.

There is no such thing as a deer-proof plant. If deer are hungry, they will eat anything they can reach. The best you can hope for is planting deer-resistant plants your particular herd doesn't like. Your local Master Gardener program will have the best experience-based list of deer-resistant plants for your area. A few of the more reliable resistant plants are listed at the end of this section.

The best way to ensure deer stay out of your garden is to erect a 7- to 8-foot-tall fence of field wire or heavy polypropylene mesh. Wire fencing can be heavy and hard to handle while the polypropylene mesh is lightweight and easy to

Deer can easily jump short fences. This 7.5-foot, heavy-duty polypropylene mesh fence keeps the deer at bay. Be sure to anchor it to the ground—they will crawl under it.

install. Deer can crawl under fences so be sure to anchor them to the ground. Both are available at farm and agricultural supply stores or online.

If you can't put up a fence, your next best deterrent are repellant sprays that are applied to the plants. There are a number of commercially prepared deer repellant sprays on the market, and the Internet has dozens of recipes for homemade repellants. Most repellants discourage deer by using the scent of things deer don't like or that remind them of a predator. Garlic, hot pepper, putrefied egg, blood, and coyote urine are common ingredients in these mixes. Homebrewed deer repellent recipes are inexpensive to make but they need to be reapplied frequently. Commercial repellents contain fixative agents to keep the chemicals on the plant leaves for several weeks.

There are a number of deer deterrent devices on the market that purport to keep these marauders out of the garden. Unfortunately, deer that spend a lot of time around humans become *very* accustomed to our scents and actions. As a result, deterrents like soap bars or human hair hung in plants rarely work for long. Deer also become accustomed to motion-activated sprinklers, lights, and radios after a few weeks, and they just ignore them when they are turned on.

In some parts of the Northwest, elk and moose are common. These are very large, unpredictable animals that can walk through a fence and are not deterred by stinky sprays. If you encounter them, especially moose, *leave them alone* as they will charge you or your dogs. They can do a lot of damage with their big antlers and sharp hooves.

Skunks, raccoons, and squirrels will hang around if there is a dependable food source such as birdseed, pet food, pond plants, or fish. Skunks prefer seeds and insects while raccoons are omnivores that will eat *everything* from the expensive koi fish in your pond to the ripe plums that were ready to harvest. Squirrels will dig up spring bulbs and find their way into bird feeders. Rabbits will dig under fences, unless the fences are buried a foot down, to nibble on tender shoots and plants.

The best way to control these critters is to remove pet food and spilled birdseed and to put low fences around ponds. Close off holes in home foundations and roof eaves. If these critters become a serious nuisance or take up residence in crawlspaces, attics, or outbuildings where they can be unexpectedly encountered, it's best to call a critter removal professional who is licensed to humanely trap and relocate them. Never handle any of these animals as they will bite and can carry diseases, including rabies in isolated cases.

Moles and gophers are ground dwellers that are responsible for the mounds of dirt that pop up in your lawn or garden. While both are burrowers, moles primarily feed on insects in the soil while gophers feed on roots and plants. Both animals are solitary creatures so the damage you see in a lawn is likely caused by a single animal. Gopher mounds are distinguished by a mound of dirt pushed to the side of a small hole while mole mounds appear as a cone of soil with a smaller plug of soil at the top. Moles and gophers are found together west of the Cascades while east of the Cascades, gophers are predominant.

The most reliable way to control these animals is to use body gripping traps inserted into the animal's runs. That said, the use of body gripping traps is illegal in Washington even though it is legal to sell the traps in the state. Deterrents—such as inserting moth balls into runs, soil vibrators, or flooding tunnels—are not reliable and have not stood up to scientific testing. Poison baits are strongly discouraged because they can affect other animals like cats, dogs, hawks, and owls that try to make a meal out of the dead mole or gopher.

TAKING A SOIL SAMPLE

As was discussed previously, taking care of your soil—above everything else—will go a long way towards creating a healthy, sustainable garden. The first step is to establish a baseline of information on what your soil type is, its nutrient and organic matter content, and its pH level. This is done by taking soil samples around your garden and having them analyzed by a laboratory. There are DIY kits

available in garden centers but they are not as accurate as laboratory tests nor do they offer recommendations on how to correct deficiencies.

To take a soil sample you will need a shovel, a plastic bucket, a plastic trowel to mix the soil, and some closable freezer bags. (Note: Using plastic is important because metal buckets and trowels can contaminate a sample via metallic ions that are picked up in the micronutrients tests.) Individual samples will need to be taken from several different areas of your garden or yard and then blended together to make one sample that will be submitted. If you have a large garden with high and low spots or a couple of different types of soil, it may be necessary to take multiple sets of blended samples.

With the shovel, dig a hole about 8 to 12 inches deep. Take a representative slice of the soil down

Collect small soil samples from several spots in your yard, and from multiple depths. You can use a shovel, trowel, or even a spoon to collect the samples. Mix the soil samples together in a small, clean plastic bucket, and blend the samples thoroughly.

the side of the hole. Push all but the middle 2-inch column off the shovel and put that soil column in the bucket. Take five to ten separate samples from an area. Once you have collected your samples, mix the soil thoroughly to blend the individual samples. Take 2 cups of this soil, put it in the plastic bag, and prepare the package to ship it to a soil laboratory.

Our region's land grant universities are no longer testing soil samples for the public. There are, however, commercial soil labs throughout the Northwest that can do them for a fee. Ask your local Master Gardener program or conservation district for a list of local labs. Laboratories located in your area will be familiar with your soils and will give you a much more accurate set of recommendations than if you send it out of the region. Call the lab and ask for the cost of the test and how to prepare and label the sample.

There are two types of tests: A basic nutrient test for nitrogen, phosphorus, potassium, organic matter, and pH and a more detailed test that also measures the soil's micronutrients and trace elements. The latter test also includes heavy metals such as lead, cadmium, and arsenic that can be health hazards, especially in areas that could be planted with edible crops. Along with the information of what is in your soil, the soil report will have recommendations on how much fertilizer, sulfur, or agricultural lime you might need to add.

DEALING WITH SOIL ACIDITY AND ALKALINITY

Soil acidity or alkalinity can be a challenge when it comes to growing certain plants in a Northwest garden. Generally, the soils found west of the Cascades tend to be more acidic than those east of the Cascades. Acidity and alkalinity are measured by a 14-point pH scale, with 7 being the neutral point. Soils with a pH below 7 are considered acidic while those above 7 are considered alkaline. Most plants do well in a pH range of 5.5 to 7.0. The pH scale is a measure of bacterial and chemical interactions in the soil that affect the availability of nitrogen, phosphorus, potassium, iron, copper,

boron, zinc, sulfur, calcium, and manganese for proper plant growth and development.

In the Northwest, rhododendrons, azaleas, blueberries, and camellias thrive in acidic pH soils but struggle in more alkaline soils. Acid-loving plants in this condition often turn yellow because the higher pH chemically ties up the availability of iron in the soil and disrupts the chlorophyll production that makes the plant green.

Because of the popularity of these acid-loving plants, many Northwest gardeners—especially those east of the Cascades—go to great lengths to create a more acidic soil to successfully grow these plants. However, changing the pH in a large area is difficult; it may be more practical to group these finicky plants in raised beds or large pots than to create a more acidic soil. To lower the pH, the soil needs to be amended with granular or powdered sulfur, which oxidizes into sulfuric acid. Plants will then need to be fertilized with acidifying fertilizers such as ammonium sulfate, ammonium nitrate, and urea (which are often sold as rhododendron fertilizers). Granular sulfur is easier to use than powdered and both are available at garden centers that stock a good line of soil amendments.

When acidic soils need to be shifted to a more neutral or alkaline pH, agricultural limestone or gypsum is added to the soil. Vegetable crops grown in high rainfall areas of the region often benefit from an application of lime or gypsum. Many of the drought-tolerant plants recommended for low-water use or xeric gardens prefer a more alkaline soil.

USING COLOR IN THE GARDEN

In the Northwest, where many of our gardens are set against a backdrop of green forests or subtly colored desert landscapes, the interplay of color draws our landscapes together and creates a lively atmosphere through the four seasons. Unity and coordination of color creates cohesion in a landscape by drawing together shapes, focal points, and leaf textures. It creates a rhythm that ties the garden together.

This container planting uses plants with colorful leaves to provide season-long interest.

Color can be split into the warm colors and the cool colors. Warm colors are the reds, yellows, and oranges. Their brightness draws your attention to wherever they are in the garden. They lead your eye through the garden or highlight a particular point. They evoke a sense of warmth, security, and excitement that creates vibrancy in the garden. Warm colors make large spaces seem smaller.

Cool colors are the blues, greens, and purples. Their coolness creates a serene, calm, and relaxing mood in a garden. They can even create a bit of a mysterious feel in the right setting. Cool colors tend to make a small space seem larger, which makes them particularly useful in a small garden.

Neutral colors like whites, grays, and silvers often soften the warm, vibrant colors, especially the very intense ones. They also help create transitions between different colors in a bed. There are few gray and silver flowers so these colors are introduced by plants with gray leaves like the sages, lamb's ears, and lavenders. Whites can be more intense than some of the hotter warm colors so they need to be used carefully.

Always use fewer warm-colored plants than cool-colored ones, especially if they are the really hot colors. To give a bed depth, plant warm colors at the front and plant cool colors behind them starting with the darker shades graduating into lighter shades as you go farther back. Use masses of the same plants rather than individual plants to give a bed weight and cohesiveness. A bed full of individual plants creates a cluttered, unorganized look. Use groupings of odd numbers of plants (three, five, seven) as it is easier to create balance in a planting.

Most perennials, shrubs, and trees only bloom for a short time, so a good garden design should have different plants that bloom in succession through the spring, summer, and fall. This creates an ever-changing tapestry of color and texture through the seasons. Choose shrubs and trees not only for their spring color but also for their summer and fall leaf colors. For winter interest, consider shrubs and trees with colorful bark, stems, or seed clusters.

There are no hard and fast rules for using color in the garden. It comes down to personal choice and the look you are trying to create. Be adventurous; paint the shed purple and then use complementary colors in your plantings. If you aren't sure what would look good, buy some annuals and experiment for the year. You can always hit the fall sales to pick up perennials, roses, shrubs, and trees that fit your newly discovered color palette.

STARTING PLANTS FROM SEEDS

Starting your own plants from seed or cuttings is a fun and inexpensive way to get more of your favorite plants or grow unusual ones you don't normally find at the garden center. It isn't hard but it does take some attention to detail.

Quality plants come from quality seed so buy from reliable sources. There are hundreds of seed companies out there so ask your local garden experts and fellow gardeners whom they recommend. Several Northwest regional seed companies are noted on pages 238 to 239; these specialize in plants that do well in the Northwest. Read the seed packet carefully before starting your seeds. It will have all the information on when to plant, how deep to plant the seeds, how long it will take for them to germinate, when to fertilize them and when to plant them outdoors. Keep in mind that some seeds need light to germinate and are planted *on* the soil surface.

Most seeds need to be started indoors in a warm place four to twelve weeks ahead of the date recommended for transplanting them into the

2 Carefully sow the seeds on the surface and cover with the appropriate amount of medium.

1 Fill containers to within about a half-inch of the top with soilless mix and place in a tray of water to saturate the soil. You want to be sure to use a purchased lightweight, soilless mix that is sterilized and free of disease organisms rather than garden soil, which is usually too heavy, poorly drained, and can contain harmful fungi or bacteria.

3 Put the container in a plastic bag and seal it to maintain humidity. Place the containers in a warm spot out of direct sunlight. The top of a refrigerator or freezer works well. Check daily for germination. You may need to open the bag for a little while to prevent excessive moisture buildup, which can lead to damping off.

④ Remove the plastic bag when the seedlings first start showing up and place the container under fluorescent lights, leaving about 1 inch between the tops of the plants and the light. Adjust the light as needed to keep it 1 to 3 inches above the seedlings as they grow.

⑥ Transplant seedlings into individual pots when they have two sets of leaves, gently prying seedlings out of the soil and separating the roots, if necessary. Place pots back under lights.

⑤ When seedlings have one or two sets of leaves, use small, pointed scissors to thin out excess seedlings. Avoid pulling the unwanted seedlings because it can uproot nearby seedlings.

garden. That translates to starting seeds indoors in February and March and transplanting them into the garden in May. Seeds started too early become overgrown and stunted before their set-out date; it's a condition they usually don't recover from. Seeds started too late produce plants that are not strong enough to withstand the variable spring weather conditions in the garden.

Seeds germinate best at about 70 degrees Fahrenheit so warm basements or extra bedrooms are perfect for starting seeds. Seeds can also be started on heat mats in heated greenhouses in the warmer areas west of the Cascades. As the seedlings grow, they will need temperatures more in the 60-degree range to do well.

Start your seeds in a soilless potting mix that contains finely milled peat to hold moisture, sand for drainage, and perlite or vermiculite to improve texture. This mix is light, drains quickly, and doesn't form a crust that can stop seedlings from poking through the surface. The mix is also sterile, which reduces the occurrence of diseases that can kill your seedlings. These soil mixes are sold in a dry form that will need to be thoroughly moistened

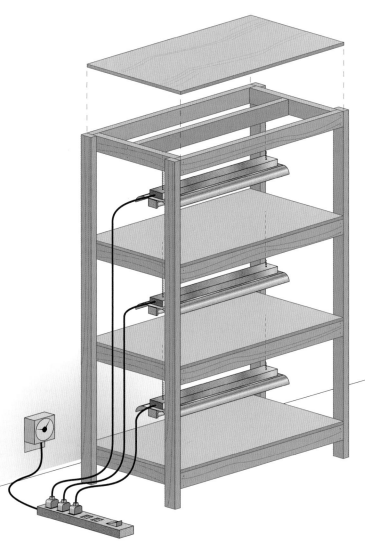

This easy-to-build starter rack holds up to twelve full-sized seedling flats or trays and can be located practically anywhere with an accessible electrical outlet. The top shelf offers a handy space for storing extra flats and other supplies. Use one or two light fixtures above each shelf, as appropriate for your needs.

before use. They are available at garden centers as germination or seed starting mixes.

Seeds can be started in almost any container as long as it drains well. Household containers like cottage cheese cartons, margarine tubs, and milk jugs cut to the proper size are easy to handle and provide enough space for root development. Be sure to punch several quarter-inch holes in the bottom of a container for drainage. Egg cartons do *not* make good starting containers because they don't provide enough space for root development and it's difficult to remove seedlings without damaging roots.

Commercially available wood or plastic flats, peat or plastic pots, compressed peat pellets, and plastic cell packs are also a good choice for seed starting. The advantage of the commercial containers is that they are easier to fit under a light system and offer more space for roots to grow. These containers can be purchased new or you can recycle ones from the plants you've bought. Used containers should be rinsed in a solution of one part bleach to ten parts water to kill bacteria and disease pests.

In the Northwest, our natural light is limited in the winter by persistent clouds, short day lengths and a low sun angle. This means seedlings need to be started indoors under artificial lights programmed to stay on for twelve to fourteen hours a day. Use 4-foot long grow lights or fluorescent shop light fixtures set 2 inches above the seedlings. Ordinary fluorescent lights are much less expensive than grow lights but they don't offer as broad a spectrum of light. Suspend the lights in such a way that they can be raised as the seedlings grow.

PROPAGATING SHRUBS AND PERENNIALS

Many herbaceous perennials and woody plants can be multiplied by taking root divisions or softwood stem cuttings at the right time of the year. Spring-flowering perennials can be divided after they finish blooming while summer and fall bloomers can be divided in the late fall or early spring. As always, do a little research on the particular requirements of the plants you want to divide.

Many shrubs can be propagated from softwood cuttings taken in the spring. Cuttings are made of the current year's stems with three to four leaf buds attached. Strip the stems of all but the top two sets of leaves and then dip them in rooting hormone powder (available at garden centers). Then plant the cuttings in a flat of sterile, moistened perlite and cover loosely with a plastic bag or cover. Place the flats of cuttings in shaded cold frames outdoors or under lights in a cool room indoors until they develop enough roots to be planted in a regular growing medium. Keep them moist but not overwatered. The rooting process may take several months depending on the variety of shrub. Keep this in mind—many popular, hybridized plants are protected under plant patents that do not permit reproduction in mass quantities.

SAVING SEEDS

Saving your own seeds is a fun way to preserve plants that are not commonly available commercially. The catch is that they must be from plants that are "open-pollinated," meaning that the seed was naturally

To divide perennials, smaller rootballs can usually be cut into pieces using a sharp knife. Larger clumps can be sliced with a sharp spade or pried apart using two back-to-back garden forks.

fertilized and not hybridized or propagated from cuttings. Seeds from hybridized plants often are sterile, have low germination rates, and more often than not do not reproduce true to type. This means you will get a plant that doesn't look like the plant you started with. If you plan to save your own seed, make sure the package says the seed is either heirloom or open-pollinated. Designations on the package like "F1" or "F2" indicate hybridized seed.

Seeds must be mature or ripe when you harvest them in the fall so do some research so you know when the time is right. Label and store seeds in paper envelopes in a cool, dry place until you need them. Properly stored seed can remain viable for two to three years or longer. To test germination rates, roll twenty seeds in a damp paper towel and set it in a warm place to sprout. Calculate the germination percentage to determine how many seeds you need to plant in order to grow the plants you need.

GARDENING IN SMALL SPACES

In recent years, as housing costs rise and people move back into the urban core of many Northwest cities, small gardens have become popular. Gardening practices in a small garden are no different than those used in larger spaces; they are just done on a smaller scale.

Small gardens need particular attention paid to their design. There is often little or no room for experimenting so starting with a well-thought-out plan is critical. Each plant, structure, bench or pathway will need to serve more than one function.

The first design consideration in a small garden is how will people move through it? How will they get from the small front yard around to the equally small backyard? Oftentimes a simple, gently curving path with narrow planting beds along the side works well. Make the path as wide as you can, as this adds a feeling of space to the garden. If your space demands long straight paths, soften the path's boundaries with billowy plants to hide its hard edges.

Dividing a small garden into even smaller spaces can actually make it seem bigger. However, instead of using tall, dense hedges or fences to divide the space, use mid-height plants and structures that

Large containers planted with unusual plants are a great way to add sculpture to a small garden.

you can see over and through to keep a broader view. Open-weave lattice fencing is easy to see through while still defining a smaller area. Arches over pathways frame an entrance to the new space. Fruit trees can be espaliered on a wire fence between sections not only to break up the space, but to provide flowers and fruit.

Changing levels also creates the sense of space. Stepping up or down a few steps puts the space into a different visual context and adds a third dimension to its visual impact. A small raised deck with a place to sit gives the garden a focal point and a different view of the garden.

Another way to add space to a small garden is to "borrow" views from outside the garden. Maybe you can see your neighbor's beautiful tree or the more distant views of some of the Northwest's spectacular volcanic peaks, the ocean, Puget Sound, or countless rivers and streams. Frame that view with plants or structures and make it a focal point for a sitting space. Drawing even a distant view gives your garden a completely different feel.

Choosing the right color combinations can also change space perceptions. As was discussed in the color section, cool colors can make a space seem larger than it is while warm colors will draw your eye to particular point in the garden. To create depth in beds, plant pastel-colored flowers at the front of the bed and then site plants of a darker color immediately behind it. Then, as you plant in back of this darker color, use successively lighter shades to extend the feeling of depth.

Small gardens are a perfect place for using large containers, especially when planting space is limited and the garden is shaded by tall fences and buildings. Large ceramic, plastic, or wood containers can be planted with a wide variety of edible and ornamental plants, small shrubs, and trees. The pots themselves can become architectural elements, especially if their colors and shapes are coordinated in the design. Containers can also be moved around in a small garden to take advantage of sunny spaces that move with the seasons. Tomatoes that need a lot of sun to ripen can be planted in a large pot on wheels and moved to a new sunny spot as needed.

While almost any smaller plant can be grown in a container, in the colder parts of the Northwest containerized plantings will need winter protection or should be treated as annual plantings that are replaced each year. Pots can be grouped together and wrapped with a wind barrier or moved into a sheltered corner. Dormant deciduous plants can be moved into a garage. Small herbaceous plants can be removed from the pots and planted in in-ground holding beds and mulched. As a rule, when selecting shrubs and trees for containers in cold areas, choose those whose cold-hardiness is rated as hardy to a USDA zone lower than your local zone so they have a better chance of surviving the winter freezes and thaws.

HOW TO GARDEN IN RAISED BEDS

If you'd like to grow your own food, but need the garden to be low-maintenance, highly productive, and attractive, raised beds are a perfect solution. Here's why:

- The soil in the beds stays loose because you walk around them rather than across them. This makes it easier for the plants' roots to develop, especially for root crops like carrots, parsnips or turnips.
- In the spring, the sun heats the sides and tops of the beds, warming the soil which will give you a head start on the gardening season. The warmer soil increases the activity of microbes that break down organic matter and make nitrogen available to plants.
- Raised beds are easier to tend because you only have to weed the tops of the beds. If you cover the pathways in between the beds with landscape fabric (also called weed-block) and a layer of bark mulch or gravel, it will really cut down on the time you'll spend weeding.
- If your soil doesn't drain well or your garden soil is mostly comprised of rocks, build some raised beds and you've solved those frustrating problems.
- And last but not least, their more formal appearance creates an aesthetically-appealing garden that looks great no matter where you locate it.

When designing your beds, remember they can be any size or shape as long as you can reach into the center from either side without having to step into the beds. A width of 3 to 4 feet is ideal.

The most common heights of raised beds are 6 to 12 inches, which provides the plants' roots with plenty of growing space, but they can also be as high as you want. If you have difficulty bending down to the ground, or if you use a wheelchair or walker, building a taller bed will allow you to continue gardening. Remember to make the pathways between the beds wide enough to maneuver in. You might also need to make the beds a little narrower for easier reaching.

To frame the beds with wood, select lumber that hasn't been treated with preservatives or other chemicals. Research has shown those materials leach into the soil and that plant roots will absorb them. Standard lumber made from fir or pine works well, as does cedar and redwood which weather the elements well.

Using wood is only one of your options, however. One alternative is non-toxic, recycled plastic lumber made from plastic milk jugs. This type of lumber is long-lasting and resistant to rot and mildew. And it's environmentally-friendly because it keeps that plastic out of the landfills. Some gardeners construct their raised beds from concrete blocks, which retain the sun's heat—something that heat-loving crops like tomatoes, peppers, eggplants, and melons thrive on.

Constructing a raised bed is pretty straightforward. If you're using standard or recycled plastic lumber, cut the boards to your specifications. Remember to use long decking screws (4-inch screws work well) to join the boards together. Nails have a tendency to pop out of the joints over time.

If pocket gophers or voles are a problem in your garden, staple hardware cloth or 1-inch poultry netting onto the bottom of the beds before filling them with soil.

Once the bed is assembled, set it into its permanent location and check to see that it is both level and square. Since pathways between the beds should be able to accommodate garden equipment like wheelbarrows and carts, make the pathways 3 to 4 feet wide.

The next step is to fill the beds with soil. If you don't have enough available from your garden, purchase a soil mix—usually a combination of sand, compost, and sandy loam soil—from landscaping supply companies. It takes a while to build fertile soil, so add in organic amendments such as compost, composted animal manure (i.e., cattle, horse, goat, llama, or poultry), or shredded leaves to accelerate the process. For the best success, you should add soil amendments at the beginning or end of each growing season.

Providing water to the plants in your raised beds is essential to gardening success. To be the most efficient, water only the tops of the beds rather than wasting water on the pathways. Consider installing soaker hoses or a drip-irrigation system set on an automatic timer to deliver water right to the plants' roots. Consult local or online sprinkler distributors for help with planning a system. The plants' moisture needs will change as the season progresses, so be sure to monitor it regularly by checking the moisture levels in the soil and make adjustments to the watering schedule as needed.

You'll be amazed at how productive a raised-bed garden can be and quickly find it has become an attractive and integral part of your landscape.

Raised beds are good choices for growing vegetables and herbs, especially where soil conditions or drainage problems make gardening difficult.

ANNUALS
for the Northwest

There is always room for the spots of color annuals can bring to a garden even if they take more work and resources to manage. Annuals can be hardy, half-hardy, or tender indicating their tolerance to cold temperatures early and late in the year. Hardy annuals can handle hard frosts and cooler spring soil and air temperatures. Half-hardy annuals will need the warmer soil and air temperatures of May before transplants or seeds can go out in the garden. They can tolerate light frosts but keep frost protection handy, just in case. Tender annuals can be transplanted into the garden after all danger of frost has passed and the soils have warmed. If conditions are too cold, they become stunted and don't recover very quickly, if at all.

ANNUALS IN THE LANDSCAPE

In a young garden, annuals can provide color, shape, and form for a couple of years while the perennials and shrubs fill in. They can fill bare spaces left when bulbs and early-blooming perennials go dormant after blooming. Colorful annuals can be color coordinated with equally colorful perennials, shrubs, and trees creating continuity in the garden and helping perennials transition through their bloom seasons. In the hot, dry areas east of the Cascades, annuals can carry color when perennials go into a heat-induced dormancy in late July and August. Finally, hardy annuals like petunias and flowering kales and cabbages can carry their color into the fall when everything else has finished blooming. In warmer areas west of the Cascades, the kales and cabbages will provide color through the winter.

ANNUALS SHINE IN SMALL SPACES

Annuals can be planted in containers, hanging baskets, and tucked into small garden spaces where larger plants don't fit. Overflowing hanging baskets and pots of bacopa (*Sutera cordata*), petunias (*Petunia* × *hybrida*), and fuchsias (*Fuchsia* spp.) hung at an entry point or along a porch invite people into the space. Window boxes hung on a wall make a

boring, harsh surface come to life. A recent trend in container gardening has led to impressive collections of coordinated plantings in huge ceramic pots. The architecture and color of the pot sets the theme and the plants—often a mix of annuals, tender perennials, and grasses—lend their colors, forms, and shapes creating a living sculpture and a garden focal point.

GROWING ANNUALS

Annuals need a well-drained soil rich in organic matter, regular fertilizing, and deep, regular watering to grow vigorously and bloom profusely. Work organic matter and a slow-release fertilizer into your beds at planting time. Follow up with monthly fertilizer applications of a low-nitrogen fertilizer. Don't count on time-release fertilizer pellets to do the job in the early summer. Those aren't activated until soil temperatures reach 70 degrees Fahrenheit. Annuals are shallow-rooted

The versatility of annuals is seen in this display in Manito Park's Duncan Gardens in Spokane, Washington.

so they will need frequent watering, especially in hot weather. From a sustainable gardening perspective, plant them in beds so you can give them a quick soak if needed. Annuals need to be deadheaded regularly to prevent the plant from putting its energy into seed development instead of flower production. Many annuals benefit from a shearing in late summer to stimulate new growth once the weather cools in September.

Annuals start appearing in the garden centers in late February to March west of the Cascades and by early April east of the Cascades. After months of gray clouds, rain, and snow, it's hard to resist taking a few of them home. While it's tempting to pick the biggest plants with the most blooms, instead pick plants with healthy (but a smaller show of) leaves and enough color so you know what you're getting. These smaller plants will transplant more easily and perform better over the season. East of the Cascades, limit your early-season purchases to hardy plants.

Garden centers will have a good selection of the ordinary types and colors of annuals but they are not going to have the unusual varieties that come in a broader spectrum of colors, shapes, and sizes. To get those, you have to grow your own from seed.

Start annuals under lights in late January to early February so they have enough time to grow to size. Read the directions on seed packets carefully. Some seeds will need to be planted into the soil; others will need light to germinate and are scattered on the surface of the soil. Cover flats with plastic covers or plastic wrap held off the soil surface with toothpicks or tongue depressors to capture the humidity from the soil. Keep the soil moist, but not soggy.

Place seed-starting trays in a warm space under fluorescent lights set 2 inches above the plants on a timer set for fourteen to sixteen hours a day. Four-foot shop lights with ordinary fluorescent bulbs work well. Once seeds germinate and have a few true leaves, transplant them into a larger container so their roots can expand. Position your lights so they are within 2 inches of the tops of the plants. Fertilize every two weeks with a half-strength liquid plant food. Check out page 50 for a layout of a lighting system.

When it is time to plant them outdoors, introduce them gradually to the outside temperatures over a five-day period by putting them outdoors in a protected spot during the day and bringing them back inside in the evening. Don't expect your home-grown annuals to look like the ones in the nursery. Commercially grown annuals are often treated with growth regulators to control their size.

WINTERING OVER TENDER ANNUALS

Some tender annuals like geraniums, coleus, and begonias can be successfully dug and overwintered in a greenhouse west of the Cascades or a cool basement under lights east of the Cascades. This is a good way to save money and to preserve unusual cultivars that are hard to find.

Whole plants can be dug from the garden before the first frost and repotted in a good quality houseplant mix. Their foliage should be cut down by half to adjust for a smaller root mass. Set the plants in a shaded area outdoors for a week or two to get them used to lower light levels before bringing them in.

PROPAGATION OF ANNUALS

Tip cuttings can also be made from your favorite annuals before the first frost. Using sharp pruners, cut a stem with three to four sets of leaves. Remove one-third of the leaves from the bottom of the stem and dip the cutting into rooting hormone, available from garden centers. Place them in a flat of moistened perlite or vermiculite and lightly cover them with plastic and place them under lights.

Once they have grown half-inch roots, pot them up into larger containers using a good potting mix. Keep them watered regularly. Lightly fertilize them with a half-strength liquid fertilizer every two weeks. Pinch fast-growing tips back to keep the plants bushy.

Annuals can be likened to an artist's paint box. They come in so many colors and textures that they can be blended into your landscape to provide unlimited combinations that tie the garden together and fit any theme the gardener chooses to create.

ALYSSUM
Lobularia maritima

Why It's Special—Alyssum's pleasantly sweet fragrance attracts bees and butterflies. They are prolific bloomers, so much so that they often obscure the foliage beneath. Because of their dainty size, they make good fillers for the front of borders, in rock gardens, and beneath shrubs, perennials, and other annuals. Suggested varieties are 'Carpet of Snow', 'Dwarf Purple', 'Easter Basket', and 'Rosie O'Day'.

How to Plant & Grow—Plant in all light conditions; in areas with hot summers, pick a location with afternoon shade. If growing from seed indoors, start them six weeks before your last frost date. If seeding directly in garden, sow them a month before the last frost. Purchased or started seedlings can be transplanted outdoors two weeks before last frost.

Care & Problems—Cut plants back after they bloom to encourage more flowering. Plants easily self-seed. See page 57 for fertilizing needs. Alyssum has minimal pest or disease problems.

Bloom Color—White, pink, lavender, apricot

Peak Season—Spring through frost

Mature Size (H x W)—4 to 8 in. x 10 to 15 in.

Water Needs—Medium. Provide regular watering throughout the season.

BACOPA
Sutera cordata

Why It's Special—Bacopa is a perky annual primarily used in container plantings because it blooms profusely and spills over the edges nicely. Plants are covered with cheerful little white, lavender, or pink flowers and attractive deep green leaves. Use in window boxes, hanging baskets, or at border fronts. White cultivars include Giant Snowflake™ and 'Snowtopia' while Snowstorm™ Blue, Abunda™ Colossal Blue and 'Blue Showers' all feature lavender blossoms. Abunda™ Colossal Pink has dainty pink flowers.

How to Plant & Grow—After frost, plant in full sun or part shade in well-drained soil. In areas with hot summers, make sure it gets some afternoon shade. Space plants 8 to 10 inches apart.

Care & Problems—Flowers are self-deadheading. Feed a slow-release fertilizer monthly. Bacopa does not have any serious pest or disease problems, although whiteflies can occasionally be an issue.

Bloom Color—White, lavender, pink

Peak Season—Summer to fall

Mature Size (H x W)—4 to 8 in. x up to 36 in.

Water Needs—Medium. Water regularly to keep the blooms coming and to prevent soil from drying.

BEGONIA
Begonia spp.

Why It's Special—The *Begonia* genus comprises more than 1,500 species worldwide, all having exotic-looking foliage and/or blossoms. While only hardy in zones 10 to 12, they are worth growing as annuals, usually in containers or hanging baskets. Wax and tuberous begonias (*B. semperflorens*) are loved for their beautiful blossoms and lush foliage. Rex begonias (*B. rex-cultorum*) are prized for their knockout foliage in stunning colors and patterns. Angel wing begonias (*B. coccinea*) have upright growth habits, winglike leaves that are frequently mottled, and brightly colored flowers.

How to Plant & Grow—Transplant bedding plants after frost. Light requirements vary by species; refer to plant tags before selecting a location.

Care & Problems—Begonias prefer moist, acidic soil as long as it's well drained. See page 57 for fertilizing needs. Remove spent flowers and dead leaves to keep plants healthy and tidy. Begonias are susceptible to fungal diseases and mealybugs.

Bloom Color—Flower color varies by species; many have colorful foliage

Peak Season—Summer to frost

Mature Size (H x W)—Up to 4 ft. x up to 1 to 2 ft.

Water Needs—Medium. Water regularly.

BIDENS
Bidens ferulifolia

Why It's Special—Also known as Apache beggarticks, bidens is perfect for that hot spot in your garden because they love the heat. The plants are covered with fragrant, golden flowers from spring through the first fall frosts. The blossoms, which don't require deadheading, attract butterflies and bees. Bidens' foliage is delicate and fernlike. Recommended varieties are 'Goldilocks Rocks', 'Sunbeam', 'Gold Carpet', or 'Golden Star'. The bright yellow blossoms are stunning when combined with blue- or purple-flowered perennials such as clustered bellflowers (*Campanula glomerata*), *Salvia × superba* hybrid 'Blue Queen', or the annual mealycup sage (*S. farinacea*).

How to Plant & Grow—After last frost, plant bedding plants in a sunny location with well-drained soil. Space plants 1 foot apart.

Care & Problems—Pinch back branch tips one to two weeks after planting to encourage new, bushy growth. See page 57 for fertilizing needs. They can have problems with aphids or thrips but plants are otherwise low maintenance.

Bloom Color—Bright yellow

Peak Season—Spring through fall

Mature Size (H x W)—12 to 14 in. x 14 to 18 in.

Water Needs—Low. Plants become drought tolerant once established.

BLUE SALVIA
Salvia farinacea

Why It's Special—Also known as mealycup sage, this member of the sage family is known for its profuse and showy flower spikes in blue, purple, or white. The flowers attract butterflies and hummingbirds and are attractive in floral arrangements. It's ideal for cottage gardens and borders and is deer resistant. Blue cultivars are stunning when paired with yellow- or red-flowering plants. 'Victoria' has deep blue flowers and 'Blue Frost' features purple flowers with a hint of white. 'Cirrus' has white flower spikes while 'Evolution' has deep purple flowers.

How to Plant & Grow—Choose a location in full sun to part shade with average soil that is well drained. Once all danger of frost is past, purchase bedding plants from a nursery and plant them 12 to 18 inches apart.

Care & Problems— They are low maintenance. See page 57 for fertilizing needs. They have minimal pest or disease problems.

Bloom Color—Violet blue, purple, lavender, white

Peak Season—Late spring to frost

Mature Size (H x W)—1 to 3 ft. x 1 to 2 ft.

Water Needs—Medium. Plants become drought-tolerant once they are established.

CALENDULA
Calendula officinalis

Why It's Special—Calendula is known for its bright, perky flowers in shades of yellow and orange. The blossoms are pretty as cut flowers and attract butterflies and bees. It's also referred to as pot marigold or English marigold. Try 'Art Shades', 'Touch of Red' with red-tipped petals, pompon-style 'Bonbon' series, and double-flowered 'Calypso' series.

How to Plant & Grow—Plant in full sun (cool summers) or partial shade (areas with hot summers). Calendulas aren't picky about the soil type as long as it's well drained. Start seeds indoors eight weeks before the last frost date or sow seeds directly in the garden four weeks before the last frost. Bedding plants are also an option.

Care & Problems—As plants begin to grow, pinch them back to encourage bushy growth. Deadhead flowers to extend the bloom period. See page 57 for fertilizing needs. Calendula has minimal pest or disease problems and is easy to maintain. Plants are deer and rabbit resistant.

Bloom Color—Yellow, orange, cream

Peak Season—Spring to fall

Mature Size (H x W)—12 to 18 in. x 12 to 18 in.

Water Needs—Medium. Water regularly.

COLEUS

Solenostemon scutellarioides

Why It's Special—Coleus proves you don't need season-long flowers to brighten up the garden. While they do have small blue flower spikes, it's the brightly colored leaves that stand out. Eye-catching varieties include 'Saturn' (burgundy and chartreuse), 'Strawberry Drops' (chartreuse leaves, burgundy veins with strawberry-and-cream highlights), 'Sedona' (rusty red), 'Black Magic' (nearly black, chartreuse margins).

How to Plant & Grow—Coleus prefers part to full shade but tolerates sunny spots as well. Purchase started plants at nurseries or start them indoors from seed two to three months prior to your last frost date. Transplant outdoors into any soil after all danger of frost is past, spaced 12 to 18 inches apart.

Care & Problems—Pinch back stems and flower buds to keep plants bushy. See page 57 for fertilizing needs. Container-planted coleus can be brought indoors for overwintering or take cuttings in fall to root in water. It has minimal problems.

Bloom Color—Foliage combinations of green, chartreuse, burgundy, salmon, orange, red, brown, gold

Peak Season—Season-long foliage

Mature Size (H x W)—6 to 24 in. x 12 in.

Water Needs—Medium. Don't let planting beds dry out.

COSMOS

Cosmos spp.

Why It's Special—Cosmos is an old-fashioned cut flower with delicate, fern-like leaves. *Cosmos bipinnatus* is the more familiar species with large pink, white, or magenta blooms that dance in the breeze. Try white 'Purity', white-with-magenta-center 'Sensation Day Dream', 'Pied Piper Red' with tubular petals, 'Double Click Rose Bonbon', or 'Gazebo Mixed'. *C. sulfureus* has more compact growth with brilliant flowers in warm colors; consider 'Cosmic Red' or 'Bright Lights'.

How to Plant & Grow—Purchase seedlings or start your own from seed indoors eight weeks before the last frost date, or directly in the garden two weeks before last frost. Plant seeds or starts in a sunny, sheltered location with average soil. Space plants 12 to 18 inches apart or closer for support.

Care & Problems—Pinch back plants to encourage bushy growth. See page 57 for fertilizing needs. Cosmos is low maintenance and generally free of insects and disease.

Bloom Color—Yellow, orange, red, white, pink, rose, purple

Peak Season—Summer until frost

Mature Size (H x W)—12 to 72 in. x 12 to 24 in.

Water Needs—Medium. Cosmos benefits from regular watering.

DUSTY MILLER
Senecio cineraria

Why It's Special—The slightly fuzzy, gray foliage of dusty miller adds a welcome contrast to bright beds and border plantings. 'Silver Dust' has deeply dissected leaves. Lacy-leaved varieties include 'Silver Queen' and 'Silver Lace' while 'Cirrus' has lobed leaves.

How to Plant & Grow—While you can start your own plants from seed three to four months before the last frost date, it's much easier to purchase seedlings. Select a location in full sun to part shade. Dusty miller is not particular about soil type as long as it is well drained. Space 6 to 12 inches apart.

Care & Problems—Trim back plants occasionally to retain a bushy shape and pinch off flowers to encourage foliage growth. See page 57 for fertilizing needs. They are easy to maintain and have minimal insect or disease problems. Plants are deer resistant. Foliage is toxic if eaten.

Bloom Color—Silvery white foliage

Peak Season—Season-long foliage

Mature Size (H x W)—6 to 15 in. x 6 to 15 in.

Water Needs—Medium to low. Dusty miller becomes drought tolerant once it is established.

FLOWERING KALE
Brassica oleracea

Why It's Special—This is a group of ornamental cabbage and kale plants that are popular in fall and winter gardens. For fall, consider grouping them with chrysanthemums and different types of pumpkins and gourds. Because of their uniform growth, they're perfect for formal plantings and in window boxes. Look for 'Crispa', 'Tokyo Pink', 'Crane Pink', 'Fresh Violet', 'Nagoya White', or 'Chidori Red'.

How to Plant & Grow—Plants thrive in the cool temperatures of fall and winter. Plant in full sun to part shade in average soil. Purchase plants in late summer or start from seed in midsummer; transplant seedlings in late August.

Care & Problems—See page 57 for fertilizing needs. Remove lowest leaves when they turn brown. Flowering kale is susceptible to aphids and green cabbage loopers. Remove aphids with a strong jet of water and use *Bacillus thuringiensis* (Bt) products to eliminate caterpillars.

Bloom Color—Green, white, gray, pink, rose, or purple foliage; many bicolors

Peak Season—Fall to winter

Mature Size (H x W)—1 to 1½ ft. x 1 to 1½ ft.

Water Needs—Medium. Keep soil moist.

FLOWERING TOBACCO

Nicotiana spp.

Why It's Special—Flowering tobacco is known for its tubular, sweetly scented flowers that attract hummingbirds and butterflies. The plants do well in cottage gardens and containers. *Nicotiana sylvestris*, also called shooting stars because of clusters of long, white, trumpet-shaped flowers, grows up to 5 feet tall. The flowers of *N. alata* are fragrant in the evening; plants grow from 15 inches to 5 feet tall. Suggested varieties are 'Lime Green', 'Grandiflora' (considered the most fragrant), and 'Crimson Bedder'.

How to Plant & Grow—Sow seeds indoors six to eight weeks before the last frost date or directly in the garden once the danger of frost has passed. Plants prefer full sun to part shade and average soil.

Care & Problems—Deadhead flowers to keep plants tidy and promote additional blooming. See page 57 for fertilizing needs. Taller species might require staking. Plants have minimal insect or disease problems.

Bloom Color—White, red, pink, lavender, pale green, yellow

Peak Season—Summer until frost

Mature Size (H x W)—10 in. to 5 ft. x 6 to 24 in.

Water Needs—Medium. Water plants regularly throughout summer.

FOUR O'CLOCK

Mirabilis jalapa

Why It's Special—Four o'clocks, also known as marvel-of-Peru, open late in the afternoon and bloom until early the following morning. The fragrant, funnel-shaped flowers attract butterflies and hummingbirds. Noteworthy varieties are 'Salmon Sunset', 'Marrakesh' (pink and yellow stripes), 'Lemon Swirl', and 'Yellow and Red Marbles' (marbled blossoms).

How to Plant & Grow—Plant seeds indoors six to eight weeks before the last frost date or sow seeds or transplants directly in the garden after the danger of frost is past. Grow in full sun to part shade.

Care & Problems—See page 57 for fertilizing needs. The plants grow from tuberous roots, which can be dug in fall and stored over winter in a cool, dark location. After the tubers are replanted again the following spring, plants should bloom even more profusely. They have minimal disease or insect problems. The plants are rabbit and deer resistant. Note: All plant parts are toxic.

Bloom Color—Pink, red, magenta, white, yellow, some are striped

Peak Season—June to frost

Mature Size (H x W)—2 to 3 ft. x 2 to 3 ft.

Water Needs—Medium. Water regularly.

GERANIUM
Pelargonium spp. and hybrids

Why It's Special—Geraniums are much-loved plants, particularly for window boxes, flower beds, and hanging baskets. Regal or Martha Washington (*Pelargonium × domesticum*) features leaves with serrated or crinkled margins. Common or zonal geranium (*P. × hortorum*) has leaves with circular dark bands running through them. Both species have the easily recognizable, large flower heads. Ivy geranium (*P. peltatum*) has shiny, deep green leaves with trailing branches that cascade attractively from hanging baskets or over rock walls.

How to Plant & Grow—Grow in full sun (cool areas) or choose part shade in areas with hot summers. Plants need well-drained, average soil or potting soil.

Care & Problems—Deadhead regularly to prolong blooming and keep plants tidy. Fertilize plants two to three times during the growing season. Aphids, thrips, or spider mites may be a problem. If desired, overwinter plants indoors in a cool, dark location or take cuttings before fall frosts for growing the following year.

Bloom Color—Red, pink, rose, violet, salmon, white

Peak Season—Summer until frost

Mature Size (H x W)—12 to 20 in. x 12 in.

Water Needs—Medium. Water regularly.

GLOBE AMARANTH
Gomphrena globosa

Why It's Special—The main attraction of this bushy, hairy plant is its globe-shaped, long-blooming bracts. The flowers attract butterflies and work equally well in fresh arrangements or dried for crafts. These deer-resistant plants tolerate heat well and work in a variety of settings, from rock gardens to containers. Look for 'Strawberry Fields', 'All Around Purple', 'Bicolor Rose' (rosy flowers fade to white on the top), 'Lavender Lady', and 'Woodcreek Mixed' (dusty pink, purple, and white mix).

How to Plant & Grow—Start seeds indoors six to eight weeks before last frost date or directly in the garden once the danger of frost is past. Purchasing bedding plants is another option. Plant in full sun in average to sandy soil.

Care & Problems—Pinch back plants to encourage compact growth. Taller plants may require support. See page 57 for fertilizing needs. Plants have minimal insect or disease problems and are low maintenance.

Bloom Color—Magenta, pink, red, white, or violet bracts

Peak Season—June to frost

Mature Size (H x W)—1 to 2 ft. x ½ to 1 ft.

Water Needs—Medium. Plants become drought tolerant once established.

LANTANA

Lantana spp. and hybrids

Why It's Special—Common lantana (*Lantana camara*) is very popular as a bedding and container plant. The showy, multicolored flowers draw butterflies in droves and leaves are aromatic. Lantana looks stunning when combined with other annuals in large containers. Recommended cultivars are 'Miss Huff' (yellow, orange, and coral), 'Lavender Swirl' (light to dark lavender), 'Luscious Citrus Blend' (yellow, red, and orange), 'Landmark Pink Dawn' (lavender and creamy white), 'Pink Caprice' (magenta and yellow), and 'Dallas Red' (red and coral). Trailing lantana (*L. sellowiana*) has masses of lavender blooms and is used in hanging baskets or as groundcovers.

How to Plant & Grow—Grow in full sun and average, well-drained soil. Purchase bedding plants and plant after danger of frost has passed; space 12 inches apart.

Care & Problems—Fertilize container plants monthly. Lantana has minimal insect or disease problems. All plant parts are toxic when ingested; leaves irritate the skin.

Bloom Color—Red, peach, purple, pink, orange, white, yellow, often bicolored

Peak Season—Summer to frost

Mature Size (H x W)—12 to 20 in. x 12 to 15 in.

Water Needs—Medium. Keep soil moist for the first few weeks.

LOBELIA

Lobelia erinus

Why It's Special—Annual lobelias are perfect for filling gaps in container plantings, as edging plants at the fronts of borders and rock gardens, and in formal gardens. They have delicate leaves and softly hued flowers that attract butterflies to the garden. There are two groups: *Lobelia erinus compacta* has compact growth and *pendula* has a trailing habit.

How to Plant & Grow—Plant in full sun to part shade in average to acidic soil. Lobelia is difficult to start from seed, but if you decide to go that route, start them indoors two to three months before the last frost date. Otherwise, purchase bedding plants and transplant them after all danger of frost is past.

Care & Problems—Fertilize every two weeks until hot weather arrives, which causes plants to stop blooming and languish. Trim them back to promote fall rebloom. Plants have minimal insect or disease problems. Plants are deer resistant.

Bloom Color—White, blue, rose, purple

Peak Season—Spring and fall

Mature Size (H x W)—4 to 8 in. x 6 to 18 in.

Water Needs—Medium. Water regularly but do not overwater.

LOVE-IN-A-MIST

Nigella damascena

Why It's Special—Love-in-a-mist is a must for all cutting gardens. The plants have eye-catching flowers—highly prized both fresh-cut or dried—and intricate foliage. 'Persian Jewels Mix' has blue, white, rose, and violet flowers while 'Persian Jewels Indigo' has amazing, deep violet-blue blossoms. 'Miss Jekyll Blue' features intense blue flowers and 'Red Jewels' is covered in rosy red blooms.

How to Plant & Grow—For best results, sow seeds directly in the garden as soon as soil can be worked. Plants will grow in full sun or partial shade, in average, well-drained soil.

Care & Problems—See page 57 for fertilizing needs. Deadhead flowers to extend blooming period or leave spent flower heads on plants to develop showy, puffy seedpods. Plants easily self-seed, coming back each year. Love-in-a-mist is an easy-care annual that isn't bothered by pests or disease.

Bloom Color—Blue, white, pink, purple, rose

Peak Season—June to August

Mature Size (H x W)—1½ to 2 ft. x 1 to 1½ ft.

Water Needs—Medium. Don't let soil dry out.

MARIGOLD
Tagetes spp.

Why It's Special— Marigolds are one of the most popular annuals. Their bright, cheery blooms light up the garden and their pungent aroma helps repel damaging insects. African marigolds (*Tagetes erecta*) are the tallest species, growing to 4 feet tall, with large white, yellow, or orange blossoms. French marigolds (*T. patula*) are more compact at 6 to 12 inches tall, and yellow, orange, red, or bicolor blooms. Signet marigolds (*T. signata*) grow 1 foot tall with lacy foliage and single blossoms in yellow, red, or orange.

How to Plant & Grow—Select a sunny location with average, moist, well-drained soil. Sow seeds indoors six to eight weeks before the last frost date or purchase bedding plants. Set out seedlings once frost danger has passed.

Care & Problems—Deadhead flowers regularly to promote a continuous bloom. See page 57 for fertilizing needs. Taller species may require staking in windy locations.

Bloom Color—Yellow, orange, gold, bronze, creamy white

Peak Season—Summer through fall

Mature Size (H x W)—6 to 48 in. x 6 to 15 in.

Water Needs—Medium. Water regularly initially; then only during dry periods.

MEXICAN SUNFLOWER
Tithonia rotundifolia

Why It's Special—If you want to attract butterflies, hummingbirds, and bees from miles around, this is the plant for you. With its sunny blossoms, impressive height, and lush foliage, Mexican sunflower is a standout in any garden. They are best used at the backs of borders or grouped as specimens. Plants are deer resistant and *love* the heat. Popular cultivars are red-orange 'Torch', golden yellow 'Aztec Sun' and orange, 30-inch-tall 'Fiesta del Sol'.

How to Plant & Grow—Select a sunny location with average soil. Sow seeds indoors six to eight weeks prior to last frost date or plant seeds or nursery plants directly in the garden after the frost danger. Space 2 feet apart.

Care & Problems—Avoid high-nitrogen fertilizers, which cause weak growth; use fertilizers containing more phosphorus. Plants require staking in windy areas. Deadhead flowers regularly to prolong bloom. They do not have insect or disease problems.

Bloom Color—Orange, red, yellow

Peak Season—July to September

Mature Size (H x W)—3 to 6 ft. x 2 to 3 ft.

Water Needs—Medium to low. Water regularly initially; they become drought tolerant once established.

MILLION BELLS
Calibrachoa

Why It's Special— Million bells are easy-care, prolific bloomers that live up to their name. Because of their trailing habit, they are commonly grown in hanging baskets or window boxes but are also ideal for cascading over the edges of rock garden walls and at the fronts of border plantings. Color selections are endless, with some featuring golden eyes, and many double forms. Plants tolerate heat. Notable hybrids include Superbells® 'Lemon Slice', 'Dreamsicle', and 'Grape Punch'; Noa™ series 'Ultra Purple', 'Dark Pink Carnival', and 'Sunrise'; MiniFamous™ series 'Double Rose Chai' and 'Tangerine'.

How to Plant & Grow— Plants perform best in full sun and rich, well-drained soil. Purchase plants from a nursery and transplant into the garden after danger of frost is past.

Care & Problems—Plants are self-deadheading. Feed monthly with slow-release fertilizer. They are not bothered by insects or disease.

Bloom Color—Pink, red, magenta, purple, blue, violet, yellow, white, bicolor

Peak Season—June to frost

Mature Size (H x W)—3 to 9 in. x 6 to 24 in.

Water Needs—Medium. Water regularly.

MOSS ROSE

Portulaca grandiflora

Why It's Special—Moss rose has showy, cactus-like blossoms and succulent foliage that brings a refreshingly different texture to the garden. While it is ideal for use in rock gardens, along walkways, in hanging baskets, and cascading over rock walls, this attractive plant has a secret: It will thrive in areas where little else will grow.

How to Plant & Grow—Select a sunny location with average, well-drained soil. Sow seeds indoors six to eight weeks before the last frost date, or sow seeds directly in the garden after the danger of frost is past. An easy option is to purchase seedlings; space 8 inches apart.

Care & Problems—Plants prefer hot conditions and are low maintenance. See page 57 for fertilizing needs. They easily self-seed but are not invasive and do not have any serious insect or disease problems.

Bloom Color—Red, rose, orange, yellow, white

Peak Season—June to frost

Mature Size (H x W)—3 to 9 in. x 6 to 12 in.

Water Needs—Low to medium. Water regularly as seedlings first grow, then water only when soil is dry.

NASTURTIUM

Tropaeolum majus

Why It's Special—Nasturtiums have long been popular with their distinctive, colorful flowers and parasol-shaped leaves that flutter in the breeze. Blossoms are edible—provided you don't use chemicals near them—with a pleasing, peppery flavor. They are commonly used in salads and hors d'oeuvres. Plants have a compact or vining growth habit. Nasturtiums are ideal for hanging baskets, rock gardens, border plantings, and cottage gardens. 'Empress of India' has dark leaves and scarlet blossoms. 'Alaska Mix' features unusual, variegated leaves and flowers in warm colors. 'Vanilla Berry' has creamy blossoms with strawberry throats.

How to Plant & Grow—They grow in average to poor soil. Sow seeds directly in a sunny area once the danger of frost has passed. Space seeds 4 inches apart; thin later to 8-inch spacing.

Care & Problems—Nasturtiums don't require fertilizer. Aphids love nasturtiums; gardeners frequently plant nasturtiums next to susceptible vegetables to draw aphids to the nasturtiums.

Bloom Color—Yellow, orange, red, white

Peak Season—Summer to frost

Mature Size (H x W)—12 in. x 12 to 14 in.

Water Needs—Medium. Water regularly but do not overwater.

PANSY

Viola × wittrockiana

Why It's Special—With their perky, face-like flowers, pansies make garden visitors smile. The blossoms come in solid colors and bicolors in many shades. The plants are perennial in zones 6 to 10 and annual in colder regions. In warmer areas, they bloom in fall; elsewhere, they're early-spring bloomers. Look for 'Fizzy Lemonberry', 'Bowles Black', orange 'Padpardja', and Bolero, Inspire, and the Colossus series.

How to Plant & Grow—Pansies do grow in all types of light but they perform best in sun to part shade; they are adaptable to all soil types. Purchase bedding plants and transplant them in early spring or start them indoors from seed three months before the last frost date.

Care & Problems—Deadhead flowers to prolong the bloom and trim plants as needed to keep them looking tidy. See page 57 for fertilizing needs. Slugs may be a problem but plants generally have few problems.

Bloom Color—White, blue, purple, yellow, dark red, rose, apricot

Peak Season—Spring to early summer and fall

Mature Size (H x W)—4 to 8 in. x 9 to 12 in.

Water Needs—Medium. Water regularly.

PERSIAN SHIELD

Strobilanthes dyerianus

Why It's Special—Persian shield has striking purple leaves with deep green veins and a touch of iridescent silver. They add beautiful color to container plantings and are often grown as houseplants. Outdoors, plant them in borders with other brightly colored annuals and perennials or as a contrast to silver-leaved plants. They tolerate heat and are hardy to zones 9 and above. When grown as an annual, plants don't always bloom but their fabulous foliage more than makes up for it.

How to Plant & Grow—Plant in part shade in areas with hot summers and full sun where summers are cooler. Persian shield prefers rich, well-drained soil.

Care & Problems—Pinch back occasionally to keep plants from becoming leggy. If possible, water with soaker hoses as overhead watering can cause leaves to stain. See page 57 for fertilizing needs. Plants have minimal insect or disease problems and need little care. Propagate by cuttings in spring or summer.

Bloom Color—Violet; grown for foliage

Peak Season—Fall

Mature Size (H x W)—1 to 3 ft. x 1 to 3 ft.

Water Needs—Medium. Water regularly.

PETUNIA
Petunia × hybrida

Why It's Special— This cheerful, dependable annual has been a garden favorite for many years. Their funnel-shaped flowers come in every color imaginable; some are fragrant and all attract butterflies and hummingbirds. There are both trailing and upright types. Plant them in borders, next to walkways and driveways, and in hanging baskets or window boxes. Consider cultivars in the Wave™, Double Wave™, Summer Madness™, and Supertunia™ series.

How to Plant & Grow—Petunias thrive in full sun but also tolerate part shade. They prefer moist, well-drained soil. Purchase bedding plants and transplant them into the garden after all danger of frost is past; space plants 12 inches apart. Or start from seeds three months before last frost.

Care & Problems—Water plants regularly and deadhead to prolong the bloom. See page 57 for fertilizing needs. Pinch back plants in summer as needed to keep them bushy. Aphids and slugs can be a problem.

Bloom Color—Pink, red, violet, lavender, yellow, salmon, white, bicolored

Peak Season—Spring through fall

Mature Size (H x W)—6 to 18 in. x 6 to 36 in.

Water Needs—Medium. Water regularly.

SCARLET RUNNER BEAN
Phaseolus coccineus

Why It's Special—As its name implies, this colorful plant produces an edible crop. A type of pole bean, scarlet runner beans grow vertically and soon become covered in profuse, deep red blossoms that draw in hummingbirds. The beans are edible while they're young and tender and the edible flowers are often used in salads. They are more cold tolerant than other beans.

How to Plant & Grow—Sow seeds indoors two to three weeks prior to the last frost or directly in the garden after the danger of frost has passed. When sowing, place the seeds scar side facing downward for best germination. In the garden, select a sunny location with fertile, well-drained soil. Space seeds or seedlings 4 to 8 inches apart. Provide a tall trellis for plants to climb up and over.

Care & Problems—Pick beans frequently to prolong the bloom. See page 57 for fertilizing needs. Slugs may bother seedlings in spring.

Bloom Color—Red

Peak Season—Midsummer to frost

Mature Size (H x W)—6 to 8 ft. x 1 ft.

Water Needs—Medium. Water regularly.

SCARLET SAGE
Salvia splendens

Why It's Special—A native of Brazil, scarlet sage has fragrant, fiery-red flower clusters that draw in hummingbirds and butterflies. The plants are deer tolerant. Hybrids are available in white, pink, or deep purple. Varieties include (red) 'Saucy Red' and dwarf 'Firecracker'; (purple) 'Saucy Wine', 'Lighthouse Purple', and 'Phoenix Bright Lilac'; (white) 'Salsa White' and 'Sizzler White'; (salmon) 'Sizzler Salmon'; and (pink) 'Burgundy Bicolor'.

How to Plant & Grow— Sow seeds indoors six to eight weeks before the last frost date or purchase bedding plants. Once the danger of frost is past, transplant seedlings into the garden where plants will get full sun to part shade. Plants aren't particular about soil type as long as it is well drained.

Care & Problems—This easy-care plant isn't bothered by pests or disease. See page 57 for fertilizing needs. Plants can self-sow; deadhead spent flowers if you don't want them to spread.

Bloom Color—Red, salmon, pink, blue, lavender, purple, white

Peak Season—Summer until frost

Mature Size (H x W)—8 to 30 in. x 8 to 12 in.

Water Needs—Medium. Water regularly but don't overwater.

SNAPDRAGON
Antirrhinum majus

Why It's Special—As kids, most of us probably played with snapdragon flowers, pretending they were dragons whose jaws would snap when we pinched the sides together. As adults, we enjoy having the cheerful, fragrant flowers in cutting gardens, borders, and rock gardens. They are deer resistant. The blooms attract hummingbirds and butterflies. Dwarf, intermediate, and tall types are available, and there are now double and bicolor flowers to choose from.

How to Plant & Grow—Plant seeds indoors six to eight weeks before last frost date or purchase bedding plants. Plant seedlings outdoors after danger of frost is past in all light conditions, although shade works best in hot summer regions. Space 6 to 12 inches apart.

Care & Problems—See page 57 for fertilizing needs. Deadhead flowers to prolong bloom and pinch back plants in summer to promote bushy growth. Taller cultivars may need staking. Aphids, mildew, and rust can be problems.

Bloom Color—White, yellow, bronze, purple, pink, red, peach

Peak Season—Spring and fall

Mature Size (H x W)—6 to 48 in. x 6 to 24 in.

Water Needs—Medium. Water regularly.

SPIDER FLOWER

Cleome hassleriana

Why It's Special— Spider flower is named for its graceful, delicate flowers borne on tall stalks. The fragrant flowers make a wonderful addition to cottage and butterfly gardens, in borders, and along fences. Plants are rabbit resistant and heat tolerant. They have thorns at the base of each leaf. Look for white 'Helen Campbell', rosy purple 'Violet Queen', and dwarf 'Sparkler Blush'.

How to Plant & Grow—Plant in full sun or part shade, in average, well-drained soil. Sow seeds indoors six to eight weeks before last frost, or sow directly in the garden after frost danger has passed, or purchase bedding plants. Space plants 18 to 24 inches apart. It's most impressive when planted *en mass*.

Care & Problems—Plants are low maintenance, just requiring deadheading especially to prevent self-seeding. See page 57 for fertilizing needs. They have minimal insect or disease problems.

Bloom Color—White, pink, rose, purple

Peak Season—Summer through fall

Mature Size (H x W)—Up to 6 ft. x 1 to 2 ft.

Water Needs—Low to medium. Water regularly early in the season; after that they tolerate dry conditions.

SUNFLOWER

Helianthus annuus

Why It's Special—There's something very uplifting about large groupings of cheery sunflowers in borders, cottage or children's gardens, along fence rows, or tucked into the vegetable garden. They come in many shapes, heights, and colors, featuring brown to golden center disks and bright petals. The fast-growing plants are deer resistant and attract birds, bees, and butterflies. Save flower heads in fall for local birds to enjoy; the blooms are also prized as cut flowers. Varieties range from dwarf 10-inch 'Big Smile' up to 15-foot 'Titan'.

How to Plant & Grow—Select a sunny location with average, well-drained soil. Sow seeds directly in the garden after the danger of frost has passed, using a 12- to 18-inch spacing.

Care & Problems—Plants need minimal fertilization. Sunflowers are very easy to grow and have minimal problems. Taller plants may require staking in windy areas.

Bloom Color—Yellow, white, and bronze with yellow, brown, purple, or crimson center

Peak Season—Midsummer to frost

Mature Size (H x W)—15 in. to 15 ft. x 12 to 24 in.

Water Needs—Low to medium. Water deeply when soil is dry.

SWEET POTATO VINE
Ipomoea batatas

Why It's Special—It's pretty difficult for Northwest gardeners to grow sweet potatoes but the colorful leaves of the newer ornamental cultivars look stunning as "spillers" in container plantings. They also are a good choice for the fronts of borders, cascading over rock walls, and as annual groundcovers. Most vines grow 3 feet long but can grow longer under ideal conditions. Plants rarely bloom but they are deer resistant. Recommended varieties are 'Sweet Caroline Light Green', 'Blackie', variegated 'Pink Frost', and chartreuse 'Margarita'.

How to Plant & Grow—Sweet potato vine grows best in sunny locations but tolerates shady sites. They're not particular about soil type as long as it's well drained. Plant nursery seedlings after danger of frost is past, spacing 18 to 24 inches apart.

Care & Problems—Plants are easy to maintain; just remove spent leaves from the vines. See page 57 for fertilizing needs. Slugs may be a problem.

Bloom Color—Lime green, purple, variegated green, cream, and pink foliage

Peak Season—Season-long foliage

Mature Size (H x W)—Up to 3 ft. or more in length

Water Needs—Medium. Water regularly.

VERBENA
Verbena hybrids

Why It's Special—Trailing verbenas are popular in hanging baskets, as "spillers" for large containers, and as annual groundcovers. Plants love the heat and are profuse bloomers with flat flower clusters that attract butterflies. Two series of verbena hybrids are Babylon™ and Superbena™. Available seed mixes are 'Florist Mix' and 'Mammoth Mix', as well as hybrids such as 'Apricot', 'Scarlet', 'Rose', or 'White'.

How to Plant & Grow—Sow seeds indoors eight to ten weeks before last frost date or plant nursery seedlings after danger of frost is past. Select a sunny site with well-drained soil enriched with compost or slow-release fertilizer; space plants 8 to 12 inches apart.

Care & Problems—Verbena is low maintenance although powdery mildew may be a problem. They are deer and rabbit resistant. Flowers do not require deadheading but trim back plants after initial flowering to encourage more blooms and branching.

Bloom Color—White, lavender, purple, blue, pink, red, apricot

Peak Season—Summer till frost

Mature Size (H x W)—Up to 15 in. x up to 20 in.

Water Needs—Medium. Water regularly until plants become established, then decrease watering.

ZINNIA
Zinnia elegans

Why It's Special—Zinnias are much-loved, old-fashioned plants with large, daisylike blossoms that attract bees and butterflies. They are heat tolerant and make excellent cut flowers. These versatile plants work well in children's and cottage gardens, mixed border plantings, or along driveways and walkways. The flowers come in single, semidouble, and double forms and are either dahlia- or cactus-flowered. They have compact to tall growth habits.

How to Plant & Grow—Sow seeds indoors four to six weeks prior to last frost, or sow directly in the garden after danger of frost has passed, or plant purchased seedlings. Choose a sunny location with well-drained soil. Space compact plants at 6 to 8 inches and taller cultivars at 12 inches.

Care & Problems—Extremely easy to grow, the long-lived flowers of zinnias should be deadheaded to encourage additional blooms. See page 57 for fertilizing needs. Zinnias can be susceptible to powdery mildew; choose mildew-resistant varieties.

Bloom Color—White, yellow, green, red, orange, apricot, rose, violet

Peak Season—Summer to frost

Mature Size (H x W)—6 to 36 in. x 18 to 24 in.

Water Needs—Medium. Water regularly; avoid overhead watering.

JANUARY

- Develop your planting plan for beds and containers. Refer to your garden journal for new ideas and changes you noted during the height of the growing season. Check out online garden planning software to help you lay out the garden and keep records this year. It could save you a lot of time.

- Read the seed catalogs that are piling up. Order catalogs from suppliers you want to try. Work with your garden plan to make the final selections you will grow. Get your order in early: popular varieties will go fast.

- Begin seeding early spring annuals under lights so they are ready when the weather warms. An unused basement or bedroom is a good place to set up your light stand. Start seedlings on the tops of the light stand racks where the air is warmer and move them to the bottom racks as the plants get bigger.

- Frequently check soil moisture of overwintering annuals you have under lights, but water only when the soil has dried out slightly. Low light levels and cooler temperatures slow a plant's ability to use water during winter.

FEBRUARY

- Attend local and regional winter flower and garden shows to learn about new plants, design, and planting ideas. Seattle, Portland, and Vancouver, B.C. all have good shows this month.

- Repot seedlings to larger pots as they develop two sets of true leaves. Repot cuttings you took from plants in the fall and rooted over the winter into larger pots. Pinch back plants as they grow to encourage bushy growth. Begin a biweekly fertilization program with a half-strength, low-nitrogen organic fertilizer.

- Continue seeding annuals indoors. Seed those that can tolerate cool spring conditions first and follow with plants that will need warmer temperatures later in spring.

MARCH

- West of the Cascades, when the soil is dry enough to work, begin bed preparation by pulling weeds and adding compost. East of the Cascades, you will have to wait for the ground to thaw.

- Buy a few primroses and put them in your windows to make believe it is spring.

- Don't hurry to plant outdoors. The ground is still cold and wet and frosts can still kill plants.

- Pot up seedlings that are outgrowing their containers. Check for bugs. Trim any leggy growth.

APRIL

- West of the Cascades, begin planting hardy annuals outdoors around the middle of the month. Harden off seedlings for five days before planting them outdoors by setting them outdoors during the day and bringing them back into a garage at night. If the spring has been dry, water them regularly.

- Start a regular weeding program early and mulch areas you weed so you don't have to do it again. Don't let weeds go to seed.

- Prepare containers for planting. Existing potting soil can be mixed half-and-half with fresh potting mix or compost. Add slow-release fertilizer to the top 6 inches of the soil and set the pots in the sun to warm the soil.

- East of the Cascades, gardeners can begin early bed preparations as the weather warms and the soil dries out. Put mulch down immediately after working beds to reduce weed problems.

MAY

- Mother's Day signals the beginning of the gardening season. Gift certificates to nurseries are always a good gift. Better yet, take Mom to her favorite nursery and help her pick out plants.

- If it has been a cold spring, most plants will be slow to show signs of growth. Be patient.

- Now is the time to plant your large containers. Plant tall, showy plants in the middle of the pot and surround the edges of the pot with plants that trail down the sides. Plant shorter, bushy plants to tie the tall and trailing plants together. Nursery professionals call these "thrillers, spillers, and fillers."

- If you haven't mulched your beds, pull the weeds and do so. Next year you will do it earlier, Pat can assure you.

JUNE

- Plant the last of the annuals early in the month. Traditional cool June temperatures will give plants a good opportunity to set out roots before the heat of July really gets them growing.

- As early-blooming annuals finish their first flush of blooms, start deadheading them for another round of blooms.

- Weeds love cool weather so stay on top of the weeding and get the mulch down.

- Annuals are heavy feeders so begin fertilizing every two weeks with a quality, organic fertilizer. Stake up plants that will grow taller than 24 inches with bamboo stakes or wire cages as they begin to grow. Several stakes can be placed around plants and string woven between them to create a support lattice.

JULY

- If you plan on going on vacation, put your pots on a timed, drip-irrigation system. They will get watered and you won't have to rush home. Otherwise, arrange for a gardening friend or neighbor to come in and water regularly.

- Keep up with your deadheading, trimming, and fertilization schedules.

- As the weather turns hot east of the Cascades, double-check watering schedules, especially on hot windy days. A couple of hours of hot wind can fry a pot in no time.

- Seed fall annuals like flowering kale and cabbages in the garden early in the month. They will grow to size by September, ready to add color to the fall garden.

AUGUST

- August is the driest month in the Northwest and southern British Columbia. Check watering systems for plugged heads. Make sure annuals get an inch of water per week, more in hot windy weather.

- Decide what worked and what did not in the garden and note it in your garden journal so you can modify your plans for next year.

- Shear back scraggly annuals mid-month to encourage new growth. Once the temperatures moderate in early September, annuals will put on a new show of flowers.

- Catch up on your weeding and reapply mulch so you maintain a 2-to-3-inch layer. The weeds will be back as the weather cools.

- Identify plants that you want to save seed from and mark the flower stalk with a piece of ribbon. Allow seedheads to dry and then shake the seeds gently out of the seedhead. Lay the seeds on a paper towel to dry for a week and then store them in a paper envelope. Label the envelope. Too much moisture damages seeds, so store in a refrigerator only if the seeds have been hermetically sealed in a moisture-proof pouch or can.

SEPTEMBER

- Trim up sun- and heat-damaged plants. They will revive as the weather cools early this month.

- Dig up any frost-sensitive annuals you want to overwinter and pot them up into potting soil. Put them in a shady place to acclimate to lower light levels and a smaller root system. Be sure to bring them indoors before frosts occur.

- Prepare for the first light frosts east of the Cascades by staging tarps, old blankets, large cardboard boxes, and buckets close at hand. Remove covers in the mornings as the days are still warm enough to create heat under the covers.

- As temperatures cool, plants will be using less water so adjust your watering schedules accordingly.

OCTOBER

- Enjoy the last of the hardy annuals this month. Look for spaces you can plant more in next year.

- As frost takes out the annuals, pull them out of the ground or their containers and add them to the compost pile. They are considered green material so mix them half-and-half with shredded brown material as you add them to the pile.

- Monitor the plants you brought indoors. Set grow lights within 2 inches of the plants. Check for pests and treat them. A good drowning in a cool shower will wash many of them off.

NOVEMBER

- Clean out the rest of your beds and pots. Shred the discards and add them to the compost pile.

- Clean pots and store them in a dry place. Terracotta clay and some concrete pots will absorb moisture and crack or spall in below-freezing weather. If they are too big to move, cover them with a large plastic bag or tarp and tie it down securely.

- West of the Cascades, dig some of your ornamental kale or cabbage plants and plant them in your frost-resistant-but-now-empty pots for winter color.

DECEMBER

- Review your seeding schedule. Clean up seed-starting equipment and purchase new germinating soil mix. Change the fluorescent tubes in your grow lights.

- Check overwintering indoor plants for water and bugs.

- Drop hints about what you want for Christmas. Yes, you really do want a yard of compost.

BULBS, TUBERS, CORMS & RHIZOMES
for the Northwest

The Northwest's cool, moist winters and warm, dry summers are perfect for growing bulbs. So much so that the Skagit Valley north of Seattle is one of the best places in the world for the commercial production of daffodils and tulips. Each March, the Skagit Tulip Festival draws thousands of people to the area to see the acres of colorful flowers.

WHAT IS A BULB, TUBER, CORM, OR RHIZOME?

The generalized term "bulb" refers to several different root structures each with their own growth habit and purpose. True bulbs, including tulips (*Tulipa* spp.), daffodils (*Narcissus* spp.), hyacinths (*Hyacinthus orientalis*), and snowdrops (*Galanthus* spp.), grow from an onionlike bulb with scales attached to a basal plate that generates new bulblets at its base. Corms such as crocosmia (*Crocosmia* spp.), gladiolus (*Gladiolus* spp.), and freesia (*Freesia* spp.) are a food storage structure used up by the plant each year. Tubers including tuberous begonias (*Begonia × tuberhybrida*), dahlias (*Dahlia* spp.), and daylilies are modified stems that generate new plants from underground growing points. Finally, rhizomes including iris (*Iris* spp.) and canna (*Canna*) are underground stems that generate new plants from a growing point on the stem. To simplify things, we will use the generic term "bulbs" to refer to all of these in this chapter.

DESIGNING WITH BULBS

Bulbs are an integral element in good garden design. In the informal garden, they add punches of color early in spring and offset blooming perennials and shrubs as they transition between seasons. Iris, Oriental lilies, and daylilies add bold leaves as well as flowers to the garden's architecture.

Plant bulbs in clusters rather than as individual bulbs to create a more dynamic show. When planting a bed, plant ten to twelve shorter bulbs at the front of the bed and then clusters of thirty to forty bulbs in the middle ground followed by eighty- to one hundred-count groupings of taller bulbs at the back.

Mass plantings of a single type of bulb are often used in more formal gardens to create unity and sweeping patches of color and texture. Designers recommend using no more than two or three colors in an area. This is expensive because the bulbs are cleared out of the bed after blooming and replaced with something else each year.

Randomly scattered or naturalized clusters of bulbs mimic nature's way of growing things. Naturalizing is best done in well established but undisturbed areas or areas that are not mowed or trimmed until after the bulb's foliage matures. Following the principle of planting in clusters, scatter bulbs across an area and plant them where they land.

In containers, early spring daffodils and tulips can provide spots of color long before the rest of the garden is awake. They are perfect for doorsteps, front porches and decks where there isn't a "garden" per se. You can force daffodils and tulips by planting them, in the fall, in large pots and overwintering

Groupings of tulips add splashes of color to the spring garden.

To plant bulbs in pots, place the bulbs in the pot, pointy end up. You can place the bulbs so they're almost touching one another. A secret of the pros: more bulbs equals more excitement. You can also plant a mixture of bulbs that bloom at different times to extend the flower show on your front porch.

them in a very cool shed, garage, or heeled into a garden bed. Put them out in the sun in late winter to start growing for an early show. Many better garden centers will have pre-planted pots of bulbs available in the spring for an instant bulb garden without the work.

GROWING BULBS IN THE NORTHWEST

Bulbs can be purchased from a wide variety of local and online sources and are priced by the bulb or in multiples for bulk quantities. Price is a reflection of quality so be prepared to pay a fair price for larger, top-quality bulbs. Choose plump, heavy bulbs that are free of cuts, bruises, or discoloration that might be a sign of disease. If you can't plant them right away, store them in a mesh bag in a cool place. If you purchase online, avoid the bargain sites and buy the best you can afford.

With a few exceptions, most bulbs require full sun and well-drained soil rich in organic matter. They should be fertilized with a bulb fertilizer or a good 10-10-10 fertilizer in early spring so that nutrients are available when the bulbs emerge.

Early spring bulbs like tulips, daffodils, and hyacinths need to be planted in fall to develop a good root system. Summer- and fall-flowering bulbs including lilies, daylilies, and crocosmia can be planted in early spring. Tropical bulbs like cannas, elephant ears, and calla lilies need to be planted after the soil has warmed up and the danger of frost has passed.

Planting depths vary for many bulbs. Most true bulbs and corms can be planted two to three times their height. Tubers and rhizomes need to be planted horizontally just below the surface of the soil. Irises need to be planted so the top of the rhizome is at the surface of the soil.

To quickly plant a large quantity of spring bulbs in fall, dig and level a space 6 to 8 inches deep in an area of several square feet. Add some bulb fertilizer and bonemeal and set the bulbs upright about 2 to 3 inches apart. Amend the soil with compost and backfill the hole. Mark the area with stakes so you don't dig into the cluster next spring when you are planting something else.

Leave bulb foliage on the plant for at least six to eight weeks after they finish blooming to replenish the bulb's food stores for next year's show. Dying bulb foliage can be hidden nicely by planting them behind and among taller perennials.

In general, when the number of flowers begins to dwindle on hardy bulbs, it is time to dig and divide them. Spring-flowering bulbs should be dug in early fall. Iris should be dug and divided in mid-July. Replant the largest and plumpest of the bulbs or roots. Frost-tender gladiolus, begonia, dahlia, and the tropical bulbs should be divided when they are dug up for winter storage.

DEALING WITH CRITTERS

Squirrels, deer, voles, and gophers love bulbs and their foliage and can destroy a whole planting in a few hours. If you are plagued with deer and don't have a fence, skip the tulips, crocus, and Asiatic lilies. Deer repellant only works on older foliage and even then, the marauders will come in broad

daylight and eat them to the ground—even in urban areas.

Voles, squirrels, and gophers will snack on the bulbs through the winter. Squirrels will dig them up—usually shortly after you plant them. Gophers and voles will eat them from below ground and you will only know it when your feet sink about 6 inches in the area you planted them. Squirrels can be deterred by laying chicken wire or metal hardware cloth over a bed after you plant it. Voles and gophers can be slowed down by planting your bulbs in hardware cloth baskets they can't chew through.

Bulbs are some of the easiest garden plants to grow and care for. Year after year, their bright color in April is a cheery reminder that spring has arrived. Summer-flowering bulbs help perennials and shrubs transition through the season. All they need for years of enjoyment is water and a light dose of fertilizer.

To plant bulbs outdoors, toss the bulbs into the garden, and then even out spacing as needed, avoiding straight planting lines.

AUTUMN CROCUS
Colchicum autumnale

Why It's Special—Despite its name, autumn crocus isn't technically a crocus but it sure looks like one. In spring, the bulbs send up leaves, which die back in summer. After a dormancy period, beautiful, crocus-like blossoms appear in fall. The foliage is deer resistant. Pink is the most common color; *Colchicum autumnale* 'Pleniflorum' is an early double pink cultivar that starts blooming in late summer. 'Alboplenum' has striking double white flowers with yellow centers. 'Tenorii' has single blue-violet blooms. 'Major' has large single pink flowers.

How to Plant & Grow—Select a sunny planting site in well-drained soil. If possible, plant at the front of a border or along a pathway so they are easy to see and enjoy. Plant corms 3 inches deep, 6 inches apart, in August. Plants bloom that fall.

Care & Problems—Dig corms to divide while plants are dormant, if needed. No pests will bother it.

Color(s)—Pink, white, violet, purple

Peak Season—August to September

Mature Size (H x W)—12 in. x 3 to 12 in.

Water Needs—Low. Water regularly during its flowering period.

CALADIUM
Caladium bicolor

Why It's Special—Also known as angel wings, caladiums have beautifully marked, arrowhead-shaped leaves. They are commonly grown as houseplants but can be grown outdoors in zones 9 to 10 or kept outdoors for summer before being overwintered inside. 'Freida Hemple' has red centers and deep green margins. 'Florida Sweetheart' has similar markings although the red centers are larger. 'White Queen' is stunning with nearly white leaves and bright red veins. 'Blushing Bride' features straplike leaves with white veins and green-and-red mottling.

How to Plant & Grow—Caladiums prefer rich, acidic soil and part to full shade. Once soil temperatures reach 60°F, incorporate balanced fertilizer into the soil. Plant 2 inches deep and 8 to 12 inches apart, depending on tuber size.

Care & Problems—Divide tubers in spring, as needed. They have minimal insect or disease problems.

Color(s)—Plants rarely flower; grown for foliage

Peak Season—All season

Mature Size (H x W)—1 to 2½ ft. x 1 to 2½ ft.

Water Needs—Medium. Water regularly but don't allow soil to become waterlogged.

CALLA LILY
Zantedeschia spp. and hybrids

Why It's Special—Native to South Africa, calla lilies have graceful, exotic blooms. Grow year-round in zones 8 to 10 or outdoors in containers, then bring inside during winter. *Zantedeschia aethiopica* is a bog plant that can also be container-grown on pond shelves. Hybrids include 'Millennium Gold' with bright gold spathes (petal-like bract) and spotted foliage, 'Majestic Red' features rosy pink spathes and spotted leaves, and 'Flame' has yellow and orange spathes with red stripes. *Z. albomaculata* has white spathes and mottled leaves.

How to Plant & Grow—Grow in full sun to part shade. Plant rhizomes 3 to 4 inches deep and 12 to 18 inches apart after danger of frost is past. Mulch plants to keep roots cool.

Care & Problems—After bloom period, leave foliage on plants until they yellow. Dry bulbs; store in cool location for next year.

Color(s)—White, pink, yellow

Peak Season—June to July

Mature Size (H x W)—2 to 3 ft. x 1½ to 2 ft.

Water Needs—Medium to high. Keep soil damp but not soggy or bulbs will rot.

CAMAS

Camassia spp. and hybrids

Why It's Special—Native to the Northwest, camas have showy, star-shaped flowers growing on spikes and are hardy in zones 4 to 8. Allow them to naturalize with yellow daffodils or narcissus. *Camassia leichtlinii* (up to 4 feet) has flowers in blue, purple, white, or cream. 'Blue Danube' features dark blue flowers and 'Alba' has white flower spikes. Small camas (*C. quamash*) 'Blue Melody' (1 to 2 feet) features variegated foliage while 'Orion' (15 inches) has violet-blue flowers.

How to Plant & Grow—In fall, plant in full sun to part shade in rich, acidic soil. Incorporate bulb fertilizer into the hole. Plant multiples for best effect, with bulbs 4 to 6 inches deep and 6 inches apart.

Care & Problems—Plants go dormant in late summer; foliage can be removed at this time. Minimal amounts of pest or insect problems.

Color(s)—White, cream, blue, purple

Peak Season—May, June, and July, depending on elevation and temperatures

Mature Size (H x W)—12 to 36 in. x 3 to 6 in.

Water Needs—Low to high. Provide regular moisture through their blooming period, then decrease watering.

CANNA

Canna spp.

Why It's Special—To add a tropical look to your garden, try cannas. They are hardy to zone 7 so are usually grown as annuals in containers, next to house walls or fences, or at the back of borders. Flowers come in warm colors and many cultivars have captivating striped or variegated leaves. 'Wyoming' features bright orange blossoms and bronze-red foliage. 'Praetoria' has orange flowers and variegated leaves. 'Pink Magic' features hot pink flowers while 'Island Gran Canaria' has creamy yellow blossoms with yellow centers.

How to Plant & Grow—Plant rhizomes in full sun, 2 inches deep and 12 to 18 inches apart. Cannas can be started indoors or in greenhouses in pots eight weeks before the last frost date or outdoors after frost date. Amend soil with compost and feed with high-nitrogen fertilizer.

Care & Problems—Deadhead to keep plants tidy. Slugs or snails may chew on foliage; use slug bait.

Color(s)—Orange, yellow, salmon, red, pink, bicolors

Peak Season—July through September

Mature Size (H x W)—3 to 6 ft. x 3 ft.

Water Needs—Medium to very high. Water regularly.

CROCOSMIA

Crocosmia spp. and hybrids

Why It's Special—With its bright flower stalks and sword-shaped leaves, crocosmia (or montbretia) is an attention-grabber in the garden. Hardy in zones 5 to 10, it attracts hummingbirds and makes a great cut flower. *Crocosmia x crocosmiiflora* 'Emily McKenzie' has orange flowers with red centers and grows 1½ feet tall. 'Lucifer' is deep red and grows 3 to 4 feet tall. 'Solfaterre' features sulfur yellow blooms and bronze foliage. *C. masonorum* 'Saffron Fire' has orange blossoms with red margins.

How to Plant & Grow—In spring, plant corms in full sun to part shade in average, well-drained soil. Add a balanced fertilizer to the soil. Plant corms 5 to 6 inches deep and spaced 4 to 5 inches apart, or start with nursery-grown plants. Grow in multiples for best effect.

Care & Problems—Divide bulbs in fall once they've finished blooming. No pest or disease problems. Plants are rabbit- and deer-resistant.

Color(s)—Orange, red

Peak Season—July to September

Mature Size (H x W)—1½ to 4 ft. x 1 to 2 ft.

Water Needs—Medium. Water regularly but do not overwater.

CROCUS

Crocus spp.

Why It's Special—One of the earliest bulbs to flower, crocuses are a heartwarming sight in late winter and early spring. They naturalize well and are ideal for woodland or cottage gardens. Dutch crocus (*Crocus vernus*) comes in many colors: 'Twilight' (purple), 'Jeanne d'Arc' (white), 'Grand Maitre' (lavender-blue), 'Pickwick' (white with purple stripes), and 'Yellow Mammoth' (gold). Woodland crocus (*C. tommasinianus*) 'Barr's Purple' has deep purple petals while 'Rosaeus' features pale violet flowers. Saffron crocus (*C. sativus*) has lilac-purple flowers with orange stigmas that are used in gourmet cooking; it blooms in fall and is hardy to zone 6.

How to Plant & Grow—In the fall, plant in full sun to part shade, in a density of ten bulbs to 1 square foot, 2 inches deep.

Care & Problems—Apply balanced fertilizer after bulbs finish blooming. Squirrels have been known to dig up the bulbs.

Color(s)—White, pink, lavender-blue, blue, violet, yellow, gold, bicolors

Peak Season—February to April

Mature Size (H x W)—4 to 6 in. x 3 to 6 in.

Water Needs—Low. Water if soil dries out.

CYCLAMEN

Cyclamen spp.

Why It's Special—Hardy cyclamen is a wonderful naturalizer grown from a tuber. Use in shady rock or woodland gardens and along pathways. *Cyclamen hederifolium* is hardiest with light to deep pink blossoms. *C. purpurascens* features fragrant blooms in light pink to magenta. Both are dormant in early summer and bloom from late summer and fall. The leaves appear during or after flowering. They grow in zones 5 to 9.

How to Plant & Grow—In spring, plant tubers in light to medium shade in average, well-drained soil. Add bonemeal to soil. With the growing points facing upward, cover the tops of *C. hederifolium* bulbs with ½ inch of soil; plant other species as deep as 4 inches. Space 6 to 12 inches apart.

Care & Problems—No fertilizer is needed. During early summer dormancy, mulch bulbs to conserve moisture. Plants have minimal problems.

Color(s)—Pink, white, magenta, red

Peak Season—Late summer into fall

Mature Size (H x W)—2 to 6 in. x 6 in.

Water Needs—Medium. Water in late summer to early fall; then only when soil is dry.

DAFFODIL

Narcissus spp. and hybrids

Why It's Special—Daffodils are reliable, easy-to-grow bloomers. The flower size stays consistent over time and bulbs naturalize well. They are hardy in zones 3 to 9. 'Ceylon' has yellow petals and orange cups, 'Intrigue' has pale chartreuse blooms, and 'Accent' has white petals with a salmon trumpet. 'Ice Follies' features cream petals and a pale yellow cup and 'Thalia' is completely white with delicate, outward-facing petals.

How to Plant & Grow—Plant bulbs in full sun or dappled shade in autumn in slightly acidic but well-drained soil. Incorporate bulb fertilizer into planting holes. Refer to package directions for depth and spacing as it varies by type; plant in multiples for best effect.

Care & Problems—Deadhead flowers but don't remove leaves until they turn brown so bulbs can store energy for the following year. Bulbs are toxic so they're left alone by rodents.

Color(s)—White, yellow, salmon, bicolors

Peak Season—Early to late spring

Mature Size (H x W)—6 to 18 in. x 6 to 8 in.

Water Needs—Low to medium. Water only during very dry periods.

DAHLIA

Dahlia spp. and hybrids

Why It's Special—Dahlias come in an impressive number of colors, forms, and sizes. Combine that with their attractive, bushy growth habit, and you've got a winner whether you grow individual plants as specimens or mass plantings for effect. Dahlia types include single-flowering (such as anemone, orchid, and peony style) and double-flowering (such as cactus, ball, water lily, and pompon).

How to Plant & Grow—Select a sunny location with well-drained soil. Place a stake in the ground for each plant first, then plant tubers 4 to 6 inches deep after all danger of frost is past. Stake plants as they grow.

Care & Problems—Feed with a balanced fertilizer once plants are established. Slugs can cause damage. In zones 7 and below, tubers must be lifted and stored over winter. For advice on this technique and for more dahlia care information, contact your local Master Gardener program.

Color(s)—Every color except blue

Peak Season—Mid- to late-summer

Mature Size (H x W)—1 to 7 ft. x 1 to 2 ft.

Water Needs—Medium. Water regularly.

ELEPHANT EARS

Colocasia esculenta

Why It's Special—For a tropical look, add elephant ears to your garden. They also can be grown as aquatic plants, in outdoor containers, and as showy houseplants. Their large leaves are striking in appearance and the blooms are reminiscent of calla lilies. 'Black Magic' has purplish black leaves while 'Pink China' has pink stems and deep green, heart-shaped leaves. 'Mojito' features green leaves with large black splotches. 'Hilo Bay' has crinkled, green leaves on black stems, whereas the stems and leaves of 'Diamond Head' are both black.

How to Plant & Grow—After the danger of frost is past, plant in full sun to part shade in rich, moist soil, 2 to 4 inches deep. If grown as aquatic plants, place them in water that is no more than 6 inches deep.

Care & Problems—Plants have minimal problems. In zones 7 and below, lift and store tubers in a cool, dry location over winter.

Color(s)—Purple-black or green foliage, white flowers

Peak Season—Summer to fall

Mature Size (H x W)—3 to 6 ft. x 3 to 6 ft.

Water Needs—High. Do not allow soil to dry out.

FOXTAIL LILY

Eremurus spp.

Why It's Special—With tall flower spires looking like shooting fireworks, foxtail lilies are showy and colorful. The flowers are fragrant and stunning in floral arrangements. Plants are drought tolerant and grow in zones 5 to 8. *Eremurus robustus* (10 feet) has pale pink flowers. *E. stenophyllus* 'Bungei' (6 feet) has yellow-orange flowers . *Eremurus* x *isabellinus* 'Cleopatra' has orange-red flowers while 'Pinocchio' features orange flower spikes; both grow to 6 feet tall.

How to Plant & Grow—In the fall, plant in full sun in rich, well-drained soil preferably sheltered from wind. In fall, dig a hole about 6 inches deep with a mound in the bottom. Spread crowns and their roots over the mound and carefully refill the hole. Space 2 to 3 feet apart and plant in multiples for best effect.

Care & Problems—Stake plants in windy areas. No fertilizer is required. Plants have minimal insect or disease problems.

Color(s)—Pink, yellow, white

Peak Season—June to July

Mature Size (H x W)—5 to 10 ft. x 2 to 3 ft.

Water Needs—Medium. Plants become drought tolerant once established.

FRITILLARY
Fritillaria spp. and hybrids

Why It's Special—These specialty bulbs are just plain fun! From the dainty Guinea hen flower (*Fritillaria meleagris*) with unusual, checkered flowers to the more imposing crown imperials (*F. imperialis*) with huge red or yellow flowers and 3-foot-tall height, they look fabulous wherever they're planted. *F. verticillata* features delicate, bell-shaped flowers hanging from 2-foot-tall stalks; the pale yellow flowers have burgundy webbing inside. Persian lily (*F. persica*) has deep purple, bell-shaped flowers on stems up to 3 feet tall. Zones 4 to 8.

How to Plant & Grow—In fall, select a site in full sun to part shade with well-drained soil. Plant smaller fritillaries in 2- to 3-inch-deep holes and larger species 8 inches deep. For the best effect, plant in multiples.

Care & Problems—Fertilize with bonemeal or bulb food in early spring. Once the bulbs have finished blooming, don't remove leaves until they turn brown so bulbs can store energy for next year. They have no pests.

Color(s)—Purple checkered, orange, yellow, white

Peak Season—Spring to early summer

Mature Size (H x W)—Varies from 1 to 4 ft. x 1 to 1½ ft.

Water Needs—Medium. Water regularly.

GLADIOLUS
Gladiolus spp.

Why It's Special—Gladiolus species are showy, colorful additions to the garden and even more impressive as cut flowers. *G. grandiflorus* is the tallest type and blooms from spring to fall. *G. nanus* grows 1 foot tall and blooms from June to July. *G. primulinus* grows to 2 feet tall and blooms all summer.

How to Plant & Grow—Choose a sunny location and moist, well-drained soil. Plant corms from mid-spring to early summer, every two weeks to extend blooming period. Small bulbs should be planted 2 inches deep and large bulbs up to 6 inches deep. Space them 6 inches apart. Initially cover corms with 2 inches of soil, backfilling the planting holes as the plants grow.

Care & Problems—Stake plants as needed. Feed a balanced fertilizer when plants are 6 inches tall. Deadhead when blooms fade. In zones 6 and below, corms must be lifted and stored over the winter.

Color(s)—Every color except true blue

Peak Season—June through August

Mature Size (H x W)—1 to 5 ft. x 6 in.

Water Needs—Medium. Water well when soil is dry.

GLORY-OF-THE-SNOW
Chionodoxa luciliae

Why It's Special—Hardy down to zone 3, this specialty bulb provides splashes of color early in spring when the landscape looks pretty bleak. The flowers are borne in clusters on stems, with most having contrasting white centers. The bulbs naturalize easily and do well in rock gardens or under trees. Plants are deer tolerant. Choose other early-blooming bulbs for attractive combination plantings. Most bulbs have blue star-shaped flowers but *Chionodoxa luciliae* (formerly *gigantea*) 'Alba' has white flowers and grows 5 to 10 inches tall while 'Pink Giant' grows to 1 foot in height. 'Violet Beauty' features pink-violet blossoms.

How to Plant & Grow—Plant in fall in full sun to part shade. Bulbs are not particular about soil type as long as it's well drained, but add bulb food to the planting hole. Plant 3 inches deep and 2 inches apart.

Care & Problems—Plants have minimal insect or disease problems.

Color(s)—Blue, white, pink

Peak Season—Early spring

Mature Size (H x W)—4 to 12 in. x 4 in.

Water Needs—Medium. Early spring moisture should suffice but water during dry periods.

GRAPE HYACINTH
Muscari spp.

Why It's Special—Grape hyacinths are petite, early-blooming bulbs that are ideal for rock gardens, under trees and around shrubs, in the fronts of borders, and along pathways. The bulbs can be forced to bloom indoors as well. *Muscari armeniacum* 'Blue Spike' has double blue flowers while 'Lady Blue' has white and pale blue flowers. *M. aucheri* 'Mount Hood' is unusual, having blue flower spikes capped in white. *M. latifolium* has two-toned flowers with dark blue at the bottom and light blue at the top. *M. botryoides* 'Album' features white flowers. It's hardy in all zones.

How to Plant & Grow—Choose a site in full sun to part shade with average, well-drained soil; incorporate bulb food into the hole. Plant bulbs 3 inches deep and 3 inches apart in fall. Plant in multiples for best effect, although bulbs easily naturalize.

Care & Problems—Plants have minimal insect or disease problems but deer and rabbits find the foliage and flowers tasty.

Color(s)—White, blue, violet, yellow, bicolors

Peak Season—Early spring

Mature Size (H x W)—4 to 8 in. x 3 in.

Water Needs—Low. Water only during excessively dry periods.

IRIS
Iris spp. and hybrids

Why It's Special—In Greek mythology, Iris is the Goddess of the Rainbow, and with all of the colorful species and cultivars available, irises truly bring color to the garden. Their fragrant flowers have three outer petals (falls) and three inner, upright petals (standards). Hardy to zone 3; deer resistant. Recommended species: bearded iris (*Iris germanica*), 8 inches to 4 feet; dwarf bearded iris (*I. pumila*), 6 inches; dwarf crested iris (*I. cristata*), 4 inches; Siberian iris (*I. siberica*), 3 feet; Japanese iris (*I. ensata*), 3½ feet; and sweet iris (*I. pallida*), 3 feet.

How to Plant & Grow—Plant in full sun to part shade in well-drained soil between July to September. The rhizomes should be planted shallowly, at or just below the soil surface.

Care & Problems—Provide balanced fertilizer in early spring and after blooming. Divide clumps every three years. Minimal pest or disease problems.

Color(s)—All colors

Peak Season—Late spring to midsummer

Mature Size (H x W)—4 in. to 4 ft. x 1½ to 2 ft.

Water Needs—Medium (most species) to high (*I. siberica* and *I. ensata*). Water regularly.

NAKED LADY
Amaryllis belladonna

Why It's Special—A native of South Africa, naked lady (also called amaryllis) is known for its stems and stunning pink flower clusters. It is winter-hardy in zone 7 and above. This is not the same as the popular bulb that is forced to bloom indoors, which is *Hippeastrum*. The flowers of naked ladies are trumpet-shaped and very fragrant.

How to Plant & Grow—In fall, plant bulbs in a sunny location in well-drained soil. Incorporate bulb fertilizer into the soil at planting time, then place bulbs 6 inches deep with the pointed end facing upward. Plant up to three bulbs per square foot. The bulbs will send up a tall stem and flower in late summer before plants develop leaves.

Care & Problems—Fertilize each spring with bulb food or balanced fertilizer. Remove flowers after blooming but leave stems in place until they begin to dry. Continue to water until leaves turn yellow. Trim leaves back. Plants are deer resistant.

Color(s)—Pink; also red or white hybrids

Peak Season—Summer to fall

Mature Size (H x W)—2 to 3 ft. x 1 ft.

Water Needs—Medium. Plants will become drought tolerant once established.

ORIENTAL LILY

Lilium spp.

Why It's Special—With their exotic blossoms and intoxicating fragrance, Oriental lilies command attention in perennial borders and cottage gardens. Hardy to zone 4, they're extremely easy to grow. Plant where you can easily view the stunning blossoms. 'Stargazer' is magenta with red freckles while 'Casablanca' is pure white. 'Virginale' has white petals with yellow stripes and 'Salmon Star' features pale orange and white blossoms. Orienpets, hybrids of Oriental and trumpet lilies, have more heat tolerance and bloom earlier.

How to Plant & Grow—Plant bulbs in spring or fall in full sun; provide afternoon shade in areas with hot summers. Plants tolerate most soil types as long as they drain well. Incorporate bulb fertilizer in soil and plant bulbs 8 inches deep and space 8 to 12 inches apart.

Care & Problems—Taller cultivars may need staking in windy areas. Fertilize each spring with high-phosphorus fertilizer. Deadhead flowers after blooming; cut foliage back in fall. Plants have minimal problems.

Color(s)—White, pink, salmon, yellow, magenta

Peak Season—Late summer

Mature Size (H x W)—2 to 4 ft. x 1 ft.

Water Needs—Medium. Water regularly.

ORNAMENTAL ONION

Allium spp. and hybrids

Why It's Special—Hardy to zone 4, ornamental onions add a "wow" factor to perennial borders and cottage gardens. Most naturalize well. Flowers are long-lasting and can be used in dried floral arrangements. 'Globemaster' is 4 feet tall with full, pink globes. 'Purple Sensation' is 3 feet tall with rosy purple globes while foot-tall 'Millennium' has rosy pink flowers. 'Mount Everest' features white globes on 3-foot stalks. The popular star of Persia (*A. christophii*) has pink, 8-inch flower heads on 2-foot stalks. *A. caeruleum* 'Blue' has soft blue flowers and grows 2 feet. Lily leek (*A. moly*) has butter yellow flowers and is 8 inches tall. Drumstick allium (*A. sphaerocephalon*) has oblong magenta flower heads on 3-foot stalks.

How to Plant & Grow—In fall, plant bulbs in full sun where soil drains well. For best effect, plant in multiples at the depth recommended on packaging.

Care & Problems—Fertilize in fall and spring with bulb food. Minimal problems.

Color(s)—Blue, purple, yellow

Peak Season—Late spring through summer

Mature Size (H x W)—8 to 48 in. x 20 in.

Water Needs—Low. Water only when soil is dry.

SIBERIAN SQUILL

Scilla siberica

Why It's Special—One of the hardiest bulbs is Siberian squill, which will grow in zone 2. Plants have straplike leaves and nodding blue or white bell-shaped flowers. It is deer resistant and naturalizes beautifully. Due to their dainty size, plant them at the front of borders or rock gardens, along pathways, and under trees and shrubs. You can even plant them in your lawn. 'Spring Beauty' has intense blue flowers, a highly desirable color for the landscape, while 'Alba' has heavenly white blossoms. Attractive companions include other early-blooming bulbs like crocus, snowdrops, and glory-of-the-snow.

How to Plant & Grow—In fall, plant in full sun to part shade in well-draining soil. For best effect, plant groupings of the bulbs at a depth of 2 to 3 inches and spaced 3 inches apart.

Care & Problems—Fertilize each spring with bonemeal or high-phosphorus fertilizer. Plants are low maintenance and have minimal pest or disease problems.

Color(s)—Blue, white

Peak Season—April

Mature Size (H x W)—5 to 8 in. x 3 to 6 in.

Water Needs—Medium. Early spring moisture should be adequate; water only if very dry.

SICILIAN HONEY LILY

Nectaroscordum siculum var. bulgaricum

Why It's Special—Related to the allium, Sicilian honey lily has 2- to 3-foot stalks topped by cream, maroon, and green bell-shaped flowers hanging from long stems. The baseball-sized flower heads make these plants real attention-getters in border plantings and are attractive in floral arrangements despite their garlic scent. The seedheads can be dried for use in arrangements and crafts. They are easy to grow in zones 6 to 10.

How to Plant & Grow—In fall, select a site in full sun to part shade. Plants are not particular about soil type as long as it is well-drained soil. Plant bulbs 4 inches deep. To make an impact, plant in groups with 5-inch spacing between each bulb.

Care & Problems—Fertilize in spring with a balanced fertilizer. Plants have minimal insect or disease problems but will easily self-seed; deadhead to control, if desired. Plants are deer and rodent resistant.

Color(s)—Cream with maroon and lime green

Peak Season—May, June, July, depending on elevation and temperatures

Mature Size (H x W)—12 to 36 in. x 3 to 6 in.

Water Needs—Low. Water regularly during growing season.

SNOWDROPS

Galanthus spp. and hybrids

Why It's Special—With their nodding white and green blossoms, snowdrops are welcome sights in late winter and early spring. They grow best in zones 3 to 7. Add to woodland gardens, along walkways, and around deciduous trees and shrubs. These deer-resistant plants need a year to establish but will naturalize. *Galanthus nivalis* 'Flore Pleno' has double flowers while 'Sandersii' features yellow, rather than green, markings on the flowers. *G. plicatus* 'Wendy's Gold' also has yellow markings. Giant snowdrop (*G. elwesii*) has larger flowers and wider leaves and grows to 1 foot tall.

How to Plant & Grow—In fall, plant in full sun to part shade in moist, well-drained soil; incorporate bulb food in planting holes. Plant bulbs 2 to 3 inches deep with 3-inch spacing.

Care & Problems—Snowdrops are low maintenance with minimal problems. Wait until foliage dies before removing so bulbs can store energy for next year.

Color(s)—White

Peak Season—February and March

Mature Size (H x W)—6 to 12 in. x 4 to 6 in.

Water Needs—Medium. Early spring moisture is adequate; water only if very dry.

SPANISH BLUEBELLS

Hyacinthoides hispanica

Why It's Special—Easy to grow in a variety of conditions, Spanish bluebells have attractive bell-shaped flowers that dangle from rigid stems. Their straplike foliage grows in dense clumps. They are ideal for woodland gardens, rock gardens, perennial borders, and in drifts under deciduous trees. Their flower stalks make delightful additions to floral arrangements. Late-blooming tulips are good companion plants. 'Excelsior' has large, violet-blue flowers while 'White Triumphator' is covered in white blossoms. 'Queen of Pinks' has lavender-pink flowers. Zones 3 to 8.

How to Plant & Grow—Select a site in full sun to full shade with average soil. In fall, plant bulbs 3 inches deep and space them 4 to 6 inches apart; add bulb food to planting holes. For the best effect, plant bulbs in large drifts.

Care & Problems—Fertilize with bulb food each spring. Bulbs will naturalize through division and self-seeding. Plants have minimal insect or disease problems and are low maintenance.

Color(s)—White, pink, blue

Peak Season—May and June

Mature Size (H x W)—16 in. x 4 to 6 in.

Water Needs—Low. Water regularly early in the season to produce the most flowers.

SPIDER LILY

Lycoris spp. and hybrids

Why It's Special—A member of the Amaryllis family, spider lilies are known for their beautiful, fragrant blossoms atop 2-foot-tall stems. The leaves die back during summer, followed by the appearance of flower stalks. Most *Lycoris* species will grow to zone 5 but resurrection lily (*L. squamigera*) is considered the hardiest. Surprise lily (*L. sprengeri*) has pink flowers with blue tips and grows up to 18 inches tall. Peppermint spider lily (*L. incarnata*) has white-and-red striped flowers, and hardy spider lily or long-tube surprise lily (*L. longituba*) features 3-foot-tall flower stems with white to pale yellow blossoms.

How to Plant & Grow—In spring, plant in full sun to part shade where soil is well drained. Incorporate compost into planting holes that are 6 inches deep and space bulbs 6 inches apart.

Care & Problems—Plants do not require annual fertilization but benefit from the addition of compost to the bed. Mulch planting beds for winter. Minimal problems.

Color(s)—Pink

Peak Season—August to September

Mature Size (H x W)—1 ½ to 3 ft. x 1 ½ to 2 ft.

Water Needs—Medium. Water moderately after foliage dies back and before flower stems emerge.

TULIP
Tulipa spp.

Why It's Special—The most-loved spring bulb, tulips bring color and drama to perennial borders and cottage gardens. Their showy flowers come in many colors and bloom in early, mid-, or late spring. The graceful petals of lily-flowering tulips have curled, pointed tips. Peony tulips have long-lasting double flowers resembling peony blossoms. Parrot tulips are riots of color, usually two-toned, with fringed petals. Apeldoorn Darwin hybrids have large, single flowers.

How to Plant & Grow—Plant in autumn in full sun. Incorporate bulb fertilizer into planting bed. Refer to package label for planting depth and spacing; rule of thumb is a depth of 8 inches for large bulbs and 6 inches for smaller ones.

Care & Problems—Apply bulb fertilizer in spring. Deadhead blooms as soon as they fade. Do not remove leaves until they wither to allow bulbs to store energy for next season. Deer and rabbits eat foliage; pocket gophers eat bulbs.

Color(s)—All colors except true blue and black

Peak Season—March, April, and May

Mature Size (H x W)—4 to 28 in. x 10 to 12 in.

Water Needs—Medium. Water when soil is dry.

WINDFLOWER
Anemone blanda

Why It's Special—These showy, daisylike flowers work well in border plantings, in woodland gardens, and as groundcovers. Plants are deer resistant and make cheerful additions to floral arrangements. They naturalize well, spreading by rhizomes and self-seeding to form a brightly colored mat. While windflowers are rated to grow in zone 5, they perform more reliably in zones 6 or higher. 'White Splendour' has white flowers with yellow centers. 'Blue Star' features lavender-blue blossoms while 'Pink Star' has pale pink flowers with white centers.

How to Plant & Grow—In fall, plant in full sun to part shade in an area sheltered from wind. The soil should be moist but well drained; add bulb food to planting holes. Soak tubers in water for several hours before planting. Plant 3 inches deep and 4 inches apart. For the most impact, plant *en masse*.

Care & Problems—Fertilize with bulb food each spring. Plants have minimal pest or disease problems and are low maintenance.

Color(s)—Pink, blue, lavender, white

Peak Season—Early to mid-spring

Mature Size (H x W)—3 to 12 in. x 3 to 4 in.

Water Needs—Regular. Water regularly throughout the growing season.

JANUARY

- Catalogs of summer- and fall-blooming bulbs will be out now. Order something different like a few unusual lilies to experiment with. If bulbs arrive before the ground is workable, store them in a cool, frost-free place until conditions improve.

- West of the Cascades, clear away leaves left from the fall from early snowdrop plantings this month. They will be the first bulbs to show up about the end of the month.

- If you are planning a major spring bulb-planting project, start putting your ideas on paper so you know how many bulbs to order. Crocus should be spaced at eight to twelve bulbs per square foot and daffodils at four to five per square foot. Tulips can be spaced between five to nine per square foot, depending on how much of a show of color you want.

FEBRUARY

- Visit Portland's Yard, Garden and Patio Show; Seattle's Northwest Flower and Garden Show; or the Vancouver B.C. Home and Garden Show for design ideas. Vendors will have a wide selection of spring and summer bulbs for sale. Store any bulbs you purchase in a cool, frost-free place until the soil has warmed and the weather has settled.

- Check for squirrel, gopher, and vole damage early. Squirrels will dig bulbs up while gophers and voles will nibble them from underground. Lay hardware cloth or chicken wire over beds to keep squirrels from digging.

- West of the Cascades, remove mulch or heavy deposits of leaves from beds so the bulbs get light as soon as they emerge.

- After a heavy rain or snow melt, check for standing water around bulbs. Bulbs rot very quickly if they stay wet too long. Consider planting bulbs in raised mounds or beds that get them out of the standing water or find a new place to plant.

MARCH

- West of the Cascades, the early-season bulbs will be blooming this month. As they emerge, work bulb fertilizer in around them. Be sure to apply deer repellant to tulips and crocus as they emerge. The deer will be looking for any tender, green shoots.

- Bring out your stored pots of bulbs where they can get light and warmth from the sun.

- Feed them with a good bulb food or low-nitrogen balanced fertilizer and water them well. After they finish blooming, heel them in, pot and all, into an out-of-the-way spot so the foliage can mature. After it has died back, remove the bulbs and plant them in the garden. Be aware that not all of them will survive this process.

- Gardeners east of the Cascades will see their first snowdrops early in the month. Snowdrops often emerge from under the last of the melting snow. Remove any remaining fall leaves gently from beds where they are planted so as to not damage the emerging foliage.

APRIL

- Late frosts can damage bulb foliage. Bulbs often send up enough foliage to break the soil surface and then stop growing until the weather is more to their liking. The flower buds are still underground and emerge after the foliage is up, reducing the chance that they will be damaged by a late frost.

- Fertilize bulbs as soon as the ground can be worked with a quality bulb or 10-10-10 fertilizer and bonemeal. Work it into the soil gently around emerging plants.

- Take pictures of your blooming bulbs to record their location so you avoid digging into them while adding new plants in fall. Make notes in your journal of the performance of various bulbs and where you want to add more in fall.

- If you see bulbs with yellowing or distorted foliage or blooms prior to full flowering, remove them from the garden. They may be diseased. Throw them in the trash to reduce the potential of spreading the disease to compost.

MAY

- Midseason bulbs will be at their glory this month as the early bloomers fade. To extend the blooming of tulips and daffodils, consider adding a mix of early, midseason, and late-blooming varieties in fall.

- West of the Cascades, it may be warm enough to plant out tender cannas, tuberous begonias, dahlias, and calla lilies by mid-month. Gardeners east of the Cascades should wait until early June when the soil is warmer.

- Deadhead any daffodil or tulip flowers to allow a plant to put its energies into bulb development instead of seed development. This will prolong the overall life of the planting.

- Keep bulb plantings weeded. Apply a layer of mulch to keep weeds in check. If you use a different type of mulch over bulb plantings, it will be easier to spot them after the foliage dies down.

JUNE

- The last of the late-blooming daffodils and tulips will be in full bloom now. Early spring bulb foliage will be close to finishing late this month and can be removed from the garden.

- Continue deadheading spent flowers.

- Gardeners east of the Cascades can put out tender bulbs early in the month if the weather has reliably warmed up.

- Stake tall-growing bearded iris, dahlias, and gladiolas to keep them tidy and upright. Be careful not to spear the bulbs with your stakes. Stakes can be wood or bamboo stakes or lengths of sturdy wire set a foot or so into the ground and tall enough to tie the flower to it.

- Early spring bulb foliage will be dying back by the end of the month. Gently remove it with a gentle tug or cut back with pruners.

- Pinch back dahlia plants when they get about 18 inches tall to force them to bush out and eventually produce more flowers.

JULY

- Early dahlias, daylilies, Asiatic lilies, and gladiolas will start blooming mid-month. Be sure to stake the plants, especially if you live in a windy area. Remove some of the smaller dahlia buds to direct more energy into the larger buds.

- With so many plants in bloom this month, pick some bouquets to enjoy indoors. Cut the blooms early in the day and immediately place them in a deep bucket of cool water. Arrange them in vases as soon as possible. Be sure to remove the lily stamens as the yellow pollen can stain fabric.

- Iris will be ready to divide towards the end of the month. Trim back foliage to 6 inches. Divide the roots and replant the largest rhizomes with a fan of foliage so the top of the rhizome is at the soil surface. Water in well and cover lightly with mulch.

- Deadhead finishing flowers to keep them looking neat. Clean up any remaining spent bulb foliage and trim off scraggly iris leaves.

AUGUST

- Keep summer-flowering bulbs moist but not soggy through the summer heat.

- Continue to clean up dying foliage and trim down Asiatic lily stalks as they dry out. Remove any plants that appear to be yellowed or distorted prior to flowering. They may be diseased. Throw them in the trash.

- Begin planning where you want to add fall-planted bulbs. Bulb catalogs will be arriving about now and bulbs will be in the local nurseries by early September.

SEPTEMBER

- Fall colchicum and cyclamen blooms will emerge this month for the last hurrah of the bulb season. Enjoy them while they last.

- Review your planting plan and make your purchases of fall-planted bulbs while there is a good supply. Plant them soon after you buy them to preserve their quality.

- Dig frost-tender bulbs like dahlias, gladiolas, and cannas immediately after the first frost. Clean them gently and cure them in a warm, dry place out of direct light. Write the cultivar name on the bulb with a felt marker. Store all but gladiolas in peat moss in a dry place between 45 to 50 degrees Fahrenheit. Glads can be stored loose in mesh bags.

OCTOBER

- This is planting month for spring bulbs so have fun tucking those little balls of color into their winter homes. If squirrels are a problem, cover the bed area with chicken wire pinned to the ground with stakes.

- If gophers and voles ate their way through your tulip, crocus, and lily bulbs last winter, plant this year's plantings in hardware cloth baskets set in the planting hole. Gopher-resistant bulbs include *Allium*, *Anemone*, *Narcissus*, *Freesia*, *Hyacinthus*, *Scilla*, *Iris reticulata*, *Fritillaria*, *Galanthus*, *Lycoris*, and *Muscari*.

- To extend the length of the bloom season next spring in a particular area, plant early, midseason, and late-blooming tulip and daffodil bulbs in the same space.

- Bulbs planted by mid-October in pots will be ready for forcing by February. Plant them in good potting soil and then heel them into a garden bed or put them in an unheated shed. They will need about thirteen to fifteen weeks with temperatures of no more than 35 to 40 degrees Fahrenheit before they are ready to force into bloom.

NOVEMBER

- If you want the bright red, pink, and white flowers of amaryllis for the holidays, purchase them now. If they don't come in a container, pot them up in a container an inch or two bigger than the bulb. Use a good potting mix for soil. Set the bulb one-half to two-thirds into the soil. Set them in a 60-degree Fahrenheit, brightly lit space, and keep the soil moist but not soggy. Long strappy leaves will appear shortly, followed by the tall flower stalk. Insert a stake at the edge of the pot to hold up the flower stalk if needed.

- Give your potted bulbs a good drink. Water them about once a month during winter.

DECEMBER

- Pot up some paper-white narcissus. They do not need chilling so they will bloom in a matter of weeks just as the dark, gray days of January start getting to us.

- Check stored bulbs for rot. Treat with a fungicide if needed. Water potted bulbs lightly.

- If you didn't get around to planting tulips and daffodils you bought in fall, get them into the ground as early as you can. If your ground is frozen, pot them up into large containers, water them well, and store them in a dark place at about 35 degrees Fahrenheit. Check them frequently and moisten the soil lightly. Don't water them heavily until the tips begin emerging.

EDIBLES, HERBS
& FRUIT
for the Northwest

In the Northwest, being a successful vegetable gardener means understanding your local climate, the intricacies of the microclimates within your own garden, and the length of your growing season. It also requires a sense of adventure in finding the varieties that will do best in your corner of the region.

Rainfall amounts and temperatures can vary widely, even in small areas, depending on three factors: Elevation; proximity to large bodies of water; and whether you are on the windward or leeward side of a mountain range. These conditions can be distilled into what you can expect for a growing season in your area. The growing season is the number of days between the last frost of spring and the first frost of the fall. Its length will determine which varieties of vegetables—especially the warm-season crops—you can successfully grow. Keep in mind they are only averages and can fluctuate by year. They can also vary depending on your elevation or distance from a large body of water.

SELECTING VEGETABLE VARIETIES

With this much season length and temperature variation, selecting the right varieties for your area is critical. Generally, short-season vegetables and fruits are best. Tomatoes, peppers, corn, and melons that mature in fewer than 75 to 80 days from transplant will more reliably ripen fruit than those requiring longer growing seasons. Unfortunately, many popular heirloom vegetables like 'Brandywine' tomatoes (90 to 110 days) often aren't ready to set fruit during the warmest part of summer. Oregon State University has developed a number of tomato varieties like 'Oregon Spring' (75 to 80 days) and 'Siletz' (70 to 75 days) specifically for the Northwest's short seasons. Ask your local Master Gardener program for recommendations.

Surprisingly, it isn't the high daytime temperatures that induce fruit set in tomatoes, peppers, and eggplant; it is regular exposure to nighttime temperatures above 55 degrees Fahrenheit. Temperatures generally don't reach this level until early July in warmer parts of the region and start fading by mid-August. Areas at high elevations or close to large bodies of water may not have nights that regularly reach 55 degrees Fahrenheit.

LOCATING YOUR VEGETABLE GARDEN

Edible plants need a minimum of six to eight hours of sunlight a day to produce heavy crops; otherwise, you will get a lot of leaves and few fruits. Midday to afternoon sun is especially important west of the Cascades, where morning fog and low clouds can block the sun. In the hotter, drier climates to the east of the Cascades, most gardens benefit from a little late-afternoon shade from the hot sun. Gardens also must be located on level land to ensure that water flows evenly around the plants. Slopes can be terraced or raised; beds can be built across a slope to provide a level space.

SOIL REQUIREMENTS

Vegetables, herbs, and fruits need well-drained soil rich in organic matter. Apply 3 or 4 inches

Drip irrigation systems are an efficient way to water vegetable crops.

of organic matter every two to three years in the fall to keep the soil in good shape. If you have clayey or sandy soil, organic material will mitigate the clay's density and increase the sand's water-holding capacity. Cover crops can be planted in empty beds and turned under to provide additional organic matter.

WATERING

Edible garden plants need at least an inch of water weekly—more in hot, dry, or windy weather. Consider putting the vegetable garden on a drip or micro-spray watering system hooked to an electronic timer that turns the water on and off automatically. Drip systems use water much more efficiently than conventional sprinklers and are quite cost-effective to install. Older, conventional sprinkler systems can be easily retrofitted. Inconsistent watering practices can cause blossom-end rot in tomatoes and knobby potatoes.

FERTILIZING

Vegetables, fruits, and herbs use varying amounts of fertilizer: Light feeders need fertilizer only when planted; heavy feeders need several applications throughout the season. Legumes fix nitrogen in the soil and are often planted with heavy feeders to restore nitrogen.

NUTRIENT REQUIREMENTS FOR SELECTED VEGETABLES

HEAVY FEEDERS	LIGHT FEEDERS	LEGUMES
Asparagus	Carrot	Alfalfa
Beet	Garlic	Bean
Broccoli	Leek	Clover
Cabbage	Mustard	Edible pea
Cantaloupe	Onion	Field pea
Cauliflower	Parsnip	Hairy vetch
Celery	Pepper	Soybean
Collards	Potato	
Corn	Rutabaga	

Source: Sustainable Gardening: The Oregon-Washington Master Gardener Handbook, 1999, page 142

The natural fertility of your soil will determine how much fertilizer you need, so do a soil test before applying. Fertilizers can be applied in dry or liquid forms. Dry fertilizers are applied alongside a row of plants and gently worked into the soil.

Liquid fertilizers are sprayed on the soil or the foliage. Conventional fertilizers generally have higher nitrogen, phosphorus, and potassium ratings than organic fertilizers, providing a quick blast of food that lasts only a short time. Organic fertilizers release their nutrients slowly, so the plants get steady doses. Manure and compost provide a limited amount of nutrients and are better as sources of organic matter than nutrients.

RELATIVE NUTRIENT CONTENT OF ORGANIC AND CONVENTIONAL FERTILIZERS

MATERIALS	NITROGEN	PHOSPHORUS	POTASSIUM
ORGANIC FERTILIZERS			
Bonemeal (steamed)	0.7 to 4	10 to 34	0
Compost	1.5 to 3.5	0.5 to 1	1 to 2
Cotton Seed Meal	6	2.5	1.7
Blood Meal	12	1.5	0.57
Alfalfa Meal	2.5 to 5	1	1
Fish Meal (dry)	10	4	0
Feather Meal	7 to 12	.5	0
Fish Meal	10	6	2
Liquid Fish Emulsion	4	2	2
Peat and Muck	1.5 to 3	.25 to .5	.5 to 1
Cattle (aged)*	1.1	.7	1.2
Horse (aged)*	.7	.2	.7
Sheep (aged)*	0.7	0.5	1.3
Poultry (aged)*	3.5	2	2
COMMERCIAL FERTILIZERS			
Urea**	42 to 45	0	0
General Garden Fertilizers**	10 to 15	10 to 15	10 to 15

Adapted from Soil Fertility Note 12 - Fertilizing with Organic Nutrients, North Carolina DA&CS Agronomic Division, 2013
* N-P-K numbers are quite variable and should be taken as a general indicator of nutritional value
** Nutritional value of commonly available commercial fertilizers

COLORADO
POTATO BEETLE

WEEDING

The best way to control weeds in a vegetable garden is to *prevent* them from taking hold in the first place. Weed gardens early, then spread a 2- to 3-inch layer of mulch over your growing beds, covering all the bare ground. When it's time to plant, clear enough space in the mulch in rows to plant seeds and transplants. The mulch will prevent most weeds from coming up.

BUGS AND DISEASE

The best way overall to approach bug and disease issues is to use Integrated Pest Management (IPM) principles: early prevention and strict maintenance. First, don't let the weeds get an initial foothold. Keep the garden clean and neat. Water and fertilize your plants well; healthy plants handle bugs and disease better. To keep beneficial insects in the garden when the bad bugs aren't around, plant some of their preferred nectar and shelter plants around the garden. Check out the list in Chapter 13. Second, scout regularly for bugs and diseases, particularly under leaves and on stems. Properly identify them at your local Master Gardener office, where you can get free fact sheets that will tell you about the insect or disease and suggest organic and conventional treatments.

If you find a harmful bug, keep an eye on it and let the beneficial insects catch up with the intruder. If the beneficial insects don't show up, you can blast bugs off your plants with a hard stream of water or handpick them off. If, after all your other efforts, the bugs are still eating your garden, it may be time for insecticidal soap. This organic chemical degrades the waxy coating on insects' bodies so they dehydrate and die. Carefully read and follow label directions for application times and quantities.

DON'T HAVE SPACE FOR A VEGETABLE GARDEN?

Even gardeners who only have room for deck pots can still grow delicious raspberries, squash, and tomatoes with a little planning and the right plant varieties. Breeders have developed several miniature vegetable varieties over the last ten years

Floating row covers provide a few degrees of frost protection, enabling gardeners to extend the season both earlier and later.

just for this purpose. Take advantage of the leaf textures, shapes, and colors of many edible plants and use them in ornamental plantings. Dwarf fruit trees espaliered on a sunny fence or trellis are easy to incorporate into a small garden. They can also be planted in large pots.

EXTENDING THE GROWING SEASON

In the Northwest's short growing season, being able to extend both the spring and fall growing seasons by as much as a month can mean the difference between getting a full crop and none at all. You can start cool-season vegetable seedlings in midwinter in cold frames for setting out in early March. West of the Cascades, temporary hoop houses—made of floating row covers and greenhouse plastic set over hoops—can keep plantings of cool-season vegetables going through the winter. In very short-seasoned areas east of the Cascades, some gardeners grow warm-season crops like tomatoes, peppers, basil, cucumbers, and melons in hoop houses all summer to hold in heat and keep errant

frosts at bay.

Edible plants aren't just for the rectangular garden plot out in the back corner of the yard any more. Be creative, try them in unconventional places. Have fun with them. That evening walk through the garden just might include a bowl and some salad dressing along with a glass of wine.

Zucchini planted in a plastic hoophouse will survive frost any time in the season.

APPLE
Malus domestica

Why It's Special—Apples are one of the most delicious and productive fruits to grow in a home garden. Apple trees require cross-pollination by another variety; your local Master Gardener program can suggest varieties that bloom at the same time.

How to Plant & Grow—Select bare-root or potted dwarf or semidwarf trees; plant in spring or fall. Choose a location that gets at least six hours of sunlight daily. Dig a planting hole that will have plenty of room for all of the roots. Spread the roots and backfill the hole, keeping the graft union 2 to 4 inches above soil surface. Do not amend soil. Water in well; add more soil if settling occurs. Stake trees their first year to provide support.

Care & Problems—Water trees regularly. In late winter, apply dormant oil to kill overwintering scale or aphids. Prune in late winter/early spring. Once developing apples are the size of marbles, thin them by removing all but the largest apple in each cluster. Established fruit trees don't require fertilization unless soil or tissue samples indicate deficiencies. Apple trees are susceptible to many pests and diseases. Consult your local Master Gardener program for advice on organic controls.

Harvest & Best Selections—Apples ripen between midsummer and fall, based on variety. A taste test will determine their ripeness. Reliable varieties for coastal areas include 'Liberty', 'Williams' Pride', 'Red Free', and 'Jonafree'; recommended inland varieties are 'Liberty', 'Enterprise', and 'GoldRush'.

APRICOT
Prunus armeniaca

Why It's Special—Apricots are attractive fruit trees that reward you with huge crops of golden, sweet orbs to savor. They are good fresh, baked in pies, dried, canned, or made into jam. Apricots are self-fruitful but will produce more if cross-pollinated by another apricot variety.

How to Plant & Grow—Because apricots bloom in early spring, they aren't reliably hardy enough to grow in all areas of the Northwest. Select late-blooming varieties and plant in spring. Choose a sheltered, sunny location. Select bare-root or potted dwarf or semidwarf trees. Dig a planting hole with room for all roots. Spread out roots and backfill the hole, keeping the graft union 2 to 4 inches above the soil surface. Do not amend. Water trees in well; add more soil if settling occurs. Stake trees the first year to provide support.

Care & Problems—Established fruit trees don't require fertilization unless soil or tissue samples indicate deficiencies. In late winter, apply dormant oil to smother overwintering scale or aphids. Prune in early spring. Thin young fruits to 2 inches apart to get larger apricots. Water deeply once a week. Apricots are susceptible to some insect pests and diseases; consult your local Master Gardener program for advice on organic controls.

Harvest & Best Selections—Most varieties ripen in July and should be harvested as they begin to soften. Late-blooming, hardy cultivars include 'Harcot', 'Moongold', 'Perfection', 'Sungold', and 'Westcot'.

ARTICHOKE
Cynara scolymus

Why It's Special—Artichokes can be grown in all areas of the Northwest, as annuals in cooler locations, and as perennials in milder zones. The plants' gray foliage and interesting texture are striking in the vegetable garden but can be grown as specimens elsewhere in the landscape. The buds are absolutely delicious when steamed or they can be left on the plants to mature and used in floral arrangements. The plants are easy to care for and grow rapidly.

How to Plant & Grow—Start seeds indoors eight to twelve weeks before the last frost date and transplant into a larger container once seedlings have a pair of true leaves. Transplant them into the garden after all danger of frost has passed. Artichokes require a minimum of six hours of sunlight daily and should be spaced 3 feet apart since they will grow quite large.

Care & Problems—Feed with half-strength, high-nitrogen fertilizer every two to three weeks while plants are actively growing. Water regularly. Plants do not require pinching or thinning. Stink bugs and earwigs can be a problem; handpick or catch them in pheromone traps to control. After a hard frost, cut down plants; in milder zones, leave in place for next year.

Harvest & Best Selection—Using a knife, harvest mature artichokes when they are fist-sized and scales are tightly closed. Recommended varieties: 'Green Globe' and 'Imperial Star'. Artichokes mature in 85 to 95 days once transplanted.

ASIAN GREENS
Brassica rapa spp.

Why It's Special—Asian greens are a diverse group of leafy vegetables that can be sweet, spicy, or quite pungent. Besides adding color, flavor, and texture to salads, they are frequently added to soups and stir-fries. They are very nutritious and simple to grow. Types of Asian greens include these: Mizuna, Tatsoi, Hon Tsai Tsai, Yukina Savoy, and Komatsuna. Look for mixes of several types at garden centers.

How to Plant & Grow—Sow seeds directly in the garden from early spring to midsummer; these plants will tolerate light shade. If you plan to harvest baby leaves, sow the seeds over the soil surface at least ½ inch apart. To grow bunches, sow seeds in 2-inch-wide bands, with rows spaced 12 to 18 inches apart. Cover seeds with a fine layer of peat moss or germination mix to keep the soil surface from becoming crusty. Sow succession plantings every two to three weeks for a longer harvest.

Care & Problems—Water regularly; give fish fertilizer early on. To protect against flea beetles and other insects, place a floating row cover over the entire bed at planting as an insect barrier. Use organic controls if slugs are troublesome

Harvest & Best Selection—For baby leaves, harvest when they are 3 to 6 inches tall. Harvest bunches after 40 days. 'Dark Purple' Mizuna has a mustard flavor, 'Tokyo Bekana' grows like a small Chinese cabbage, and 'Summerfest Komatsuna' is heat tolerant.

ASPARAGUS
Asparagus officinalis

Why It's Special—It's pretty hard to top picking your own asparagus for use in stir-fries, as a side dish, in soups, and risottos. The plants send up spears in early spring; any that aren't harvested grow into tall, feathery ferns that remain well into fall. They die back over winter, only to begin the cycle again in spring.

How to Plant & Grow—Asparagus is a long-lived perennial so choose a sunny, permanent location to grow it. It can be grown from seeds or plant starts, but for fastest results, purchase and plant crowns in early spring. Dig the planting bed deeply and add compost to the top few inches of soil. Plant crowns, with their small buds pointing upward, 5 inches deep and spaced 10 to 15 inches apart.

Care & Problems—Water 1 inch per week and frequently feed with organic fertilizer. Keep beds weed-free but be careful to avoid damaging any spears near the surface. Once the ferns turn yellow in fall, cut them down to the ground. If asparagus beetles are a problem, handpick or cover spears with floating row covers until harvest is over.

Harvest & Best Selection—Harvest lightly the first spring after they were planted. In subsequent years, harvest more heavily over the course of two to three weeks. Best varieties are 'Jersey Supreme', 'Jersey Knight', 'Pacific Purple', and 'Millennium'.

BASIL
Ocimum basilicum

Why It's Special—This delicious herb is easy to grow and fabulous in homemade pesto, on pizza, and when added to soups and Italian dishes. Basil is a good companion plant for tomatoes.

How to Plant & Grow—Grow basil from purchased seedlings or grow unusual, hard-to-find types from seed. The most important thing to remember is that basil likes warm weather. This means plant seedlings or seeds in the garden well after the danger of frost has passed or they will languish. Plant seeds 2 to 3 inches apart and cover lightly with soil. As the plants grow, thin them 5 to 8 inches apart and pinch out the centers to encourage bushy growth.

Care & Problems—Basil plants are easy to care for once they are up and growing. Regularly water throughout the summer and lightly feed with half-strength, liquid organic fertilizer. If they begin to develop flower stalks, snip them off to force the growth of more leaves. Snails or slugs can be troublesome; use organic slug bait.

Harvest & Best Selection—Harvest leaves regularly once plants are established. When making pesto, consider freezing some in ice cube trays, then storing them in the freezer for year-round use. There are many varieties, so choose based on your preference or sense of adventure. Consider 'Lettuce Leaf', 'Siam Queen', 'Purple Ruffles', 'Sweet Thai', 'Spicy Globe', or 'Genovese'.

BEAN, GREEN
Phaseolus vulgaris

Why It's Special—Bush and pole beans are productive, nutritious crops for the garden. They also improve the soil by fixing nitrogen for subsequent crops. Bush beans have a shorter harvesting season than pole beans but you can extend it by planting seeds every two weeks.

How to Plant & Grow—Choose a sunny location with well-drained soil. Sow bush or pole bean seeds with the scar side pointing down, after all danger of frost is past. Seeds can be started indoors two weeks before the last frost if birds in your garden have a habit of nibbling freshly sprouted seeds. When sowing or transplanting, use 2-inch spacing for pole beans and 6-inch spacing for bush beans. Provide pole beans with a vertical support like an arbor, trellis, wire fencing, or netting; it should be 5 to 6 feet tall.

Care & Problems—Beans have medium water needs early in the season. Increase watering once they flower and throughout the harvest. Feed young seedlings an organic fertilizer such as fish emulsion once they have two pairs of true leaves. They have minimal insect or disease problems.

Harvest & Best Selection—Pick beans every two to three days, while pods are relatively small and most tender. Beans mature in 50 to 60 days. This encourages plants to bloom and develop more pods. Varieties are (bush) 'Provider', 'Rocdor', 'Maxibel' and 'Jumbo', and (pole) 'Fortex', 'Blue Lake', 'Helda', and 'Scarlet Runner'.

BEET
Beta vulgaris

Why It's Special—Growing beets is glamorous now that so many gourmet varieties are available. The bulbs develop quickly, in 45 to 60 days, beet greens are delicious when steamed, and the bulbs can be stored well into winter.

How to Plant & Grow—Plant in full sun (although beets will tolerate light shade). Prepare planting beds by loosening the soil to a depth of 10 inches and working in a few inches of compost. Two to four weeks before the last frost, plant seeds ½ inch deep and 1 inch apart, thinning seedlings later to 3- or 4-inch spacing. Since beets mature fairly quickly, consider planting a fall crop by sowing seeds again in midsummer.

Care & Problems—Water plants regularly throughout the season. Feed growing beets with a fertilizer high in phosphorus for root growth. If you plan to eat the leaves and leaf miner insects are an issue in your area, cover the entire bed with floating row cover all season to act as a barrier.

Harvest & Best Selection—For best flavor, harvest beets when they are no larger than 2½ inches in diameter. Harvesting after the first frost makes them sweeter. Store beets in bags in the refrigerator or layer them in bins filled with damp sand; keep the bins in an uninsulated garage or a root cellar. Try 'Bull's Blood', 'Chioggia', 'Early Wonder Tall Top', and 'Golden'.

BLACKBERRY
Rubus spp.

Why It's Special—Is there anything more delectable than popping a sun-ripened blackberry into your mouth? They are easy to grow and each plant will provide quarts of berries. While wild blackberries grow with abandon in many coastal areas, most gardeners prefer growing domesticated varieties that are more prolific and thornless.

How to Plant & Grow—Blackberries are self-fruitful so they do not require another variety for cross-pollination. Plant bare-root or rooted 1-year-old vines in spring. Select a sunny area that has well-drained soil and work in a few inches of compost. Since plants are productive for about twenty years, it is important to prepare the ground well. Space plants 6 feet apart and trim the canes back to about 8 inches in length. For best results, provide trellises to keep plants off the ground. Contact your local Master Gardener program for advice on trellising methods and for help with any pests.

Care & Problems—In spring, feed an organic fertilizer high in phosphorus. Water regularly. Blackberries bear fruit on last year's growth. Once they stop bearing, prune fruiting canes down to the ground.

Harvest & Best Selection—Harvest blackberries every few days, from summer into fall, selecting ones that easily pull from their stem. Store berries in heavy-duty bags in the freezer or process them right away to use in jams or pies. Thornless, semi-erect varieties include 'Chester', 'Black Satin', and 'Triple Crown'.

BLUEBERRY
Vaccinium spp.

Why It's Special—Blueberries are easy to grow and bring many desirable qualities to the landscape: bell-shaped blossoms in spring; abundant, healthful berries in summer; and bright red foliage in fall.

How to Plant & Grow—Blueberries are self-fruitful but more productive if you plant more than one variety. Select ones that will be in bloom at the same time. Because they require acidic soil with a pH range of 4.5 to 5.5, test your soil before planting. Decomposed sawdust or ammonium sulfate can increase soil acidity. Plant bare-root or potted plants in fall in coastal areas and early spring in inland regions. Space 4 to 6 feet apart. Water well; do not fertilize at planting time. Prune branches back at planting by 30 percent to encourage new growth.

Care & Problems—Water about 1 inch per week. For root and branch growth, remove blossoms the first year. In spring, fertilize with a balanced organic fertilizer. Once established, prune for a balance of one-, two- and three-year-old canes, with an average of six to eight canes per plant. Blueberries have few pest or disease issues.

Harvest & Best Selection—Berries ripen from July to September. Pick them at their sweetest, when they are deep blue in color. For the longest harvest, choose a couple of varieties each that produce in early, mid-, and late season. Prolific cultivars include 'Patriot', 'Bluecrop', 'Liberty', and 'Draper'.

BROCCOLI
Brassica oleracea

Why It's Special—In addition to the delicious taste of freshly harvested broccoli, it provides our bodies with calcium; vitamins B, C, and K; and antioxidants. Broccoli is popular both steamed and raw.

How to Plant & Grow—Choose a sunny area that has well-drained soil; amend with rich, organic compost. Plants prefer cooler weather and will suffer in hot summers. Plant broccoli seeds indoors eight weeks before your average date of last frost. Transplant seedlings after danger of frost has passed. Plant in midsummer for a fall harvest. Space seedlings 12 to 18 inches apart. Closer spacing results in stunted growth and smaller harvests.

Care & Problems—Water regularly and feed monthly with a balanced, organic fertilizer. Broccoli is susceptible to aphids and cabbage loopers. To keep these insects away from plants, cover beds with a floating row cover for the entire season. Also use a strong jet of water to knock the aphids off the plants and use *Bacillus thuringiensis* (Bt) products found at garden centers to eliminate cabbage loopers.

Harvest & Best Selection—Broccoli matures in about 55 days. Harvest primary heads while buds are still firm and tight, which encourages the growth of smaller, secondary heads lower on the stalk. Always harvest before the buds start blooming. Suggested varieties are 'Packman', 'Fiesta', 'Umpqua', and 'Southern Comet'.

BRUSSELS SPROUTS
Brassica oleracea

Why It's Special—Brussels sprouts look like little cabbages and are packed with vitamins, fiber, and antioxidants. They add a cool factor to the garden as the mini heads develop in fall and extend your harvest, after most crops have finished growing. The plants are very cold-hardy.

How to Plant & Grow—For best results, time the planting of Brussels sprouts for a fall harvest when the sprouts will have tight leaves and the best flavor. They require about 90 days to reach maturity so plant seeds or seedlings in the garden in May or June. Since plants will be large, space them 18 inches apart. Topdress beds with compost.

Care & Problems—Water regularly and feed monthly with a balanced fertilizer. Brussels sprouts are susceptible to aphids and cabbage loopers. To keep these insects away from plants, cover beds with a floating row cover for the entire season. Or you can use a strong jet of water to knock the aphids off the plants and use *Bacillus thuringiensis* (Bt) products, which can be found at garden centers, to eliminate cabbage loopers.

Harvest & Best Selection—The best time to harvest is after the first fall frosts, when the flavor is intensified, or pick them when they are about 1 inch in diameter and firm. Harvest from the bottom of the stem and work your way up. Varieties include 'Franklin', 'Jade Cross E', and 'Early Marvel'.

CABBAGE
Brassica oleracea

Why It's Special—Cabbage is a perfect food rich in vitamins C and K, fiber, and antioxidants. There are more than one hundred types grown around the world.

How to Plant & Grow—Grow from seeds planted indoors two months before the last spring frost or purchase started plants. Plant them outdoors two to four weeks before average last frost; plants tolerate light shade. For a fall crop, plant seeds or seedlings in the garden in midsummer. Space plants 18 to 24 inches apart.

Care & Problems—Plants need consistent watering and are heavy feeders; feed with a balanced fertilizer every two to three weeks while they're actively growing. Cabbage is susceptible to aphids and cabbage loopers. Use organic controls such as covering the bed with a floating row cover for the entire season, using a strong jet of water to knock the aphids off the plants, and *Bacillus thuringiensis* (*B.t.*) products, which can be found at garden centers, to eliminate caterpillars. However, most damage tends to be on outer leaves that can simply be peeled off at harvest. Mature cabbage heads may split from rapid new growth, which can happen after a downpour or if watered heavily after a dry spell.

Harvest & Best Selection—Harvest tight heads in late summer through fall. Solid head varieties are 'Caraflex', 'Early Jersey Wakefield', and 'Ruby Ball'; Savoy types are 'Alcosa', 'Famosa', and 'Red Express'.

CARROT
Daucus carota var. sativus

Why It's Special—First cultivated in Afghanistan about 5,000 years ago, carrots were every color but orange. Orange varieties were developed in the 16th and 17th centuries in the Netherlands. They provide vitamin A and beta-carotene.

How to Plant & Grow—In early spring when the soil is dry, loosen it 12 inches deep; incorporate compost and organic high-phosphorus fertilizer to promote root growth. Do not add manure; it causes roots to split and fork. Plant seeds from early spring to midsummer. Plants will tolerate light shade. Seeds are slow to germinate so try this: sprinkle them onto soil surface; cover lightly with peat moss or germination mix; water in gently. Cover rows with boards to prevent a soil crust from forming. Remove boards after one week and watch them sprout. Seeds are viable for up to three years; plant older seeds thickly.

Care & Problems—Thinning is crucial for root growth. Once seedlings are 3 inches tall, thin to 2 inches apart. Carrots have few pests and require medium watering.

Harvest & Best Selection—Harvest anytime, although they become sweeter after the first frosts. Store carrots in bags in the refrigerator or layer in bins filled with damp sand kept in cool areas such as uninsulated garages or root cellars. Varieties range in size and color; try 'Chantenay', 'Bolero', 'Scarlet Nantes', 'Purple Haze'. Most mature in 55 to 75 days.

CAULIFLOWER
Brassica oleracea

Why It's Special—An ancient vegetable, cauliflower was first cultivated in areas of Asia Minor and the Mediterranean. It has a delightful, nutty taste and can be eaten raw, steamed, mashed, or roasted.

How to Plant & Grow—For best results, start seeds indoors four to six weeks before average last frost. In the garden, add compost to the cauliflower bed prior to planting. Transplant seedlings outdoors when they have two sets of true leaves; space them 12 to 18 inches apart.

Care & Problems—Water evenly and fertilize with fish emulsion every two to three weeks during the season. White-headed varieties will turn yellow from sun exposure. To prevent this on varieties that don't have self-wrapping leaves, tie the outer leaves around the developing head to blanch it. Aphids and cabbage loopers are attracted to cauliflower plants. You can cover the bed with a floating row cover at planting. Leave it on for the entire season. Or use a strong jet of water to knock the aphids off plants and *Bacillus thuringiensis* (Bt) products to eliminate caterpillars.

Harvest & Best Selection—Cauliflower reaches maturity about 60 to 80 days after being transplanted into the garden. Harvest when florets just begin to separate or a few days after tying leaves. Recommended varieties are 'Snow Crown', 'Amazing', 'Absolute', 'Early Dawn', and 'Cheddar', which has a pale orange curd.

CHERRY

Prunus avium (sweet); *Prunus cerasus* (sour)

Why It's Special—Cherry trees have delicate flowers in spring, tasty fruits in summer, and attractive foliage and bark. Sour or pie cherries are used for cooking, and sweet cherries for eating fresh. While pie cherry trees are self-pollinating, sweet cherries are not. They require pollen from another variety. Consult planting guides to select appropriate varieties.

How to Plant & Grow—Select bare-root or potted dwarf or semidwarf trees and plant them in spring or fall. Choose a location that gets at least six hours of sunlight daily. Dig a planting hole large enough to hold all the roots. Spread the roots and backfill the hole, keeping the graft union 2 to 4 inches above the soil surface. Do not amend the soil. Water the tree in well; add more soil if settling occurs.

Care & Problems—Water trees regularly. In late winter, apply dormant oil to smother overwintering scale or aphids. Prune in late winter/early spring. Thinning the cherries is generally unnecessary. Established fruit trees don't need fertilization unless soil or tissue samples indicate deficiencies. Cherry trees are susceptible to cherry fruit flies and some diseases. Consult your local Master Gardener program for organic controls.

Harvest & Best Selection—Cherries are ripe when firm, full-sized, and the appropriate color. Sweet cherries include 'Lambert', 'Van', and 'Rainier'; pie cherry varieties are 'Montmorency' and 'English Morello'.

CHINESE CABBAGE

Brassica spp.

Why It's Special—Also referred to as Napa cabbage, this Oriental vegetable is used in stir-fries, salads, and wraps, or boiled and eaten as greens. It originated in China around 500 A.D. and is widely used in Asian cuisine. The plants are very attractive in the vegetable garden, looking like a curly-leaved head of romaine lettuce.

How to Plant & Grow—Choose bolt-resistant varieties as plants do not tolerate the heat well. Sow seeds indoors four to six weeks before last frost or outdoors after all danger of frost has passed. Transplant seedlings after all danger of frost is past; add compost to bed. Space plants 12 inches apart. For a fall crop, plant seeds or seedlings in the garden in midsummer.

Care & Problems—Water regularly and provide nitrogen by feeding plants with diluted fish emulsion every two weeks. Chinese cabbage leaves are relished by caterpillars and slugs. To keep them away, cover bed with a floating row cover for entire season. You can also use *Bacillus thuringiensis* (Bt) to eliminate caterpillars. Use slug traps and organic baits for slugs.

Harvest & Best Selection—Chinese cabbage matures in about 50 days from its transplant date. Harvest after heads are a suitable size. Heads that have been wrapped in newspaper will store in root cellars for up to two months. Try these slow-bolting varieties: 'Minuet', 'Rubicon', 'Bilko', and 'Tenderheart'.

CHIVES

Allium spp.

Why It's Special—For a mild oniony flavor, you can't beat chives. They are an easy-to-grow perennial in a permanent garden bed or on a sunny windowsill for easy access year-round. In addition to adding flavor to baked potatoes, the chopped leaves are used in herb butters, sauces, omelets, and soups.

How to Plant & Grow—One or two plants are sufficient for most needs; purchase transplants from a garden center and plant in spring or early summer. Chives aren't particular about soil type and do not require fertilization or soil amendments. In colder areas, the plants will die back to the ground during winter and sprout again in spring.

Care & Problems—Water regularly. Chive plants easily self-sow, becoming invasive in the garden. An easy solution is to remove flowers before they set seed. Plants are free from pests and disease.

Harvest & Best Selection—The best time to harvest the leaves is before the plants begin to bloom, while leaves are their most tender and flavorful. Do not trim off all the leaves at one time. Harvested leaves can be stored in a container in the refrigerator for a few days. While fresh leaves are the best, you can also snip and dry them in a dehydrator or a microwave oven for year-round use. The flowers are edible, having a stronger, more oniony flavor. Two reliable varieties are 'Fine Leaf' and 'Purly'.

CILANTRO/ CORIANDER
Coriandrum sativum

Why It's Special—Not everyone is aware that cilantro and coriander are related: Cilantro is grown for its foliage and used in Latin American cooking. Coriander are the seeds of the cilantro plant and lend a spicy flavor to Asian and Indian sauces, curries and other dishes. Plants also attract beneficial insects to the garden.

How to Plant & Grow—Although you can purchase cilantro plants from nurseries, it's better to grow them directly from seed since transplanting stresses the plants. Work compost into the planting bed first, then sow seeds after all danger of frost has passed. If you intend to harvest the leaves, provide plants with a bit of shade. For a season-long supply of cilantro, do successive plantings every three weeks.

Care & Problems—Water regularly to prevent plants from bolting; they don't tolerate summer heat very well. No fertilization is needed. Plants do not have insect or disease problems.

Harvest & Best Selection—To harvest cilantro, pick the plant once it is several inches tall. If you want to save the coriander seeds, let some of the plants go to seed. Harvest them in the fall when they will be mature. Remove the seedheads and place them upside down in a paper bag. The seeds will drop and dry over the following week or two. Store in an airtight container. Varieties are 'Santo' and 'Slow Bolt'.

CORN
Zea mays

Why It's Special—Homegrown sweet corn is the freshest way to enjoy its delectable goodness. A member of the grass family, it is indigenous to the western hemisphere and was a staple of Native Americans.

How to Plant & Grow—Prepare the bed by adding compost or well-rotted manure to the soil. For best results, sow seeds directly into the garden after all danger of frost has passed. Space seeds 6 to 8 inches apart, later thinning seedlings 12 inches apart. Always plant corn in multiple-row blocks rather than a single row for the best pollination of the plants.

Care & Problems—Provide plants with regular watering and an organic fertilizer rich in nitrogen throughout the season as they are heavy feeders. Keep the bed weeded. Corn plants have shallow, stubby roots. If your garden is in a windy area, hill up the plants by mounding extra soil around the bases or surround the bed with stakes and twine to provide support. Earwigs and earworms can be a problem; contact your local Master Gardener program for advice on organic controls.

Harvest & Best Selection—Once silks at ends of ears have completely dried and tip of ear feels rounded out with kernels, it's ripe. Cook the ears as quickly as possible after harvesting while they are sugar-sweet rather than starchy. Reliable varieties are 'Silver Queen', 'Luscious', 'Bodacious', 'Earlivee', 'Illini Xtra-Sweet', and 'Trinity'.

CUCUMBER
Cucumis sativus

Why It's Special—Cucumbers have been cultivated for more than 3,000 years, originating in India and heavily used by the Romans for culinary and medicinal purposes. Today, we enjoy fresh cucumbers in salads and sandwiches and make pickles and relishes with them. They don't require much room in the garden as they can be grown vertically on trellises, although there are also bush-type cucumbers.

How to Plant & Grow—Sow seeds indoors two to three weeks before the average date of last frost. Prepare a bed by incorporating compost into the top few inches of soil. Cucumbers prefer warm growing conditions; cover the bed surface with a sheet of plastic mulch to increase soil temperature and cut an "X" where each seedling will be planted. After the danger of frost has passed, plant in clusters of three on hilled-up soil or place a trellis in the bed and plant seedlings 1 foot apart. Space bush-type cucumbers in a zigzag pattern 2 feet apart. Cover beds with floating row covers for the first couple weeks for extra warmth.

Care & Problems—Give cucumbers a medium to heavy amount of water. Fertilize every two weeks with organic fertilizer. Remove row covers once plants flower.

Harvest & Best Selection—Harvest as soon as they are a desirable size. Those left on the vines too long become pithy and filled with seeds. Try 'Marketmore', 'Olympian', 'Burpless', or 'Spacemaster'.

DILL

Anethum graveolens

Why It's Special—Dill is an easy-to-grow annual herb. The leaves can be harvested for use in fish dishes and sauces, and the seeds are an essential ingredient for pickled vegetables. As a member of the carrot family, it will attract beneficial insects to your garden. While dill likely originated in the Mediterranean region thousands of years ago, it is widely used around the world.

How to Plant & Grow—For best results, plant dill seeds in a sunny location as soon as the ground can be worked in spring. Incorporate compost into the planting bed. Seedlings do not transplant well. If you love dill, successively plant seeds every three weeks. Seeds only need a light covering of soil to grow. Thin plants to 18 inches apart. They will grow 3 to 4 feet tall.

Care & Problems—Dill requires lots of water throughout the season to produce a lot of leaves. Dill plants don't tolerate intense summer heat. The plants easily self-seed so deadhead flowers before they mature if you are only growing plants for the foliage. There are no serious pest or disease problems.

Harvest & Best Selection—Most varieties mature in 40 to 55 days. Harvest leaves as soon as the plant establishes. Remove seeds from plants once they turn light brown; store them in a paper bag until the seeds have dried. Recommended varieties are 'Dukat', 'Fernleaf', 'Bouquet', and 'Long Island Mammoth'.

EGGPLANT

Solanum melongena

Why It's Special—Eggplants are heat-loving plants that do best in regions with hot summers. When it comes to cooking, most folks think of ratatouille but they're also used to make hummus-like baba ganoush, served oven-roasted, or sliced and breaded for eggplant Parmesan dishes.

How to Plant & Grow—Start eggplants from seeds indoors eight to ten weeks prior to the average last frost date or buy starts at a nursery. To avoid soilborne disease, choose an area in the garden where eggplants, potatoes, tomatoes, tomatillos, or peppers have not been grown for the past few years. Incorporate compost and fertilizer high in phosphorus and potassium into the planting bed. To increase soil temperature, cover the soil with plastic mulch and cut an "X" where each seedling will be planted. Space eggplants 18 inches apart. For extra warmth, place a floating row cover over the plants for the first 2 to 3 weeks; remove it when they start to bloom so pollinators can get to the flowers.

Care & Problems—Plants require heavy watering throughout the season. They can be susceptible to Colorado potato beetles; handpick them from plants or contact your local Master Gardener program for advice on other organic controls.

Harvest & Best Selection—Eggplants are ripe when their skin is smooth and shiny. Try varieties like 'Rosa Bianca', 'Millionaire', 'Orient Express', and 'Black Beauty'.

FRENCH TARRAGON

Artemisia dracunculus

Why It's Special—This perennial herb is delightful in Béarnaise sauce, flavored vinegars, chicken, and fish dishes. Its flavor is similar to licorice. Tarragon is a member of the daisy family with woody, aromatic stems and foliage.

How to Plant & Grow—French tarragon cannot be grown from seed so purchase plants from a nursery. Make certain you are getting a French tarragon plant rather than other types that are less desirable for culinary uses. Because plants can reach a height of 3 feet, it is unlikely you'll need more than one. Tarragon is hardy down to zone 4 so it can be planted in spring once the soil is dry enough to be worked. Plant in a sunny location where the soil is well drained. You can grow it in containers on a deck or balcony, or on a sunny windowsill indoors.

Care & Problems—Tarragon has low water needs and does not require fertilization. The plants will die back to the ground in colder regions but sprout again in spring. Propagate by division or cuttings. It is not bothered by insect pests or disease.

Harvest & Best Selection—Leaves can be harvested anytime during the season, but preferably after plants have grown for four to six weeks after transplanting. In addition to using fresh leaves in cooking, you can dry leaves for year-round use.

GARLIC
Allium spp.

Why It's Special—Garlic has become so popular over the years that it's hard to imagine not using it for nearly all types of cooking. It is easy and fun to grow. There are two main types: hard-neck and soft-neck. Consuming garlic is believed to boost the immune system.

How to Plant & Grow—To avoid soilborne disease, choose a garden spot where onions, leeks, shallots, or garlic have not been grown for the past few years. Plant individual garlic cloves in fall, about six weeks before the ground freezes, in soil that has been amended with compost. Place cloves 2 inches deep with the point facing up and spaced 6 inches apart. Cover the soil with a few inches of mulch as a layer of insulation over winter.

Care & Problems—Remove mulch in early spring when the bulb tops start to break through the soil surface and top-dress with a thin layer of compost. Garlic has low water needs during the season; water should be cut back once the leaves begin drying later in summer. Plants have minimal insect or disease problems.

Harvest & Best Selection—Harvest garlic bulbs when the lowest two leaves have turned brown to ensure the bases of the remaining leaves cover and protect the bulbs. Tie bunches together; hang in a protected area to dry for storage. Reliable varieties: 'Music', 'German Red', 'Spanish Roja', and 'Inchelium Red'.

GOOSEBERRY
Ribes uva-crispa

Why It's Special—Gooseberries are ideal for the home landscape because the bushes are small in size, hardy, easy to grow, and provide tasty berries for use in jams, jellies, and pies. Depending on the variety, berries are red or pale green and some plants have small spines.

How to Plant & Grow—Gooseberry bushes are self-fruitful, meaning they don't require cross-pollination, but having more than one variety will increase their productivity. For coastal areas, choose a sunny location; in inland regions where summers can be very hot, grow gooseberries in part shade. Well-drained soil is crucial; incorporate organic compost into the top few inches. Select 1- to 2-year-old bare-root or potted plants in early spring. Space plants 3 to 4 feet apart and prune back all branches to 6 inches to encourage new growth.

Care & Problems—Plants require 1 inch of water per week once they start to set fruit. Mulch beneath the plants to save water and impede weed growth. Do not fertilize until their second year, then apply a balanced organic fertilizer. Consult with your local Master Gardener program if there are problems with pests or disease.

Harvest & Best Selection—Harvest gooseberries in mid-July when they reach mature size. The first year harvest will be light but heavier once the plants are well established. Try varieties 'Pixwell', 'Poorman', 'Captivator', and 'Oregon Champion'.

GRAPE
Vitis × hybrids

Why It's Special—Use homegrown grapes for jellies, juice, eating fresh, or making wine. The three types of grapes available are American and European cultivars and French-American hybrids. There are early-, mid-, and late-season varieties.

How to Plant & Grow—Select a sunny location with good air circulation and well-drained soil; amend with organic compost. Grapes are self-fertile so do not require cross-pollination. Buy bare-root or potted plants in early spring. Remove any broken roots and all but two canes before planting. Space plants 6 to 8 feet apart, in rows 9 feet apart. Provide a trellis system to support the vines. Consult your local Master Gardener program for help choosing the best regional varieties, to learn about pruning and trellising techniques, and for advice on controlling diseases organically.

Care & Problems—Once established, grapes have low water requirements. Do not water overhead as this can cause grapes to rot; use soaker hoses or drip irrigation instead. In spring, you can add small amounts of compost or manure to the beds or fertilizer high in phosphorus and potassium. Prune the vines in late winter or early spring each year.

Harvest & Best Selection—Vines begin to produce after about three years. For eating fresh and making jelly or juice, harvest grapes when they taste ripe. Varieties are 'Glenora', 'Vanessa', 'Concord', and 'Interlaken'.

KOHLRABI
Brassica oleracea

Why It's Special—Kohlrabi may look like it came from another planet but it actually originated in northern Europe. The thickened purple or green stems are the edible part and have a sweet flavor. They are tasty when eaten raw or cooked.

How to Plant & Grow—In spring, once the ground can be worked, add compost to the soil. Sow seeds an inch apart after danger of frost is past. Once seedlings are 3 inches tall, thin plants 4 inches apart. For fall crops, plant seeds in midsummer.

Care & Problems—Plants need lots of water until fall and should be fertilized with fish emulsion every two to three weeks. Kohlrabi is susceptible to aphids and cabbage loopers. To keep these insects away from plants, cover the bed with a floating row cover for the entire season. You can also use a strong jet of water to knock aphids off plants and *Bacillus thuringiensis* (Bt) products to eliminate caterpillars. If slugs become a problem, use an organic control.

Harvest & Best Selection—Kohlrabi takes about 65 days to reach maturity but you can begin harvesting as soon as the stems reach 2 inches in diameter. Remove the leaves before storing stems in the refrigerator for one to two months, or in a root cellar. Recommended varieties are purple 'Kolibri', white 'Winner', purple or white 'Delicacy', and purple or white 'Early Vienna'.

LEMON BALM
Melissia officinalis

Why It's Special—This attractive perennial herb is used for tea, in salads, for flavoring fish and herb butters, and dried for sachets. Just rubbing fresh leaves together provides a delightful burst of lemon scent. Native to the Mediterranean region, lemon balm has also been known for its medicinal qualities. Plants have small white flowers in summer, which attract honey bees.

How to Plant & Grow—You likely will only need one plant for your herb bed so it's best to purchase one from a nursery (although you can also grow lemon balm from seed) in the spring. The plants aren't particular about soil type and do not require fertilization or soil amendments. They will grow in full sun to part shade and are hardy down to zone 3. In colder areas, plants will die back to the ground during winter and sprout again in spring.

Care & Problems—Plants can reach 2 feet in height and will become drought tolerant once established. Lemon balm does not have any insect or disease problems. As a member of the mint family, it is an aggressive grower, although its reputation is not quite as bad as mint plants. Propagate by seed or from cuttings. Shear back foliage to keep plants looking tidy as needed.

Harvest & Best Selection—Pick fresh leaves and always add to dishes at the last moment for the best flavor.

LETTUCE
Lactuca sativa

Why It's Special—One area of your garden where you can be really diverse is in the lettuce patch. There are so many types—Bibb, butterhead, iceberg, leaf, romaine, and oakleaf, to name a few—that your most difficult decision will be which types and cultivars to choose. Lettuce is cold-hardy and easy to grow.

How to Plant & Grow—Lettuce seeds can be planted directly in the garden as soon as the soil is dry enough. The plants will tolerate light shade. Work compost into the top few inches of soil. If you intend to harvest leaves every couple of days, thin seedlings 2 inches apart; if you wish to grow and harvest whole heads, space them 8 to 10 inches apart. For best results, successively plant lettuce every three weeks to extend the harvest into fall.

Care & Problems—Provide light to medium water and an initial feeding with fish emulsion or other high-nitrogen fertilizer. Slugs find lettuce leaves delicious; choose organic slug bait. Lettuce has minimal disease problems. If birds are a problem, cover beds with netting.

Harvest & Best Selection—Pick individual leaves rather than whole heads for a longer harvest; this also prevents leaf rot by increasing air circulation within the bed. Noteworthy varieties include 'Red Sails', 'Buttercrunch', 'Flashy Trout's Back', 'Outredgeous', 'Salad Bowl', 'Garnet Rose', and 'Red Saladbowl'. Some types like romaine are more heat tolerant.

MELON

Cucumis × hybrids

Why It's Special—Melons are one of the most delectable warm-season crops you can grow.

How to Plant & Grow—Choose a sunny, well-drained location. A spot next to a driveway or wall will give plants extra warmth. Start from seed indoors two weeks prior to the last frost or buy seedlings. Incorporate compost and fertilizer high in phosphorus and potassium into the bed. To increase soil temperature, cover the soil with a sheet of plastic mulch and cut an "X" into it for each plant. Transplant seedlings into the garden after all danger of frost has passed. Plant in a zigzag pattern and space 2 feet apart. For extra warmth, cover the bed with a floating row cover for their first two to three weeks; remove when plants start blooming so pollinators can reach flowers.

Care & Problems—Water moderately throughout the season. Pinch back the vine tips once young melons are developing so plants focus energy on ripening existing melons. There are minimal insect or disease problems.

Harvest & Best Selection—Ripe melons will pull away from their stem; the rind of most varieties changes to yellow or orange. Melons do not keep for long; eat them as soon after harvesting as possible. Varieties to try include 'Hale's Jumbo', 'Edens Gem', 'Hearts of Gold', 'Alaska Hybrid', and 'Minnesota Midget'.

MINT

Mentha spp.

Why It's Special—This attractive herb is very invasive but has many desirable culinary and medicinal purposes, and it will repel some types of damaging insects. Mint leaves can be used for tea, potpourri, and to flavor sauces, meat, vegetables, or rice. Tea made with peppermint leaves is a well-known treatment for upset stomachs. Most mints are hardy in zones 3 to 8.

How to Plant & Grow—Mint grows best in part shade but will tolerate a sunny location. They prefer moist soil. Buy plants from a nursery in spring and grow in containers to keep them from spreading or give them their own bed. To use them to repel insects, place containers of mint in the areas where insects are a problem.

Care & Problems—Water regularly and trim plants to keep in bounds. Plants multiply by underground stems. Remove flowers from stems to avoid self-seeding. To propagate, divide the clumps. Mint has minimal insect or disease problems.

Harvest & Best Selection—To harvest, clip stems from plants and strip the leaves. For dried mint, hang branches in bunches upside-down or dry in a food dehydrator or microwave oven; then remove leaves from stems. Commonly grown species are peppermint (*Mentha* × *piperita*), spearmint (*M. spicata*), apple mint (*M. suaveolens*), and Corsican mint (*M. requienii*). Suggested varieties are apple, orange, *M. piperata* 'Chocolate', or variegated pineapple mint (*M. suaveolens* 'Variegata').

ONION

Allium spp.

Why It's Special—Onions are one of the most versatile vegetable crops you can grow. They can be used fresh, sautéed, baked, fried, and in every type of savory dish you can imagine. They require a minimal amount of attention and care, yet will reward you with a bountiful harvest.

How to Plant & Grow—You can grow onions from seeds, sets, or from plant starts. For best results, select long-day varieties, which take advantage of the Northwest's long daylight hours in summer. Incorporate high-potassium fertilizer like bonemeal into the bed in spring when soil is dry. Sow seeds, sets, or starts with an initial spacing of 2 inches between plants and 8 inches between rows.

Care & Problems—Onions require a medium amount of watering during summer. Weed beds regularly. They have minimal insect or pest issues and can repel pests from other nearby crops.

Harvest & Best Selection—Harvest every other onion as a scallion earlier in the season; leave remainder to develop into large bulbs. Once plant stalks bend and fall over, withhold water and pull bulbs to the soil surface so they can begin drying. After a few days, move bulbs onto a tarp in a sheltered area to continue drying. Store onions in a dark, cool location such as a basement or garage. Long-day varieties are 'Copra', 'Big Daddy', 'Walla Walla Sweet', 'Highlander', and 'Red Zeppelin'.

OREGANO
Origanum vulgare

Why It's Special—Oregano is an easy-to-grow perennial herb used primarily to season Greek and Italian dishes. It is native to the Mediterranean region and grows 1 to 3 feet tall. When planted near cabbage-family crops (broccoli, Brussels sprouts, cabbage, cauliflower, and kale), oregano is believed to repel the cabbage butterfly.

How to Plant & Grow—The plants prefer a sunny location and well-drained soil. For best results, plant transplants, although they can be started from seed about eight weeks before the average last frost date, or by dividing an existing clump.

Care & Problems—Oregano has low water needs and does not require any fertilization. The best time to trim back plants is before they start to bloom. Common oregano is more invasive than Greek oregano; consider growing either of them in a container or in their own bed to keep them from taking over the garden. Deadhead the flowers to eliminate the risk of self-seeding. Oregano has no pest or disease problems.

Harvest & Best Selection—To force plants to put on new growth, harvest frequently by clipping stems from plants and stripping the leaves. To dry leaves, either hang branches in bunches upside-down or dry them in a food dehydrator or microwave oven. While Greek oregano (*O. vulgare hirtum*) is considered to have the most intense flavor, you can also try common oregano, which is milder.

PARSLEY
Petroselinum spp.

Why It's Special—Parsley is a lush, attractive, biennial herb. It focuses its energy on growing leaves in the first year and will flower in the second year. It imparts flavor to soups, sauces, rice dishes, and meat, and is frequently used as a decorative garnish. It has a mounding growth habit in the garden. There are two types of parsley: curly-leaf and flat-leaf. Flat-leaf parsley is considered more flavorful and is preferred for gourmet cooking. Parsley is hardy in zones 3 to 9.

How to Plant & Grow—Prepare a planting bed in spring, once the soil is dry enough to be worked; add compost to the top couple of inches of soil. Parsley seeds take three to four weeks to germinate. Since you will probably only need one or two plants, it's easier to purchase seedlings. Plants should be spaced 8 inches apart and grown in partial shade; in a sunny garden, plant them next to taller crops.

Care & Problems—Provide regular watering to keep the leaves healthy and encourage new growth. Parsley has minimal pest or disease problems.

Harvest & Best Selection—Harvest outer parsley leaves to protect the central growing point. To harvest, clip stems from plants and strip the leaves. To dry leaves, hang branches in bunches upside-down or dry them in a food dehydrator. Recommended varieties are 'Giant of Italy', 'Moss Curled', and 'Dark Green Italian'.

PARSNIP
Pastinaca sativa

Why It's Special—Parsnips are often overlooked as a highly desirable vegetable crop. While they may look like robust, white carrots, the surprise is the sweet, nutty flavor they impart in savory dishes. They can be used in soups, combined with potatoes for au gratin dishes, roasted, or served mashed. Parsnips originated in the Mediterranean and are indeed related to carrots.

How to Plant & Grow—Plant seeds directly in the garden in early spring as soon as the soil can be worked. Parsnips require a sunny location and well-drained soil. While loosening the soil to a depth of 12 to 16 inches, work in compost and a fertilizer high in phosphorus such as bone-meal to encourage strong root growth. Sow seeds 1 inch apart; when the seedlings are 3 inches tall, thin them to 4-inch spacing.

Care & Problems—While parsnips need medium watering throughout the season, they are otherwise maintenance-free, with minimal pest or disease problems. Gophers and voles do enjoy nibbling on the roots.

Harvest & Best Selection—Parsnips mature in about 110 days. Since they actually become sweeter after a few frosts, they may be left in the garden until the ground freezes. Store them in plastic bags in the refrigerator or between layers of sand within a container kept in a root cellar or an unheated garage. Popular varieties include 'Hollow Crown', 'Albion', 'Harris Mode', 'Javelin', and 'Turga'.

PEA

Pisum sativum and cultivars

Why It's Special—There are three types of peas: shelling, snap, and snow. They can be eaten fresh, steamed, or in stir-fries and soups. The leaves also taste like peas, making them a delightful addition to salads and hors d'oeuvres. Peas improve the soil by fixing nitrogen for subsequent crops.

How to Plant & Grow—Plant seeds directly in a full-sun site in the garden in early spring as soon as the soil can be worked. Add compost to the top few inches of soil. If birds are a problem for newly sprouted seeds, start them indoors and transplant outside once they are 4 to 6 inches tall. Handle the root systems carefully. Whether sowing seeds or transplanting seedlings, space 2 inches apart and provide a 4-foot-tall trellis, netting, or wire for them to climb, although there are some varieties that do not require support. If there is the threat of frost, cover young plants; they can be killed or damaged by frigid temperatures.

Care & Problems—Medium water is needed through the season. Plants are susceptible to powdery mildew; avoid overhead watering. Once hot weather hits, pea plants cease growing.

Harvest & Best Selection—Harvest pea pods while they're young and tender so plants will continue to bloom and produce pods. Freeze or can the harvest. Varieties are 'Green Arrow' and 'Lincoln' (shelling), 'Super Sugar Snap' (sugar), and 'Oregon Giant' (snow).

PEACH

Prunus persica

Why It's Special—One of the nicest summertime treats is eating a fresh, juicy peach. Because peaches bloom in early spring, they vary in hardiness and aren't suitable for growing in all regions of the Northwest. Most are self-fruitful so you only need one variety.

How to Plant & Grow—Plant bare-root or potted dwarf or semidwarf trees in the spring where they'll get at least six hours of sunlight daily. Dig a planting hole with plenty of room for the roots. Spread the roots and backfill, keeping the graft union 2 to 4 inches above the soil surface. Do not amend. Water the tree in well; add more soil if settling occurs. Stake trees the first year to provide support.

Care & Problems—Water regularly. In late winter, apply dormant oil to smother overwintering scale or aphids. Prune in early spring. Established fruit trees don't require fertilization unless soil or tissue samples indicate deficiencies. Once developing peaches are marble-sized, thin 4 to 8 inches apart so they have room to grow to full size. Peach trees are susceptible to some insects and diseases such as peach leaf curl and coryneum blight. Consult your local Master Gardener program for advice on organic controls.

Harvest & Best Selection—Peaches should ripen on the tree. Press into the flesh at the base of the fruit near the stem to determine ripeness. 'Blushingstar', 'Redstar', 'Rosa', and 'Red Haven' are hardy varieties.

PEAR

Pyrus communis (European);
Pyrus pyrifolia (Asian)

Why It's Special—Both European and Asian pears make lovely additions to the landscape with their white blossoms, shiny leaves, and heavy fruit production. Because pear trees aren't self-fruitful, they require cross-pollination by another variety; nursery planting guides list suitable cross-pollinators that bloom at the same time.

How to Plant & Grow—Select bare-root or potted dwarf or semidwarf trees and plant in the spring or fall, where they'll get at least six hours of sunlight daily. Dig a planting hole with plenty of room for the roots. Spread roots and backfill, keeping the graft union 2 to 4 inches above soil surface. Do not amend. Water the tree in well; add more soil if settling occurs. Stake trees their first year to provide support.

Care & Problems—Water regularly. In late winter, apply dormant oil to smother overwintering scale or aphids. Prune in late winter/early spring. Established fruit trees don't require fertilization unless soil or tissue samples indicate deficiencies. Once pears are marble-sized, thin to one per cluster for larger fruit and to reduce stress on trees. Pear trees are susceptible to insect pests and diseases; consult your local Master Gardener program for advice.

Harvest & Best Selection—Ripe pears change color and seeds turn brown. Recommended varieties are (European) 'D'Anjou', 'Comice', 'Bosc', 'Bartlett', and (Asian) '20th Century'. Many Asian pear varieties aren't suitable for zone 5 or lower.

PEPPER, HOT
Capsicum annuum

Why It's Special—Hot peppers love to grow in the heat of summer. They come in an amazing variety of sizes, shapes, and "heat" based on how much capsaicin they contain.

How to Plant & Grow—Start peppers from seeds indoors eight weeks prior to the average last frost date or purchase seedlings. Transplant seedlings after all danger of frost has passed. To avoid soilborne disease, choose an area where peppers, eggplants, potatoes, tomatoes, or tomatillos have not been grown for the past few years. Work compost and fertilizer high in phosphorus and potassium into the planting bed. Increase soil temperature by covering the soil with plastic mulch. Cut an "X" into it for each plant. Space plants 12 inches apart. Cover the bed with floating row covers for the first two to three weeks to provide extra warmth; remove it when plants start blooming so pollinators can get to the flowers.

Care & Problems—Plants require medium watering until peppers start developing; then reduce water somewhat. Peppers are generally pest- and disease-free.

Harvest & Best Selection—Harvest when peppers reach their mature color. In addition to drying, peppers can be sliced or chopped and then frozen. The seeds contain the heat so do not touch your eyes while processing them. Recommended varieties are 'Early Jalapeño', 'Ancho Magnifico', and 'Red Rocket' cayenne.

PEPPER, SWEET
Capsicum annuum

Why It's Special—Sweet peppers come in a variety of shapes and colors, adding beauty and interest to the vegetable garden. Peppers are used fresh and in a wide array of cooking, from omelets to Italian dishes.

How to Plant & Grow—Sow seeds indoors two months before last frost or buy transplants. Transplant seedlings into the garden after all danger of frost has passed. Choose a sunny location that has well-drained soil, and where peppers, eggplants, potatoes, tomatoes, or tomatillos have *not* been grown for the past few years. Work in compost and a balanced organic fertilizer. To increase soil temperature, cover the soil with plastic mulch and cut an "X" into it for each plant. Space peppers 12 inches apart. To provide extra warmth, place a floating row cover over the plants for the first two to three weeks; remove it when they start to bloom so pollinators can get to the flowers.

Care & Problems—Provide plants with a medium amount of water while they're actively growing; decrease water somewhat as fruits develop. Peppers have minimal pest or disease problems.

Harvest & Best Selection—Harvest peppers when they are green and reach full size, or wait until they turn their mature color. They can be sliced or chopped and frozen. Try 'California Wonder', 'Golden Bell', 'Lipstick', 'Italian Sweet', or 'Sweet Chocolate'.

PLUM
Prunus domestica

Why It's Special—Besides being the easiest fruit trees to grow and maintain, plums produce bountiful crops. Gardeners in warmer regions of the Northwest can grow European and Japanese varieties, but European varieties are hardier for those in zone 5 or lower. While most European plum trees are self-fruitful, Japanese plums require cross-pollination from another variety; contact your local Master Gardener program for variety recommendations.

How to Plant & Grow—Plant bare-root or potted dwarf or semidwarf trees in the spring or fall. They'll need at least six hours of sunlight daily. Dig a hole that will have plenty of room for all the roots. Spread the roots and backfill, keeping the graft union 2 to 4 inches above the soil surface. No amendments are needed. Water the tree in well; add more soil if settling occurs. Stake trees their first year.

Care & Problems—Established fruit trees don't need fertilization unless soil or tissue samples indicate deficiencies. In late winter, apply dormant oil to smother overwintering scale or aphids. Prune in late winter/early spring. Water regularly during the growing season and avoid using high-nitrogen fertilizers. Fruit thinning isn't needed. Plums have minimal insect or disease problems.

Harvest & Best Selection—Plums are ripe when the flesh is soft. European plums turn yellowish. Varieties are (European) 'Italian', 'Earliblue' and 'Stanley' and (Japanese) 'Santa Rosa', 'Shiro', and 'Satsuma'.

POTATO
Solanum tuberosum

Why It's Special—The Northwest is an excellent region for growing potatoes. Digging up the tubers in fall is like searching for buried treasure.

How to Plant & Grow—Select a well-drained, sunny location in an area of the garden in which eggplants, potatoes, peppers, or tomatoes have not been grown for the past few years. Plant them in early to mid-spring. Add compost to beds; avoid using manure. Start with certified disease-free seed potatoes from garden centers. If they are small, plant whole. Otherwise, slice them into large chunks with two eyes each; air-dry for a few hours. Plant seed potatoes 4 inches deep and 6 inches apart. Cover soil with mulch to keep any potatoes growing near the surface from being exposed to sunlight, which creates a natural toxin called solanine and turns some of the skin and flesh green.

Care & Problems—Provide medium amounts of water while plants are blooming and young potatoes are developing. Handpick Colorado potato beetles if they appear on plants.

Harvest & Best Selection—A few new potatoes can be harvested from each plant once they start blooming. Plants die back in fall. Dig up tubers and let their skins dry in a shady, protected area before storing. Varieties include (standard size) 'Yukon Gold', 'Sangre', German Butterball', and 'Kennebec', and (fingerlings) 'Austrian Crescent', 'Red Thumb', and 'Butterfinger'.

PUMPKIN
Cucurbita maxima

Why It's Special—Nothing says autumn like festive pumpkins of varying shapes and colors. If you have a warm spot in your garden, they are easy to grow. Be sure to save space for pie pumpkins because nothing tops a homemade pumpkin pie.

How to Plant & Grow—Start from seed indoors two weeks prior to the last frost or purchase seedlings. Work compost and balanced fertilizer into the planting bed. To increase soil temperature, cover soil with plastic mulch and cut an "X" for each plant. Transplant seedlings into garden once the danger of frost has passed. Space them 18 inches apart in a zigzag pattern. Place a floating row cover over the plants for two to three weeks to increase soil temperature; remove it when they bloom so pollinators can access the flowers.

Care & Problems—Water heavily throughout the summer. Pinch back the vine tips once young pumpkins are developing so plants focus energy on ripening them. Plants are susceptible to squash beetles, which can be handpicked. Pumpkins have minimal disease problems.

Harvest & Best Selection—Pumpkins are ripe when you can't pierce the skin with your thumbnail. Cut from the vine with a 2-inch stem attached. Cure in a sunny, protected area for two weeks before storing. Recommended varieties include (pie) 'New England Pie' and 'Winter Luxury', and (decorative) 'Casper' and 'Rouge Vif d'Etampes'. Most mature in 90 to 120 days.

RADISH
Raphanus sativus

Why It's Special—Radishes might seem like an inconsequential crop but they have a lot going for them. They germinate quickly, making them a fun veggie for kids to grow. Plantings can be used to mark the rows of other, slow-germinating crops like carrots, parsnips, or parsley. They make a crunchy addition to salads and hors d'oeuvres. They are native to China. There are more than 200 varieties of radishes, so there are sure to be some that appeal to you.

How to Plant & Grow—Radishes will tolerate light shade. Prepare the planting bed as early as the ground can be worked in the spring by adding compost or shredded leaves to the soil. Sow seeds directly outdoors ½-inch deep. Once plants are growing, thin seedlings to 1- or 2-inch spacing, depending on the mature size of the radish. To harvest radishes throughout the season, plant seeds every ten days. For a fall harvest, plant seeds in mid- to late summer.

Care & Problems—It is important to provide radishes with regular, medium watering throughout their growing season. The plants have minimal insect or disease problems.

Harvest & Best Selection—Most radishes only require three weeks to reach maturity so harvest them while they are young and crisp. Radishes that are past their prime tend to be spicier and tough. Fun varieties to grow are 'Cherry Belle', 'Easter Egg', 'French Breakfast', and 'Watermelon'.

RASPBERRY
Rubus idaeus

Why It's Special—Raspberries are long-lived perennials that produce biennial canes: the first year, it is a primocane that only grows leaves; the second-year floricane will bear fruit. There are two main types of raspberries: summer-bearing, which are more productive, and fall-bearing. Plants will produce for about 20 years.

How to Plant & Grow—Select a sunny location with well-drained soil. Loosen soil and add organic amendments and a balanced fertilizer. In early spring, purchase bare-root canes from a nursery and plant them 2 feet apart. Provide plants with a trellis for ease of harvest and to keep canes off the ground. There are several trellis types so consult your local Master Gardener program for details.

Care & Problems—Water 1 inch per week during the growing season and keep weeds under control. Fertilize with 10-20-20 in early spring. Prune floricanes of summer- and fall-bearing varieties down to the ground once they've borne fruit. Fall crops will be produced on the primocane tips of fall-bearing varieties. If you're growing this type, the easiest way to know which canes not to prune is to wait until early spring to see which ones are sprouting new leaves.

Harvest & Best Selection—Pick berries while at their peak every two to four days. Recommended varieties include (summer-bearing) 'Canby', 'Chilcotin', and 'Willamette', and (fall-bearing) 'Fallgold' and 'Heritage'.

RHUBARB
Rheum rhabarbarum

Why It's Special—Did you know rhubarb is a vegetable? That's because veggies produce leaves, stems, or roots for us to eat, while fruits contain seeds. Rhubarb stalks are the only edible part of the plants and are used for making pies, jams, and jellies. Note: while the foliage is attractive in the garden, it is also poisonous.

How to Plant & Grow—Planting crowns purchased from nurseries gets plants off to a speedy start although you can also start from seed. Since rhubarb plants can last for many years, select a sunny, well-drained location where the roots will not be disturbed. If your soil doesn't drain well, try growing rhubarb in a raised bed. Add a balanced fertilizer or composted manure to the soil. Plant crowns in early spring with 3-foot spacing from other plants or crops.

Care & Problems—Plants need regular watering and either composted manure or a balanced fertilizer each spring. Trim plants back to five buds every five years. Rhubarb goes dormant during winter and will sprout again in early spring. Plants have minimal insect or disease problems.

Harvest & Best Selection—Wait two years before harvesting a few stalks; each year after that, harvest more heavily over the course of two months. Cut stalks at the soil line; remove leaves. Recommended varieties are 'Cherry Red', 'Victoria', and 'Valentine'.

ROSEMARY
Rosmarinus officinalis

Why It's Special—Rosemary is an attractive and useful herb for the garden. Its needle-like foliage adds texture and interest to its surroundings, the purple or white flowers draw bees to the garden like magnets, and the flavorful leaves are used in a variety of meat and vegetable dishes. It is native to the Mediterranean region.

How to Plant & Grow—Most rosemary varieties are hardy in zones 7 and above and will retain their leaves year-round. In colder zones, plants can be grown either as an annual or grown in pots and brought indoors to overwinter for the following season. You will probably only need one or two plants in your herb bed so it's easiest to purchase plants at a garden center in early spring. If you decide to start your own plants from seed, know that they are slow to germinate and usually don't have good germination rates. Select a sunny location with well-drained soil.

Care & Problems—Rosemary plants have low water and nutrient requirements. They grow 2 to 3 feet tall so trim the plants occasionally to keep the foliage tidy. Rosemary has no serious pest or disease problems.

Harvest & Best Selection—Clip rosemary branches from plants as needed and strip off the leaves. Branches can be dried by hanging upside-down in bunches and then stored in jars. Two varieties to try are 'Arp' and 'Roman Beauty'.

SAGE
Salvia officinalis

Why It's Special—Culinary sage is an evergreen, perennial herb that is hardy to zone 5. It's used primarily to season meat, poultry, fish, sauces, and soups. Sage makes a nice addition to the garden because the gray-green leaves are attractive, even in winter. The violet-blue flowers are popular with bees and butterflies. An added bonus is that members of the sage family repel deer and damaging insects.

How to Plant & Grow—You will only need a plant or two in your garden so it's easiest to purchase seedlings at a local nursery in the spring. If you want to start sage from seeds, plant them indoors about two months before the last frost. When planting outdoors, select a sunny location although sage will tolerate some shade; make sure the soil is well drained as sage plants do not like to have wet feet.

Care & Problems—Provide a low amount of water during dry periods. Plants grow 1 to 2 feet tall; trim them back occasionally to keep them tidy. Sage does not have any serious pest or disease problems.

Harvest & Best Selection—Leaves can be harvested anytime, although flavor will be the most intense while its flowers are blooming. Leaves can also be dried in a dehydrator and stored for year-round use. Suggested varieties of common sage are 'Garden Broadleaf' and 'White Edge'. Purple sage (*Salvia officinalis* 'Purpurea') is hardy down to zone 6.

SPINACH
Spinacia oleracea

Why It's Special—Spinach is a hardy, cool-season crop. It can be grown in early spring or late summer as a fall crop in all regions because it tolerates frost. Spinach is very nutritious, providing us with vitamins, minerals, and antioxidants. Use it raw for salads, steamed, or in soups and casserole dishes.

How to Plant & Grow—In addition to growing in full sun, spinach can be planted in part shade. Add compost or other organic amendments to the planting bed. Sow seeds directly in the garden as soon as the soil can be worked. Space plants 8 to 12 inches apart.

Care & Problems—Keep beds evenly moist throughout the season. Once hot weather hits, spinach plants will stop growing and bolt. Two insects to be aware of are leaf miners, which are larvae that ruin the leaves by tunneling through them, and slugs. Cover the bed with floating row covers for the entire season to prevent leaf miner adults from laying eggs on the leaves. Leaf miners are more prevalent during particularly wet springs. For slug problems, use traps or organic bait.

Harvest & Best Selection—Harvest individual leaves as soon as they are large enough, or cut back an entire plant to 1 inch tall, which causes it to grow new leaves. Spinach can be blanched and frozen for later use. Recommended varieties include 'Bordeaux', 'Tyee', 'Space', 'Olympia', or 'Bloomsdale Savoy'.

STRAWBERRY

Fragaria spp.

Why It's Special—The first berry crop to ripen each year, strawberries are an excellent source of vitamin C. While they are at their best when eaten fresh, they are also delicious in smoothies, jams, and pies. There are three types: June-bearing, which are the most productive and earliest ripening; ever-bearing, which bear fruit in spring and late summer; and day-neutral, which produce berries from spring to fall. The plants are productive for four to five years.

How to Plant & Grow—Select a sunny location with well-drained soil; add compost and fertilizer high in phosphorus and potassium. Purchase disease-free strawberry crowns from a garden center in early spring. Dig a planting hole that will accommodate spread-out roots and keep the crown of the plant even with the soil surface. Press soil firmly around the roots to eliminate air pockets. Space plants 1 foot apart.

Care & Problems—Mulch around the plants to conserve soil moisture and impede weed growth. Keep weeds that do sprout under control but be careful with cultivation as strawberries have shallow roots. Water plants regularly all season. Fertilize after harvest with balanced fertilizer. Remove runners from mother plants; start with new plants every four to five years. Contact your local Master Gardener program for advice if pest or disease problems arise.

Harvest & Best Selection—Pick berries as they ripen. Varieties are (June-bearing) 'Rainier' and 'Shuksan'; (ever-bearing) 'Quinault' and 'Ogalalla'; and (day-neutral) 'Tillicum', 'Tristar', and 'Tribute'.

SWISS CHARD

Beta vulgaris subsp. *cicla*

Why It's Special—Swiss chard is a hardy, cool-season yet heat-tolerant plant that lasts longer in the garden than spinach. It's available in a rainbow of colors. The leaves and stalks are delicious when steamed and served with butter and a wedge of lemon. It can be used like spinach in salads, soups, or casseroles. This crop rarely bolts to seed. Plants grow well into fall and will occasionally overwinter in zone 5 gardens when protected by a floating row cover, a plastic-covered hoop tunnel, or when mulched with leaves or pine needles.

How to Plant & Grow—Sow seeds directly outdoors in a sunny location as soon as the soil can be worked; chard will tolerate light shade. Incorporate compost in the soil and fertilize seedlings with fish emulsion. Thin plants to an 8- to 10-inch spacing.

Care & Problems—Provide regular, medium watering throughout the season. Swiss chard is susceptible to leaf miner larvae—which ruin the leaves by tunneling through them—and slugs. Cover the bed with floating row covers for the season to keep leaf miner adults from laying eggs on the leaves. Use organic slug controls.

Harvest & Best Selection—Harvest individual leaves, instead of whole plants, to prolong the harvest. Leaves can be lightly steamed and frozen for later use. Try 'Bright Lights', 'Charlotte', 'Fordhook Giant', or 'Pot of Gold'.

THYME
Thymus vulgaris

Why It's Special—Thyme is a hardy perennial herb that imparts a distinctive, delicious flavor to meat, poultry, soups, or vegetable dishes. It has a compact, fairly tidy growth habit and has pest-repelling qualities. Plants are covered with small pale pink blossoms in June and July. Thyme has also been used for medicinal purposes such as soothing a sore throat and aiding digestion.

How to Plant & Grow—Since thyme plants are long-lived, select a permanent growing bed that gets full sun and has well-drained soil. You will likely only need one or two plants so purchase them at a nursery. Plants grow to 1 foot tall; space them 8 inches apart. Thyme can grow well in containers on patios or decks, and on a sunny windowsill indoors.

Care & Problems—Thyme has medium to low water requirements. Plants may need an occasional light trimming to keep them tidy. It can be propagated by digging up rooted stems from the mother plant. Thyme has no serious pest or disease problems and it's deer-resistant.

Harvest & Best Selection—Thyme can be harvested anytime. To dry, snip branches from plants and hang them upside-down; once dry, strip the tiny leaves from the woody stems and store them in airtight containers. The hardiest varieties include 'English' and 'German Winter'. 'French' thyme, sometimes referred to as 'Summer' thyme, is hardy in zones 6 and above.

TOMATILLO
Physalis ixocarpa

Why It's Special—While tomatillos are related to tomatoes, they are not as commonly grown in this region as they are in the Southwest. Used in Mexican dishes, they are a popular ingredient for making salsa verde (green sauce). Tomatillos are easy to grow.

How to Plant & Grow—Sow seeds indoors one month before the average date of last frost. Select a sunny location with well-drained soil; add compost to bed. To avoid soilborne disease, choose an area where tomatillos, eggplants, potatoes, tomatoes, or peppers have *not* been grown for the past few years. After all danger of frost is past, plant seedlings deeply, just as you would a tomato, by burying all but the top few leaves, and space plants 3 feet apart. Because tomatillos are heat lovers, cover the bed with a floating row cover for the first two or three weeks; remove when plants start to bloom so pollinators can get to the flowers.

Care & Problems—Plants tend to be leggy so stake them as they grow, although they are just as happy to sprawl on the ground. Water a medium amount throughout the season. They have few pest or disease problems.

Harvest & Best Selection—Harvest begins 60 days after transplanting, when the fruit feels plump and the husk has split open. Tomatillos can be stored in the refrigerator two to four weeks. Recommended varieties are 'Toma Verde', 'Mexican Strain', and 'De Milpa'.

TOMATO

Solanum lycopersicum

Why It's Special—Tomatoes are the most popular home garden crop. And why not? The flavor of a homegrown tomato is unsurpassable. There are varieties suitable for all zones of the Northwest.

How to Plant & Grow—Sow seeds indoors eight weeks before the last frost date or purchase seedlings. Select a sunny location where the soil drains well. To prevent soilborne disease, choose a site where tomatoes, eggplants, potatoes, tomatillos, or peppers have not been grown for the past few years. Incorporate compost into the soil. To increase soil temperature, cover soil with plastic mulch; cut an "X" into it for each plant. Once danger of frost is past, strip off the lowest leaves and plant seedlings in deep holes with only the top few leaves above ground. Space seedlings 2 to 3 feet apart and feed with fish emulsion. To provide extra warmth, use a floating row cover for two to three weeks; remove once plants start flowering. Provide plants with a sturdy cage or stakes for support.

Care & Problems—Water regularly until tomatoes start ripening, then cut back. Feed plants organic fertilizer high in phosphorus every two weeks. Tomato hornworms can be controlled by handpicking.

Harvest & Best Selection—Harvest tomatoes when they are plump and the appropriate color and size for their variety. Try (cherry) 'Sungold' and 'Sweet 100'; (paste) 'Roma' and 'San Marzano'; (salad/eating) 'Oregon Spring', 'Early Girl', 'Early Goliath', and 'Legend'.

TURNIP

Brassica rapa subsp. *rapa*

Why It's Special—Turnips are fast-growers that provide both greens and bulbous roots for us to eat. Cultivation goes back many centuries, with use by the early Greeks and Romans. It was grown in India around the 15th century B.C., not for the bulbs but for the oil in its seeds.

How to Plant & Grow—Select a sunny location with well-drained soil. To prevent soilborne disease, don't grow turnips where other cabbage family members have been grown in recent years. Add compost and high-phosphorus organic fertilizer to encourage good root development. Sow seeds outdoors in early spring for a midsummer harvest or in mid- to late summer for a fall harvest. Space seeds 4 inches apart.

Care & Problems—Regularly water at soil level rather than wetting foliage. Flea beetles can attack leaves, and roots are susceptible to root maggots; cover a bed with a floating row cover. Leave in place for entire season.

Harvest & Best Selection—Harvest turnips when roots are 1 to 3 inches in diameter. Fall crops taste best when harvested after a few frosts. Turnips can be stored in the ground until the soil freezes. Store in plastic bags in the refrigerator or between layers of sand within a container kept in a root cellar or an unheated garage. Recommended varieties include 'Purple Top White Globe', 'Scarlet Queen Red Stems', 'Hakurei', and 'Golden Ball'.

WATERMELON
Citrullus lanatus

Why It's Special—There's nothing quite like eating a juicy watermelon in the heat of summer. In the Northwest, we don't always have the best conditions for growing them but if you choose a short-season variety and use a few tricks, you'll be successful.

How to Plant & Grow—Select a sunny location with well-drained soil; add compost to the bed. A site next to a driveway or wall will give plants extra warmth. Start seed indoors two weeks prior to the last frost or purchase seedlings. Incorporate fertilizer high in phosphorus and potassium into the bed. To increase soil temperature, cover the bed with plastic mulch and cut an "X" into it for each plant, 2 feet apart. Transplant seedlings after all danger of frost has passed. For extra warmth, cover the bed with a floating row cover for two to three weeks; remove when plants start blooming.

Care & Problems—Water a medium amount throughout the season. Pinch back vines once you see young melons developing; this forces plants to focus energy on ripening melons instead of blooming more. Most plants will produce one to three melons each. Plants have minimal pest or disease problems.

Harvest & Best Selection—Harvest a watermelon when it begins pulling away from the vine and the bottom of the melon has turned yellow. Short-season varieties worth trying are 'Sugar Baby', 'Blacktail Mountain', 'Icebox Mickylee', and 'Sweet Beauty'.

ZUCCHINI
Cucurbita pepo cultivars

Why It's Special—Zucchinis are one of the most popular and productive garden crops. They grow in bush form and are used in relishes and a wide variety of dishes and baked goods.

How to Plant & Grow—Select a sunny location and add organic matter to the soil. Start seeds indoors two weeks prior to average last frost date, or sow directly in garden once all danger of frost is past. Transplant started seedlings into the garden after all danger of frost has passed; space them 2 feet apart. Zucchini plants usually don't require plastic mulch but it is helpful to cover the soil with grass clippings from an untreated lawn to conserve moisture and impede weed growth. To get plants off to a good start, cover the bed with a floating row cover for the first couple of weeks; remove it when plants start blooming so pollinators can get to flowers.

Care & Problems—Zucchini plants need lots of water all summer. Lack of pollination can sometimes be a problem early in the season, which will resolve as the temperatures warm and more pollinators are active in the garden. Plants have minimal insect or disease problems.

Harvest & Best Selection—Harvest zucchini while they are small and tender; if left on vines too long, they become tough. Recommended varieties are 'Romanesco', 'Goldmine', 'Yellowfin', 'Eight Ball', and 'Geode'.

JANUARY

- Go over your garden journal and note anything you want to change or add. Lay out your garden beds or pots for the new season. Remember to rotate your crops to different beds so that nitrogen fixers like beans and peas follow heavy feeder crops like corn and beets. Crop rotation also breaks many insects' life cycle and reduces infestations.

- Pour a cup of coffee, settle in with a stack of garden catalogs and dream a bit. Order early to ensure you get what you want.

- Clean seed-starting equipment. Buy new fluorescent tubes, germinating mixes, labeling tags, pots, and flats if you need them. Wash existing flats and pots in a 10-percent bleach solution to kill any bacteria or fungus.

- Gardeners west of the Cascades need to stay on top of the cool-season weeds like chickweed and annual bluegrass.

- If you are in an area that is warm enough for winter crops, check that plants growing under plastic row covers are getting enough water.

FEBRUARY

- West of the Cascades, gardeners can seed early cool-season cole crops like spinach, kale, lettuce, and chard indoors early in the month. This will speed up the germination process so that you will be able to plant early crops outdoors by mid-March.

- If you are overwintering herb plants indoors, keep them watered and trim back scraggly growth. Begin fertilizing them towards the end of the month with a half-strength houseplant food.

- Fruit tree pruning can be done this month throughout the region. Use sharp tools and a sturdy ladder. If you are renovating a large tree, take only one-third of the wood each year for three years.

- Toward the end of month, apply dormant oil to fruit trees to reduce the presence of insect eggs and some diseases. Spray peach trees with lime sulfur before the buds begin to swell to prevent leaf curl.

MARCH

- West of the Cascades, gardeners can begin preparing growing beds as soon as the soil is workable. Peas and potatoes can be planted mid-month. Gardeners east of the Cascades will likely have to wait until April to begin bed preparation and planting.

- Start warm-season crops like tomatoes, peppers, and eggplant under lights later in the month so they have eight weeks to grow before transplanting in late May. If they spend too much time in their pots, they become rootbound and stunted, which will reduce fruit production.

- Fertilize perennial crops like berries, rhubarb, and asparagus with a good slow-release 10-10-10 fertilizer late in the month.

APRIL

- Cool-season crops can be planted outdoors in all but the coldest areas of the region this month. East of the Cascades, keep some frost blankets handy for that unexpected late snow or hard frost. Seedlings will be available in the nurseries if you didn't grow your own.

- About ten days after petal fall, begin spraying apple and pear trees for codling moths and cherry trees for cherry fruit flies (cherry worms). Use organic insecticides, such as sprays containing spinosad, whenever possible. Spray late in the evening after honey bees have returned to their hives as even organic sprays can kill bees and their larvae. Read the label and follow directions carefully.

- Check that indoor seedlings are getting enough light and water. Repot them to bigger pots so they have plenty of room to grow. Fertilize every two weeks with half-strength, low-nitrogen fertilizer.

MAY

- Melon, cucumber, and squash seeds can be planted indoors in pots early in the month and set out around the end of May. Use pots such as peat or coir fiber that can be planted directly in the ground to avoid disturbing the roots. Tear off the top of the pot or cover it with soil to prevent moisture from being "wicked" out of the soil.

- Pick up your favorite vegetable starts at the nursery early. Popular ones will go fast. If it is still too cold to plant, put them in a cold frame or in a well-lit spot in the house.

- West of the Cascades, warm-season crops and transplants can be hardened off and planted by early to mid-month. Gardeners east of the Cascades need to wait until late May or early June to plant tender crops.

- Stay on top of weeds: they will grow fast in the early warmth. Apply mulches as you weed. Lay sheets of mulch over an entire bed and then make spaces to plant seeds or plants.

- If it has been a dry spring, make sure new plantings have enough water. Get your watering system tuned up now while the weather is still cool.

JUNE

- Keep cool-season crops picked; they are at their prime for flavor this month. Crops like spinach may start bolting by the end of the month. Pull them and replant with another crop.

- Thin root crops when they are 3 inches high so there are about 3 to 4 inches between each carrot or parsnip or four to 6 inches between beet plants.

- Scout for Colorado potato beetles, aphids, flea beetles, and cabbage moths. Begin an integrated pest management program (IPM). See Chapter 2 for a description of IPM.

- In dry areas, start a regular watering program early in the month. Give vegetables and fruit about an inch of water a week. Make a simple drip irrigation system by laying soaker hoses down plant rows and hook them to a timer.

JULY

- Prune back herbs to prevent flowering and keep them bushy. The air and soil temperatures have warmed enough by the beginning of the month to allow direct seeding of basil. Basil loves warm soil and will grow quickly for a mid-August harvest.

- Fertilize heavy-feeding crops such as beets, corn, cole crops, and melons around the first part of July with a 10-10-10 fertilizer as they begin to put on good growth. Side-dress asparagus ferns with the same fertilizer to help the roots build reserves for next spring.

- Continue scouting for bugs. If you can't identify them, take them to your local Master Gardener office for proper identification and IPM-based control methods.

- Towards the end of the month, harvest garlic when half of each top turns yellow. Hang the garlic to cure in a cool, dark place for a month. It can then be stored in cool, dry place for the winter. Use up softneck garlic first. It will store only about three months. Hardneck garlic will store well into late winter.

AUGUST

- Most crops will begin to ripen this month, so stay on top of picking to extend the harvest. See the individual profiles for specifics.

- Early in the month, replant spaces left bare by early maturing crops with new plantings of carrots, lettuce, beets, and kale for a fall harvest.

- Keep tomatoes and other vegetables evenly watered through the heat. Both blossom-end rot and cracking in tomatoes are caused by irregular watering. Adjust your watering schedule to ensure that plants are watered deeply and that the soil stays evenly moist.

- Powdery mildew will likely appear on squash and cucumber leaves as the weather begins to cool and humidity rises in the evening hours. Treat the plants with a mixture of 4 teaspoons of baking soda and 2½ tablespoons of Neem oil to a gallon of water before the mildew appears. Spray the leaves lightly as too much can damage them.

- If you're in the higher elevations east of the Cascades, get the frost protection covers ready. Frosts often occur when cool sunny days are followed by clear, windless nights.

SEPTEMBER

- Consider extending the season in the garden by making temporary hoop houses. Bend 10-foot sections of PVC pipe over a bed and cover it with a floating row cover. The row cover holds in heat, especially at night, while still allowing air, water, and light to reach the plants.

- Finish harvesting vegetables as they ripen. Most production will trail off as the nights cool and sunlight levels drop with the shortening days.

- Leave root crops such as carrots, parsnips, and beets in the ground until after a good frost. The frost helps increase the sugars in the roots and makes them sweeter.

OCTOBER

- Pick winter squash and pumpkins when your fingernail doesn't dent their skin. Cure them in a warm place for a week before storing them somewhere cool and frost-free.

- Harvest root crops and store them for winter use in damp sand in a cool, dark place.

- Plant garlic and shallots mid-month and cover them with 6 to 12 inches of mulch.

- Start a new compost pile by mixing spent vegetable plants and grass clippings with fall leaves. Spread finished compost from older piles on your beds to prepare for the spring.

NOVEMBER

- Cut down woody single-crop raspberry and blackberry canes that produced this year and tie up the new canes to a trellis.

- Catch up on your journal; keep track of all the changes and new ideas you want to implement for next year.

- Spread mulch on empty beds to keep the winter weeds at bay.

DECEMBER

- Gardeners west of the Cascades will be able to harvest late crops of hardy vegetables well into the month.

- Plan a winter stew with vegetables you canned or froze from the garden.

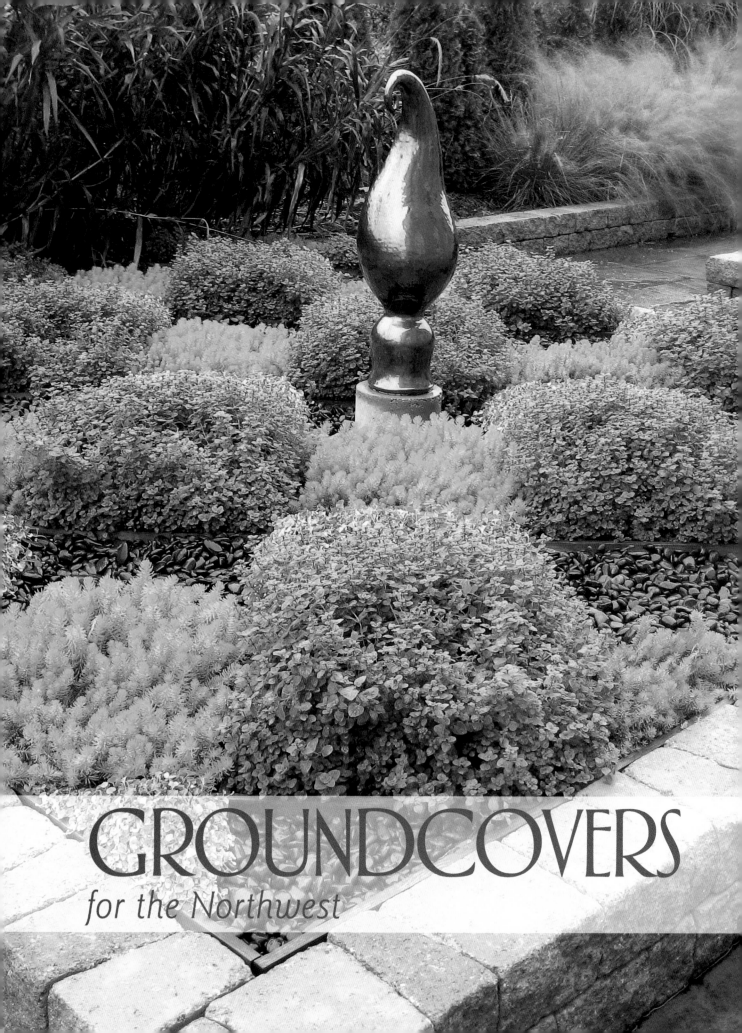

GROUNDCOVERS
for the Northwest

Groundcovers are the underappreciated workhorses of the garden. They are a large group of evergreen and deciduous plants that include low-growing, creeping, or spreading shrubs; perennials; vines; and a few annuals. Groundcovers come in such a wide variety of textures, heights, growth habits, and leaf and flower colors that they can fit into any landscape design. In a small garden, fine-textured groundcovers make the space seem larger and more lush to the visitor. In a larger garden, they can help create a smooth flow between beds and other garden features. When planted between pavers or trained to spill down walls, they can soften the harsh edges of angular hardscapes. In the shady garden and under large trees where lawn grasses struggle, groundcovers can thrive and provide an alternative to bare ground. Some groundcovers are tough enough to grow in narrow parking strips where many plants won't survive.

For homeowners who are tired of dealing with thirsty and high-maintenance lawns, groundcovers can make a good replacement. They use *far* less water than an average lawn and need much less fertilizer to look good. You may even be able to sell the lawn mower and free up the space in your garage for something more useful. Groundcover lawns won't take the heavy wear kids or dogs can dish out, but they will take light foot traffic with little problem.

Groundcovers can also help stabilize steep slopes that would otherwise be prone to erosion during the Northwest's frequent winter storms. A plant's leaf cover breaks up the raindrops before they can hit the soil surface, and its dense root systems hold soil particles in place. In the drier parts of our region, groundcovers can improve air quality by reducing the dust kicked up by summer winds. They can also cover rough, rocky areas that are too hard to maintain with any other kind of garden.

PLANTING AND MAINTAINING GROUNDCOVERS

Groundcovers spread by a variety of methods. Some grow from the tips of their stems, expanding as they go. Others send out runners that take root when they touch the soil surface, then send out new runners. Another type expands by sending out stolons (underground roots) into new territory. Keep an eye on your groundcovers. They all grow at different paces; if not monitored, they may invade areas where you don't want them.

Most groundcovers require little maintenance beyond a yearly raking in fall and some trimming back of errant plants. Most of them do well in average-to-poor soil with low-to-average watering and a spring feeding with a slow-release fertilizer.

When planting a groundcover, good weed control is critical for establishment. The area must be well-weeded prior to planting, with particular attention paid to the tough perennial weeds. Once the area has been cleared, water it well and leave it for a couple of weeks so that some of the remaining weed seed can sprout and be pulled. Another option is to mulch the weeded area with 2 to 3 inches of shredded leaves or needles, then simply plant the new groundcover through the mulch.

Most groundcovers are planted as small plugs or cut as chunks from full flats of plants. Small plugs are often cheaper to buy, especially if you are covering a large area. Research the spacing recommended for your chosen groundcovers; it will

Groundcovers spread over a basalt outcrop where nothing else will grow.

depend on the growth rate of the plant and how quickly you want it to fill in the space. One method of planting is to calculate the recommended planting distance and then lay out a diamond-shaped grid over the area. This way, each plant will be equidistant from its neighbors. Keep the plantings well watered for the first year to get them established.

As a rule, don't put aggressive growers in a small space. They will quickly outgrow it and become very difficult to control. To keep groundcovers in check, edge them regularly or install a barrier of wood, metal, or stone 6 inches into the soil. When buying groundcovers, be wary of tags that state the plant is a vigorous grower or spreads widely.

Many groundcovers are quite shade and drought tolerant, which makes them the perfect choice for difficult areas of the garden. The table below compares several commonly used groundcovers for their sun, shade, and drought tolerance and notes which ones grow quickly.

ENGLISH IVY IS A NOXIOUS WEED

For decades, English ivy was a popular groundcover west of the Cascades. It was used liberally in private and public landscapes because it covered the ground quickly and took little maintenance. Unfortunately, it grew so well that over time it began invading native landscapes. As a result, five species and cultivars of English ivy (*Hedera helix* 'Baltica', *H. helix* 'Pittsburgh', *H. helix* 'Star', *H. helix* 'California', and *H. hibernica*) have been declared Class C noxious weeds in western Washington and Class B noxious weeds in western Oregon. Both designations mean that these cultivars of ivy are mandated for control by landowners. In British Columbia, English ivy is not on the noxious weed list but it is a major problem in some park areas including Vancouver's Stanley Park. Ivy spreads rapidly when established, crowding out all other native vegetation on the ground and smothering trees as it climbs. Birds eat the berries and deposit seeds that grow into new colonies in forests and woodlands. The sale of these cultivars in nurseries in western Oregon and Washington is prohibited. East of the Cascades, the colder winter temperatures and drier climate seem to keep the plant in check.

Ivy is not easy to remove. There are no bio-controls or reliable herbicides that will control the plant. Removal generally involves digging out the roots by hand. The Oregon Department of Agriculture estimates it costs upwards of $2,000 an acre to remove infestations from some of the state parks.

GROUNDCOVER SUN, SHADE, AND DROUGHT TOLERANCE

PLANT	SUN	PART SHADE	SHADE	DROUGHT TOLERANT	FAST GROWING
Bellflower	X	X		X	
Bishop's weed	X	X			X
Brass buttons	X	X			
Bugleweed		X		X	X
Creeping Jenny		X	X		X
Creeping thyme	X	X		X	
Hardy ice plant	X	X		X	
Hardy verbena	X	X		X	
Japanese spurge	X	X			X
Kinnikinnick	X	X		X	
Lily-of-the-Valley	X	X		X	
St. John's wort	X	X			
Scotch moss		X	X		
Snow-in-Summer	X			X	
Sweet woodruff		X	X	X	

BELLFLOWER
Campanula spp.

Why It's Special—Bellflowers make stunning groundcovers. These are easy to grow, providing colorful accents in the landscape: clustered bellflower (*Campanula glomerata*) 'Superba' grows 2 feet tall and has purple flower clusters in spring. *C. punctata* 'Cherry Bells' grows to 30 inches and has large tubular flowers in cherry-rose. Siberian bellflower (*C. poscharskyana*) 'Blue Waterfall' grows 8 to 10 inches tall and has delicate blue flowers; great for cascading over a rock wall. Goldleaf Adriatic bellflower (*C. garganica*) 'Dickson's Gold' is 4 inches tall and features golden foliage with contrasting deep blue flowers.

How to Plant & Grow—All these named bellflowers thrive in full sun to part shade and tolerate all types of well-drained soil. Grow from bedding plants in spring.

Care & Problems—Apply a balanced fertilizer in early spring. Deadhead flowers to extend bloom. Plants are low maintenance; divide every three years in spring.

Hardiness—Zones 4 to 7

Color(s)—Purple, blue, pink

Peak Season—Late spring into summer

Mature Size (H x W)—4 to 30 in. x 6 to 30 in.

Water Needs—Medium. Water regularly.

BISHOP'S WEED
Aegopodium podagraria

Why It's Special—This attractive perennial establishes quickly wherever it's planted. The aromatic foliage brightens up shady areas of the garden, underneath trees or next to buildings and is an excellent choice for growing in dry shade. It tolerates all types of soil and is deer resistant. It is also known as snow-on-the-mountain and bishop's goutweed. 'Variegatum' has variegated leaves and is not as aggressive as the species.

How to Plant & Grow—Plant in sun to part shade in average, well-drained soil.

Care & Problems—Bishop's weed requires the least amount of maintenance when grown in a container or by itself rather than in mixed plantings. It can become very aggressive so take care when choosing its location. If leaves scorch in intense summer heat, set your lawn mower on high and mow the leaves to renew plants.

Hardiness—Zones 4 to 9

Color(s)—Green

Peak Season—Spring through fall, white blooms in midsummer

Mature Size (H x W)—10 in. x 12 in.

Water Needs—Low to medium. Water regularly until established and during periods of drought.

BRASS BUTTONS
Leptinella squalida

Why It's Special—Originating from New Zealand, brass buttons has an exotic look. Fortunately, it's hardy to zone 4 so Northwest gardeners can enjoy it. The tiny, fernlike leaves are green in spring and summer, turning bronze in fall. The plants are members of the Daisy family, and as such, have the disc-like flower center but no petals. Plants tolerate moderate foot traffic so this is a good choice for planting between steppingstones. 'Platt's Black' features darker leaves than the species.

How to Plant & Grow—Plants are very adaptable to different soil types. Choose a sunny site or part shade in regions with hot summers. In spring, plant nursery plugs on 8-inch spacing to quickly fill in an area.

Care & Problems—Plants are easy to care for, requiring only annual fertilizing. Easily propagate by dividing clumps into small pieces in spring or fall. Plants have minimal problems.

Hardiness—Zones 4 to 10

Color(s)—Tiny green and bronze leaves, yellow flowers

Peak Season—Summer

Mature Size (H x W)—3 in. x 12 in.

Water Needs—Medium. Plants require regular watering.

BUGLEWEED
Ajuga reptans

Why It's Special—Bugleweed's beautiful intense blue flowers borne on 6-inch spikes make it a great choice for a groundcover. Its glossy leaves are a combination of maroon, bronze, and green. It can be used as a lawn substitute in the more challenging areas of your yard and is deer resistant. 'Burgundy Glow' has variegated foliage with deep red and pink splotches. 'Black Scallop' features the darkest foliage and rich blue blossoms.

How to Plant & Grow—Plants grow in full sun to part shade and handle all types of soils. In spring, purchase nursery plants, or propagate by planting runners or dividing clumps once blossoms have faded in early summer.

Care & Problems—Fertilize in spring or late summer. If plants form too thick of a mat, rot can be a problem but bugleweed is generally trouble-free.

Hardiness—Zones 3 to 8

Color(s)—Blue flower spikes, bronze or green leaves

Peak Season—Spring to early summer

Mature Size (H x W)—3 in. x 12 to 18 in.

Water Needs—Low. Water once a week or more often during drought.

CREEPING JENNY
Lysimachia nummularia

Why It's Special—Creeping Jenny is an herbaceous perennial with many attractive uses: It naturalizes the edges of water features, trails over rock garden walls, and works well in hanging baskets and containers. It softens the borders of pathways and will tolerate light foot traffic. While it's primarily grown for its glossy foliage, the yellow flowers really brighten up the garden in early summer. 'Aurea' has golden to lime green leaves. 'Goldilocks' has shiny chartreuse foliage.

How to Plant & Grow—Creeping Jenny does well in part shade to full sun, provided it receives some afternoon shade. It adapts to all soils but prefers moist growing conditions. To establish, space plants about 12 inches apart.

Care & Problems—Plants do not require deadheading or pruning but can be very aggressive, forming a thick mat of roots and crowns. Avoid planting in areas adjacent to lawns or you'll have a nightmare on your hands. Do not fertilize!

Hardiness—Zones 3 to 8

Color(s)—Chartreuse foliage, yellow flowers

Peak Season—May to June

Mature Size (H x W)—1 to 2 in. x as permitted

Water Needs—Medium. Water regularly.

HARDY ICE PLANT

Delosperma spp.

Why It's Special—Hardy ice plant is frequently seen growing along coastal cliffs, where its tough nature is impressive. The evergreen, succulent gray-green foliage forms a dense mat, making it a good choice for controlling erosion. The vibrant pink flowers have a long bloom period and the plant is drought tolerant once it becomes established. The best uses for hardy ice plant include rock gardens, rocky slopes, and near the seashore where it can handle salt spray. *Delosperma cooperi*, with its hot pink flowers, and *D. nubigenum*, which has bright yellow blooms, are both hardy to zone 5.

How to Plant & Grow—This plant grows best in full sun and, although it prefers rocky, well-drained soil, it tolerates all soil types. Plant in spring and space plants 1 foot apart.

Care & Problems—Plants need little care and have few problems.

Hardiness—Zones 5 to 10

Color(s)—Deep purple-pink, yellow

Peak Season—Summer

Mature Size (H x W)—3 in. x 12 to 18 in.

Water Needs—Low. Water regularly its first year to allow a strong root system to develop.

HARDY VERBENA

Verbena canadensis

Why It's Special—Despite its name, hardy verbena won't grow in many inland regions but it has desirable attributes that make it a must for warmer gardens. It has attractive, evergreen leaves and fragrant purple flowers that have a long bloom period and are butterfly magnets. It's drought tolerant once it has become established. The popular 'Homestead Purple' and 'Apple Blossom', with pale pink petals and deep pink centers, are excellent choices.

How to Plant & Grow—Plant bedding plants in the spring in full sun. To establish as a groundcover, space plants 2 to 3 feet apart, or closer to fill in more quickly.

Care & Problems—Mulch to conserve soil moisture and impede weed growth. Fertilize in mid- to late spring. Trim plants as needed to keep tidy. Plants can be susceptible to powdery mildew.

Hardiness—Zones 7 to 9

Color(s)—Purple

Peak Season—Summer through fall

Mature Size (H x W)—6 to 8 in. x 18 to 24 in.

Water Needs—Low to medium. Water well during its first year so plants form a strong root system.

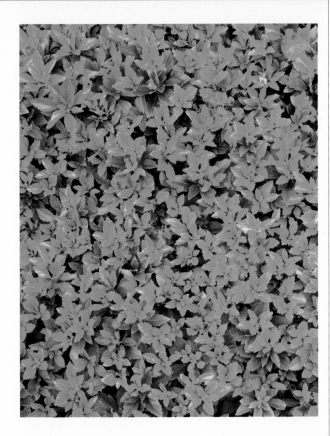

JAPANESE SPURGE
Pachysandra terminalis

Why It's Special—This evergreen plant has glossy, serrated leaves and white, non-showy flowers in spring. Spreading by rhizomes, it is hardy and easy to grow. The plants are ideal for shady areas, particularly underneath trees where little will grow. It works well for erosion control and fire-wise landscaping. 'Green Carpet' and 'Green Sheen' have waxy leaves. Slower-growing 'Variegata' ('Silver Edge') has mottled foliage that provides attractive accents in shade and is hardy to zone 3.

How to Plant & Grow—In spring, plant in full to part shade in slightly acidic soil. Space plants 2 to 3 feet apart.

Care & Problems—Mulch to conserve moisture and impede weeds. Fertilize each spring. Plants are easy to propagate by division in spring or by cuttings in early summer. Slugs may cause damage. Deer and rabbits leave it alone.

Hardiness—Zone 4

Color(s)—Green foliage, small white flowers

Peak Season—Spring and summer

Mature Size (H x W)—6 to 10 in. x 12 to 18 in.

Water Needs—Medium. Water regularly throughout the season to help plants establish strong root systems.

KINNIKINNICK
Arctostaphylos uva-ursi

Why It's Special—Also known as common bearberry, this native has shiny, evergreen leaves and pink, bell-shaped flowers in late spring. The bright red fruits, which persist from late summer through winter, attract birds. It has a prostrate growth habit, is used for erosion control as well as fire-wise landscaping, and provides year-round interest. Generally slow-growing, 'Vancouver Jade' is a more vigorous cultivar with bronze-colored leaves in fall. 'Massachusetts' has red-gold autumn foliage.

How to Plant & Grow—Kinnikinnick prefers acidic soil in full sun to part shade. Plant anytime, spacing 5 feet apart or closer to more quickly fill in an area. Mulch to control weeds under plants while they are becoming established.

Care & Problems—Plants are slow to establish and difficult to transplant although they can be propagated by cuttings. Do not fertilize. Plants are low maintenance, with minimal insect or disease problems.

Hardiness—Zones 2 to 6

Color(s)—Pink flowers, red fruit

Peak Season—Spring and summer

Mature Size (H x W)—½ to 1 ft. x 1 to 3 ft.

Water Needs—Low to medium. Water well until established, then water sparingly.

LILY-OF-THE-VALLEY
Convallaria majalis

Why It's Special—This delightful flowering plant is native to North America. The plants have fragrant, bell-shaped flowers that hang downward from arching stalks. They naturalize well in woodland gardens and around shrubs. The flowers look enchanting in floral arrangements. It can be invasive, spreading by rhizomes, but grows well under trees and other difficult locations. 'Flore Pleno' features double white flowers, 'Prolificans' has profuse clusters of white bells, and 'Rosea' has unusual, dainty pink blossoms.

How to Plant & Grow—In spring, select a location in full to part shade where they'll have room to spread. Plants prefer moist but well-draining soil although they tolerate tough soil conditions. Space 2 to 3 feet apart.

Care & Problems—Mulch to impede weeds while plants establish. Feed with balanced fertilizer after blooming. Propagate by division. Pests are rare. Plants are rabbit and deer resistant. Note: All plant parts are toxic.

Hardiness—Zones 3 to 8

Color(s)—White, pink

Peak Season—May

Mature Size (H x W)—6 to 12 in. x 18 to 24 in.

Water Needs—Low to medium. Water regularly to establish a strong root system.

ST. JOHN'S WORT
Hypericum calycinum

Why It's Special—While St. John's wort has an exotic appearance with its showy yellow flowers and lush foliage, it's actually hardy and low maintenance. Plants do well in rock gardens and under shade trees, and they naturalize well in their surroundings. They are often used to control erosion on slopes. Plants are also referred to as Aaron's beard. 'Brigadoon' has chartreuse and gold foliage with smaller golden flowers and tolerates heat well.

How to Plant & Grow—Plant in spring or fall in full sun to part shade. It tolerates all types of soil as long as it drains well. Space 18 inches apart.

Care & Problems—The foliage dies to the ground in regions with cold winters. St. John's wort can become aggressive if conditions are optimal. Prune back old growth in late winter. They have a minimal amount of insect or disease problems. Do not fertilize!

Hardiness—Zones 5 to 9

Color(s)—Bright yellow

Peak Season—July to August

Mature Size (H x W)—1 to 1½ ft. x 1½ to 2 ft.

Water Needs—Medium. Established plants are drought tolerant.

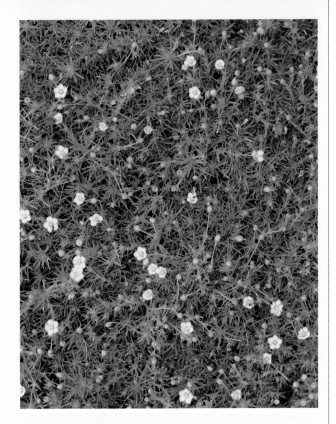

SCOTCH MOSS
Sagina subulata

Why It's Special—This evergreen perennial works beautifully in rock or alpine gardens, along pathways, and between steppingstones. It forms a soft, dense mat that tolerates a moderate amount of foot traffic. Scotch moss provides a soothing appearance in Zen gardens, is low maintenance, and deer resistant. It blooms in late spring. 'Aurea' has bright chartreuse foliage.

How to Plant & Grow—Purchase nursery plants in spring. They will grow in part to full shade and are not particular about soil type as long as it has good drainage. If soil is too wet, the moss will rot. Space plants 6 to 8 inches apart.

Care & Problems—To propagate, divide clumps in early spring. Fertilize with fish emulsion in spring and summer. No deadheading or pruning is necessary. Slugs or cutworms can be a problem.

Hardiness—Zones 4 to 8

Color(s)—Chartreuse to yellow foliage with small white flowers

Peak Season—Spring

Mature Size (H x W)—1 to 2 in. x 12 in.

Water Needs—Medium. Water regularly in spring and increase watering during intense heat or droughts.

SNOW-IN-SUMMER
Cerastium tomentosum

Why It's Special—A member of the Carnation family, snow-in-summer has attractive gray foliage and showy white flowers. Plants work well in rock gardens, spilling over rock walls, over bulb plantings and where they can naturalize. While this plant is an herbaceous perennial, they are short-lived. 'Silver Carpet' has frosty-looking foliage, and both 'Columnae' and 'YoYo' have compact growth.

How to Plant & Grow—Plant in spring in a sunny location. They prefer dry soil, but will adapt to most soil types. Space them 9 to 12 inches apart.

Care & Problems—Snow-in-summer spreads by runners. After the late spring/early summer bloom period, trim or mow foliage on a high setting to tidy the plants and encourage new growth. Divide plants in spring or fall. They have minimal pest or disease problems and are deer and rabbit resistant.

Hardiness—Zones 3 to 7

Color(s)—Silver foliage with white blossoms

Peak Season—Spring

Mature Size (H x W)—6 to 12 in. x 24 to 36 in.

Water Needs—Low. Plants become drought tolerant once established.

SWEET WOODRUFF
Galium odoratum

Why It's Special—With its carpet of green foliage and dainty white flower clusters, sweet woodruff is perfect for growing under rhododendrons, roses, and other shrubs and perennials. It quickly spreads by creeping roots, although it will self-sow. This plant is an herb, with fragrant leaves and blossoms. Its palmate leaves can be dried to make May wine and also for sachets and potpourri. It will grow under trees, is attractive in rock gardens or when tucked into rock walls, and is a good addition to shady borders.

How to Plant & Grow—Sweet woodruff thrives in part to full shade and prefers moist soil. Plant in spring and space plants 8 to 12 inches apart.

Care & Problems—Even though this plant is low-maintenance, it can become aggressive when grown under ideal conditions. It does not have insect or disease problems. No need to fertilize.

Hardiness—Zones 4 to 8

Color(s)—Green foliage with tiny white blossoms

Peak Season—April to May

Mature Size (H x W)—6 to 8 in. x 18 to 24 in.

Water Needs—Medium. Water regularly, especially in the heat of summer.

THYME
Thymus spp.

Why It's Special—Several species make excellent groundcovers. Woolly thyme (*Thymus praecox arcticus*) has soft, fuzzy, gray-green leaves but rarely blooms. 'Hall's' woolly thyme has greener leaves and profuse pink blossoms. Creeping thyme (*T. serpyllum* and *praecox* 'Coccineus') features more succulent leaves and deep pink flowers. 'Highland Cream' has attractive variegated leaves. A slow-growing thyme, petite 'Elfin' has pink flowers and works well between steppingstones. Caraway thyme (*T. herba-barona*) is a fast-grower with rosy flowers and the added bonus of a caraway scent. All are easy to grow, deer resistant, evergreen, and tolerate foot traffic.

How to Plant & Grow—Plant in the spring in full sun to part shade. It grows in most soil types with good drainage. Plant 12 inches apart.

Care & Problems—Trim off winter damage in early spring. Moist soil can cause root rot; plants are otherwise trouble-free.

Hardiness—Zones 4 to 10

Color(s)—White to pink flowers, green and silvery gray foliage

Peak Season—Late spring, summer

Mature Size (H x W)—3 in. x 12 to 24 in.

Water Needs—Low. Water until well-established, then decrease.

JANUARY

- Take a survey of your evergreen groundcovers to see how they are faring in the winter weather. Make notes on where they are thin and could use a few more new plants in spring.

- Browse the catalogs for new groundcovers to try out.

- Apply a commercial deer repellant to evergreen groundcovers being browsed by deer. If your plants are being heavily browsed, surround the area with deer fencing. Secure the netting *firmly* to the ground. Hungry deer can crawl under fencing if they are desperate enough.

FEBRUARY

- If your area is snow-free, visit some local public gardens to see how groundcovers are used in the garden for winter interest. Make notes of those that have a good winter appearance.

- If you are planning a large groundcover project for the year, check with your local nursery about what stock they will be getting in. Order ahead if you can.

- West of the Cascades, begin looking for the early spring bulbs you planted among the groundcovers. This should reassure you that spring is indeed coming.

- Trim back winter- and deer-damaged groundcovers as you see damage. If you have die-back of individual stems or branches in a clump, check the branches for bark damage caused by mice or voles gnawing on the bark. This is particularly prevalent during long, snowy winters when the critters can't find other food sources. Trim out dead branches and thin out dense undergrowth to take away their hiding places.

MARCH

- West of the Cascades, you can begin planting new groundcovers. Make sure the soil is dry enough to work by squeezing a handful together and then poking it; it is workable if the ball falls apart easily. Plant groundcovers in a diamond-shaped pattern so they are evenly spaced across the bed.

- If you order groundcovers from mail order sources, request delivery later in the month when the ground is more likely to be ready to work. The plants often come as small plugs just a couple of inches wide. Plant them immediately or heel them into an empty garden bed until you are ready to plant.

- Remove any remaining winter debris and renew mulches. If the weather is dry, water your plantings.

- Start patrolling for early weeds.

- Fertilize groundcovers with a slow-release, 10-10-10 organic fertilizer late in the month.

APRIL

- This is planting month throughout the region. If you are doing a big project, get to the nursery early for the best selection.

- Pay particular attention to weeding this month. Removing weeds now will save you hours of work later in summer. If your groundcovers are thin, apply mulch on the bare spots to keep them from sprouting.

MAY

- This month is a good time to divide established groundcovers either to fill in thin spots or plant a new bed. Incorporate some compost in the new bed then dig fist-sized clumps with vigorously growing shoots and replant them immediately. Set them at the same depth they were originally planted.

- Check out the nurseries for their last shipments of the season. You never know what you might find.

- East of the Cascades, begin a regular watering schedule, especially if you have new or young groundcover plantings. Add a 2- to 3-inch layer of mulch in thin spots to slow down water loss and keep weeds at bay.

- If groundcovers are getting out of bounds, trim them back this month by edging the bed with a sharp shovel. Dig a 3-inch-deep trench along the edge to expose roots to the air and slow them down. Vigorous growers like bishop's weed (*Aegopodium podagraria*) and sweet woodruff (*Galium odoratum*) spread by underground roots. You may need to install a 6-inch-wide wood or plastic edging around a bed to control them.

- Trim back the foliage of spring-flowering groundcovers after they finish blooming to encourage new growth and keep them bushy.

JUNE

- Finish up any dividing and planting before mid-month when the dry summer season will start.

- Early spring weeds will be setting seed; pull them so they don't spread in your groundcover beds.

JULY

- Make sure you irrigate new plantings regularly as the hot season arrives.

- Shear down the dead flower stalks of early summer bloomers, like bugleweed, so they stay neat.

- Give scraggly growers a trim to keep them tidy. Dig out plantings that are getting out of bounds.

- At the end of the month, give creeping thymes a serious reshaping and clean out debris from around and under the leaf mats.

AUGUST

- This is a good time to assess what is, and is not, working in the garden so you can plan your fall renovation projects.

- Hot weather will take a toll on many plants. Trim off tattered leaves and keep the moderate to high water-users hydrated, especially young plantings. Drought-tolerant groundcovers appreciate a good soaking every two to three weeks to keep them looking good.

SEPTEMBER

- The plant sales will start this month, so visit your local nurseries to see what you can find.

- Keep irrigating until the fall's first soaking rain shows up.

- As the weather cools, look out for new crops of weeds to pop up and remove them as soon as they appear.

- Early fall is a good time to apply finished compost to garden beds in preparation for the new crop of fall leaves. Apply an inch of compost to groundcover beds and rake it in gently.

OCTOBER

- Fall leaves and needles will be coming down this month. Lay bird netting over your groundcovers before the leaves fall. After the leaves and pine needles have come down, simply pick up the netting with its load and dump it in the compost pile. Rake groundcovers gently to settle smaller conifer needles from spruce and fir to the soil surface.

- Visit public gardens and parks to look for groundcovers with fall interest. Think about where you can incorporate them into your garden.

- Apply deer repellent to evergreen groundcovers to protect them from deer and elk. Apply once a month through the winter when the ground is snow-free. Consider setting up deer fencing if your groundcovers were heavily browsed last winter.

NOVEMBER

- Many of the evergreen groundcovers begin to show off their foliage as deciduous plants go dormant for the winter. These will hold interest in the garden through the winter.

- West of the Cascades, visit some of the Chinese and Japanese gardens in your area to see how they use moss as a groundcover. Maybe that moss-infested patch of lawn could become your new moss garden.

DECEMBER

- Remove the last of the fall leaves from groundcover beds and compost them.

- Catch up on your journal notes before the holidays get too busy. Note what worked and what you want to change next year.

- Make your Christmas list. Gift cards from your favorite nursery or cash for plants will be easy for non-gardeners in the family to provide.

LAWN & ORNAMENTAL GRASSES
for the Northwest

There will always be a place for lawns in Northwest gardens, even if they do take a lot of water, fertilizer, and care. We need soft, level places for our kids and pets to play. Lawns can cool summer temperatures around a house and provide a fire break from wind-driven wildfires. Curved patches of lawn serve to draw you through a garden and frame a particularly lovely border of mixed perennials.

TURF CHOICES FOR THE NORTHWEST

The turfgrasses you select for your lawn will depend heavily on which side of the Cascades you live on. West of the Cascades and in southwestern British Columbia and Vancouver Island, turf-type perennial ryegrass, bentgrass, and fine fescues (Chewings, red creeping, sheep, and hard fescues) do well in the cooler and wetter conditions there. East of the Cascades and in southern interior British Columbia, Kentucky bluegrass, fine fescues, and turf-type tall fescues are more adapted to the region's cold winters and hot summers. All of these are cool-season grasses, which means they green up early in the spring and stay green after the fall frosts. Warm-season grasses, like buffalograss and blue grama grass, don't green up until late May and go dormant after the first frosts.

Lawn seed is sold as a blend of several turfgrass varieties, drawing on the best characteristics of each variety for a stronger, more durable lawn. There are dozens of cultivars of each variety, so your final choice will depend on your needs and location. Read the bag label and always buy certified, weed-free seed. Perennial ryegrass tolerates heavy traffic use better than Kentucky bluegrass and fine fescues. The fine fescues are generally more tolerant of partial shade than Kentucky bluegrass and perennial ryegrass. No turf will do well in heavy shade, so consider groundcovers or other alternatives for these areas. Below is a summary of the characteristics of Northwest turfgrasses.

ESTABLISHING A LAWN

A new lawn site should be weed free, well drained, and as smooth as possible. Weed-free organic matter should be worked into the top 6 to 8 inches of the soil, then carefully leveled and packed with a roller. Water the area for two weeks to germinate weed seed at the soil surface. Grass seed should then be broadcast with a spreader in two perpendicular directions, then very lightly raked to cover the seed with a quarter inch of soil. Apply a thin mulch and roll again to create good soil contact. Water lightly twice a day until the seed germinates, and again every day until the first mowing. Sod can be laid in a brick pattern on the prepared soil, rolled, and then watered daily for two weeks to allow the roots to establish. The best time to seed on either side of the Cascades is in May or September to avoid summer heat.

To renovate established lawns, rake out the thin, existing turf, apply 1 inch of compost, and then overseed with new seed. Apply a light mulch and roll the lawn. Water daily until the new lawn emerges and then frequently until the first mowing.

CHARACTERISTICS OF NORTHWEST TURFGRASSES

TURF TYPE	EAST/WEST	DROUGHT TOLERANT	LEAF TEXTURE	MOW HEIGHT (inches)	SUN/SHADE	NITROGEN NEEDS
Kentucky bluegrass	East	No	Medium	1½–2½	Sun	High
Fine fescues	Both	Yes	Fine, narrow	1½–2½	Both	Low
Perennial ryegrass	West	No	Medium	1½–2½	Sun	High
Turf-type tall fescues	East	Yes	Fine	2½–3	Sun	High
Colonial bentgrass	West	No	Very fine	½–¾	Both	Low
Buffalograss	East	Yes	Medium	2–3	Sun	Low
Blue grama	East	Yes	Fine	Once a year	Sun	Low

Set out a straight-sided container in the approximate middle of the area your sprinkler covers. (A short, straight-sided drinking glass works well for this.) Then let the sprinkler run for fifteen minutes. Use a ruler or measuring tape to measure the amount of water in the cup. You'll now know how much water the sprinkler puts out in fifteen minutes.

Rain sensors detect when a prescribed amount of rain has fallen and can be programmed to shut your automatic sprinkler system off, avoiding redundant watering. Other electronic systems pick up broadcasting weather forecasting information and adjust to the automated system that takes the weather into account.

MAINTAINING A LAWN

A healthy lawn needs proper mowing, the right amount of water and fertilizer, and proper weeding. In general, if you take care of the first three, you won't have to worry about the weeding.

Mowing height depends on the turf type. See the table in this chapter for recommended heights for Northwest grass varieties. Lawns that are cut too short are more susceptible to weed invasions and water loss. In the heat of the summer, it's better to cut lawns a little taller to provide shade for the soil and to reduce water loss.

Most lawns, except the most drought-tolerant fescues, require at least an inch of water a week. In July and August they need an inch-and-a-half, especially east of the Cascades. It is better to water longer and do it less often than to water briefly every day. Watering for longer periods allows the water to soak down into the root zone, which forces the roots to grow deep. To measure how much water your sprinkler system puts out, set a series of empty, shallow tuna or cat food cans around the lawn and turn the sprinklers on for fifteen minutes. Measure the water in the cans. This will tell you how many fifteen-minute periods it will take in a week to apply an inch of water.

The three most important times to fertilize a lawn are in the early spring, early September,

and at the beginning of November. Secondary applications can be made around the end of May and early July but aren't necessary. This schedule provides the lawn with the nutrients it needs when it is growing the fastest or getting ready for winter.

A good fertilization program will reduce the development of weeds, mosses, and certain diseases. Before establishing your program, get a soil test of your lawn to accurately determine how much and what types of nutrients are needed. The best fertilizers to use are slow-release organics that release their nutrients gradually over a couple of months. This gives the lawn the food it needs without forcing it into wild growth that the roots can't support.

Lawn fertilizers have been implicated as a key source of non-point water pollution in the region's rivers and lakes, Puget Sound, Straits of Juan de Fuca, and the Georgia Straits. Nitrogen and phosphorus increase the growth of algae and reduce dissolved oxygen levels in the water, which negatively affects marine life. As of January 1, 2013, Washington homeowners can no longer buy lawn fertilizers containing phosphorus for use on established turf. This means the bag of lawn fertilizer you buy in Washington will have a zero as the second number on the listed nutrient analysis. Fertilizers containing phosphorus can still be used on *new* turf installations and for all other garden uses. The only exception for its use on established turf is if a soil test performed in the last three years indicates a need for phosphorus. Fortunately, the region's soils naturally contain plenty of phosphorus.

Proper watering, fertilization, and mowing will reduce weed problems and the need for herbicides by creating a thick turf that crowds out weeds. If weeds do get established, properly identify them before starting a control program. Initially, try removing small infestations by hand or by spot-spraying where they occur. Avoid using weed and feed products that apply a herbicide with the fertilizer when you only have a few patches of weeds; overuse of herbicides only leads to more pollution. If you have to apply a herbicide for a particularly bad problem, do it before the weeds go to seed and on a day when temperatures are below 80 degrees Fahrenheit and the wind is still. Read and follow label directions. Organic herbicides on the market are not as effective as the conventional herbicides. Therefore, if you want to avoid using harsh herbicides, make sure to water, feed, and mow your turf properly to keep it healthy.

Regular core aeration with a hollow-core aerator opens the soil and allows air, water, and fertilizer to reach the grass roots. The machines can be rented from equipment rental places or you can hire someone to do it. Core aerating also helps remove thatch, thus reducing the need for the de-thatching process that can tear up sod. It is best done in the early spring just as the lawn comes out of dormancy or in the fall.

DEALING WITH MOSS

Moss in Northwest lawns is a given, especially in areas that receive a lot of rain. Moss takes over when lawns are weakened, which can be caused by several factors: too much shade, improper watering and fertilization, oversaturation, heavy compacting, or high acid levels. The only way to eliminate moss completely is to correct these conditions, which can be difficult. Make sure you are using a shade-tolerant type of grass, and thin the branches of shrubs and trees above the area to increase light levels. Aerate mossy areas to open the soil to air and water. Don't overwater the lawn, and be sure to provide enough fertilizer. When even these changes don't eliminate the moss, give in to nature and turn the area into a moss garden. Check out the chapter on groundcovers for suggestions.

Rent a core aerator and aerate the lawn once yearly in the fall to keep the soil from becoming compacted.

To eliminate moss, raise the soil pH by adding lime, prune the tree branches so that more light reaches the ground, and rake compost into the area.

USING ORNAMENTAL GRASSES IN THE GARDEN

We enjoy most plants in the garden because the intermingling of their flowers, shape, texture, and/or size creates a pleasant place to relax or enjoy nature. Ornamental grasses, on the other hand, capture the wind and sunlight and in doing so add movement to the garden. The wispy grass leaves and seedheads easily catch any air movement in the garden and sway gently back and forth. The shiny leaf blades reflect sunlight in a pattern influenced by air movement. The thin leaf blades also send a blaze of color through the garden when they are backlit by sun.

Ornamental grasses also add a lot of fall and winter interest to the garden. Many grasses turn shades of gold, red, tan, and yellow in the fall, completely changing the look of the garden. This color hangs on well into the fall and then fades to tan into the winter, adding interest to the otherwise dormant winter garden. Most grasses will stand up through all but the heaviest snows.

Ornamental grasses add winter interest to Ferris Perennial Gardens in Manito Park, Spokane, Washington.

Tall grasses are best at the back of borders and make neat hedges to divide spaces and block out unwanted views. Smaller, low-growing grasses can be used to soften the edges of planting beds and along walkways. Some of them can add an upright note to a container planting.

GROWING ORNAMENTAL GRASSES

There are two general types of ornamental grasses; cool-season and warm-season growers. Cool-season grasses like blue moor grass (*Sesleria caerulea*) and blue oat grass (*Helictotrichon sempervirens*) sprout in the early spring and are blooming by early summer. Warm-season grasses like Japanese forest grass (*Hakonechloa macra*) and feather reed grass (*Calamagrostis* × *acutiflora*) need warm soil to begin growing and generally don't sprout until late May. They send up their flowers in the late summer.

Ornamental grasses can grow in a wide range of sunlight or light shade and usually need a medium amount of water through the growing season. Most need a light fertilization in the spring with a balanced organic fertilizer.

Because ornamental grasses are kept for their winter interest, the best time to trim them down and divide them is in the early spring. Except for the evergreen grasses like blue oat grass and the ornamental blue fescue (*Festuca glauca*), grass clumps can be cut back to 6 inches tall. Gather the clump together and tie it up with a string. Then use clippers to cut it off. This makes a very neat, tidy package for cleanup. Most ornamental grasses can be dug up with a shovel and the clumps divided and replanted.

Strategically placed patches of lawn and ornamental grasses can add a lot of useful features and texture to a garden. Lawns can be used to frame garden beds and provide paths through the garden as well as provide a place to sit or for children and pets to play. Ornamental grasses, on the other hand, pick up light and the wind in ways most other plants can't and bring in light and motion to the garden. Experiment with them and enjoy the results of your efforts!

BENTGRASS
Agrostis spp.

Why It's Special—Bentgrass is a turfgrass widely grown throughout North America and is recommended for lawns west of the mountains. It has a very fine texture and usually spreads through rhizomes. Bentgrass is used for home lawns, golf course grounds, and athletic fields. Colonial bentgrass (*Agrostis capillaris*) grows well in coastal areas and prefers cool, humid locations. It's considered fairly high maintenance due to its need for regular watering and fertilizer as well as de-thatching. 'Highland' (*A. castellana*) is more tolerant of heat. Native bentgrass (*A. pallens*) is a good choice for naturalized lawns, can be cut short, and is drought tolerant; it tolerates foot traffic and grows thickly, which keeps weed growth to a minimum.

How to Plant & Grow—Bentgrass is a cool-season grass planted from seed in fall or spring. It grows in full sun to part shade.

Care & Problems—Mow at ⅓ to ¾ inch in height. Refer to sections on "Establishing a Lawn" and "Maintaining a Lawn" for more care information. It's susceptible to turfgrass diseases.

Texture—Fine

Peak Season—Entire growing season

Water Needs—Water regularly.

BLUE FESCUE
Festuca glauca

Why It's Special—Blue fescue is an ornamental grass prized for its finely textured, blue-gray foliage and small mounding habit. In late spring to early summer, greenish purple inflorescences on 8-inch stems appear, which mature into light gold seedheads. They work well as a groundcover, in rock gardens, and in containers. 'Elijah Blue' is one of the most popular varieties because of its hardiness and heat tolerance.

How to Plant & Grow—Plant in full sun to part shade, although full sun yields the most striking foliage color. It is not particular about soil type. If growing as a groundcover, space 10 inches apart.

Care & Problems—Plants are short-lived and tend to die out in the center, so replace them every few years. If the foliage turns brown during drought conditions, trim it back. Lightly trim in early spring. No fertilizer is necessary.

Hardiness—Zones 4 to 8

Texture—Medium

Peak Season—June to July

Mature Size (H x W)—9 to 12 in. x 12 to 18 in.

Water Needs—Blue fescue is drought tolerant once established.

BLUE GRAMA GRASS
Bouteloua gracilis

Why It's Special—Blue grama grass is a versatile ornamental grass; use it as a groundcover, in rock gardens or naturalized areas, in mass plantings, or even as a lawn since it tolerates regular mowing. Its blue-gray foliage changes to golden hues in autumn. It has horizontal purple inflorescences on 6- to 8-inch stems during summer and seed spikes that attract birds. 'Blonde Ambition' has golden flowers, is hardy to zone 4, and grows up to 3 feet.

How to Plant & Grow—Easy to grow from seed or nursery plants, blue grama grass prefers full sun although it tolerates part shade as well. It grows in any soil type as long as it is well drained.

Care & Problems—Trim to the ground in late winter before new growth starts. Avoid fertilizing as this causes weak growth. They have minimal insect or disease problems.

Hardiness—Zones 3 to 10

Texture—Medium

Peak Season—June to August

Mature Size (H x W)—9 to 36 in. x 18 to 24 in.

Water Needs—Plants become drought tolerant once established.

BLUE MOOR GRASS

Sesleria caerulea

Why It's Special—Blue moor grass features twisting foliage that is blue on one side and green on the other. A clump-forming ornamental grass, it is native to Europe where it grows on the moors. The plant produces purple flower spikes in spring to early summer that mature into eye-catching, silvery inflorescences as the season progresses. Grow it as a groundcover, in perennial borders or rock gardens, or for edging around steppingstones. It grows particularly well in coastal regions and is deer resistant.

How to Plant & Grow—Plant blue moor grass in spring or fall in full sun to part shade; in areas with hot summers, choose a location that gets afternoon shade. Space plants 1 to 2 feet apart.

Care & Problems—It has minimal problems, doesn't need fertilizing, and is low maintenance.

Hardiness—Zones 5 to 8

Texture—Medium

Peak Season—March to June

Mature Size (H x W)—6 to 12 in. x 9 to 12 in.

Water Needs—Water regularly until plants are well established; after that, they tolerate drought.

BLUE OAT GRASS

Helictotrichon sempervirens

Why It's Special—Blue oat grass has appealing blue foliage and blue-brown flower spikes that turn golden in fall. An ornamental grass with a clumping habit, it does well in coastal gardens and is deer resistant. Plant them in rock gardens, as a taller groundcover, and in foundation plantings. It makes a stunning specimen when grown next to plants with chartreuse or purple foliage. 'Sapphire' (or 'Saphirsprudel') has been bred for a more intensely blue foliage, increased disease resistance, and heat tolerance.

How to Plant & Grow—Blue oat grass thrives in full sun but tolerates partial shade. It has better foliage color when grown in average soils that are on the dry side. Plant in spring or fall.

Care & Problems—They are low maintenance and have minimal insect or disease problems. Cut back the foliage in late winter before new growth begins. No fertilizing is necessary.

Hardiness—Zones 4 to 8

Texture—Coarse

Peak Season—June

Mature Size (H x W)—2 to 3 ft. x 2 to 2½ ft.

Water Needs—Plants are drought tolerant once they establish.

BUFFALOGRASS

Buchloe dactyloides

Why It's Special—Buffalograss is a prairie grass native to the North American plains. It spreads by stolons and is often used for erosion control because of its strong root system. It can be grown as a mowed turfgrass or unmowed, naturalized grass that grows between 4 and 6 inches tall. Seeded cultivars include 'Sharp's Improved', 'Cody', and 'Legacy' and are favored for their ability to stay greener longer, with less water than turfgrasses like 'Kentucky Blue'.

How to Plant & Grow—Plant in full sun to part shade. Start buffalograss by seed, or from sod or plugs in spring to midsummer. It's not picky about soil. Refer to the section on "Establishing a Lawn" for more information.

Care & Problems—It rarely needs to be fertilized and is low maintenance. Mow weekly at 2 inches. It doesn't tolerate much foot traffic and can become invasive.

Hardiness—Zones 3 to 9

Texture—Fine

Peak Season—Entire growing season

Mature Size (H x W)—3 to 6 in. x 6 in.

Water Needs—Buffalograss is very drought tolerant once sod establishes; water every one to two weeks.

FEATHER GRASS

Stipa spp.

Why It's Special—Feather grass is an evergreen, grasslike plant with soft stems topped by feathery, golden panicles. Locate where the sunlight highlights the attractive foliage. Feather grass does well in coastal gardens. Plant as a specimen or near the back of borders, preferably against dark backgrounds for good contrast. Grow as an annual in colder zones. Giant feather grass (*Stipa gigantea*) has 2- to 3-foot-tall clumps and up to 7-foot-tall flowering stems; Mexican feather grass (*S. tenuissima* or *Nasella tenuissima*) grows 1 to 2 feet tall. New Zealand wind grass (*S. arundinacea*) is hardy in zones 8 to 10, grows 1 to 2 feet tall, and features stunning orange-brown fall foliage.

How to Plant & Grow—Plant in spring or fall in full sun to light shade. It prefers rich, well-drained soil.

Care & Problems—Trim back foliage in late winter. No fertilizing is necessary.

Hardiness—Zones 7 to 9

Texture—Medium

Peak Season—Spring to fall

Mature Size (H x W)—Up to 6 ft. x 2 to 3 ft.

Water Needs—Water regularly until plants establish; then they'll tolerate drier conditions.

FEATHER REED GRASS

Calamagrostis × acutiflora

Why It's Special—Feather reed grass is one of the most attractive ornamental grasses you can grow. It has a clean, vertical growth habit and beautiful golden inflorescences from summer through fall. This grass behaves itself because it has sterile seeds. Grow as a vertical accent in your landscape or in a mass planting for impact. They are deer resistant. 'Karl Foerster' blooms early and will grow in moist soil. 'Avalanche' features variegated foliage and also tolerates moist soil. 'Overdam' has variegated foliage and a shorter height of 2½ to 3 feet. 'Eldorado' features gold-and-green foliage and stems.

How to Plant & Grow—Plant in spring or fall in full sun to part shade. This grass does well in average, well-drained, or moist soil.

Care & Problems—Trim clumps back to the ground in late winter before new growth begins. Plants have minimal insect or disease problems and don't require fertilizing.

Hardiness—Zones 5 to 9

Texture—Coarse

Peak Season—Late spring through fall

Mature Size (H x W)—3 to 5 ft. x 2 ft.

Water Needs—Water regularly, especially during hot spells.

FINE FESCUE

Festuca spp.

Why It's Special—Fine fescues are ideal for homeowners faced with shady conditions and lack of time for mowing and other lawn maintenance. They blend well with other types of turfgrass. Fescues that grow well in the Northwest are red (*Festuca rubra*), Chewings (*F. rubra* subsp. *commutata*), sheep (*F. ovina*), and hard (*F. longifolia*). They require less fertilization, less watering, and consequently, less frequent mowing. As a bonus, they demonstrate good cold tolerance.

How to Plant & Grow—Plant from seed in fall or spring in all light conditions. Because Chewings, sheep, and hard fescue are bunchgrasses, uniform seeding is important. Refer to the section on "Establishing a Lawn" for more information.

Care & Problems—Mow to 1½ to 2½ inches. They have moderate tolerance to foot traffic. Fescues are susceptible to the fungal disease red thread; look for resistant varieties. Since it only infects older growth, another solution is to apply a nitrogen fertilizer to green up the lawn, making the fungus less noticeable.

Hardiness—Zones 2 to 7

Texture—Depends on variety

Peak Season—Entire growing season

Water Needs—Water deeply once a week.

FOUNTAIN GRASS
Pennisetum alopecuroides

Why It's Special—Fountain grass is a showy ornamental grass with gracefully arching leaves. Bristly flower spikes appear in late summer and mature into brown seedheads that persist into winter. The leaves turn golden in fall. Grow as an accent or grouped for more impact. They are deer resistant. 'Hameln' is more compact at 2 feet tall. 'Red Head' features profuse burgundy inflorescences while 'Moudry' has purplish black flower spikes. Dwarf cultivars include 'Little Bunny' at 12 to 18 inches and 'Piglet' with a height of 18 inches.

How to Plant & Grow—Plant in spring in full sun to part shade, although it flowers more in sunny locations. Fountain grass is easy to grow in average soil and even tolerates moist soil.

Care & Problems—Plants are low maintenance and can become drought tolerant. In late winter, cut foliage to the ground before new growth begins. Propagate by division.

Hardiness—Zones 6 to 9

Texture—Medium

Peak Season—July to February

Mature Size (H x W)—2½ to 5 ft. x 2½ to 5 ft.

Water Needs—Water until plants establish; then only occasionally.

JAPANESE BLOOD GRASS
Imperata cylindrica

Why It's Special—Japanese blood grass is a low-growing, colorful ornamental grass. The foliage is bright green with blood-red tips in spring, completely turning a lovely burgundy color by fall, and coppery in winter. Consider planting multiples in a border, rock garden, or planter. Plants are deer resistant. Since the species has been labeled a noxious weed, it is not available at nurseries. Try 'Rubra', also known as var. *koenigii* 'Red Baron', which is much better behaved.

How to Plant & Grow—While plants grow in full sun to part shade, choose full sun for the best foliage coloration. They adapt to different soil types that are moist but well drained.

Care & Problems—Plants go dormant in winter. Cut back foliage in late winter or early spring before new growth emerges. They have minimal pest or disease problems.

Hardiness—Zones 5 to 9

Texture—Medium

Peak Season—Entire growing season

Mature Size (H x W)—1 to 1½ ft. x 1 to 1½ ft.

Water Needs—Water regularly but do not overwater.

JAPANESE FOREST GRASS
Hakonechloa macra

Why It's Special—With its delicately arching, variegated leaves, Japanese forest grass is perfect for a shady area in the garden. In midsummer, yellow-green flower spikes of this slow-growing ornamental grass emerge. It makes a delightful addition to woodland gardens, shady borders, Japanese-style gardens, and along the edge of walkways. 'Aureola' has variegated, golden leaves although it's less hardy than the species. 'All Gold' has even brighter color. 'Beni Kaze' foliage turns red in fall; hardy to zone 6. 'Naomi' features burgundy-hued fall foliage. 'Fubuki' has white-and-green variegated leaves.

How to Plant & Grow—Plant in spring or fall in partial shade. Too much sun or shade can affect leaf color. Plants prefer moist, well-drained soil with compost incorporated into it. Mulch the plants.

Care & Problems—Cut back foliage to the ground in late winter before new growth emerges. Propagate by division in spring. No fertilizing is needed.

Hardiness—Zones 5 to 9

Texture—Medium

Peak Season—July to August

Mature Size (H x W)—1 to 3 ft. x 1 to 3 ft.

Water Needs—Water regularly.

KENTUCKY BLUEGRASS
Poa pratensis

Why It's Special—Kentucky bluegrass is the most widely planted turfgrass in the U.S. and Canada. It's prized for its fine texture, appealing color, ability to withstand heavy foot traffic, and longevity. It's a good choice for inland regions that receive more sunshine and warmer temperatures than coastal areas. This grass is typically sold in mixtures containing other grasses. Drought-tolerant varieties include 'Adelphi', 'Banff', 'Baron', and 'Touchdown'.

How to Plant & Grow—Plant in full sun from seed or sod, in spring or fall when moisture levels are high. Refer to sections on "Establishing a Lawn" and "Maintaining a Lawn" for more information.

Care & Problems—Mow regularly at 1½ to 2½ inches. Extended periods of heat and drought cause grass to turn brown but it recovers well when extra moisture is provided. It's susceptible to necrotic ring spot. Other diseases include anthracnose, powdery mildew in shady areas, brown patch, and fairy ring. Pests include sod webworms and European crane fly.

Hardiness—Zones 2 to 7

Texture—Fine

Peak Season—Entire growing season

Water Needs—Water 1 inch per week.

LITTLE BLUESTEM
Schizachyrium scoparium

Why It's Special—Little bluestem is a native grass commonly found in North America and is now grown as an ornamental. The foliage changes from green to reddish gold in fall and the fluffy seedheads are quite showy. Its densely formed root system is helpful for erosion control. They're attractive in native-plant gardens, border plantings, and cottage gardens. The seeds attract birds, and plants are deer resistant. 'Blaze' has bright red fall foliage while 'Blue Heaven' has blue-gray foliage that changes to burgundy-red. 'Standing Ovation' has stronger stems that hold up against winds. 'Carousel' grows to 3 feet and has attractive fall color. 'The Blues' has blue-green stems that turn orange.

How to Plant & Grow—Plant in spring or fall in full sun in average, well-drained soil.

Care & Problems—Plants are low maintenance and have minimal insect or disease problems. Fertilizing is not needed.

Hardiness—Zones 3 to 9

Texture—Medium

Peak Season—August to February

Mature Size (H x W)—2 to 4 ft. x 1½ to 2 ft.

Water Needs—Water only until established.

MAIDEN GRASS
Miscanthus sinensis

Why It's Special—Maiden grass is admired for its dense growth and gracefully arching foliage. This ornamental grass is attractive year-round and can be grown singly, in groupings, as a privacy screen, or next to water features. 'Gracillimus' has long, very fine foliage and silver inflorescences; 6 feet tall. 'Morning Light' features green leaves with white margins, pink flowers; 4 feet tall. 'Purpurascens' is popular with its wide leaves that change from green to red-orange in fall and purple inflorescences; 4 feet tall. 'Zebrinus' is striking for its green leaves with horizontal, cream bands; 5 to 8 feet tall.

How to Plant & Grow—Plant in spring or fall in full sun to part shade in all well-drained soils.

Care & Problems—Propagate by division every few years. They have minimal insect or disease problems. In late winter to early spring, cut back old foliage to 3 inches to encourage new growth.

Hardiness—Zones 5 to 9

Texture—Coarse

Peak Season—August to February

Mature Size (H x W)—3 to 15 ft. x 4 to 6 ft.

Water Needs—Water regularly; plants become drought tolerant once established.

MONDO GRASS

Ophiopogon spp.

Why It's Special—For a bold look, consider mondo grass with its dense, deep green or black foliage. It's easy to grow and deer resistant. They are most effective in groupings, particularly along border edges or walkways, and next to plants with wildly contrasting foliage colors. They're ideal container plants and can be used as groundcovers. Black mondo grass (*Ophiopogon planiscapus*) 'Nigrescens' is prized for its deep purple to black, strappy leaves that grow 6 to 12 inches tall; its pink flower spikes mature into purple berries. Dwarf mondo grass (*O. japonicus*) 'Nana' grows in 2- to 3-inch-tall clumps and features green leaves and white flower spikes; hardy in zones 7 to 8.

How to Plant & Grow—Plant in spring in part to full shade. They prefer moist, rich soil; incorporate compost into the planting bed.

Care & Problems—Slugs can be a problem, but plants are otherwise trouble-free and don't require fertilizing.

Hardiness—Zones 6 to 10

Texture—Fine to medium

Peak Season—June to July

Mature Size (H x W)—2 to 12 in. x 12 in.

Water Needs—Water regularly.

MOOR GRASS

Molinia caerulea

Why It's Special—Moor grass is an easy-to-grow ornamental grass that has narrow, arching foliage. In midsummer, purple flower spikes grow well beyond the clump. Both the spikes and grass blades make a pleasing rustle whenever a breeze blows. The foliage turns orange in fall. The plants are appealing when grown as an accent, especially when surrounded by plants with contrasting darker foliage. 'Variegata' features variegated, yellow-and-white foliage, purple-tinged flower spikes, and grows in 1- to 2½-foot-tall clumps. Tall purple moor grass (*Molinia caerulea* subsp. *arundinacea*) 'Skyracer' has 3-foot-tall foliage that is surpassed by 3- to 4-foot-tall, airy panicles.

How to Plant & Grow—Plants perform best in full sun but tolerate light shade in areas with hot summers. Plant in spring or fall in acidic, well-drained soil. Incorporate compost in the planting bed.

Care & Problems—Plants don't need fertilizing and have minimal insect or disease problems. Foliage disintegrates over the winter.

Hardiness—Zones 5 to 8

Texture—Coarse

Peak Season—July to September

Mature Size (H x W)—2 to 8 ft. x 2 to 4 ft.

Water Needs—Water regularly.

NORTHERN SEA OATS

Chasmanthium latifolium

Why It's Special—For year-round interest, add northern sea oats to your landscape. The bright green, bamboo-like foliage gently rustles in the breeze. In midsummer, chevron-shaped seedheads develop. The foliage turns a bronze color in fall and the seedheads persist into winter; consider leaving them to provide food for wintering birds and to add texture to the garden. They last a long time in floral arrangements. The plants are attractive in sunny borders and woodland gardens and make good specimens.

How to Plant & Grow—Plant in spring or fall in full sun to part shade in moist, well-drained soil.

Care & Problems—Plants are very low maintenance yet perform well year after year. They have no insect or disease problems and don't need fertilizing. Plants may require staking in windy locations. They self-seed easily. Trim back to the ground in late winter before new growth.

Hardiness—Zones 3 to 8

Texture—Medium

Peak Season—August to September

Mature Size (H x W)—2 to 5 ft. x 1 to 2½ ft.

Water Needs—Water regularly but do not overwater.

PEARL MILLET
Pennisetum glaucum

Why It's Special—Native to Africa, pearl or ornamental millet has glorious, deep purple foliage and erect growth. In summer, sturdy flower spikes shoot up from its base. They later become laden with millet seeds, which attract birds to the garden. Use this plant in borders as a stark contrast to perennials with green or chartreuse foliage. The flower spikes make great cut flowers. 'Purple Majesty' is 4 to 5 feet tall. 'Purple Baron' and 'Purple Jester' grow to 3 feet. 'Jade Princess' only reaches 2 feet but features chartreuse leaves and purple flower spikes.

How to Plant & Grow—This plant easily starts from seed indoors a few weeks before the last frost date or you can purchase potted nursery plants. It tolerates many soil conditions.

Care & Problems—Plants can be susceptible to aphids but are otherwise trouble-free and don't require fertilizing.

Hardiness—Zones 9 to 11

Texture—Coarse

Peak Season—Summer

Mature Size (H x W)—2 to 6 ft. x 2 to 6 ft.

Water Needs—Water regularly early in the season but plants are drought tolerant once established.

PERENNIAL RYEGRASS
Lolium perenne

Why It's Special—Perennial ryegrass is commonly used as a turfgrass because it tolerates heavy foot traffic and has an appealing dark green color. The seeds, which germinate quickly, should be mixed with other grasses, typically Kentucky bluegrass. It grows rapidly and fills in quickly, which helps suppress weed growth. This grass is more suited to coastal regions because of their milder temperatures. It is often used for pasture grass and erosion control, and has good resistance to necrotic ring spot disease.

How to Plant & Grow—Perennial ryegrass performs best in full sun but tolerates some shade. Plant seed mixtures in spring or fall, and sod in spring. Refer to sections on "Establishing a Lawn" and "Maintaining a Lawn" for more information.

Care & Problems—Mow at 1½ to 2½ inches. This grass is short-lived, generally for two to three years. It has low tolerance for heat, drought, or heavy shade. Red thread is a fungal disease that commonly afflicts perennial ryegrass.

Hardiness—Zone 5 and above

Texture—Medium

Peak Season—Entire growing season

Water Needs—Water deeply when soil is dry.

PINK MUHLY GRASS
Muhlenbergia capillaris

Why It's Special—Pink muhly grass is native to much of North America and is grown as an ornamental grass. While this clumping plant is attractive during summer, its fall display of fuzzy pink inflorescences is what makes it a standout in the garden. It's ideal for perennial borders, rock gardens, or native plant gardens. This plant attracts beneficial insects and is deer resistant. It's also known as hairawn muhly. Cultivars include 'Pink Flamingoes', 'Regal Mist', and 'White Cloud'.

How to Plant & Grow—Plant in full sun to part shade, although sun is best for optimum color. Plant in groupings for impact. This grass tolerates all soil types as long as they are well drained.

Care & Problems—Trim back old growth in late winter before new sprouts appear. It has minimal insect or disease problems. Only feed with balanced fertilizer in spring if plants aren't growing vigorously.

Hardiness—Zones 6 to 10

Texture—Coarse

Peak Season—September to November

Mature Size (H x W)—2 to 3 ft. x 2 to 3 ft.

Water Needs—Water regularly, especially in areas with hot summers. Established plants are drought tolerant.

RAVENNA GRASS

Saccharum ravennae

Why It's Special—Ever wish you could grow pampas grass but your winters aren't mild enough? Ravenna grass is a much-hardier substitute. Also known as plume grass, this ornamental grass has attractive purple inflorescences that change to bronze in fall before fading to silver. They are commonly used in floral arrangements. The blue-gray foliage rustles pleasantly anytime the wind blows. It is deer resistant. Use ravenna grass as a privacy screen, in naturalized gardens, or individually as an accent.

How to Plant & Grow—Plant in spring or fall in full sun and in dry, average soil for best results. Mulch heavily around the plants to provide roots with winter protection.

Care & Problems—Trim back to the ground in late winter before new growth emerges. Plants have minimal insect or disease problems and do not require fertilizing. If grown in moist conditions, they might require staking.

Hardiness—Zones 5 to 10

Texture—Coarse

Peak Season—September to October

Mature Size (H x W)—6 to 12 ft. x 4 to 6 ft.

Water Needs—Plants become drought tolerant once established.

SEASHORE PASPALUM

Paspalum vaginatum

Why It's Special—Seashore paspalum is a turfgrass native to the coastal regions of the southeastern U.S. It has coarse, blue-green blades that tolerate heavy foot traffic, which makes it useful for home landscapes. It spreads by rhizomes and grows aggressively. This grass does particularly well in coastal areas of the Northwest as it tolerates salty soil and can even be irrigated with saltwater. It is frequently used for erosion control. Seashore paspalum has a higher ability to compete with weeds than other turfgrasses. 'Adalayd' looks similar to Kentucky bluegrass.

How to Plant & Grow—Plant in spring in full sun to light shade. It's typically grown from plugs and sod. Refer to sections on "Establishing a Lawn" and "Maintaining a Lawn" for more information.

Care & Problems—Mow regularly to ¾-inch to promote dense shoot growth. The grass can be susceptible to scalping injury. Fertilize in fall and spring. This grass has minimal insect or disease problems. It goes dormant over winter.

Hardiness—Zones 8 and above

Texture—Coarse

Peak Season—Entire growing season

Water Needs—Water regularly; it tolerates occasional dry periods.

SEDGE

Carex spp.

Why It's Special—Sedge is a grasslike plant that is grown as an ornamental. It's native to North America, with over 200 species native to the Northwest alone. Many are found in wetlands and are used for erosion control. One of the hardiest, morning star sedge (*Carex grayi*) grows in zone 3 and reaches 2 feet tall. Both black-flowered sedge (*C. nigra*), at 10 inches tall, and palm sedge (*C. muskingumensis*), 2 feet tall, are hardy to zone 4. Zone 5 sedges include 6-inch-tall blue sedge (*C. glauca*); 1-foot-tall Japanese grass sedge (*C. morrowii*) 'Aurea Variegata'; drooping sedge (*C. pendula*), 2 to 4 feet tall; and tufted sedge (*C. elata*) 'Bowles' Golden' at 1 to 3 feet tall.

How to Plant & Grow—Plant in spring or fall in full sun, although part shade works well in hot summer regions. Soil should be moist but well drained.

Care & Problems—In late winter, trim back the foliage by one-third to rejuvenate plants. No fertilizing is necessary.

Hardiness—Varies by species

Texture—Medium

Peak Season—Varies by species

Mature Size (H x W)—Varies

Water Needs—Water regularly.

SWITCH GRASS

Panicum virgatum

Why It's Special—Switch grass is native to the tall-grass prairies of North America. Its blue-green foliage grows 3 feet tall. In the summer, wheat-colored panicles easily double the plant's height. It's a tough plant grown for privacy screens, as accents, and often used for erosion control. The seeds provide food for birds in winter. 'Shenandoah' (2 to 3 feet) has bright red foliage while 'Cheyenne Sky' (3 feet) features blue-green leaves that turn red in early summer, later followed by purple panicles. 'Northwind' (to 6 feet) has blue-green foliage and a highly desirable vertical growth habit.

How to Plant & Grow—Plant in spring or fall in full sun to part shade; plants may fall over when grown in shade. It's adaptable to all soil types.

Care & Problems—They self-seed easily; deadhead to control. Trim back old growth in late winter before new sprouts appear.

Hardiness—Zones 5 to 9

Texture—Coarse

Peak Season—July to September

Mature Size (H x W)—3 to 6 ft. x 2 to 3 ft.

Water Needs—Water regularly until plants establish.

TUFTED HAIR GRASS

Deschampsia cespitosa

Why It's Special—Grown as an ornamental grass, tufted hair grass is a real attention-getter when in bloom. In summer, 3-foot-tall flower spikes emerge with long panicles of gold, silver, and purple flowers, creating an ethereal appearance. The seedheads persist into winter, attracting hungry birds. This grass is attractive as a groundcover, in woodland gardens, alongside ponds, and in perennial borders. 'Pixie Fountain' is hardy to zone 2 and has silvery white flowers while 'Goldtau' has golden inflorescences. 'Northern Lights' has variegated foliage.

How to Plant & Grow—Plant in spring or fall in full sun to part shade. Since flowering is highly desirable, avoid too much shade where it won't bloom. This grass prefers moist, well-drained soil with compost incorporated into the planting bed.

Care & Problems—Trim foliage to the ground in late winter before new growth begins. It has minimal pest or disease problems and does not require fertilizing.

Hardiness—Zones 4 to 9

Texture—Coarse

Peak Season—May to August

Mature Size (H x W)—2 to 3 ft. x 1 to 2 ft.

Water Needs—Water regularly but do not overwater.

TURF-TYPE TALL FESCUE

Festuca arundinacea

Why It's Special—Turf-type tall fescue has denser blades than those of tall fescues commonly used for forage grasses, making them more suitable for turfgrass. Their attributes include tolerance for high foot traffic, drought, shade, and resistance to necrotic ring spot. They're particularly well suited for inland regions and tolerate poorly draining soils. Recommended varieties for inland regions include 'Arid', 'Rebel II', 'Jaguar', 'Olympic', 'Falcon', and 'Maverick'. Cultivars adapted for coastal regions include 'Adventure', 'Bonanza', 'Jaguar II', 'Monarch', and 'Trailblazer'.

How to Plant & Grow—Plant seed in full sun. The best planting time is in early fall to avoid summertime drought stresses while plants are establishing. Refer to "Establishing a Lawn" for more information.

Care & Problems—These grasses germinate and grow slowly. Mow at 2½ to 3 inches. They need a medium amount of fertilization, at a rate of one pound of nitrogen in mid-May and mid-August. Tall fescues are susceptible to cutworms.

Hardiness—Zones 2 to 11

Texture—Coarse

Peak Season—Entire growing season

Water Needs—Water deeply in spring, then as needed to prevent a lawn from going dormant.

JANUARY

- On the east side of the Cascades, your lawn will either be frozen solid or covered with snow—or both. Go enjoy some winter activities.

- West of the Cascades, winter rains will show you where there might be soggy spots in your lawn. Make plans to improve drainage in those areas.

- Visit local botanical and public gardens to observe the winter colors of ornamental grasses. Make a list of some you could add to your garden.

FEBRUARY

- Rake up any winter storm debris that has come down on the lawn.

- Watch wild birds finish cleaning out ornamental grass seedheads. Keep track of which species you see.

- Take your lawn equipment in for servicing now so you can beat the rush. If you are doing your own maintenance, change the oil and grease wear points. Replace the spark plug and clean the air filter. Sharpen the blade so it will cut grass cleanly.

- Dandelions may start popping up by the end of the month west of the Cascades. Wait until there is a good crop of them on a sunny day before treating them with a broadleaf herbicide. Alternatively, leave them as an early pollen source for foraging honeybees and mow just when their fluffy white seedheads form.

- West of the Cascades, lawns may start growing near the end of the month as the weather and the soil warms up. Apply pre-emergent weed controls now before the crabgrass and chickweed get a good foothold. Wait until lawns thaw out east of the Cascades to apply pre-emergents.

MARCH

- Cut down ornamental grasses, except the fescues and blue oat grass, leaving 6 inches of stem. Loop string around the grass bunches before you cut them to make a neat bundle and easy clean-up.

- As the snow melts off lawns east of the Cascades, rake up dead grass and leaves that weren't picked up in the fall. If they are present, rake out snow mold patches to help dry out the ground. If voles left trails in the lawn surface, rake them out to remove the dead grass. The grass will grow back.

APRIL

- If you can't leave the dandelion flowers for the honey bees, treat them with a broadleaf herbicide following label directions. If you haven't applied pre-emergence herbicides for crabgrass, do so early in the month.

- Apply a slow-release, preferably organic, fertilizer to lawns in all areas of the region this month. Remember: fertilizers purchased in Washington for established lawns will not contain phosphorus. Slow-release organic fertilizers release their nutrients over a period of time. As a result, you do not have to apply them as often. You will not need to apply them again until early September when the weather cools and grasses resume growing and then again in late October to prepare them for winter.

- Check sprinkler systems for damaged, broken, or plugged heads. Now is a good time to retrofit an older system with more efficient heads and timers. Consult a local sprinkler design company to evaluate your options and then either hire someone to do the work or do it yourself. The retrofit may only mean changing the old heads for more efficient ones.

- Fertilize ornamental grasses late this month with a slow-release 10-10-10 fertilizer. Cool-season ornamental grasses will begin emerging about mid-month. Ornamental grasses do not require as much fertilizer as a lawn so this will be their important feeding for the year.

MAY

- New lawns can be planted from seed or sod early in the month so they have a chance to establish before the dry season begins.

- This is a good time to aerate your lawn with a hollow-core aerator. Run over the lawn in two directions at 90 degrees to each other. This will open the soil to water and air. Aerators can be rented or you can hire a professional.

- In dry areas, it may be necessary to begin irrigating your lawn. Water deeply so the water gets to a depth of 6 to 8 inches to force the grass roots to grow deep into the soil. Deep roots help the grass withstand hot weather later in the summer.

- Spot-treat any remaining weed issues. Avoid using weed and feed products if you have just a few weeds. Applying herbicides all over a lawn when there are only a few patches of weeds can lead to unnecessary expense and contribute to pollution of groundwater and nearby bodies of water.

JUNE

- Blue oat grass and the fescues will be sending out delicate seedheads this month. Watch how they catch the slightest breeze.

- Adjust your sprinkler system as the weather warms up to give ornamental and turfgrasses at least an inch of water a week.

- Sharpen your mower blade after a couple months of mowing. Dull blades tear, rather than cut, leaving the tips of the grass blades ragged and the lawn with a rough texture.

JULY

- Drought-stressed lawn grass will appear gray and dull as the hot weather sets in. Water long enough to wet 6 to 8 inches into the soil.

- Don't fertilize grass during hot weather. Growth normally slows when it's hot, so you will only waste fertilizer.

- All of the ornamental grasses will be in full leaf. Watch how they catch light and the wind and bring motion into the garden. They are particularly pretty when they are backlit by the sun in the early morning or evening.

AUGUST

- Cut your lawn as high as your type of lawn grass allows in hot weather. Tall grass helps shade the soil which reduces water loss and prevents weeds from sprouting.

- Continue deep-watering lawns and ornamental grasses this month.

SEPTEMBER

- Early this month is perfect for new lawn installation or renovation and repair projects. The soil is warm so seed should sprout quickly. If you are using seed, prepare a weed-free seed, smooth the bed and spread certified lawn seed over the area and gently rake it in lightly. Roll the area and cover lightly with a mulch and water twice a day to keep the seed bed moist until the grass is 2 inches tall. If you are laying a sod lawn, level the area carefully and then butt the edges of the sod firmly together. Roll the sod to set it firmly on the soil. Water every two or three days through mid-October or until the steady falls rains appear.

- Cooler temperatures will bring out the fall weeds. Spot-treat as needed.

- Apply a second round of slow-release organic fertilizer to your lawn early in the month.

- Adjust your sprinkler cycles as cooler temperatures reduce the lawn's need for water. Continue watering until the fall rains begin.

OCTOBER

- Frosts this month will turn many ornamental grasses to gold, rust, and yellow. Watch how they catch the fall light. Look for more places to plant them where they can be backlit by the fall light.

- Aerate your lawn now if you didn't do it in the spring.

- If you live east of the Cascades, turn off your sprinkler system and get the system blown out around mid-month before a cold snap catches you by surprise. Keep a hose and sprinkler handy to water newly-seeded or sodded areas if it is still dry.

- Rake up leaves so they don't smother the lawn over the winter. One easy way to clean up leaves and pine needles is to mow over them as you do your last rounds of mowing. This will shred and pre-mix green and brown materials for your compost pile.

- Apply a slow-release fall-winter fertilizer blend at the end of the month or in early November. The roots will store the nutrients and be able to get a head start next spring.

NOVEMBER

- Clean up any remaining leaves and needles so they don't smother the grass over the winter.

- Take your lawn mower in for service now before the shop gets busy with snow blowers. Run fuel out of all yard equipment engines or add a fuel stabilizer to the gas tank. Drain and store hoses.

- Join Project Feeder Watch in the U.S. or Bird Studies Canada in British Columbia and tally the species of birds that show up at your feeders through the winter. Check it out at www.feederwatch.org/about/project-overview/.

DECEMBER

- Relax. Even the weeds will have slowed down or frozen solid by now.

- Observe how much color and life ornamental grasses add to the now-dormant garden. Where can you plant more?

PERENNIALS
for the Northwest

Perennials are the party dresses of the garden: With each change of seasons they create an entirely new celebration of color and texture. They are very tolerant of a wide range of soils, light, and moisture levels, which makes them versatile in any garden setting. Many of the perennials on the plant list in this chapter are Northwest and British Columbia natives.

WHAT IS A PERENNIAL?

Perennials are plants that live longer than three years. Some will fade after a few years, while others will live many more. Perennials come in three categories: Tender, half-hardy, and hardy. Tender perennials should be treated as annuals or taken indoors during the winter. Half-hardy perennials can survive outdoors with a protective mulch west of the Cascades where winter temperatures don't get far below freezing; east of the Cascades, they should be treated as annuals or dug and brought indoors in the winter. Hardy perennials can usually handle very cold winter temperatures without much protection. Be sure to check hardiness ratings when you purchase plants.

Herbaceous perennials die down to the ground either when the plant finishes blooming or at the end of the growing season and will regrow in the spring. Woody perennials develop woody stems that produce new shoots each spring.

PLANTING AND CARING FOR PERENNIALS

Many perennials prefer full sun while others will need shade. Sun-loving perennials will need a minimum of six to eight hours of full sun to grow and bloom to their full potential. Those that prefer partial or full shade will often burn and wither when planted in too much sun. That said, west of the Cascades where low clouds and fog persist in the mornings, many perennials that prefer partial shade can be grown in almost full sun. In interior areas, even sun-loving perennials often benefit from some shade from the hot afternoon sun. Avoid planting perennials that are not adapted to heat

close to a south-facing concrete or rock wall or building; they will cook quite quickly.

Perennials can tolerate a wide range of soils and moisture levels, but most prefer well-drained soil of average fertility and a medium amount of water. Some, like native penstemons (*Penstemon* spp.) and sedums (*Sedum* spp.), are very tolerant of gravelly, sandy soils and dry conditions. Others, like herbaceous peonies (*Paeonia lactiflora*) and delphinium (*Delphinium* spp.), prefer a moist soil rich in organic matter.

Proper drainage is critical for most perennials especially in the Northwest's notoriously soggy winters. Plant roots can quickly rot if left in standing water for too long. If soggy soils are a major problem, it may be necessary to install some French drains around the property to channel away excess water. Another solution is to build raised planting mounds 1 or more feet high to get above the water level. Raised beds should be built on top of a few inches of sandy loam or fine gravel to further improve drainage. In areas where the ground freezes, frost heaving of young plants can

Sun damage on hosta

occur as the soil freezes and thaws through the winter. To prevent this, mulch new plantings of perennials with straw or pine needles to keep soil temperatures even.

Most perennials need fertilization in the early spring just as new growth begins to emerge and a second one in mid-June to give the late summer bloomers an extra kick. Use a low-nitrogen, slow-release fertilizer (10-10-10 or less) at each feeding. You want to give them enough nutrients to do well but not so much that they grow rampantly and take over their neighbors.

GROWING PERENNIALS FROM SEED OR STARTS

For the adventurous gardener, starting perennials from purchased or saved seed is a good way to save money and to get unusual varieties of plants not available in the nurseries. There are several mail order and online seed companies that specialize in perennials. Many perennials such as foxglove (*Digitalis* spp.), hollyhock (*Alcea rosea*), and lupine (*Lupinus* spp.) will self-sow if their seedheads are left to ripen. Simply shake the dry seeds from the stalks over areas where you want to establish new plants. In the spring, you will have a new crop of seedlings to use in other places around the garden. Be aware that these seeds may have a lower germination rate than purchased seed. Seed companies can sort and clean seed to increase the amount of viable seed in a package.

If you are seeding purchased seed outdoors, read the packet description for the best time to sow the seed and how deep it needs to be planted. Most will say in the spring, but a few can be seeded in the fall and left to overwinter. Many perennial seeds need to be at or barely below the soil surface to germinate properly. You can scatter the seed in the garden and then cover it lightly with no more than ⅛ inch of soil or vermiculite if needed to help with moisture control.

Starting perennial seeds indoors is usually done in the early winter under grow lights in a heated basement in cold areas, or in a greenhouse in warmer coastal areas. Seed is sown in flats or other well-drained containers of germination mix and set under lights (see page 48 for more details about starting seed indoors). Once a seed germinates and produces its first set of true leaves, it will need to be transplanted into a larger container and grown until the plant is big enough to move outdoors into the garden. In some cases it might be better to transplant these young seedlings into a nursery bed in the garden where they can grow for a year and develop a strong set of roots and leaves before you plant them out into the open garden.

If starting your own seeds isn't for you, the nurseries and many online and catalog perennial suppliers will be full of good choices in the spring. Keep in mind that mail-ordered plants will be small and often arrive bareroot or in very little soil (it saves on shipping costs) so it is important to plant them quickly. If you can't, at least heel them into a nursery bed and keep them watered until you have the time to properly plant them.

Perennials may take one to three years before they are large enough to bloom or reach their full size so be patient. The general rule is the first year after planting, they will sleep while they develop roots; the second year they will creep as they begin to expand their crown; and by the third year they will leap into full bloom and foliage.

DEALING WITH SLUGS, APHIDS, AND POWDERY MILDEW

Slugs and aphids are the biggest pests of perennials. Slugs will appear in the early spring just as tender new growth is emerging and soon will be chewing holes in the foliage of hostas, iris, true lilies (*Lilium* spp.), and daylilies (*Hemerocallis* spp.) to name a few. Slugs feed at night so it's hard to find them in the day. Clean out dead foliage under susceptible plants early in the spring and lightly cultivate the soil to disturb the slug eggs. During the day, patrol the garden, looking under leaves and large objects and drop any slugs you find in a container of soapy water. If they get really bad, apply iron phosphate-based slug baits liberally around your plants as the slugs emerge in the spring. These slug baits are non-toxic to other animals and insects.

Aphids also like tender new foliage and can be a problem in the early spring. If they appear, start looking for predator bugs and give them a chance to come in and feast on the aphids. If the predators don't show up or you reach your tolerance level for the damage, either spray the plants with a hard stream of water to wash them off or apply insecticidal soap.

Mildew is a fungal disease that attacks a number of perennials and creates a grayish or whitish powdery coating on leaves. It most commonly appears under humid conditions when the days are warm followed by cool nights. Humidity can be created by irrigation as well as weather conditions. It usually doesn't hurt the plant but the plants look less than stellar. Some plants like lupine (*Lupinus* spp.) and bee balm (*Monarda* spp.) are quite prone to it. To reduce the potential for its appearance, plant mildew-resistant varieties and plant them where they get enough sun, good air circulation, and limited overhead irrigation. Plant susceptible varieties behind other plants so that when the mildew shows up the other plants will hide the damaged foliage. There are fungicides available that can minimize the onset of powdery mildew but they need to be applied before a problem emerges.

Gardening with perennials is like sending a gardener into the candy store with a blank check. Perennials come in so many shapes, sizes, colors, and textures that it's often hard to choose the ones you like the best. So experiment and try a few new plants every spring. It's always fun to discover new combinations.

Use beer traps to prevent slugs from damaging your plants. To make a beer trap, put a shallow jar or butter lid on the ground next to the afflicted plant. Fill the trap with beer to catch the slugs.

ARTEMISIA
Artemisia spp. and hybrids

Why It's Special—Wormwood and mugwort are two species of this plant, which includes sagebrush. The silver foliage provides contrast in herbaceous borders. Hybrid 'Powis Castle' is a bushy, woody perennial with lacy foliage, growing 2 to 3 feet tall. Beach wormwood 'Silver Brocade' (*Artemisia stelleriana*) has attractive, divided leaves and compact (6 to 12 inches) growth. 'Silver Mound' (*A. schmidtiana*) features delicate, feathery foliage and an attractive, mounding growth habit of 12 inches. Absinth wormwood (*A. absinthium*) has 2- to 3-foot-tall foliage that is deer and rabbit resistant.

How to Plant & Grow—Artemisia grows well in full sun to part shade, in average, well-drained soil. Plant nursery plants in spring or fall. Space plants 2 feet apart; they spread quickly.

Care & Problems—Trim back plants in summer; no fertilizing necessary. Propagate by division.

Hardiness—Zones 4 to 9, some cultivars only hardy to Zone 5

Color(s)—Silver-gray foliage, small white or yellow flowers

Peak Season—Late spring through autumn

Mature Size (H x W)—1 to 6 ft. x 1 to 2 ft.

Water Needs—Low. Plants are drought tolerant once established.

ASTER
Aster spp. and hybrids

Why It's Special—Asters are prolific, late-season flowers when most perennial blooms are finished. They are hardy and easy to grow. Flowers attract bees and butterflies and are good for cutting. New England aster (*Aster novae-angliae*) 'Alma Potschke' has fabulous rosy red flowers and grows 4 feet tall while 'Purple Dome' features deep purple blooms and is 18 inches tall. New York aster (*A. nova-belgii*) 'Crimson Brocade' has magenta-red blooms and reaches 3 feet. *Aster × frikartii* 'Monch' forms tidy 2-foot-tall mounds with lavender blossoms.

How to Plant & Grow—Plant in spring or fall in full sun in fertile, well-drained soil. Space 18 to 24 inches.

Care & Problems—Feed with balanced fertilizer in spring. Pinch back in early summer to keep plants bushy. Propagate by cuttings every other year in spring or fall. Asters have minimal pest or disease problems.

Hardiness—Zones 4 to 8

Color(s)—Magenta, red, blue, lavender, purple

Peak Season—Late August until frost

Mature Size (H x W)—18 in. to 4 ft. x 16 to 24 in.

Water Needs—Medium. Water regularly.

ASTILBE
Astilbe spp. and hybrids

Why It's Special—Astilbe's fernlike foliage and feathery plumes (another name is false spirea) make it an attractive choice for any planting. They attract butterflies and hummingbirds while keeping deer and rabbits at bay. Chinese astilbes (*Astilbe chinensis*) bloom later and have more sun tolerance; 'Pumila' has lilac plumes and 'Visions' is available in medium pink or white flowers. Astilbe hybrids (*A. × arendsii*) bloom from late spring to late summer: 'Burgundy Red' has deep green foliage with burgundy stems and small plumes of deep red; 'Bridal Veil' features delicate white spires.

How to Plant & Grow—Astilbes prefer part shade, but will grow in the sun if the soil is kept moist. Plant in spring or fall.

Care & Problems—Feed a balanced fertilizer in spring. Propagate by division in early spring every three years. Minimal pest or disease problems.

Hardiness—Zones 4 to 9

Color(s)—Pink, white, raspberry, red, purple

Peak Season—June to July

Mature Size (H x W)—12 to 30 in. x 12 to 24 in.

Water Needs—Medium to high. Provide plenty of water throughout the season, especially while plants are establishing.

BASKET-OF-GOLD
Aurinia saxatilis

Why It's Special—This popular, showy perennial blooms profusely in early spring. Its golden flowers are particularly attractive when cascading over a stone wall, in rock gardens, or at the front of perennial borders. It is often used in fire-wise landscaping. 'Citrina' is 10 to 15 inches tall and has lemon-yellow flowers, 'Compacta' and 'Golden Flourish' grow 8 to 10 inches tall, and 'Goldkugel' is a mere 6 inches.

How to Plant & Grow—In spring or fall, choose a full-sun location, although in areas where summers are hot, afternoon shade is very helpful. Plants tolerate most soil types as long as they drain well. Space 8 to 10 inches apart.

Care & Problems—Deer-resistant basket-of-gold tends to be pest free and requires medium maintenance. Trim back after flowering to keep plants compact. Avoid fertilizing this plant as that will cause weak growth.

Hardiness—Zones 3 to 8

Color(s)—Yellow

Peak Season—April to May

Mature Size (H x W)—6 to 12 in. x 12 to 18 in.

Water Needs—Medium to low. It's drought tolerant once established.

BEE BALM
Monarda didyma

Why It's Special—The showy flowers of bee balm *are* a favorite of bees but they're popular with hummingbirds and butterflies too. A member of the mint family, its foliage and flowers are fragrant with a citrusy scent. 'Jacob Cline' has the familiar, large red flowers. 'Purple Rooster' is 36 inches tall and covered with deep purple blooms. 'Pink Lace' features pale pink fringes on top of deep pink cushions and more compact growth than many cultivars. 'Pardon My Pink' is petite at only 12 inches tall.

How to Plant & Grow—Bee balm thrives in full sun to part shade, in rich, moist soil. Plant in spring or fall and space 12 to 15 inches apart.

Care & Problems—Deadhead to extend blooming. Divide every three years. Powdery mildew can be a problem. Plants are both rabbit and deer resistant.

Hardiness—Zones 3 to 9

Color(s)—Red, pink, purple, coral, white

Peak Season—Late June to August

Mature Size (H x W)—15 in. to 5 ft. x 18 in. to 5 ft.

Water Needs—Medium. Water regularly but do not overwater.

BLACK-EYED SUSAN
Rudbeckia spp.

Why It's Special—One of the perkiest perennials around, this tough native attracts butterflies, naturalizes well, and makes a wonderful cut flower. Black-eyed Susan (*Rudbeckia fulgida*) 'Goldsturm' has butter-yellow petals and dark centers. Gloriosa daisy (*R. hirta*) 'Prairie Sun' is stunning with its green center disk and yellow-tipped orange rays, 'Cherry Brandy' features dark maroon petals with a deep brown disk, and 'Sonora' has yellow-tipped burgundy rays. Gloriosa daisies are not reliably hardy as perennials in some zone 5 regions and must be grown as an annual.

How to Plant & Grow—Plant in spring or fall in full sun although it tolerates some light shade. Black-eyed Susans are not particular about soil type as long as it holds some moisture.

Care & Problems—Deadhead to extend the bloom. Divide every few years. Plants are low maintenance. Black-eyed Susans do not require fertilizer.

Hardiness—Zones 3 to 9

Color(s)—Yellow, red, orange, green, bronze, bicolors

Peak Season—June through September

Mature Size (H x W)—2 to 3 ft. x 1 to 2 ft.

Water Needs—Low to medium. Plants are drought tolerant once established.

BLEEDING HEART
Dicentra spectabilis

Why It's Special—Bleeding hearts are easily recognizable by their nodding, heart-shaped flowers that dangle from gracefully arching stems. Plants are long-lived and a good choice for shade, woodland, or cottage gardens. The blooms last a long time as cut flowers. 'Burning Heart' is compact with feathery, gray leaves and rose-red flowers. 'Alba' features pristine white blossoms while 'Valentine' has deep red flowers hanging from red stems. 'Gold Heart' makes a great accent plant with its bright golden foliage and dainty pink flowers.

How to Plant & Grow—Plant in spring in part to full shade and average, well-drained soil. Space 24 to 30 inches apart.

Care & Problems—Low-maintenance bleeding heart goes dormant in midsummer so plant companion perennials nearby to fill in the gaps for the remainder of the season. Minimal insect or disease problems. Plants are rabbit and deer resistant.

Hardiness—Zones 3 to 9

Color(s)—Red, white, magenta, bicolors

Peak Season—April to May

Mature Size (H x W)—1 to 3 ft. x 1½ to 2½ ft.

Water Needs—Medium. Water regularly.

CALIFORNIA POPPY
Eschscholzia californica

Why It's Special—California poppies, a wildflower native to the Columbia River Gorge south to California, are grown as short-lived perennials in warmer areas of the Northwest or as annuals in zones 5 and below. Their bright flowers light up rock gardens and pathway borders. Plants are used for erosion control and are deer resistant. 'Orange King' features bright orange flowers. 'Summer Sorbet' has rose-pink petals and 'Sunset' seed mix includes orange, yellow, cream, red, and pink blossoms.

How to Plant & Grow—California poppies grow best in sunny locations but it's not particular about soil type as long as it has good drainage. Plant directly from seed in fall in zones 6 to 10 or in spring when frost danger has passed in colder zones.

Care & Problems—They multiply through self-seeding. Minimal insect or disease problems. Fertilizing will cause a reduction in blooms.

Hardiness—Zones 6 to 10

Color(s)—Orange, yellow, red, pink, cream

Peak Season—June to July

Mature Size (H x W)—1 to 1½ ft. x 1 to 1½ ft.

Water Needs—Low. Plants become drought tolerant as they establish.

CANDYTUFT
Iberis spp. and hybrids

Why It's Special—Candytuft is such a prolific bloomer, it's difficult to see its attractive foliage underneath. This plant looks stunning along walkways, in containers, rock gardens, and perennial borders. Its mounding growth habit makes it a useful groundcover. The flowers attract butterflies. *Iberis sempervirens* 'Alexander's White' is an early bloomer. Both 'Little Gem' and 'Snowflake' are dwarfs, reaching just 6 to 10 inches. 'October Glory' is a repeat bloomer in fall. 'Pink Ice' has pink flowers and compact growth of 8 to 10 inches. *I.* × *hybridus* 'Absolutely Amethyst' has lavender blossoms.

How to Plant & Grow—Plant in full sun and in average, well-drained soil, from nursery plants or seed. Plants can grow in part shade, but won't bloom as profusely.

Care & Problems—Trim plants back one-third after blooming to encourage new growth. In cold inland regions, mulch plants over winter to prevent moisture loss. Plants are deer and rabbit resistant.

Hardiness—Zones 3 to 8

Color(s)—White, pink, purple

Peak Season—April to May

Mature Size (H x W)—6 to 12 in. x 6 to 18 in.

Water Needs—Medium. Water regularly.

CARDINAL FLOWER

Lobelia cardinalis

Why It's Special—Cardinal flower has nectar-rich showy blossoms that attract hummingbirds and butterflies. They naturalize well and are ideal for perennial beds and alongside water gardens, streams, and in bogs. Native to North America, plants are short-lived perennials. The flowers can be cut for floral arrangements. 'Queen Victoria' features red flowers and foliage, while 'Alba' has white blossoms. 'Pink Flamingo' has deep pink flowers while 'Heather Pink' has soft pink blossoms. The flowers of 'Angel Song' are a lovely combination of salmon and cream.

How to Plant & Grow—Choose a location in full sun to part shade. Plants prefer rich, moist soil. Plant in spring or fall and space 12 to 18 inches apart.

Care & Problems—These low-maintenance plants have minimal insect or disease problems. Propagate by division in spring. Cardinal flowers are rabbit and deer resistant. Fertilize every six weeks with all-purpose fertilizer.

Hardiness—Zones 3 to 9

Color(s)—Red, blue, white, rose

Peak Season—July to September

Mature Size (H x W)—2 to 4 ft. x 1 to 2 ft.

Water Needs—Medium to high. Water frequently to keep soil moist.

CATMINT

Nepeta spp. and hybrids

Why It's Special—Catmint is a tough yet attractive perennial with gray-green leaves and pastel flower spikes. It's terrific in cottage gardens, perennial borders, and rose gardens. Flowers attract hummingbirds and butterflies. *Nepeta grandiflora* 'Dawn to Dusk' has pale pink flowers and grows 2 feet tall. *N. racemosa* 'Little Titch' has blue flowers and is only 8 inches tall. Popular *N. nervosa* 'Six Hills Giant' has intense blue flowers and grows 3 feet tall. *N. x faassenii* 'Walker's Low' has violet-blue flowers and is 2 to 3 feet tall. *N. cataria* is the aromatic catmint that cats go wild over.

How to Plant & Grow—Catmint prefers full sun to part shade and adapts to all soil types. Plant nursery plants in spring or fall.

Care & Problems—Plants need minimal care though deadheading can stimulate a second blooming. Propagate by division in late spring. No fertilizing needed!

Hardiness—Zones 4 to 9

Color(s)—Blue, violet, white, pink

Peak Season—May through June

Mature Size (H x W)—12 to 36 in. x 16 to 36 in.

Water Needs—Low. Plants are drought tolerant once established.

COLUMBINE

Aquilegia spp.

Why It's Special—Columbine's showy flowers attract hummingbirds and butterflies and make great cut flowers. Plants are a delightful addition to cottage or woodland gardens because they naturalize well. *Aquilegia canadensis*, with yellow stamens and red spurs, is the native. The Biedermeier group is one of the shortest columbines at 18 inches and has white, pink, or purple flowers. *A. vulgaris* 'Clementine' features double blue or pink spurless flowers. The Winky series has beautiful ruffled blooms in red and white or blue and white. 'Lime Sorbet' has attractive double flowers in pale lime-green. 'Dorothy Rose' has full, compact flowers in rose-pink.

How to Plant & Grow—In spring, plant seeds or transplants in full sun to part shade. They grow in any soil type with good drainage.

Care & Problems—Plants self-seed but are not invasive. Columbines need minimal care and don't require fertilizer.

Hardiness—Zones 3 to 9

Color(s)—Red, pink, yellow, white, pale blue, dark blue, bicolors

Peak Season—May through July

Mature Size (H x W)—1 to 3 ft. x 1 ft.

Water Needs—Low to medium. Water when the soil is dry.

CORAL BELLS

Heuchera spp. and hybrids

Why It's Special—Even though coral bells bloom each summer, their foliage colors make them stars in the garden all season. While they add color to perennial borders, they also work as groundcovers. Plants are deer resistant and their small flowers attract hummingbirds. Cultivars include 'Berry Smoothie', 'Delta Dawn', 'Ginger Peach', and 'Shanghai'. Heucherellas are a cross between *Heuchera* and *Tiarella*. *Heucherella* 'Alabama Sunrise' is noteworthy for its lime-colored leaves with deep red veins and 'Solar Eclipse' has reddish brown leaves edged in chartreuse.

How to Plant & Grow—Plant in full sun to part shade; in areas with hot summers, place them where they'll get some afternoon shade. Coral bells prefer rich, moist, well-drained soil. Space 18 inches apart.

Care & Problems—Minimal insect or disease problems. No fertilizer is necessary.

Hardiness—Zones 4 to 9 and Zone 3 with protection

Color(s)—Bronze, purple, pink, orange, lime, apricot, variegated foliage; cream to deep red flowers

Peak Season—June through August

Mature Size (H x W)—12 to 30 in. x 12 to 24 in.

Water Needs—Medium. Water regularly but do not overwater.

CREEPING HUMMINGBIRD TRUMPET

Zauschneria garrettii

Why It's Special—Creeping hummingbird trumpet's flowers look quite exotic but this plant is a good candidate for xeriscaping. It does well in alpine and rock gardens and is attractive in containers. With its long blooming period, hummingbirds and butterflies will be visitors to your garden. One of the hardiest and easiest varieties to find is the compact 'Orange Carpet™'. At just 4 inches tall, it will be covered by bright orange flowers. 'Silver Select' is hardy to zone 6 and features attractive silver foliage that contrasts with deep red blooms.

How to Plant & Grow—Site in full sun or in afternoon shade in areas with hot summers. It tolerates most soil types. In coastal areas, good soil drainage is a must. Plant in spring from nursery plants.

Care & Problems—Plants need minimal care, just a little shearing to keep them tidy. Give slow-release fertilizer in spring. Plants are deer resistant.

Hardiness—Zones 3 to 9

Color(s)—Orange-red

Peak Season—July to October

Mature Size (H x W)—4 to 10 in. x 18 in.

Water Needs—Low to medium. Plants become drought tolerant once established.

DAYLILY

Hemerocallis hybrids

Why It's Special—Gone are the days when we only had yellow- or orange-flowering daylilies to choose from. Today, the color choice is endless, varieties are fragrant, and many are repeat bloomers. For red cultivars, try 'Chicago Apache', 'Border of Red', or 'Apple Tart'. Daylilies featuring different throat colors include 'Night Beacon' and 'Wineberry Candy'. White cultivars include 'Joan Senior' and 'Gentle Shepherd'. Rose or pink varieties are 'Ocean Rain', 'My Sweet Rose', and 'Jedi Rose Beauty'.

How to Plant & Grow—In spring, plant bare-root or container plants in full sun to part shade. Daylilies tolerate most soil types as long as they drain well. Space 18 to 24 inches apart.

Care & Problems—Daylilies are low maintenance and virtually pest free. Deadheading keeps plants looking tidy; clip stalks once blooming has finished. Divide clumps every few years.

Hardiness—Zones 3 to 10

Color(s)—Orange, yellow, red, pink, salmon, maroon, lavender

Peak Season—July through August

Mature Size (H x W)—1 to 4 ft. x 2 to 3 ft.

Water Needs—Low. Provide extra water during periods of drought or intense heat.

DELPHINIUM

Delphinium spp. and hybrids

Why It's Special—What would a cottage garden or perennial border be without delphiniums? They have a regal appearance with their tall flower spikes. Blossoms attract butterflies and make good cut flowers. They are short-lived perennials. Plants in the Pacific Giants (*Delphinium elatum*) series have white, pale to deep blue, pink, or purple flower spikes reaching 7 feet, although 'Dasante Blue' is only 3 feet tall. *D. grandiflorum* 'Summer Blues' has soft blue blossoms and 'Summer Morning' is a pink cultivar; both are 14 inches tall.

How to Plant & Grow—Plant in full sun; in areas that have hot summers, provide afternoon shade. Delphiniums thrive in rich, well-drained soil. Space 1 to 3 feet apart.

Care & Problems—Support the flower stalks, especially where windy. Provide all-purpose fertilizer after planting. Deadheading encourages additional blooming. Foliage is susceptible to powdery mildew.

Hardiness—Zones 3 to 7

Color(s)—White, blue, purple, pink

Peak Season—June to July

Mature Size (H x W)—14 in. to 7 ft. x 2 to 3 ft.

Water Needs—Medium. Water regularly.

EUPHORBIA

Euphorbia spp.

Why It's Special—If you're looking for an unusual plant, euphorbia should be at the top of your list. With its mounding habit and coloration, they make wonderful accents in borders, rock gardens, and xeric landscapes. Cushion spurge (*Euphorbia polychroma*) has yellow to chartreuse bracts while 'Bonfire' has burgundy, red, and orange foliage. Chameleon spurge (*E. dulcis*) has burgundy foliage with purple flowers. Purple wood spurge (*E. amygdaloides*) 'Purpurea' features yellow-green flower clusters above burgundy stems and foliage. The leaves turn red in fall.

How to Plant & Grow—Plant in spring or fall in full sun; in areas with hot summers, afternoon shade is helpful. Euphorbia prefers dry, well-drained soils.

Care & Problems—Plants self-seed after blooming if not deadheaded. Divide in fall or early spring every few years. Plant exudes milky sap that can irritate the skin and eyes; it's toxic if ingested. Plants are deer and rabbit resistant.

Hardiness—Zones 4 to 8

Color(s)—Yellow bracts

Peak Season—April to May

Mature Size (H x W)—1 to 1½ ft. x 1 to 1½ ft.

Water Needs—Low. It's drought tolerant once established.

FERNS

Many genera and species

Why It's Special—Ferns may look lush and tropical but there are many hardy species for Northwest gardens. These are perfect for woodland or shade gardens. Northern maidenhair fern (*Adiantum pedatum*) has black-stemmed, frilly leaves and grows 1 to 2 feet tall. Western sword fern (*Polystictum munitum*) is a 4-foot-tall evergreen featuring long, bright green fronds. Japanese painted fern (*Athyrium goeringianum* 'Pictum') has variegated fronds and red stems that will be more colorful with some morning or afternoon sun. For a bit of drama, try royal fern (*Osmunda regalis*), which can reach 6 feet and has foliage resembling locust leaves.

How to Plant & Grow—Plant in full to part shade. Soil must be moist but well drained.

Care & Problems—Feed with slow-release fertilizer each spring. Ferns have minimal pest or disease problems.

Hardiness—Zones 3 to 8 (except Japanese painted fern Zones 4 to 9)

Color(s)—Green, silver, brown, bronze

Peak Season—Early summer until fall

Mature Size (H x W)—1 to 4 ft. x 1 to 5 ft.

Water Needs—High. Water frequently to keep soil moist.

FOXGLOVE

Digitalis spp.

Why It's Special—Foxgloves are known for their stalks of colorful, tubular flowers that are popular with hummingbirds. They are ideal for cottage gardens and perennial borders. Common foxglove (*Digitalis purpurea*) is a biennial available in many colors: creamy 'Dalmatian Peach'; 'Dalmatian White', which features white trumpets filled with burgundy spots; and the Camelot series. Plants range from 3 to 6 feet tall. Perennial foxgloves include yellow foxglove (*D. grandiflora*), 12 to 16 inches tall, and strawberry foxglove (*D. × mertonensis*), which grows 2 to 3 feet tall.

How to Plant & Grow—Plant in spring in full sun to part shade. Foxgloves are easy to grow and prefer average, well-drained soil. Space 1 to 2 feet apart.

Care & Problems—Feed in spring with water-soluble fertilizer. Propagate by sowing seeds or dividing perennial types in spring or fall. Deadhead to prevent self-sowing. *Note: All parts are toxic.*

Hardiness—Zones 3 to 8

Color(s)—White, pink, rose, yellow, peach, rusty copper

Peak Season—June through July

Mature Size (H x W)—3 to 4 ft. x 1 ft.

Water Needs—Medium. Water regularly.

GAURA

Gaura spp. and hybrids

Why It's Special—Also known as wandflower or butterfly gaura, this plant's butterfly-like blossoms are graceful additions to perennial borders and cottage gardens. They naturalize well and are good container plants. The wealth of dainty blossoms attracts hummingbirds and butterflies. The flowers of *Gaura lindheimeri* are initially white, then fade to pink. 'Ballerina Blush' grows 1 to 2 feet and has pale pink flowers; 2-foot-tall 'Passionate Blush' has burgundy stems and buds that open to dark pink. 'Whirling Butterflies' is 3 feet tall and was named for the way its delicate white blossoms dance in the breeze. 'Sparkle White' has denser, more compact growth, reaching 24 to 30 inches.

How to Plant & Grow—In spring or fall, plant seeds or transplants in full sun in average soil that drains well.

Care & Problems—Deadhead to extend bloom period and prevent self-sowing. Minimal insect or disease problems. Divide in spring or fall.

Hardiness—Zones 5 to 9

Color(s)—White, pink

Peak Season—August to October

Mature Size (H x W)—1 to 5 ft. x 1 to 2 ft.

Water Needs—Medium. Water regularly.

GAYFEATHER

Liatris spp.

Why It's Special—With its tall purple flower spikes, gayfeather provides structure and height to perennial borders and cottage gardens. Blooming from the top of the spike downward, they make impressive cut flowers and attract hummingbirds and butterflies. Blazing star (*Liatris spicata*) has deep purple spikes, grows 2 to 4 feet tall, and tolerates more soil moisture. It is the easiest species to find in nurseries. Prairie blazing star (*L. pycnostachya*) has purple flower spikes and can grow up to 5 feet. The flowers on rough blazing star (*L. aspera*) are spaced farther apart on the spikes; it grows 3 to 5 feet.

How to Plant & Grow—Plant in full sun. Gayfeather is not particular about soil type as long as it is well drained.

Care & Problems—Stake taller species for support. Feed with balanced liquid fertilizer every two weeks for the first two months. Plants have minimal pest or disease problems.

Hardiness—Zones 3 to 9

Color(s)—Purple, white

Peak Season—July to August

Mature Size (H x W)—2 to 5 ft. x 1 to 2 ft.

Water Needs—Low to medium. It's drought tolerant once established.

GLOBE THISTLE

Echinops spp.

Why It's Special—Many gardeners will run the other way before considering adding a thistle plant to their gardens. Don't fear globe thistle. This knockout plant has profuse, slightly prickly globes flowering in deep blue or white. Plants grow erect and the deeply dissected leaves add texture to the garden. The flowers attract bees and butterflies and are good for fresh or dried floral arrangements. Two cultivars with intensely blue flower heads are *Echinops ritro* 'Veitch's Blue' and *E. bannaticus* 'Blue Glow'. Great globe thistle (*E. sphaerocephalus*) 'Arctic Glow' has white flower heads and silvery foliage.

How to Plant & Grow—In spring or fall, plant nursery plants in full sun. Globe thistle tolerates all well-drained soils.

Care & Problems—Because plants have a taproot, it's difficult to transplant or divide. It's low maintenance but deadhead to prevent self-sowing. They are deer and rabbit resistant.

Hardiness—Zones 3 to 8

Color(s)—Blue, white

Peak Season—July to September

Mature Size (H x W)—3 to 4 ft. x 1½ to 2 ft.

Water Needs—Medium. Water when soil is dry.

GUNNERA

Gunnera spp.

Why It's Special—The huge puckered leaves and primeval look of *Gunnera* (also called "rhubarb") provide a stunning focal point in the garden. They are commonly referred to as "dinosaur food." The plants send up huge, cone-shaped stalks bearing a brown or red inflorescence in late spring, followed by small red berries. Plants do well in boggy areas and next to water gardens; they grow quickly under ideal conditions. The leaves and stems of giant rhubarb (*Gunnera manicata*) are covered with prickly red hairs. Chilean prickly rhubarb (*G. tinctoria*) features frilly leaf margins.

How to Plant & Grow—Plant in part shade to part sun, in moist, rich soil. Give them plenty of room to grow, with 6- to 12-foot spacing depending on species.

Care & Problems—Feed a high-nitrogen fertilizer in spring. Plants have minimal insect or disease problems. *Note: No part of this plant is edible.*

Hardiness—Zones 7 to 10

Color(s)—Deep green leaves

Peak Season—June to July

Mature Size (H x W)—6 to 10 ft. x 8 to 14 ft.

Water Needs—High. Keep soil moist but not soggy.

HARDY GERANIUM

Geranium spp.

Why It's Special—Geraniums, commonly known as cranesbills, are excellent for rock gardens, perennial borders, or cottage gardens. Their mounding habit makes them ideal as a groundcover and they pair nicely with roses. *Geranium* 'Rozanne' has prolific blue flowers. *G. dalmaticum* 'Dragon Heart' is an eye-catcher with magenta blooms that have black centers. *G. pratense* 'Splish Splash' features mottled flowers with blue to violet streaks. Bloody cranesbill (*G. sanguineum*) 'New Hampshire Purple' features deeply cut foliage and magenta flowers. *G. × oxonianum* 'Wargrave Pink' is more compact and has delicate pink blossoms.

How to Plant & Grow—In spring or fall, plant in full sun to part shade, spacing 12 to 15 inches. They adapt to most soils provided they drain well.

Care & Problems—Plants are low maintenance although they are exuberant growers; deadhead to prevent self-sowing. Feed with balanced fertilizer in spring. Divide in spring or fall.

Hardiness—Zones 5 to 8

Color(s)—Lavender-blue, purple, white, pink, deep rose

Peak Season—June through September

Mature Size (H x W)—6 to 18 in. x 6 to 18 in.

Water Needs—Medium. Water regularly.

HOLLYHOCK
Alcea rosea

Why It's Special—Garden hollyhocks exude old-fashioned charm. With their tall stalks and varied flower colors, they dress up fences, border plantings, and cottage gardens. The plants are considered short-lived perennials or biennials; roots and foliage develop the first year, followed by flower stalks the second year. 'Chater's Double' is a mix of attractive double flowers in yellow, white, pink, purple, and red. The unusual 'Black Beauty' has purplish black flowers with burgundy centers. 'Fiesta Time' has striking magenta-pink blooms featuring fringed edges. 'Summer Carnival' is a mixture of single blooms in delightful colors.

How to Plant & Grow—Plant seeds or seedlings in full sun. They tolerate a variety of well-drained soil types. Space 18 to 24 inches apart.

Care & Problems—Plants will self-sow if spent flower stalks aren't removed. Feed with high phosphorus fertilizer in spring. Rust can be a problem on leaves.

Hardiness—Zones 2 to 10

Color(s)—Pink, red, white, maroon, yellow, peach, salmon

Peak Season—July through September

Mature Size (H x W)—2 to 8 ft. x 1 ft.

Water Needs—Low. Plants become drought tolerant once established.

HOSTA
Hosta spp.

Why It's Special—Hostas are highly prized for their attractive foliage in many colors and textures. They're perfect for shady areas, perennial borders, or woodland gardens. Plants vary widely in size. *Hosta* 'Sum & Substance' tolerates some sun and grows to 3 feet. *H. sieboldiana* 'Elegans' features blue-green, corrugated leaves. *H. plantaginea* has shiny green leaves and tall, fragrant flower spikes. *H. undulata* 'Variegata' features leaves with wavy margins and variegated color. *H. fortunei* 'Variegata' has variegated leaves and is 12 inches tall. Smaller hybrids include 'Little Wonder' at 9 inches tall, with variegated leaves and purple blossoms. Foot-tall 'Autumn Frost' features blue-green leaves with wide yellow margins.

How to Plant & Grow—Plant in spring in full to part shade and moist, well-draining soil.

Care & Problems—Feed with a balanced fertilizer three times per year. Divide in spring or fall. Hostas are susceptible to deer, slug, and snail damage.

Hardiness—Zones 3 to 10

Color(s)—White or lavender blossoms, showy green foliage

Peak Season—June through August

Mature Size (H x W)—6 to 60 in. x 10 to 72 in.

Water Needs—Medium. Water regularly.

JAPANESE ANEMONE
Anemone × hybrida

Why It's Special—Just when most perennials wind down, Japanese anemones come to the rescue with their late-season blooms. They are a good choice for borders and cottage gardens and they naturalize well. *Anemone × hybrida* 'Honorine Jobert' has pristine white blossoms and the popular 'September Charm' features medium pink flowers. 'Queen Charlotte' has semidouble, pale pink blossoms. *A. vitifolia* 'Robustissima' has pale pink, cup-shaped blooms. *A. hupehensis* 'Bressingham Glow' and 'Pamina' feature semidouble flowers in rose-pink. Hybrid 'Wild Swan' is less hardy (zone 6) but its white flowers are noteworthy for their violet-blue coloring on the reverse.

How to Plant & Grow—In spring or fall, plant anemones in full sun to part shade. They prefer average, well-drained soil.

Care & Problems—Plants spread by rhizomes; propagate by division in fall or early spring. They don't need feeding and are low maintenance with minimal pest or disease problems. Plants are deer resistant.

Hardiness—Zones 5 to 9

Color(s)—Pink, white, rose

Peak Season—August through October

Mature Size (H x W)—3 to 4½ ft. x 2 ft.

Water Needs—Low to medium. Water regularly.

JOE-PYE WEED

Eupatorium purpureum

Why It's Special—If you want your garden to stand out, plant a bunch of Joe-Pye weed. Their tall growth and huge, vanilla-scented flower clusters held high on burgundy stems are real eye-catchers. The flowers attract bees and butterflies and can be used fresh or dried in arrangements. *Eupatorium purpureum* subsp. *maculatum* 'Gateway' has bright pink flowers and grows 4 to 6 feet tall while 'Bartered Bride' has large creamy flower clusters and can grow 7 feet high. 'Baby Joe' is 1 to 2 feet tall with bushier growth and purple flowers.

How to Plant & Grow—Plant in full sun to part shade. They tolerate most types of soil as long as there is plenty of moisture. Plant in multiples for best effect, spacing 2 to 3 feet apart.

Care & Problems—Propagate by cuttings or division in spring. No fertilizing is necessary. Plants have minimal insect or disease problems.

Hardiness—Zones 5 to 9

Color(s)—Rose-pink, purple, cream

Peak Season—Late summer through fall

Mature Size (H x W)—4 to 7 ft. x 3 to 4 ft.

Water Needs—High. Water regularly.

LAMB'S EAR

Stachys byzantina

Why It's Special—Lamb's ear adds a tactile dimension to the garden with its long, velvety-soft leaves. The silver foliage brings in an underused but valuable color to the palette. It can be used in perennial borders, children's gardens, and as a groundcover, but plant some in containers so you can "pet" the leaves anytime you walk by. 'Silver Carpet' spreads quickly as a groundcover. 'Big Ears' ('Helene Von Stein') has 8-inch leaves and dwarf 'Silky Fleece' is only 2 inches tall.

How to Plant & Grow—Plant in spring or fall in full sun and well-drained soil. In areas with hot summers, select a spot with afternoon shade. If using as a groundcover, space 12 to 18 inches apart.

Care & Problems—Avoid overhead watering to prevent leaf problems. It's deer and rabbit resistant. Plants can be aggressive under ideal conditions. Propagate by division in fall.

Hardiness—Zones 4 to 9

Color(s)—Silvery gray foliage, rose flowers

Peak Season—Late spring to early summer

Mature Size (H x W)—12 to 18 in. x 12 to 18 in.

Water Needs—Low. Plants are drought tolerant once established.

LAVENDER COTTON

Santolina spp.

Why It's Special—Lavender cotton is an evergreen subshrub with fragrant foliage and flowers. As a Mediterranean native, this herb is drought tolerant and does well in coastal areas. Clip them for small hedges around herb gardens or use as groundcovers and in fire-wise landscaping. *Santolina chamaecyparissus* has silvery gray foliage while *S. virens*, hardy in zones 8 and 9, has bright green foliage. *S. rosmarinifolius* 'Morning Mist' has dark green foliage and unusual 'Lemon Fizz' has yellow to chartreuse foliage, depending on how much light it gets. All have yellow, button-like flowers in midsummer.

How to Plant & Grow—In spring or fall, plant in full sun. Space 3 feet apart for use as a groundcover, closer for hedges.

Care & Problems—Keep plants tidy and robust by shearing yearly after blooming. Do not fertilize. Propagate from cuttings. Plants are deer resistant.

Hardiness—Zones 7 to 9

Color(s)—Gray foliage, yellow flowers

Peak Season—Summer

Mature Size (H x W)—1½ ft. tall x 3 ft.

Water Needs—Medium to low. Water regularly the first year; established plants are drought tolerant.

LENTEN ROSE

Helleborus orientalis

Why It's Special—Lenten roses start blooming in late winter when we need reassurance that spring is almost here. With their evergreen, palmate leaves and long-blooming flowers, these plants are ideal for heavy shade and woodland gardens where they naturalize well. Notable single flower hybrids include *Helleborus* × *hybridus* 'Red Lady', yellow 'Warbler', 'Apricot Blush', and dark 'Winter Jewel Black'. Double hybrids include raspberry-colored 'Winter Jewel Berry Swirl', creamy white 'Mrs. Betty Ranicar', pale pink 'Ashwood Elegance Pearl', and deep pink 'Kingston Cardinal'.

How to Plant & Grow—In spring or fall, plant Lenten rose in full to part shade, in rich, well-drained soil.

Care & Problems—Plants are low maintenance; remove dead leaves in spring. No fertilizer is necessary. Propagate by division in spring; plants self-sow but not aggressively. Minimal insect or disease problems. Plants are deer resistant.

Hardiness—Zones 4 to 9

Color(s)—White, lime-green, pink, rose, purple, maroon, yellow, speckled

Peak Season—February through May

Mature Size (H x W)—18 to 24 in. x 12 to 24 in.

Water Needs—Low to medium. Water weekly during dry periods.

LIGULARIA

Ligularia spp.

Why It's Special—The bold leaves and bright flowers of ligularia make them standouts in Northwest landscapes. They're ideal for woodland gardens, shady perennial borders, edges of water gardens, and boggy areas. Plants grow in clumps. *Ligularia dentata* has serrated leaf margins and orange flowers. 'Desdemona' and 'Othello' feature burgundy stems and leaf undersides. 'Midnight Lady' has purple-black foliage. *L. przewalskii* 'The Rocket' has dark-stemmed palmate leaves and yellow flowers and 'Dragon Wings' features deeply cut leaves with burgundy veins and gold blossoms. *L. stenocephala* 'Little Rocket' has 2-foot-tall, heart-shaped leaves with serrated margins; flower spikes are 3 feet tall.

How to Plant & Grow—Plant in part to full shade, in rich soil, spacing 2 to 3 feet (based on mature size).

Care & Problems—Fertilize lightly with nitrogen fertilizer in spring. Leaves will wilt if plants get too much sun. Slugs and snails can damage foliage.

Hardiness—Zones 3 to 9

Color(s)—Yellow or orange flowers

Peak Season—June to July

Mature Size (H x W)—3 to 5 ft. x 2 to 4 ft.

Water Needs—Medium to high. They require plenty of moisture.

LUNGWORT

Pulmonaria spp.

Why It's Special—For color in shady areas of your garden, lungwort is a great choice with speckled foliage and colorful flowers. It grows where most flowering plants won't. Most are compact, the flowers attract hummingbirds, and they're good for cutting. 'Berries and Cream' has raspberry flowers and primarily silver foliage. *Pulmonaria saccharata* 'Mrs. Moon' surprises with pink flowers that mature to blue. *P. longifolia* 'Bertram Anderson' has attractive violet-blue flowers and silver-spotted leaves. *P. officinalis* 'Sissinghurst White' features bell-shaped white flowers and white-splotched leaves. *P. angustifolia* 'Azurea' has deep blue flowers.

How to Plant & Grow—In spring or fall, plant in full to part shade, in moist soil. Space 18 to 24 inches apart.

Care & Problems—Lungwort requires little maintenance. Its leaves are susceptible to powdery mildew but removing them will force attractive new growth. Propagate by division in spring or fall. Plants are deer and rabbit resistant.

Hardiness—Zones 3 to 8

Color(s)—White, pink, lavender-blue, violet

Peak Season—Early spring

Mature Size (H x W)—6 to 10 in. x 18 in.

Water Needs—Medium. Keep soil moist but not soggy.

LUPINE

Lupinus spp. and hybrids

Why It's Special—When it comes to planting lupines, more is better. There's nothing quite so striking as large groupings of these plants while they're in full bloom. They are showy, add height to the garden, and are a must for cottage gardens. Russell hybrids are very popular with profuse flower stalks in pastels and bicolors; they're 3 to 4 feet tall. Gallery series features more compact plants at 15 to 18 inches.

How to Plant & Grow—In spring, plant seeds or seedlings in full sun, spacing 2 feet apart. Afternoon shade helps in areas with hot summers. Lupines adapt to many soils if they're well drained.

Care & Problems—Don't fertilize. Leaves are susceptible to powdery mildew, snails, slugs, and aphids. Deadheading extends blooming and keeps plants vigorous. Taller plants may need support. *Note: All plant parts are toxic.*

Hardiness—Zones 3 to 8

Color(s)—White, pink, lavender, blue, purple, red, yellow, bicolors

Peak Season—May through July

Mature Size (H x W)—18 in. to 4 ft. x 2 to 3 ft.

Water Needs—Medium. Water regularly but avoid overhead watering.

ORIENTAL POPPY

Papaver orientale

Why It's Special—With huge flowers that look like they're made from crepe paper, Oriental poppies are absolutely stunning and available in many colors. For best effect, always plant in multiples. The leaves are deeply cut and hairy. Plants go dormant after blooming so combine with other later-blooming perennials or annuals. 'Beauty of Livermere' and 'Orange Scarlet' have large, orange-red petals with black blotches. 'Harlem' has beautiful burgundy-rose flowers and 'Patti's Plum' features purple blossoms with dark spots. 'Princess Victoria Louise' delights with salmon-pink blooms while 'Miss Piggy' has fringed white petals.

How to Plant & Grow—In spring, plant seeds or nursery plants in full sun; afternoon shade is helpful in areas with hot summers. Poppies have taproots so transplanting is difficult. Space 18 inches apart.

Care & Problems—These low-maintenance plants have few insect or disease problems. Plants can self-seed if not deadheaded.

Hardiness—Zones 4 to 8

Color(s)—White, pink, salmon, red, orange, purple

Peak Season—June to early July

Mature Size (H x W)—2 to 4 ft. x 2 to 4 ft.

Water Needs—Low. Water when soil is dry.

PENSTEMON

Penstemon spp.

Why It's Special—This native adapts to many conditions and comes in a wide range of colors and heights. Hummingbirds, bees, and butterflies love them. Tall flower stalks add movement to the garden and are good for cutting. Plants are versatile in rock gardens, perennial borders, and cottage gardens. *Penstemon digitalis* 'Husker Red' has burgundy foliage and stems and white tubular flowers while 'Dark Towers' features wine-red foliage and pale pink blossoms. Beardlip penstemon (*P. barbatus*) has red-orange flower panicles. Rocky Mountain penstemon (*P. strictus*) 'Bandera' has 2-foot-tall stems with profuse purple-blue flowers. Firecracker penstemon (*P. eatonii*) 'Richfield' grows 2 to 3 feet tall and has deep red blossoms.

How to Plant & Grow—Plant in spring or fall in full sun. Adapts to different well-drained soil types.

Care & Problems—Only fertilize if plants aren't growing vigorously. They have minimal insect or disease problems and are deer resistant.

Hardiness—Zones 5 to 9

Color(s)—White, red, pink, purple, blue

Peak Season—Late spring to midsummer

Mature Size (H x W)—Up to 5 ft. x 1 to 2 ft.

Water Needs—Low to medium. Drought tolerant once established.

PEONY, HERBACEOUS

Paeonia lactiflora and hybrids

Why It's Special—Herbaceous peonies are well known for their huge blooms in delightful colors. Many are fragrant and make wonderful cut flowers. These plants are perfect for perennial borders and cottage gardens. They become fully dormant in winter, reviving in spring. Recommended *Paeonia lactiflora* cultivars are 'Sarah Bernhardt' (double pink), 'Duchesse de Nemours' (semidouble white), and 'Buckeye Belle' (red semidouble). Notable hybrids are 'Coral Sunset' (semidouble), 'Summer Crown' (yellow Itoh hybrid) and 'Spring Carnival' (single, golden edged with rose).

How to Plant & Grow—Plant potted or bare-root peonies in full sun or filtered sunlight. Add compost to planting hole. Potted plants can be planted anytime but plant bare-root peonies in fall. Plant shallowly with the growing points just below soil surface.

Care & Problems—Feed low-nitrogen fertilizer in spring after new growth begins. Propagate by division in fall. Some peonies require support.

Hardiness—Zones 3 to 8

Color(s)—White, pink, salmon, red, rose, yellow, bicolors

Peak Season—Late spring to early summer

Mature Size (H x W)—2 to 4 ft. x 3 ft.

Water Needs—Medium. Water regularly.

PURPLE CONEFLOWER

Echinacea purpurea and hybrids

Why It's Special—Here's a plant that thrives on neglect and poor soil yet performs beautifully every year. Coneflowers draw butterflies and bees to the garden and give us wonderful cut flowers. Recommended cultivars include tried-and-true 'Magnus' with its rosy flowers, 'Ruby Star' with purple blooms, and 'White Swan', which features white blossoms with golden central cones. *Echinacea × hybrida* 'Cheyenne Spirit' is a mixture with orange, red, and yellow flowers; 'Twilight' has rosy red flowers and a wider central cone; and 'Coconut Lime' has double white flowers with lime-green centers.

How to Plant & Grow—In spring or fall, plant in full sun to part shade. Average soil with good drainage is a must.

Care & Problems—Propagate by division every few years. They are low maintenance. Coneflowers are deer resistant and have minimal insect or disease problems. Deadhead to prevent self-sowing.

Hardiness—Zones 4 to 9

Color(s)—Deep pink, orange, red, white, cream, lime-green, bicolors

Peak Season—July through August

Mature Size (H x W)—2 to 4 ft. x 18 to 24 in.

Water Needs—Low. They are drought tolerant.

RODGERSIA

Rodgersia spp.

Why It's Special—The large, palmate leaves of rodgersia make this a specimen plant but throw in some showy summertime flowers and you've got a winner. Foliage grows 3 to 4 feet tall while the flower stalks, reminiscent of astilbes, can reach up to 5 feet. The leaves of *Rodgersia pinnata* 'Superba' change to bronzy red at the end of summer. 'Fireworks' features deep pink blossoms and green leaves with bronze margins. The foliage of 'Chocolate Wing' starts out chocolate brown in spring, gradually changes to dark green. *R. aesculifolia* has crinkled green leaves with hints of bronze and creamy white flowers.

How to Plant & Grow—In spring, plant in full sun to part shade—especially in areas with hot summers—in rich, moist soil.

Care & Problems—Feed with high-nitrogen fertilizer in spring. It has minimal insect or disease problems.

Hardiness—Zones 5 to 7

Color(s)—Creamy white to pink

Peak Season—June to July

Mature Size (H x W)—3 to 4 ft. x 3 to 4 ft.

Water Needs—Medium to high. Plants need plenty of water to grow successfully.

RUSSIAN SAGE
Perovskia atriplicifolia

Why It's Special—The silvery gray foliage and tubular, pale blue flowers make Russian sage stand out in the garden. The leaves are aromatic and borne on woody stems. The long-blooming flowers attract butterflies, hummingbirds, and bees to the garden. Russian sage is perfect for dry settings and as a background plant. Even though it's a member of the mint family, it's not invasive. 'Blue Spires' is a tall, vigorous plant with deep blue flowers; 'Lacy Blue' is more compact at 18 to 24 inches, but it is covered with large, lavender-blue flowers. 'Little Spire' is compact.

How to Plant & Grow—In spring or fall, plant in full sun in average, well-drained soil. Space 2 to 3 feet apart.

Care & Problems—Plants have a tendency to sprawl later in the season. Cut plants down to the ground in early spring. No pest or disease problems; it's deer and rabbit resistant. Propagate by cuttings.

Hardiness—Zones 4 to 9

Color(s)—Lavender-blue

Peak Season—June through September

Mature Size (H x W)—1½ to 5 ft. x 4 ft.

Water Needs—Low. Plants are drought tolerant.

SALVIA, PERENNIAL
Salvia × superba

Why It's Special—Most sages are tough, deer resistant, and drought tolerant, and perennial sage (also known as violet sage) is no exception. The flowers bloom from summer to fall, attracting butterflies and hummingbirds. The leaves are lance-shaped and aromatic. 'Merleau' has compact growth and purple blooms. 'Blue Queen' has deep blue blossoms covering the prolific flower spikes while 'Rose Queen' has rose-pink blossoms; both grow in clumps. 'Snow Hill' features white flowers.

How to Plant & Grow—In spring or fall, plant in full sun. It grows in part shade but will have fewer blooms and less compact growth. Plants aren't particular about soil as long as it has good drainage. Space 15 to 18 inches apart.

Care & Problems—Feed with all-purpose fertilizer in spring. Deadhead to extend the bloom. Plants easily self-sow. Foliage is susceptible to powdery mildew.

Hardiness—Zones 4 to 8

Color(s)—White, pink, lavender-blue, purple

Peak Season—Late spring through September; heavy bloom in May and June

Mature Size (H x W)—18 to 24 in. x 18 to 36 in.

Water Needs—Low. Drought tolerant once established.

SCOTCH HEATHER

Calluna vulgaris

Why It's Special—Scotch heather is evergreen with a lot of variation in foliage and flower colors. It works well as a groundcover, in alpine or rock gardens, and in perennial borders. Bees *love* this plant. Scotch heather doesn't grow well in some of the colder, inland areas of the Northwest. 'Spring Torch' has bright green leaves with cream, orange, or red tips in spring and pink flowers in summer. 'Blazeaway' features yellow-green foliage from spring through summer, then turns orange or red during the colder months.

How to Plant & Grow—In spring, plant in full sun to part shade. It blooms more profusely in full sun but in hot summer areas, select an area with afternoon shade. Soil should be well drained.

Care & Problems—Prune each spring to regain its tidy growth habit. Do not fertilize. Spider mites can bother plants during hot summers. Mulch to protect plants from winter winds.

Hardiness—Zones 5 to 8

Color(s)—Pink, white

Peak Season—July to September

Mature Size (H x W)—I to 2 ft. x I to 2 ft.

Water Needs—Medium. Water regularly.

SHASTA DAISY

Leucanthemum superbum

Why It's Special—Shasta daisies are impossible to ignore when they're covered in blossoms. They are easy to grow and ideal for perennial borders and cottage and cutting gardens. Most flowers have white rays with golden disks. *Leucanthemum superbum* should not be confused with ox-eye daisy (*L. vulgare*), which will take over a garden. Notable hybrids include 'Becky' (3 to 4 feet tall) with a long blooming period; 'Banana Cream' (12 to 18 inches) with attractive, soft yellow flowers; 'Summer Snowball' (2 to 3 feet) with double white flowers; 'Snowcap' (14 inches) which blooms all at once; and 'Freak!' (10 to 14 inches) with its fluffy, curly petals.

How to Plant & Grow—In spring or fall, plant in full sun or choose part shade in areas with hot summers.

Care & Problems—Feed with an all-purpose fertilizer in spring. Deadhead to keep plants looking tidy and prevent self-sowing. Propagate by division in spring.

Hardiness—Zones 5 to 9

Color(s)—White, pale yellow

Peak Season—June through July

Mature Size (H x W)—3 to 4 ft. x 2 to 3 ft.

Water Needs—Medium. Water regularly but do not overwater.

STONECROP SEDUM
Sedum spp. and hybrids

Why It's Special—Sedum encompasses a wide variety of succulents prized for their attractive foliage and interesting flowers. Most bloom late in the season when many perennials are past their prime. Flowers attract bees and butterflies. *Sedum spectabile* 'Autumn Joy' has pale green foliage and large dusty pink flower heads. 'Vera Jamison' has burgundy foliage and rosy red flowers. Low-growing *S. kamtschaticum* 'Variegatum' has pale green leaves with white margins and golden flower clusters while *S. rupestre* 'Angelina' has needlelike leaves that start as bright green and change to yellow-orange in fall; both are ideal as groundcovers and in rock gardens.

How to Plant & Grow—In spring or fall, plant in full sun. Sedum isn't particular about soil type as long as it's well drained.

Care & Problems—No fertilizer is necessary. Deadhead flowers to keep plants tidy or leave in place for winter interest.

Hardiness—Zones 3 to 9

Color(s)—Pale to rosy pink

Peak Season—September to October

Mature Size (H x W)—1 ½ to 2 ft. x 1 ½ to 2 ft.

Water Needs—Medium to low. Plants become drought tolerant once established.

YARROW
Achillea spp.

Why It's Special—Yarrow is a tough plant that survives the harshest of conditions. The aromatic, fernlike foliage adds texture to planting beds and its flower colors are striking. Fern leaf yarrow (*Achillea filipendula*) 'Coronation Gold' is a good choice for hot sites as it is very drought tolerant. There are many attractive varieties of common yarrow (*A. millefolium*): 'Summer Wine' (burgundy red); 'Paprika' (dusty red); 'Pretty Belinda' (lilac-pink); and the Summer Pastels group are popular. Both species provide flowers suitable for drying and craft projects.

How to Plant & Grow—In spring or fall, plant in full sun, spaced 1 to 2 feet apart. Yarrow tolerates most soils as long as they are well drained. Plant in multiples for the best effect.

Care & Problems—Yarrow can become invasive; deadhead to prevent self-sowing. Do not fertilize. Propagate by division whenever clumps become overcrowded. Plants are deer resistant.

Hardiness—Zones 3 to 9

Color(s)—White, pink, red, yellow, gold, lilac, salmon, mixed

Peak Season—June to September

Mature Size (H x W)—1 ½ to 4 ft. x 2 to 3 ft.

Water Needs—Medium to low. Drought tolerant once established.

JANUARY

- Organize your photos and review with last year's garden notes for things you wanted to try or change. Not only will this get your planning off on the right foot, but taking a virtual garden tour will soften the winter blues.

- Check out the mail order catalogs over a cup of coffee. Order early if you are planning to start perennial seeds indoors.

- Start perennial seeds under lights at mid-month. They will need twelve to fourteen weeks of growing time before they can be set out in the garden.

- Gardeners west of the Cascades should start checking for slugs under evergreen perennials and put out slug bait if needed. They are active all winter here and a single slug can live up to five years.

FEBRUARY

- Continue to plant seeds; keep seed-starting mix evenly moist but not soggy. Some may be ready for a pot upgrade at the end of the month.

- If your ground is thawed, check for frost heaving, especially in new plantings. Gently tamp the plants back into the ground and apply mulch to insulate them from future frosts.

- West of the Cascades, early weeds will start popping up. Pull them now before they start to spread.

- Continue checking for slugs west of the Cascades. If the winter has been warm east of the Cascades, the slugs will appear late in the month.

- Note where soggy ground appears after a good rain or snow melt. Make plans to improve drainage in the area later in the spring by installing drainage pathways or building raised planting mounds. If that is not possible, consider installing plants that thrive in wet areas such as low spots where runoff collects or where clay soils drain slowly.

- The ground may still be too soggy to work but those first few sunny days are perfect for cleaning up remaining winter debris.

MARCH

- Perennials like Lenten rose (*Hellebous orientalis*) and Scotch heather (*Calluna vulgaris*) will be blooming in all but the coldest, snowiest areas early in the month.

- If the soil is dry enough, gardeners west of the Cascades can start planting new plants and dividing late summer-blooming ones this month. Dig well-seasoned manures and compost into new beds.

- Slugs will be very active now, so keep an eye out for them and have the soapy water and the slug bait ready. Lay cardboard or boards among their favorite plants. They will hide under them during the day and it will be easy to find them.

- Transplant the perennial seedlings you are growing indoors into 4-inch pots so their roots have enough room to grow. They will probably be ready to move to the garden by the end of April.

- Apply a low-nitrogen, slow-release organic fertilizer to perennials where the ground is thawed and workable. Work it gently into the top layer of soil.

- Trim back the scraggly, dead leaves and stems of last year's growth on evergreen perennials.

APRIL

- Tall-growing perennials will need staking toward the end of the month to help support the weight of the plants and their flowers.

- Continue checking for slugs. Aphids will be out, too, so watch for the appearance of beneficial insects. If they don't seem to be around, hose the aphids off with a strong stream of water.

- Pinch back the growing tips of early-summer blooming plants to force the plants to fill out more.

- Begin hardening off the seedling perennials you have been growing indoors in warmer parts of the region. Bring them outdoors during the day and back in at night for a week to get them used to outside temperatures.

- Deadhead the early-spring bloomers as they finish to keep them neat.

- Start a regular weeding program. Apply 2 to 3 inches of mulch to freshly weeded areas to prevent more from sprouting.

MAY

- Plant containers this month. Perennials mix nicely with annuals and grasses.

- Check your favorite nursery regularly for new shipments of plants. There is always room for one more.

- Plant your seedlings out in the open garden this month. Water them in well and frequently until they are established.

- Finish dividing or moving established late summer-blooming perennials early in the month. Water them in well and apply a light sidedressing of a low-nitrogen fertilizer.

- In dry areas, particularly east of the Cascades, begin a regular irrigation program especially for new plantings. Remember: Watering deeply and less frequently is best.

JUNE

- The perennial garden will transition from the spring bloomers to the early-summer bloomers this month. Take pictures to document the changes. When you look at them later, you might be surprised at how much of a change it really is.

- Finish planting new plants and seedlings this month before the heat and dryness settle in. Water them in well.

- Catch up on your weeding before they go to seed. Weeds without seeds can go into the compost pile. Seedy weeds need to go in the trash. Slugs will still be active too.

- East of the Cascades as the native foliage begins to dry out, deer will start moving into home gardens. Apply commercial deer repellants about every six weeks through the fall. Commercial repellants have a fixative agent that holds the spray on the leaves for up to two months.

- Towards the end of the month, give the late-summer bloomers an application of a slow-release, low-nitrogen fertilizer. Feed your container plantings with a half-strength fertilizer every two to three weeks.

JULY

- Check on mulches and add more if needed. The heat and dryness will reach full force this month.

- Keep deadheading plants to keep plants neat. Some perennials will send out smaller secondary blooms if old flower heads are removed promptly.

- Trim back dying foliage from spring-blooming plants that are going dormant. Lupines often get powdery mildew around this time, so cut them back to about a foot high. They will generate a few new leaves to keep them going.

- Slugs will be less of a problem as tender leaves harden off and become too tough to dine on. Aphids will still be around, though.

- Maintain a regular irrigation on perennials that aren't drought tolerant. Give drought-tolerant plants a good soaking every two to three weeks to keep them looking good.

- Do a good weeding now and you won't have as much to do in the fall. Apply mulch as needed.

AUGUST

- If you want perennials to self-sow, leave seedheads on the plants until they are very dry; then seeds can be shaken out over areas where you want more of them. Scratch them into the surface of the soil. Some of them may not sprout until next spring.

- Many perennials become semidormant during the hottest part of the summer. Keep them watered and they will revive when the weather cools. Trim off heat-tattered leaves to keep plants looking good.

- Update your journal and picture record. Plan what you want to divide and move in the fall or spring.

- If you are planning a new bed, add compost to it now and work it in several inches down.

- Late summer-blooming perennials like Autumn Joy sedum (*Sedum 'Autumn Joy'*), the asters (*Aster* spp.), and Russian sage (*Pervoskia atriplicifolia*) are honey bee and bumblebee magnets. Where can you plant more of them to help out the invaluable but struggling pollinators?

SEPTEMBER

- September is planting and dividing month for most perennials, especially the spring bloomers. Refer to the plant profiles in this chapter for the specifics of your particular plants. Invite some friends over to help and give away the extra plants.

- Give plants one last fertilization early in the month with a low-nitrogen fertilizer and continue watering until the fall rains arrive.

- Do one last good weeding as the weather cools and the weeds return.

- If you are collecting seed from perennials, wait until the seedheads are dry and then shake them out the seedhead onto a piece of newspaper. Dry them for a week or two in a cool, dark, dry place before putting them in paper envelopes. Label the envelope with the plant name and store in a cool, dry place.

OCTOBER

- Young plants can be pushed up out of the ground as the soil freezes and thaws throughout the winter. To prevent frost heaving, finish planting early in the month and mulch newly planted perennials with straw or pine needles to keep soil temperatures even.

- Continue watering if the fall rains haven't returned.

- As the frost takes down plants, clear them from the garden and add them to the compost pile.

NOVEMBER

- Check out the fall colors of your evergreen and late-fall perennials. What can you add to the garden for more late-season color and texture?

- Finish cleaning beds and marking the crowns of plants so you don't dig into them in the spring.

- Make a new compost pile with all your trimmings, leaves and lawn debris. Mix green and brown material equally and moisten it to the consistency of a wrung-out sponge.

DECEMBER

- If snow and ice cover your drive and walkways, use only potassium or magnesium chloride de-icing salts. These salts don't hurt plants.

- Review your notes and jot down ideas for next year.

ROSES
for the Northwest

Roses have a special place in the hearts and gardens of Northwest gardeners. Who can resist their colors, fragrance, or versatility as a groundcover, hedge, vine, or show-stopping specimen in the landscape? Portland, Oregon, is even known as the City of Roses and is home to the International Rose Test Garden. Located in Washington Park in the city's West Hills, the public display garden is home to over 550 varieties of roses and over 7,000 plants.

Beyond being a beautiful display garden, the American Rose Society (ARS) and other international rose breeders use the garden to test new rose cultivars for vigor, disease, and insect tolerance, and their response to the local climate and hardiness before the plants are released to growers and the public. The plants that do well here and in other test gardens around the U.S. and Canada will be the hot new introductions in the future.

With 50 different categories of roses recognized by the ARS and hundreds of cultivars within each category, it can be a challenge to find your favorites. Take some time to walk through public rose gardens in your area and identify those that will fit your space and landscape needs and are in the colors you like. In addition to the International Rose Test Garden in Portland, there are also notable public rose gardens in Longview, Seattle, and Spokane in Washington and Vancouver and Victoria, B.C.

CLIMATE: THE GOOD AND THE BAD

On one hand, the cool, damp, marine-influenced climate west of the Cascades is considered one of the best for growing roses in the world outside of England. The cooler temperatures and higher humidity allow plants to flourish and keeps flowers looking good for long periods. However, not everything is perfect in paradise. This same climate also creates conditions perfect for the development of diseases such as blackspot, rust, and powdery mildew. Cool daytime temperatures and cloudy, damp mornings don't allow the dew and irrigation water to dry off leaves quickly, creating the perfect environment for disease development. It is another

reason why rose breeders bring their new cultivars here to test. If the plant grows and blooms well and proves to be resistant to disease, then they know they have a winner.

East of the Cascades, rose gardeners have a whole different set of advantages and challenges. Disease issues are not as prevalent here because the hot, sunny days and lower humidity levels evaporate moisture off leaf surfaces quickly. On the other hand, these same conditions make regular irrigation necessary throughout the summer and early fall, especially on windy days. In the winter, many grafted and marginally hardy roses will need protective winter mulches to protect graft points and stems from temperatures that can get below zero.

USING ROSES IN THE SUSTAINABLE LANDSCAPE

As interest in sustainable gardens grows and new, more carefree roses hit the market, roses again are gaining popularity and respect for their versatility in the garden. The old varieties of shrub, old garden, and species roses that had been ignored for years are finding their way back into the garden as low-maintenance, durable border backdrops, hedges, and foundation plantings that provide structure and form to the garden. The new, more vigorous, hardy, and disease-resistant hybrid tea, grandiflora, and floribunda roses are finding their way back as specimen plantings in borders, beds, and even in patio containers. Low-growing groundcover roses are being used to cover sunny areas as a carefree alternative to higher-maintenance perennials and shrubs. Climbing and rambling roses are being trained up stout arbors and walls to soften harsh edges and cover ugly structures, all while spreading their fragrance through the garden. Miniature and smaller-growing floribundas and miniature roses can easily be grown in large containers in smaller gardens or on decks and patios.

Finally, many roses have interesting fall color and fruit in the form of rose hips at the end of the season. Birds and other wildlife seek out the rose hips for winter food and take shelter among the rose stems.

For us, rose hips are a good source of vitamin C and can be used to make jelly and tea.

GROWING ROSES IN NORTHWEST GARDENS

Roses need an average of six to eight hours of sun per day to bloom properly; they do best in morning sun with some afternoon shade, especially east of the Cascades. Afternoon shade helps prolong bloom life while morning sun helps dry the dew quickly, reducing the potential for disease. That said, *Rosa alba* and *Rosa multiflora* do well in less than six hours of sun. Roses tolerate a wide range of soils from clayey loams to the gravelly glacial soils found in the Northwest. If soggy soils are a challenge, roses can be planted in raised mounds or beds. Amend the soil with a good quality compost at planting time and as a topdressing every other year. Finally, roses need good air circulation around the plants and the space they grow in to reduce disease potential. This can be a challenge when rose plantings are surrounded by native and planted forests that block breezes. Leave a generous space between plants and thin dense stems as needed to improve air flow.

Repeat bloomers like hybrid tea, grandiflora, and floribunda roses are heavy feeders and benefit from the regular application of rose fertilizer or an organic 10-10-10 fertilizer. The first feeding should be in the early spring when winter mulches are removed, and then every month until mid-August. Single-blooming shrub, old garden, climbers, and species roses are much thriftier with nutrients and need only an early spring application and then again after they finish blooming. In general, fertilization should end no later than mid-August so that plants have time to harden off before winter.

Regular watering is *critical* for roses, especially east of the Cascades. Most plants need 1 to ½ inches of water a week, especially in hot or windy weather. Where possible, use drip irrigation or soaker hoses to keep water off the leaves.

Roses can add a touch of an English garden to the landscape. Northland Rosarium, Spokane, Washington.

HARDINESS AND WINTER PROTECTION

Roses have a wide range of tolerances to winter cold. Many of the shrub, old garden, and species roses are hardy to zones 4 to 5 and will need little winter protection. Some, particularly the Explorer and Parkland (Morden) series developed in Canada, are hardy to zone 3. Grafted roses, on the other hand, generally need a good mulch around their crowns to protect graft points from freezing. The rootstocks are usually quite hardy but the grafted top of the plant may only be hardy to zone 6. Mound soil or compost brought from another part of the garden several inches above the graft point and then cover the compost with another foot of shredded pine or spruce needles, shredded leaves, medium-texture bark, or other coarse, fast-draining material.

Apply mulch around the end of October and leave it in place until March west of the Cascades and until early April east of the Cascades.

Some gardeners protect the graft point by planting it 2 to 4 inches below the surface of the soil. This leaves a reservoir of growth buds on the blooming part of the plant above the graft point to regrow if the plant is killed to the ground. This concept comes with many differing opinions among rose experts so talk to your local Master Gardeners or rose society about what works best in your area.

OWN-ROOT OR GRAFTED ROSES

When the graft point on a grafted rose dies, the rootstock sprouts and replaces your beautiful rose with a rankly growing monster with less than stellar blooms. As gardeners began demanding grafted roses that were easier to care for and less likely to succumb to cold winters, breeders began growing some of the more vigorous varieties on their own roots. This means that if the top of an own-root plant dies to the ground for any reason, there is a reservoir of buds below ground that can easily regrow the rose. Own-root roses also tend to be longer-lived and produce more canes than grafted roses. Ask your local nursery staff or Master Gardener program about local sources or you can order them from several Northwest specialty nurseries.

DISEASE AND PEST MANAGEMENT

The best ways to reduce the potential for disease or pest outbreaks is to care for the plants properly and plant disease-resistant varieties. Providing well-drained soil, adequate water, removing dead

Blackspot

Powdery mildew

Aphids *(enlarged to show detail)*

leaves and debris, and maintaining good air circulation can go a long ways toward reducing insect and disease problems.

Even with good plant selection and cultural practices, disease issues will still arise and insects will attack. Blackspot, rust, and powdery mildew can be controlled with commercial organic fungicides including Bordeaux mixes applied at the first sign of disease. Homemade sprays containing baking soda and horticultural oil mixed with water can serve as a treatment for powdery mildew.

Aphids, curculio beetles, spider mites, and rose midges are common insects found on roses. Aphids usually appear in the spring when new growth is emerging to feed on the tips of new stems and buds. Spider mites appear later in the summer and feed on leaves, leaving them stippled with tan specks; Curculio beetles, thrips, and rose midges feed on buds and flowers, distorting them in the process.

A few insects on plants are normal. However, when the numbers of undesirable insects rise to unacceptable levels, it's time to apply IPM techniques. Begin watching for beneficial insects like lady beetles, syrphid flies, and lacewings. Be patient, it can take a couple of weeks for the population of beneficial insects to get big enough to put a dent in the pest populations. If you get impatient, use a hard stream of water to knock insects off the plants to break up their reproduction cycle. Finally, if insect infestations become overwhelming, apply an insecticidal soap according to the label instructions. Be aware that insecticidal soaps will also kill beneficial insects.

PRUNING ROSES

Roses need to be pruned for several reasons: to maintain their shape, vigor, health, and to encourage flowering. Most pruning and shearing should be done in the early spring as winter mulches are removed. Hybrid teas, grandifloras, and floribundas generally need to be pruned to several stout canes to encourage flower development. Groundcover roses need a light shearing to encourage new growth and flower production. Shrub-type roses generally need an occasional thinning and removal of an errant cane. Finally, climbing roses need to have one or two of the oldest canes cut to the ground each year to encourage new wood for flower production.

Roses have come a long way from the days when they seemed to catch every bug and disease known to gardeners or froze to the ground during a cold winter storm. Today's roses are tough, disease resistant, and easy to maintain. Where once the hybrid tea rose dominated the garden, breeders and rose aficionados have reintroduced many old standbys and created new types that can fit into nearly every garden setting. Have fun discovering them.

CLIMBING
Rosa cultivars

Why It's Special—Nothing is prettier than a climbing rose paired with a clematis, spilling over an arbor or pergola. Climbing roses can be used at garden entrances, as privacy screens, or along house walls. Once established, they'll bloom profusely. Recommended varieties include 'New Dawn', 'Fourth of July', 'Geschwind's Schonste', and 'William Baffin'.

How to Plant & Grow—Choose a sunny or partially sunny location where a climber will have plenty of room to grow. Work compost or composted manure into the soil. Mulch around base of plants to conserve moisture and impede weeds. Provide roses with a sturdy support to grow on.

Care & Problems—Fertilize with 10-10-10 in spring and high-phosphorus fertilizer after initial blooming. Only prune to remove dead wood; no other pruning is necessary. If your rose has insect or disease issues, contact your local Master Gardener program for information.

Hardiness—Varies with species

Bloom Color—Various, including red, pink, salmon, yellow, white

Bloom Period—Once, or repeat blooming summer through fall

Mature Size (H x W)—6 to 20 ft. x 3 to 6 ft.

Water Needs—Medium. Water regularly.

ENGLISH
Rosa cultivars

Why It's Special—English roses, primarily bred by David Austin, are known for their heavy fragrance, lush blossoms, ability to rebloom, and superior disease resistance. Stunning cultivars include 'Graham Thomas', 'Heritage', 'Lady of Shalott', and 'William Morris'.

How to Plant & Grow—Select a sunny location; in areas with hot summers, afternoon shade is ideal. Plant bare-root roses in spring or container-grown plants from spring to fall. Incorporate compost or composted manure into soil. Space individual roses 3 feet from other plants or groupings of English roses 18 inches apart. Mulch around the base of plants to retain moisture.

Care & Problems—Fertilize when they start growing in spring and after blooming with fertilizer high in phosphorus. Prune back by one-third to two-thirds in summer after flowering to encourage additional blooms. Roses can be bothered by some insects and diseases; contact your local Master Gardener program for advice.

Hardiness—Zone 4 and above

Bloom Color—Variety of colors

Bloom Period—Summer to fall

Mature Size (H x W)—3 to 6 ft. x 3 to 4 ft.

Water Needs—Medium. Keep soil lightly moist.

FLORIBUNDA
Rosa cultivars

Why It's Special—Floribunda roses are more compact than many other classes. These fragrant roses are a cross between hybrid teas and polyanthas. Because they flower in clusters, it's like having bouquets of roses all over the plants. They are repeat-bloomers. They're often used as hedges or planted in groupings. Suggested varieties: 'Gruss An Aachen', 'Iceberg', 'Julia Child', 'Scentimental', and 'What A Peach'.

How to Plant & Grow—Plant bare-root roses in spring or container-grown plants from spring to fall. Select a site that gets at least six hours of sun daily; provide afternoon shade in hot-summer regions. Incorporate compost or composted manure into soil. Space plants 2 to 3 feet apart; mulch around bases to retain moisture.

Care & Problems—In spring, remove dead wood and small canes. Fertilize with 10-10-10 in spring and high-phosphorus fertilizer after initial bloom. Deadhead to prolong blooming. Provide winter protection with heavy mulches. Floribundas have good disease resistance.

Hardiness—Zone 5 and above

Bloom Color—Variety of colors

Bloom Period—Summer

Mature Size (H x W)—3 to 5 ft. x 3 ft.

Water Needs—Medium. Water regularly.

GRANDIFLORA
Rosa cultivars

Why It's Special—Grandiflora roses are taller than hybrid teas and either have clusters of large, elegantly formed blossoms or single flowers, ideal for cutting. They are hardy repeat-bloomers. This rose class was developed for crosses of hybrid teas and floribundas. Recommended varieties: 'Cherry Parfait', 'Queen Elizabeth', 'Tournament of Roses', and 'Wild Blue Yonder'.

How to Plant & Grow—Plant bare-root roses in spring or container-grown plants from spring to fall. Select a site that gets at least six hours of sun daily; provide afternoon shade in hot-summer regions. Work compost or composted manure into the soil. Space plants 3 feet apart and mulch around the bases to retain moisture.

Care & Problems—Prune in early spring to remove dead, damaged, or crossing branches; remove canes smaller than the diameter of a pencil. Fertilize with 10-10-10 in spring and high-phosphorus fertilizer after initial bloom. Grandifloras have good disease resistance.

Hardiness—Zone 5 and above

Bloom Color—A variety of solids, blends, and bicolors

Bloom Period—Summer

Mature Size (H x W)—4 to 6 ft. x 3 ft.

Water Needs—Medium. Water deeply at soil level.

HYBRID TEA
Rosa cultivars

Why It's Special—Prized for their classic, long-stemmed blooms with high centers, hybrid teas are a staple of the floral industry. Many cultivars are extremely fragrant. Plant individual roses as specimens or in groupings. Recommended varieties include 'Double Delight', 'Peace', 'Elle', 'Mikado', and 'Sunset Celebration'.

How to Plant & Grow—Plant bare-root roses in spring or container-grown plants from spring to fall. Select a sunny location, although afternoon shade is helpful in areas with hot summers. Soil must have good drainage; incorporate compost or composted manure to improve fertility and water absorption. Space plants 2½ to 3 feet apart and mulch around the base of plants to retain moisture.

Care & Problems—Prune in early spring and fertilize monthly. Deadhead to encourage additional blooming. Hybrid teas are considered high maintenance compared to other rose classes and are susceptible to insects and disease; contact your local Master Gardener program for controls.

Hardiness—Zone 5 and above

Bloom Color—Variety of colors

Bloom Period—Summer

Mature Size (H x W)—2 to 6 ft. x 3 ft.

Water Needs—Medium. Water deeply once a week.

MINIATURE
Rosa cultivars

Why It's Special—While miniature roses may sound tiny and delicate, most are quite hardy and bloom profusely. They grow on their own roots and are scaled-back versions of larger roses. Most have compact, bushy growth and range from a diminutive 6 inches to 2 feet. Some have a light fragrance. They work well in rock gardens, border fronts, and in containers, and they can be grown indoors. There are many varieties available.

How to Plant & Grow—Miniature roses need plenty of sunlight. Plant them in spring as they start to bud out so they have a whole season to become established. The soil must be well drained; work compost into the top few inches of the soil.

Care & Problems—Prune back by one-third in spring. Fertilize monthly with rose food or all-purpose fertilizer during spring and summer. Mulch plants for winter protection. The same pests and diseases affect minis as full-sized roses.

Hardiness—Zone 5 and above

Bloom Color—Variety of colors

Bloom Period—Summer

Mature Size (H x W)—6 to 24 in. x 8 to 24 in.

Water Needs—Medium. Regularly water.

MODERN SHRUB
Rosa cultivars

Why It's Special—While modern shrub roses tolerate a variety of light conditions, most prefer to grow in full sun to part shade. They were bred for improved hardiness, disease resistance, and ease of care. Many are grown on their own rootstock. Some bloom continuously while others bloom once in spring. Cultivars include 'Baby Love', 'Ballerina', 'Cerise Bouquet', 'Abbaye de Cluny', and 'Scintillation'.

How to Plant & Grow—Modern shrub roses tolerate wide variety of light conditions but most can be grown in full sun to part shade. Soil must be well drained and amended with compost. Spacing varies; refer to the plant tag.

Care & Problems—Fertilize with 10-10-10 in spring and high-phosphorus fertilizer after initial bloom. Do not prune for first two years. After that, prune to shape plants as needed; remove one-third of the oldest canes each spring to renew roses. The remaining mature canes will flower. Contact your local Master Gardener program for insect and disease controls.

Hardiness—Varies by variety

Bloom Color—Variety of colors

Bloom Period—Summer

Mature Size (H x W)—3 to 8 ft. x 3 to 6 ft.

Water Needs—Medium. Water regularly.

OLD GARDEN
Rosa cultivars

Why It's Special—Old garden roses are a group of rose classes that existed before 1867. The group comprises alba, Bourbon, Centifolia, China, damask, Gallica, moss, Noisette, Portland, rambler, and tea roses. Some varieties bloom once, others are repeat-bloomers, and still others bloom constantly. Notable cultivars: 'Reine Victoria', 'Madame Hardy', 'Apothecary's Rose', 'Rosa Mundi', 'Crested Moss', and 'Rose de Rescht'.

How to Plant & Grow—Plant bare-root roses in spring or container-grown plants from spring to fall. Select an area that gets at least six hours of sunlight each day and where the soil is well drained. Give them plenty of room to grow and avoid planting near trees or shrubs since their roots will compete for moisture and nutrients.

Care & Problems—Fertilize every six weeks, from early spring until late July. Prune once-bloomers after flowering; all others bloom on both old and new wood so can be pruned before or after flowering. Old garden roses have good disease resistance.

Hardiness—Zone 4 and above

Bloom Color—Pink, red, white

Bloom Period—Summer

Mature Size (H x W)—Varies

Water Needs—Medium. Water regularly.

SHRUB
Rosa cultivars

Why It's Special—Shrub roses are ideal for rose aficionados who are looking for fragrance and performance, yet don't want to fuss over them. They are hardy, have good disease resistance and are versatile in the landscape. Many bloom just once in June, although some are repeat-bloomers. All were developed in recent times. Grow them as specimens, in perennial borders, or as hedges.

How to Plant & Grow—Shrub roses grow in full sun to part shade. They adapt to different soil types as long as it's well drained. Plant bare-root roses in spring or container-grown plants from spring to fall. For the most impact, plant them in groupings of three with 18-inch spacing or individually with 2½- to 3-foot spacing from other plants.

Care & Problems—Fertilize regularly as shrub roses are heavy feeders. In spring, prune once-bloomers lightly and prune back repeat-bloomers by one- to two-thirds.

Hardiness—Varies with species

Bloom Color—Variety of colors

Bloom Period—Early summer, many repeat throughout summer

Mature Size (H x W)—2 to 8 ft. x 2 to 8 ft.

Water Needs—Medium. Provide regular water.

JANUARY

- Check mulches around roses to make sure they haven't settled too much and exposed the graft points. Add a layer of evergreen boughs left over from your holiday decorations or extra pine needles or shredded leaves if needed.

- Review your notes and begin planning revisions to existing rose plantings or developing new plantings. Evaluate potential new garden sites for sun, air flow, and soil conditions. If needed, use the dormant season to trim back shrubs and trees around the new bed.

- Check on containerized roses you stored in the garage for winter. Water lightly only if the soil is dry and not frozen.

FEBRUARY

- Order bare-root roses while selections are still good. Gardeners west of the Cascades can designate a March delivery date while gardeners east of the Cascades should not take delivery until mid-April to avoid plants freezing in shipment. Plant them as soon as they arrive or heel them into holding beds until you can. Water them well.

- Apply dormant oil to roses that have proved to be susceptible to disease and insect damage.

- Check plants planted the previous year for frost heaving. Gently tamp them back into the soil and apply more mulch to insulate them.

MARCH

- Gardeners west of the Cascades can begin removing mulch at mid-month from roses as buds begin to swell. Gardeners east of the Cascades need to wait until April to begin any spring rose chores.

- Prune back winter-killed canes to green wood. Thin out weak or old canes to create a strong, well-spaced framework that will produce strong new canes and improve air flow in and around the plants.

- Apply a granular, slow-release, organic rose fertilizer to plants towards the end of the month as buds begin to swell. Work it into the soil surface gently so as to not disturb feeder roots. This will be the first of monthly feedings you will need to do until mid-August. Gently work the fertilizer into the surface of the soil around the plant's drip line so as to not disturb the fine surface roots the plant relies on for gathering water.

APRIL

- Gardeners east of the Cascades can remove mulches and begin their spring pruning and fertilizing early this month.

- Bare-root and container roses will be available in nurseries now. Look for plants with three to four strong, well-spaced canes and strong root systems. Plant immediately.

- Begin training climbing roses to their supports. Thin one or two of the oldest canes back to the ground each year to stimulate new growth.

- Begin watching for aphids on new growth. Watch for the appearance of beneficial insects such as lady beetles and lacewings. If these don't appear within a couple of weeks, knock aphids' numbers down by spraying the plants with a hard stream of water.

- If the aphids get really bad or you can't tolerate the invasion, apply insecticidal soap to the plants. Aphids will be active until the new growth matures and hardens.

MAY

- Early this month throughout the region, begin a monthly fertilization program for the repeat-blooming hybrid teas, grandifloras, and floribundas. Work a slow-release granular organic rose fertilizer in around the drip line of the plant.

- Bare-root roses should be in the ground by the early part of the month. Containerized plants can be planted into late June. Water them in well.

- Watch for the appearance of blackspot and powdery mildew. Select disease-resistant plants to start with. Blackspot and powdery mildew are likely to appear during warm, humid weather and are more common west of the Cascades. Remove all infected leaves and debris and throw them in the trash to prevent further spread. Thin out crowded stems to improve air flow. There is still time to transplant bushes that are growing too close together. Thin surrounding shrubs and trees to improve air flow. If you have had problems with these diseases in past years, apply commercial fungicides early in the year as leaves emerge.

- Remove any shoots that appear below the graft point. This is growth from the rootstock and it can overpower the grafted portion of the plant and take over the plant.

- Begin a regular training program for climbing roses to keep them from taking over nearby plants and to keep their blooms at a level where you can appreciate them.

JUNE

- As plants reach their full growth, begin a regular watering program early this month if you haven't already. Plants should get an inch of water a week. Avoid using overhead sprinklers in favor of drip irrigation. Overhead irrigation leaves too much water on the leaves and can result in the onset of blackspot and powdery mildew.

- June is the height of rose season. Take pictures to record their beauty and to plan any changes. Take the time to enjoy their fragrance and pick bouquets for the house and friends. To create a long-lasting bouquet, cut roses early in the day just as the bud begins to open. Cut the stem at an angle just above an outward facing five-leaf stem. Remove the lower leaves from the stem and recut the stem just before you place it in a vase. Change the water every couple of days.

- Deadhead faded blooms to prolong blooming in repeat bloomers and keep the plants neat.

- Apply mulch around plants to reduce water loss as the summer heats up and to deter weed growth.

JULY

- Continue to train climbing rose canes onto their supports as they grow.

- Watch for the emergence of insects on new foliage and flowers. Encourage beneficial insects, spray with water, or, as a last resort, treat the plants with an insecticidal soap.

- As the dry weather takes hold, check that plants are getting enough water. Water deeply so that plants get 1 to 1½ inches of water a week. Continue your fertilization program.

- Remove plants that are not thriving. Do not replant another rose in the same spot without removing all the soil from the hole. It can have an allelopathic effect on a new plant.

AUGUST

- Gardeners east of the Cascades should make their last fertilizer application by the early part of the month. Gardeners west of the Cascades should finish by the middle of the month. This will slow the development of new growth and allow plants to harden off before hard frosts occur.

- Water and check for insects and disease regularly.

- Containerized nursery plants need to be planted in the ground this month so they have enough time to establish roots before cold weather sets in. Remove all blooms so the plant can focus on root development instead of flower development.

- Catch up on weeding around rose plants. Use a scuffle hoe to reach among the thorny branches to reach the weeds. Disturb only the top inch of soil to prevent damaging surface feeder roots. Reapply mulch to prevent new weed growth.

SEPTEMBER

- Discontinue pruning and deadheading early this month to discourage new growth and to let the plants know it's time to begin going dormant.

- Take some time to makes notes on what worked and what didn't, plants that seemed to struggle, or plants that were plagued with disease and insect problems.

- Light frosts this month and next won't hurt blooms. They will continue until the hard frosts occur in late October.

OCTOBER

- Begin gathering mulching materials as you rake up leaves and needles.

- Keep up your watering program until the steady rains return.

- Gardeners east of the Cascades can begin mulching roses during the last half of the month. Shredded ponderosa pine needles make an excellent, fast-draining winter mulch. Cover the graft point and the lower canes with about a foot of mulch.

- Pick the last bouquet of roses and enjoy them. Next summer is a long way off.

NOVEMBER

- Keep a hose and sprinkler out so you can give roses one more long drink if the fall rains are slow in coming.

- Gardeners west of the Cascades can begin mulching roses this month.

- Prune canes of hybrid tea roses back by half to prevent them from whipping in the winter winds. Don't cut them any shorter as the stems have food reserves that plant will need over the winter.

DECEMBER

- Order specialty catalogs and research some new varieties to try.

- Move roses growing in containers to a protected shed or garage. Once they are dormant and the leaves have come off, they won't need much light.

SHRUBS
for the Northwest

There is no end to the versatility and beauty that shrubs can add to a Northwest garden. Deciduous and evergreen shrubs are often considered the "bones" of the garden and provide year-round permanence and structure. They bridge the vertical space between tall trees and ground-hugging plants, tying the garden together and melding our built gardens into the native landscape that is never very far away. Tall shrubs serve as privacy screens and hedges between neighbors and divide spaces in the garden. Low-growing shrubs soften the harsh edges of foundations and hide bare stems of taller plants. Mounding shrubs can cover rough areas and slopes that are prone to erosion. Smaller shrubs planted in containers make a colorful addition to a deck or patio.

GROWING SHRUBS IN THE NORTHWEST

The biggest mistake many gardeners make when selecting shrubs is to pick the wrong shrub for the wrong place. Resist falling for the "cuteness factor" at the nursery; instead, pick shrubs *whose mature size fits the space you have.* Shrubs allowed to grow this way will keep their natural shape and need little if any pruning beyond a periodic thinning and light shaping. The mature size information on plant tags is based on a ten-year estimate; they can grow much larger if left in place for a few decades.

Shrubs generally need well-drained soil with some organic matter but many do well in clayey or marginally fertile soils. They don't need much fertilizer beyond a light application of 10-10-10 garden fertilizer or rhododendron fertilizer in the spring. Many shrubs, especially native shrubs, are fairly drought tolerant and only need regular irrigation during the summer. This makes them perfect for those drier areas of the garden.

Gardeners east of the Cascades need to take into account differences in climate, plant hardiness, and soil pH when buying and planting shrubs. Gardeners in this region will have to water more frequently, especially in hot, windy weather, and be prepared for very cold temperatures in the winter. Check hardiness ratings carefully when buying shrubs to ensure your new purchases match your hardiness zone. Consult with nursery staff or your local Master Gardener program for their experiences with marginally hardy shrubs.

Soils east of the Cascades tend to be more alkaline with a pH above 6.5. Many shrubs like rhododendrons (*Rhododendron* spp.), pieris (*Pieris japonica*), and big leaf or mophead hydrangea (*Hydrangea macrophylla*) that thrive in the acidic soils west of the Cascades struggle in the more alkaline soils found here. Gardeners east of the Cascades will need to get a soil pH test and based on the results, amend their soil with granular sulfur to lower the pH before planting.

CELEBRATE OUR NATIVE SHRUBS

Many of our Northwest native evergreen and deciduous shrubs have found their way from our native landscape into our gardens as "domesticated" shrubs. Some common examples include rhododendrons (*Rhododendron* spp.), Oregon grape (*Mahonia* spp.), and ninebark (*Physocarpus opulifolius*). These shrubs are already adapted to our climate, soils, moisture, and sun and shade patterns, making them the epitome of sustainable landscaping. They generally only need extra irrigation during the hottest part of the summer, use less fertilizer, need little pruning, and are less prone to disease and insect problems than other shrubs. They also provide a familiar source of fruit, flowers, and branch structure preferred by native insects, birds, and wildlife for food, shelter, and nesting sites. Plant breeders have developed many new cultivars from our native shrubs. As an example, breeders took our native green-leaved ninebark and created cultivars *P.* 'Diablo' with dark purple leaves and *P.* 'Coppertina' and 'Dart's Gold' with copper-colored and brilliant yellow leaves. Ask your local nursery, local Master Gardener members, or native plant society for good sources of native plant stock adapted to your area.

Rhododendrons do well in the filter shade of tall trees.

GROWING THE NORTHWEST'S CLASSIC SHRUBS

RHODODENDRON

Without a doubt, rhododendrons and their cousins the evergreen and deciduous azaleas are *the* quintessential signature shrub of the Northwest, both in the wild and in our gardens. Most species thrive west of the Cascades while gardeners have to choose hardy varieties east of the Cascades.

Rhododendrons need an acidic, well-drained soil rich in organic matter. Gardeners east of the Cascades will need to amend their soil with granular sulfur to lower the pH. Considered an understory plant, they do best in the filtered shade of taller trees, especially east of the Cascades. Rhododendrons are tolerant of our dry summers but do benefit from regular watering during the hottest part of July and August, especially east of the Cascades. Plants should be fertilized with a rhododendron fertilizer in the spring just as they bloom. To encourage development of next year's flower buds, deadhead blooms right after they fade by snapping off the old bloom just above the newly emerging bud. Overgrown plants can be pruned just after flowering by cutting stems back to a bud or whorl of leaves down inside the canopy.

CAMELLIA

West of the Cascades, camellias (*Camellia* spp.) attract a lot of attention with their beautiful early-blooming, pink, red, white, or variegated flowers and dark green evergreen leaves. They are not hardy east of the Cascades. Some varieties begin flowering in the winter, adding color to the drab landscape, while others bloom well into the spring. Camellias grow as a dense shrub or small tree making nice specimen plants or hedges. They prefer a well-drained, acidic soil rich in organic matter with regular watering during the summer months and a light fertilization with rhododendron fertilizer right after flowering. They thrive in the light, filtered shade of taller shrubs and trees. The shrubs can be periodically sheared immediately after flowering to redefine their shape and size.

HYDRANGEA

Hydrangeas (*Hydrangea* spp.) with their bold leaves and huge blue, pink, and white flowers are the stars of the midsummer garden. They need an acidic, well-drained soil high in organic matter, filtered shade, especially east of the Cascades, and frequent watering through the growing season. They are one of the first shrubs to wilt when conditions get too dry. The shrubs benefit from a light, early-spring application of rhododendron fertilizer.

To grow the blue-flowered mophead hydrangea (*Hydrangea macrophylla*) east of the Cascades, gardeners will have to amend their alkaline soil with granular sulfur and aluminum sulfate to lower the pH and free up the aluminum in the soil to maintain blue flowers. Even then, it isn't easy; most of the blooms turn more pink than blue over the years. While the plant itself is hardy to zone 5, the buds are not and are frequently killed by cold unless planted in a protected spot and heavily mulched. Gardeners here would be wise to plant cultivars of the *H. macrophylla* Endless Summer series that bloom on new wood or cultivars of the white- to pink-flowering peegee hydrangea (*H. paniculata*) that are much hardier.

Gardening with shrubs in the Northwest is an adventure in shape, size, texture, and color. There is a shrub for *every* place in the garden. You can even create a colorful garden just by using shrubs with different shades of green, yellow, red, and purple. Some have great fall color and others have interesting bark during the winter. Many are native to the Northwest. Experiment with them and see what interesting gardens you can create.

Camellias bloom early in the year and provide a cheery contrast to clouds and rain.

ARBORVITAE
Thuja occidentalis

Why It's Special—Arborvitaes' conical shape makes them ideal for hedges, windbreaks, and foundation plants. Many birds seek them out as cover from predators. These shrubs grow quickly and have attractive overlapping, scalelike leaves on fan-shaped branchlets. They are also known as Eastern or American arborvitae or white cedar. 'Nigra' features dark green foliage and can reach 30 feet while 'Emerald' has bushier, more compact growth up to 10 feet. Dwarf 'Little Gem' grows just 3 feet tall.

How to Plant & Grow—Arborvitae tolerate all light conditions and soil types provided they are well drained. Plant in spring or fall.

Care & Problems—Deer think arborvitaes are *delicious*. Either plant them where deer can't get to them or consider using a deer repellent on the foliage. Spider mites can be a problem. Branches can become damaged from heavy snowfall. Prune plants as needed to keep them a manageable height.

Hardiness—Zones 2 to 7

Seasonal Color—Evergreen

Peak Season—Year-round evergreen foliage

Mature Size (H x W)—3 to 40 ft. x 4 to 15 ft.

Water Needs—Medium. Water regularly.

AZALEA
Rhododendron × spp. and hybrids

Why It's Special—Members of the rhododendron family, azaleas bloom earlier than rhodies and have smaller flowers but their profuse blooms provide plenty of color early in the season. They also attract hummingbirds and butterflies to the garden. Grow them as specimens or in groupings for more impact. Plants are evergreen in areas with milder winters.

How to Plant & Grow—Choose the hardiest varieties for your region. Select a site that is sheltered from the wind. Plant azaleas in full sun except in areas with hot summers; then grow in partial shade. They prefer rich, acidic soil with a pH of about 5.5. Plant shallowly and mulch around the plants to protect their roots.

Care & Problems—Feed with an acidic fertilizer such as rhododendron food each spring. Prune lightly as needed to retain shape. Deadhead to keep plants looking tidy.

Hardiness—Zones 4 to 9

Seasonal Color—Red, salmon, pink, white, yellow

Peak Season—Spring to early summer

Mature Size (H x W)—3 to 6 ft. x 6 to 12 ft.

Water Needs—Medium. Water regularly.

BEAUTYBUSH
Kolkwitzia amabilis

Why It's Special—Beautybush is best known for its profuse bell-shaped flowers and attractive arching growth habit. The plants have exfoliating bark that also provides winter interest. Plant one as a specimen or create a hedge with several. 'Pink Cloud' is the most commonly found cultivar with green foliage and a showy springtime display of dainty pink flowers. Dream Catcher™ 'Maradco' is prized for its golden foliage that changes to orange-red in autumn.

How to Plant & Grow—Beautybush is easy to grow. Plant it in spring or fall in full sun to get the maximum amount of blooms. It adapts to all soil types.

Care & Problems—Feed with all-purpose fertilizer in spring. Plants grow densely so they require occasional pruning to reshape them. Prune after flowering since they bloom on old wood. They have minimal insect or disease problems, and are deer resistant.

Hardiness—Zones 4 to 8

Seasonal Color—Pink with yellow throats

Peak Season—April to May

Mature Size (H x W)—6 to 10 ft. x 6 to 10 ft.

Water Needs—Medium. Water regularly, especially during hot periods.

BLUE MIST SPIREA
Caryopteris incana

Why It's Special—Also known as bluebeard, blue mist spirea bursts into bloom late in the season when most shrubs have finished flowering. Bees and butterflies love to visit its attractive blue flower clusters; it is a good choice for a butterfly garden. Since it has a mounding growth habit, some gardeners plant several to create a hedge. Both the flowers and leaves are fragrant. 'Blue Myth' features dark blue flowers and gray-green leaves. Sunshine Blue™ 'Jason' is an ideal accent plant with its purple-blue flowers and golden foliage.

How to Plant & Grow—Plant in spring or fall in full sun for best results, in average, well-drained soil.

Care & Problems—Feed a slow-release fertilizer for shrubs and trees in spring. Prune back stems during dormancy as plants bloom on new wood. They have minimal insect or disease problems.

Hardiness—Zones 5 through 9

Seasonal Color—Blue flowers

Peak Season—Late summer through frost

Mature Size (H x W)—2 to 4 ft. x 3 ft.

Water Needs—Low to medium. Plants are susceptible to root rot; monitor soil moisture and don't overwater.

BOTTLEBRUSH
Callistemon spp.

Why It's Special—Bottlebrush gets its name from its eye-catching, bristle-like flower spikes. Most won't tolerate temperatures below 20°F., although crimson bottlebrush (*Callistemon citrinus*) 'Woodlander's Hardy Red' is cold tolerant to 0°F. The long, narrow leaves are fragrant and evergreen and the flowers attract bees. Grow bottlebrush as a specimen or trained along a fence or wall, preferably south-facing. Most have red flower spikes. Another crimson bottlebrush, 'Little John', is a dwarf growing 3 to 5 feet tall. Lemon bottlebrush (*C. pallidus*) 'Eleanor' is hardy to zone 8 and has rosy red flowers. Stiff bottlebrush (*C. rigidus*) 'Clemson Hardy' also grows in zone 8 and flowers in spring and fall.

How to Plant & Grow—In spring or fall, plant in full sun, in average, well-drained soil.

Care & Problems—Fertilize lightly in spring; too much reduces blooms. Prune mature plants annually after flowering to promote bushier growth. No problems!

Hardiness—Zones 7 to 10

Seasonal Color—Red, pink

Peak Season—Summer

Mature Size (H x W)—3 to 8 ft. x 5 ft.

Water Needs—Low to medium. Established plants are drought tolerant.

BOXWOOD
Buxus sempervirens

Why It's Special—Boxwood is a popular evergreen shrub used for formal hedges, topiary, and foundation plants. 'Winter Beauty' is hardy to zone 4 and grows 3 feet high. Cultivars hardy to zone 5 include dwarf English boxwood 'Suffruticosa' (1 to 2 feet tall), 'Winter Gem' (4 to 6 feet tall), and variegated 'Silver Beauty' (2 to 3 feet tall).

How to Plant & Grow—In spring or fall, plant in full sun to part shade where it will be sheltered from the wind. Mulch around plants to protect their shallow roots.

Care & Problems—Wait until the danger of frost is past before pruning; then prune as needed. Provide high-nitrogen fertilizer in spring. Foliage can turn bronze-colored from wind and exposure to full sun during winter. It is rabbit and deer resistant. Boxwood has few insect or disease problems.

Hardiness—Zones 4 to 9, depending on cultivar

Seasonal Color—White blooms; evergreen foliage

Peak Season—Year-round foliage

Mature Size (H x W)—3 to 6 ft. x 3 to 4 ft.

Water Needs—Medium. Water well going into winter to reduce leaf desiccation.

BURNING BUSH
Euonymus alatus

Why It's Special—One of the most recognizable shrubs for its spectacular fall display, burning bush is hardy and easy to grow. It has a rounded growth habit. The deciduous leaves are dark green until fall, when they turn bright red. Plant singly as an accent, in groupings for effect, or as part of a shrub border. It is also called winged euonymus for the corky wings found on the stems of the species and many cultivars. The species can reach 15 to 30 feet, while 'Compactus' grows to 10 feet. More petite cultivars include 'Rudy Haag' at 3 to 5 feet and Little Moses™ 'Odom' at 2 to 3 feet.

How to Plant & Grow—Plant in spring or fall in full sun to part shade in average, well-drained soil. Shelter from the wind.

Care & Problems—Feed rhododendron fertilizer in spring. Plants are generally trouble-free but can get spider mites or powdery mildew.

Hardiness—Zones 4 to 8

Seasonal Color—Bright red leaves

Peak Season—Fall

Mature Size (H x W)—Varies widely by species and cultivar

Water Needs—Medium. Water regularly.

CAMELLIA
Camellia japonica

Why It's Special—Camellias are prized for their roselike flowers and dark green leaves. They are a member of the tea family. The plants have an attractive growth habit that easily lends itself to formal plantings. The semidouble to double blossoms come in a breathtaking array of colors. Plants can be grown outdoors in containers and overwintered indoors.

How to Plant & Grow—Plant in spring in part shade where it's sheltered from wind. They prefer acidic, well-drained soil. Incorporate compost into the planting bed. Mulch to protect their shallow roots and retain soil moisture.

Care & Problems—Fertilize established plants lightly with acidic fertilizer each spring. Plants should not require pruning but, if necessary, prune after flowering. Camellias are temperamental about sudden changes in light or temperature, causing them to drop their buds. If it's container-grown, watch for mealybugs or spider mites.

Hardiness—Zones 7 to 9

Seasonal Color—Pink, red, lavender, white, yellow, bicolors

Peak Season—Spring

Mature Size (H x W)—7 to 15 ft. x 5 to 10 ft.

Water Needs—Medium. Water regularly but do not overwater.

CALIFORNIA LILAC
Ceanothus spp.

Why It's Special—Many species of California lilacs are native to the western United States. As members of the buckthorn family, there are evergreen and deciduous species. They all bloom profusely, with dreamy blue, lavender, or white panicles covering the plants. Most are fragrant and attract bees. Blueblossom (*Ceanothus thrysiflorus*), hardy in zones 6 to 9, grows to 18 feet; this species is most widely grown. Snowbrush (*C. velutinus*) is hardy in zones 5 to 6, grows to 10 feet, and has fragrant foliage and white flowers. Deerbrush (*C. integerrimus*) is hardy in zones 5 to 9 and grows up to 12 feet.

How to Plant & Grow—In spring or fall, plant in full sun to part shade. Choose locations where the soil drains quickly, such as rock gardens or large containers.

Care & Problems—Do not fertilize. Shrubs are short-lived, usually no longer than ten years. Aphids, caterpillars, mealybugs, and canker can cause problems.

Hardiness—Varies by species

Seasonal Color—Blue, white

Peak Season—Spring to summer

Mature Size (H x W)—Varies by species

Water Needs—Low. Established plants are drought tolerant.

NINEBARK
Physocarpus opulifolius and hybrids

Why It's Special—This easy-to-grow deciduous shrub has attractive flower clusters that look like mini bouquets from late spring to early summer. Its peeling bark provides winter interest. Use it as an accent, for hedges, or erosion control. Summer Wine™ 'Seward' is prized for its bronze foliage and pink to dusty red flower clusters. Coppertina™ 'Mindia' features copper to red foliage and pinkish white flowers. 'Diablo' has burgundy foliage and white flowers.

How to Plant & Grow—Plants grow best in full sun but tolerate shade. They adapt to all soil types. Plant in spring or fall.

Care & Problems—Ninebark shouldn't need fertilizing. Prune for shape immediately after flowering; remove a couple of canes in late winter to early spring to rejuvenate. It doesn't have any serious insect or disease problems. Easy propagation from cuttings.

Hardiness—Zones 2 to 8

Seasonal Color—White or pink flowers in spring; red fall color; interesting bark

Peak Season—Spring to early summer

Mature Size (H x W)—5 to 8 ft. x 4 to 6 ft.

Water Needs—Low to medium. Ninebark is drought tolerant once established.

OCEAN SPRAY
Holodiscus discolor

Why It's Special—Native to western North America, ocean spray gets its name from profuse sprays of creamy white flowers that cover it from late spring to early summer. Attractive, deeply veined leaves grow along arching stems. The leaves turn red or gold in fall. The flowers attract butterflies and beneficial insects, and the seeds later bring birds to the garden. This easy-to-grow member of the rose family is also referred to as cream bush. Use it as an accent, in shrub borders or wildlife gardens, and for fire-wise landscaping.

How to Plant & Grow—Ocean spray adapts to a wide variety of soil, moisture, and light conditions. It grows more slowly in shade. Plant in spring or fall.

Care & Problems—Ocean spray does not need fertilizing. No pruning is required other than shaping, as desired. It has minimal insect or disease problems.

Hardiness—Zones 4 to 9

Seasonal Color—Creamy white

Peak Season—Spring to summer

Mature Size (H x W)—Up to 15 ft. x 5 ft.

Water Needs—Low to medium. Plants have some drought tolerance once established.

OREGON GRAPE
Mahonia spp.

Why It's Special—Oregon grape provides year-round interest with evergreen foliage, yellow flower clusters, and blue berries. The prickly foliage changes color in fall. Bees and hummingbirds come for the flowers and the berries attract birds. Plants are ideal for shade or woodland gardens and foundation plantings. They are native to western North America. *Mahonia aquifolium* 'Compacta' grows to 3 feet while 'Smaragd' ('Emerald') has purple-bronze leaves in winter and grows 4 feet. 'Orange Flame' foliage changes to red in winter; plants grow to 10 feet. Creeping Oregon grape (*M. repens*) is a 1-foot-tall groundcover.

How to Plant & Grow—Oregon grape prefers partial shade but grows in most light conditions. Plant in spring or fall in rich, acidic, and well-drained soil. Shelter from winds.

Care & Problems—Plants spread by rhizomes so can become invasive. It has minimal pest or disease problems and doesn't need fertilizing.

Hardiness—Zones 5 to 9

Seasonal Color—Yellow flowers, blue berries

Peak Season—Spring through fall

Mature Size (H x W)—1 to 10 ft. x 2 to 5 ft.

Water Needs—Low to medium. Water when soil is dry.

PACIFIC WAX MYRTLE
Myrica californica

Why It's Special—Pacific wax myrtle is a highly desirable evergreen shrub native to the West Coast. A member of the bayberry family, it has slightly aromatic, lance-shaped leaves, small yellow flowers, and purple berries that attract birds. It can be grown as a hedge or privacy screen and is particularly ideal for coastal locations where winds and salt spray would adversely affect many other shrubs. 'Buxifolia' grows up to 8 feet tall.

How to Plant & Grow—This shrub grows in all light conditions and is very adaptable to a variety of soils. Plant in spring or fall.

Care & Problems—Feed lightly with all-purpose fertilizer in spring only. Prune as desired to keep tidy or to shape as an informal hedge. Plants can be susceptible to spider mites, whiteflies, and thrips. It is deer resistant.

Hardiness—Zones 7 to 9

Seasonal Color—Yellow

Peak Season—Year-round

Mature Size (H x W)—Up to 15 ft. x up to 12 ft.

Water Needs—Low to medium. Drought tolerant once established; plants require minimal water in coastal regions, more regular water inland.

PIERIS
Pieris japonica

Why It's Special—Pieris is an evergreen shrub desirable for its drooping clusters of bell-shaped flowers and bronzy orange foliage that matures to dark green. Use for foundation plants and in borders with other acid-lovers as well as in fire-wise landscaping. The new foliage of 'Mountain Fire' is red; it grows 4 to 8 feet tall. 'Flaming Silver' is prized for its red foliage that matures to attractive, variegated silver. 'Variegata' has variegated leaves but is only hardy to zone 6, as is 'Valley Rose', which features pink blossoms.

How to Plant & Grow—Plant in spring or fall in all light conditions but where it's sheltered from wind. In inland regions with hot summers, provide afternoon shade. Pieris prefers slightly acidic, well-drained soil.

Care & Problems—Feed acidic fertilizer in spring. Plants die back after prolonged exposure to cold winter winds. They are unaffected by serious pest or disease problems and are deer resistant.

Hardiness—Zones 5 to 8

Seasonal Color—White flowers, red-tinged spring foliage

Peak Season—Spring

Mature Size (H x W)—Up to 12 ft. x 8 ft.

Water Needs—Medium. Water regularly.

RHODODENDRON
Rhododendron × spp. and hybrids

Why It's Special—While rhododendrons flourish in the Northwest, there are only a few native species here. It is prized for its clusters of five-petaled flowers in heavenly colors and attractive, evergreen foliage. Rhododendrons make wonderful foundation plants and provide structure and color for perennial borders.

How to Plant & Grow—Plant in spring in full sun to shade. In hot summers, afternoon shade is a *must*. Rhodies prefer acidic soil that is well drained to prevent root rot. Shelter plants from wind.

Care & Problems—Deadhead immediately after flowering, being careful not to break off next year's developing buds. Avoid cultivating around plants as roots are shallow. Fertilize with rhododendron food in spring and again after flowering. Black vine weevils can damage leaves by cutting C-shaped notches along the leaf margins.

Hardiness—Zones 3b to 8; varies with cultivar

Seasonal Color—Pink, purple, white, red; evergreen foliage

Peak Season—Spring

Mature Size (H x W)—Up to 6 ft. x 6 ft.

Water Needs—Medium. Water regularly during growing seasons but don't overwater. Water deeply going into winter to avoid leaf desiccation.

SALAL

Gaultheria shallon

Why It's Special—The evergreen foliage of salal will look familiar as branches are often used in floral arrangements. It features leathery oval leaves of deep green and urn-shaped, pinkish white flowers that attract hummingbirds and butterflies. Later in the season, there are plenty of edible blue-black berries that birds enjoy. Because plants have deep root systems, they are a good choice for dry shade. A native of the West Coast of the U.S., salal is deer resistant. It performs best in coastal regions and is ideal for woodland gardens and fire-wise landscapes.

How to Plant & Grow—Plant in spring or fall. This plant prefers a shady location; it can be grown in full sun, but will grow more slowly. It tolerates any soil type if well drained.

Care & Problems—Plants need minimal care. Feed high-phosphorus fertilizer in spring. If soil is too moist, plants suffer from root rot.

Hardiness—Zones 6 to 8

Seasonal Color—Pinkish white flowers; evergreen leaves

Peak Season—March to June

Mature Size (H x W)—5 ft. x 5 ft.

Water Needs—Low. Salal becomes drought tolerant once established.

SERVICEBERRY

Amelanchier spp.

Why It's Special—Native to western North America, serviceberry is one of the first shrubs to bloom. Its profuse clusters of white flowers with straplike petals are a welcome sight after a long winter. Leaf colors range from blue-green in spring to red and gold in fall; edible, dark blue berries bring in hungry birds. It's a member of the rose family. Saskatoon (*Amelanchier alnifolia*) 'Regent' grows 4 to 6 feet tall while 'Northline' can reach up to 12 feet. Shadblow serviceberry (*A. canadensis*) 'Prince William' grows to 10 feet and produces a lot of fruit.

How to Plant & Grow—In spring or fall, plant in sun to shade, with full sun being best for flowering and fall color. Serviceberry prefers well-drained soil amended with manure or compost.

Care & Problems—Plants are susceptible to leaf miners, powdery mildew, and leaf spots but they're generally low maintenance. They don't require fertilizer.

Hardiness—Zones 3 to 9

Seasonal Color—White

Peak Season—Spring

Mature Size (H x W)—3 to 25 ft. x 2 to 8 ft.

Water Needs—Medium. Water regularly to establish, then decrease.

SWEET BOX
Sarcococca spp.

Why It's Special—A relative of boxwood, sweet box has alternating, lance-shaped evergreen leaves. Fragrant white flowers bloom from late winter to early spring and berries persist into winter. They are attractive in woodlands, as a hedge, or as a foundation planting. *Sarcococca confusa* has an appealing, dense habit and grows to 5 feet. Fragrant sweet box (*S. ruscifolia*) grows up to 4 feet tall in zones 7 to 9.

How to Plant & Grow—Plant in spring in partial to full shade in moist but well-drained, acidic soil that's been amended with compost. If growing sweet box in areas with cool summers, it will tolerate *some* sun.

Care & Problems—Foliage may burn in sunny locations. Feed with all-purpose fertilizer in spring. Prune out a few old stems each spring to keep the plant structure strong and healthy. Plants have minimal insect or disease problems. *The berries are toxic.*

Hardiness—Zones 6 to 8

Seasonal Color—White flowers; dark berries

Peak Season—Spring

Mature Size (H x W)—5 ft. x 2 to 4 ft.

Water Needs—Medium. Water regularly until established, then decrease.

TREE PEONY
Paeonia × hybrids

Why It's Special—Think of tree peonies and visions of huge, often fragrant, blossoms and highly notched leaves come to mind. Unlike herbaceous peonies, these woody plants lose their leaves in winter but their stems remain above ground. They make stunning additions to perennial borders and formal gardens.

How to Plant & Grow—Although they grow and flower best in full sun, tree peonies tolerate light shade. Amend the soil with compost. Plant peonies deeply, 6 to 8 inches deeper than the container they were grown in, to develop a strong root system.

Care & Problems—Plants rarely require pruning but if you need to shape it, the best time is right after they finish blooming. They rarely require fertilizer and won't require support unless they grow very tall. Tree peonies don't like to be disturbed but if you must move them, do it in fall.

Hardiness—Zones 4 to 8

Seasonal Color—Pink, magenta, red, white, pale yellow

Peak Season—Spring

Mature Size (H x W)—Up to 6 ft. x up to 6 ft.

Water Needs—Medium. Water regularly but do not overwater.

VIBURNUM
Viburnum spp.

Why It's Special—Viburnum is a genus of hardy, attractive shrubs having beautiful, often fragrant flower clusters, dense foliage, and berries that persist into winter. American cranberry bush (*Viburnum trilobum*), zone 2, 12 feet tall, has lacecap blossoms and red berries. Arrowwood (*V. dentatum*), zone 3, 8 feet, features black berries and excellent fall color. Burkwood viburnum (*V. × burkwoodii*), zone 5, 8 feet, has fragrant blossoms. Doublefile viburnum (*V. plicatum tomentosum*), zone 5, 8 feet, has lacecap flowers, fall color, and black fruit. Koreanspice viburnum (*V. carlesii*), zone 5, 5 feet, has the most fragrant flowers. Snowball viburnum (*V. plicatum plicatum*), zone 5, 15 feet, has snowball-shaped flower clusters.

How to Plant & Grow—In spring or fall, plant in full sun to part shade in average, well-drained soil.

Care & Problems—Apply balanced fertilizer in spring. Prune after flowering. Plants have minimal problems.

Hardiness—Varies

Seasonal Color—White flowers; red, black, or blue fruit

Peak Season—Spring blooms; fall color; winter fruit

Mature Size (H x W)—Varies

Water Needs—Medium. Water regularly but don't overwater.

WITCH HAZEL
Hamamelis virginiana

Why It's Special—Common witch hazel is most loved for its fragrant and crinkly fall and winter blooms. Deeply veined, oval leaves with wavy margins turn yellow in fall. Native to central and eastern portions of the U.S., it's the hardiest of all witch hazels. Use in shrub borders, background plantings, and naturalized areas. They have an open growth habit and are deer resistant. Hardy to zone 5, *Hamamelis × intermedia* 'Diane' is a red-flowering hybrid with bright red fall foliage.

How to Plant & Grow—In spring or fall, plant witch hazel in all light conditions although the best flowering will be in sunny sites. It prefers moist, well-drained soil. Add compost to the planting hole.

Care & Problems—It rarely requires pruning but you can prune to promote strong branching structure; the best time is early spring. This plant has minimal insect and disease problems and doesn't require fertilizer.

Hardiness—Zones 3 to 8

Seasonal Color—Yellow or red flowers; fall color

Peak Season—Fall and winter blooms

Mature Size (H x W)—10 to 15 ft. x 10 to 15 ft.

Water Needs—Medium. It prefers moist soil.

JANUARY

- Remove heavy snow from shrubs with a pole or rake by gently bumping limbs from the undersides of the plant. Some areas of the Northwest are prone to ice storms. If shrubs are covered with a coating of ice, leave them alone to thaw naturally. Hitting them to knock ice off will do more damage than good.

- Walk your property after a heavy rain and note where standing water remains for long periods of time. Most shrubs do not tolerate being planted in soggy soil.

- West of the Cascades, gardeners can begin pruning summer-flowering deciduous shrubs when it's warm enough to work outdoors. Wait to prune spring-flowering shrubs until after they bloom. Follow a shrub's natural form when you prune. Check the plant profiles in this chapter for specific pruning suggestions. Don't shear shrubs into uniform round shapes; that actually creates more work for you in the long run and destroys the natural shape of the shrubs.

FEBRUARY

- West of the Cascades, remove mulch used as winter protection. Remove any cold-tolerant weeds that have sprung up and apply a 2- to 3-inch layer of mulch to prevent their return.

- Gardeners east of the Cascades can begin pruning in areas where the snow has melted.

- Apply dormant oil to evergreen and deciduous shrubs where aphids, scale, webworms, and mites were a problem last year. Always follow label directions and pay particular attention to evergreen shrubs like dwarf Alberta spruce (*Picea glauca* 'Conica'), blue-colored junipers (*Juniperus*, blue cultivars), cedar (*Thuja* spp.), and yews (*Taxus* spp.) that can't tolerate the dormant oil spray.

- Bring a little bit of spring indoors. Prune a few branches of forsythia (*Forsythia* spp.), quince (*Chaenomeles japonica*), and pussy willow (*Salix discolor*) and place them in a vase of water. They will respond to the warmer temperatures in the house and bloom weeks ahead of outdoor shrubs.

MARCH

- Continue renovating older shrubs and training young ones. Remove older stems to the ground and thin out tangled growth and weak stems. Young shrubs may need no more pruning than to remove stems headed off in the wrong direction. Finish up moving larger shrubs before they break dormancy. Dig a trench around the drip line of the shrub and then gently pry the root ball out of the ground. Slide the shrub onto a tarp and drag it to its new location. Replant it at the depth it was originally planted and water in well.

- Gardeners east of the Cascades can still apply dormant oils if buds haven't begun to swell.

- Nurseries will be fully stocked with new plants by the end of the month. Check out their selections for new introductions and old favorites.

- As soggy soils dry out west of the Cascades, gardeners can begin transplanting established plants and planting new ones. Apply 2 to 3 inches of mulch to new plantings and renew mulch around established shrubs to reduce weed growth and help retain soil moisture. Gardeners east of the Cascades need to wait until early April to start major planting.

APRIL

- As spring-flowering shrubs finish blooming, prune back up to one-third of the oldest stems to the ground on well-established plants to promote new growth and flower production next year.

- Planting season is in full swing throughout the Northwest. Be careful to plant rhododendrons and azaleas *at the soil surface*. If they are planted too deep, future flower production can be reduced.

- If you buy small, bare-root shrubs through mail order nurseries or locally, consider planting them in a nursery bed for a year to gain some size and a stronger root system.

- West of the Cascades watch for aphids on tender new growth. Sooty mold may form on the honeydew exuded by the aphids, covering the leaves with fine, black filaments. Allow beneficial insects time to do their work before applying insecticidal soap to the plants.

- If shrubs are not growing well or their leaves appear pale, lightly fertilize plants now. Evergreen and acid-loving plants need a rhododendron food while other deciduous shrubs need a rose food or 10-10-10 garden fertilizer.

- Bring containerized shrubs you stored indoors back outdoors this month after the danger of hard frosts has lessened. Keep frost protection handy in particularly cold areas.

MAY

- Deadhead rhododendrons as they finish blooming by carefully snapping off spent flower clusters just *below* the bloom but *above* the newly forming buds to encourage next year's flower production.

- Gardeners east of the Cascades need to check on irrigation system equipment and coverage to make sure they are working before the summer temperatures warm.

- Evergreen rhododendrons can be pruned this month as new growth begins. Cut back rangy branches to a bud or whorl of leaves down in the plant canopy.

- Watch rhododendrons, evergreen azaleas, pieris, and strawberry tree (*Arbutus unedo*) for notched leaf edges. This is the work of the nocturnal root weevil. Wrap masking tape tightly around the trunk a foot or so off the ground and coat it with a long-

Set the tree in the hole so that the soil surface is level with the point where the trunk flares out into the root system. If the tree is in a pot or balled and burlapped, this may require digging down into the top of the rootball to find the flare. Wholesale nursery growers tend to plant trees too deep; trees that are planted this way don't thrive and have much shorter lifespans. Backfill the hole with the native soil and water it well to settle it around the roots. Don't amend the soil, as roots tend to stay where the improved soil is rather than sending their roots far and wide. Build a 3-inch high ridge around the planting hole and fill it with water. Let the soil settle for a couple of days then fill in any low spots. If you are planting in a very windy, open area, stake the tree for the first year. Cover the twine or cord with pieces of old garden hose to protect the bark from rubbing.

FERTILIZING AND WATERING

Trees do not need much fertilizer beyond a light application of a balanced, slow-release fertilizer in the early spring for the first couple of years. If you are fertilizing plants around them that will likely be enough. Most conifers and some deciduous trees like dogwood prefer an acidic soil (pH below 6.5). West of the Cascades, this isn't much of a problem, as soils tend to be acidic. In areas with high pH soils (above 6.5), particularly east of the Cascades, use a rhododendron fertilizer or choose a different tree. Altering the pH level in a large amount of soil is difficult. A soil test will help with your decision.

All newly planted trees will need regular watering for the first two years. Deep watering is best done by setting trees on their own sprinkler circuit and then watering long enough so that the soil is wet 8 to 10 inches down. A soaker hose laid around the trees and left to run for several hours is a good alternative. How long this takes will depend on your soil type. To check, dig a shallow hole until you find dry soil.

For the most part, native trees on a site or planted in a garden will do fine without additional water after they are established. Established non-native trees will likely need regular deep soakings even during years with normal moisture levels. However, when exceptionally dry summers occur on either side of the Cascades, both native and non-native trees will benefit from a few deep soakings during August and September to reduce stress.

One classic mistake many gardeners make is to rely on sprinkler systems timed to water a shallow-rooted lawn to also water trees planted in lawn areas. Unfortunately, for trees like the European white birch, aspen, vine maple, and Japanese maple, sprinklers timed to water lawns may not apply enough water to a depth that reaches the tree roots. Set these areas on their own watering system.

PRUNING

If the right tree is planted in the right place, most trees won't need extensive pruning beyond selective removal of broken, dead, or crossing branches as they develop. Most people get into trouble when they get overzealous with the pruners and head back every branch whether the tree needs it or not. Indiscriminate pruning of branches—especially the tree's tallest branch or leader—disrupts the tree's growth-hormone balance and can send the tree into wild growth that can be controlled only by more intervention from the gardener. Over time and repeated pruning, the tree loses its natural shape and becomes weak and ugly.

Pruning techniques have changed markedly in the last twenty-five years. Gone are the days of using tree wound paints or sealers to cover a wound and cutting a branch flush with the trunk. Researchers now know that when a tree is pruned or damaged, the tree immediately seals off the damaged area and begins to grow callus wood around the wound. Over time this callus wood forms a rolled edge that grows over the wound, covering the area and sealing out rot and disease. The tree takes care of itself.

The best time to prune most established trees is in the late winter after the majority of the winter storms have done their damage, while they are dormant but before they break bud. It is easier to see the branch structure and make pruning decisions with no leaves on the trees. Start by

Place a pruning saw just outside of the branch collar, which is the bark swelling between the branch and the main trunk. Saw all the way through to remove the stub. Do not cut the branch flush with the tree trunk, or you'll hurt the tree's chances of healing itself.

By keeping the collar you will encourage callus tissue to form and heal over the cut, keeping out disease organisms from entering the cut surface.

removing the dead wood and any broken branches, then remove crossing and rubbing branches that have developed. Limbs should be cut back to an outward-facing bud or just outside the branch collar, the ridge of bark between the trunk and the branch. When planting a new tree, do not cut the tree back by one-third as was once acceptable. Instead, trim back any broken branches to an outward-facing bud and remove crossing limbs or branches that join the trunk at less than a 45-degree angle. Trim those branches back to the branch collar. Most conifers need little pruning. Use clean, sharp bypass pruners and handsaws to make cuts. Do not use chain saws up in a tree as they can be dangerous on a wobbly ladder and should only be used for cutting a tree down.

BRING IN AN ARBORIST

If you have lots of trees or even a few large ones, it may be safer to hire an arborist certified by the International Society of Arboriculture (ISA) to do your tree work. ISA-certified arborists have received extensive training on the best techniques to renovate and rehabilitate trees to preserve their health. They will have the experience, equipment, and insurance to do the work properly. Ask for recommendations from quality local nurseries and neighbors who have had work done and be sure to check references. Good arboriculture work is not cheap, so expect to pay a fair price.

Trees are an important and integral part of the Northwest landscape. In areas where there is plenty of moisture, conifers tower over the landscape and the rest of the garden to the natural environment. Trees add flowers and a wide range of leaf colors and textures to the rest of the landscape. Finally, trees help us save energy by shading our homes in the summer and sheltering us from the strong winds. Celebrate all this by planting more trees in your garden.

Kousa dogwoods are much less susceptible to anthracnose than the Florida dogwoods.

ARBUTUS
Arbutus spp.

Why It's Special—Arbutus provides year-round interest for coastal gardens: attractive red, exfoliating bark with smooth, copper bark underneath; shiny, evergreen leaves; fragrant white flower clusters; and red fruits. Pacific madrone (*Arbutus menziesii*) is native to the West Coast from southern British Columbia to California, 50 feet tall. Strawberry tree (*A. unedo*) can be pruned as a tree or grown as a dense screen, 8 to 35 feet tall.

How to Plant & Grow—In spring or fall, plant in full sun to part shade, in acidic, well-drained soil. Mulch around the base.

Care & Problems—Refer to the "Fertilizing and Watering" section on page 201 for information. Arbutus drops some of its leaves as well as bark and berries; litter will need to be cleaned up occasionally. Arbutus is susceptible to madrone canker (*Fusarium aesculi*) and basal canker (*Phytophthora cactorum*).

Hardiness—Zones 7 to 10

Seasonal Color—White flowers; red berries

Peak Season—Spring to summer

Mature Size (H x W)—Up to 50 ft. x 15 to 25 ft.

Water Needs—Low to medium. Water regularly the first year; once established it's drought tolerant.

BEECH
Fagus spp.

Why It's Special—Beeches are attractive deciduous trees with pyramidal or oval growth habits. European beech (*Fagus sylvatica*) has deep green leaves that turn reddish brown in fall, and smooth, gray bark. 'Dawyck Purple' features deep purple foliage and a columnar shape, while leaves of tricolor beech 'Roseo marginata' are purple with rose-and-white margins. Weeping beech, 'Pendula', is smaller at 12 feet. Each is hardy to zone 5. American beech (*F. grandifolia*), hardy to zone 3, grows 50 to 80 feet and has golden bronze fall foliage. Japanese beech (*F. crenata*), hardy to zone 4, grows 70 to 90 feet tall and has deep green, toothed leaves.

How to Plant & Grow—Plant in all light conditions in average, well-drained soil. See "Planting a Tree" section for detailed instructions.

Care & Problems—Refer to the section on "Fertilizing and Watering" for information. Trees can be susceptible to aphids. They rarely need pruning.

Hardiness—Varies by species

Seasonal Color—Golden bronze fall foliage

Peak Season—Fall

Mature Size (H x W)—12 ft. to 50 ft. or more x 40 ft.

Water Needs—Medium. See "Care & Problems."

BIRCH
Betula spp. and hybrids

Why It's Special—Birches are popular for their attractive bark and golden fall foliage. If you provide plenty of moisture and select a species resistant to bronze birch borers, you'll have a fine specimen to enjoy for years. River birch (*Betula nigra*), zone 4, is most resistant to borers; it has brown to black exfoliating bark, 50 feet. Canoe or paper birch (*B. papyrifera*), zone 2, has some borer resistance if it isn't subjected to drought, 70 feet. Whitespire birch (*B. playtphylla* var. *japonica*), zone 2, is somewhat resistant, and has white bark, 40 feet.

How to Plant & Grow—In spring or fall, plant in full sun to part shade in moist, well-drained soil. Read "Planting a Tree" for detailed instructions.

Care & Problems—Birches are susceptible to bronze birch borer; select resistant cultivars. Leaf miners and aphids can be problems.

Hardiness—Varies

Seasonal Color—White or brown bark; yellow fall foliage

Peak Season—Fall and winter

Mature Size (H x W)—40 to 70 ft. x 30 to 40 ft.

Water Needs—Medium to high. Water regularly.

CRAPE MYRTLE
Lagerstroemia spp. and hybrids

Why It's Special—Crape myrtle is a deciduous tree with an upright growth habit that has year-round interest. It features bronze leaves in spring that later become dark green, peeling bark, showy flower clusters that bloom from spring to fall, and attractive seedheads. In winter, it has an appealing branching structure. It tolerates heat and drought well. *Lagerstroemia indica × fauriei* 'Muskogee' has lavender panicles, cinnamon bark, and red fall foliage. 'Natchez' has dainty white flowers, cinnamon bark, and orange-red fall leaves. *L. indica* 'Red Rocket' features bright red flowers and bronze-red leaves in fall.

How to Plant & Grow—In spring or fall, plant in full sun in rich, well-drained soil. See page 200 for planting instructions.

Care & Problems—Refer to page 201 for fertilizing and watering details. Trees are susceptible to powdery mildew; choose resistant cultivars. Aphids and scale can also be problems.

Hardiness—Zones 6 to 9

Seasonal Color—Pink, purple, red, white

Peak Season—Summer to fall

Mature Size (H x W)—15 to 30 ft. x 15 to 30 ft.

Water Needs—Low to medium. See "Care & Problems."

CYPRESS
Cupressus spp.

Why It's Special—Cypress are valued for their fast growth habit, attractive evergreen foliage, and intriguing round cones. They are frequently used as windbreaks and privacy screens. Italian cypress (*Cupressus sempervirens*) has an impressively tall (to 70 feet) columnar growth habit. 'Glauca' has densely branched, blue-green foliage and can grow even taller, up to 80 feet. Arizona cypress (*C. arizonica*) grows to 40 feet tall and has stunning blue-green needles on dense sprays that provide texture and contrast in the landscape; its bark is smooth and red. All tolerate heat and drought well.

How to Plant & Grow—In early spring, plant in full sun in well-drained soil.

Care & Problems—Refer to "Fertilizing and Watering" for information. Cypress has minimal insect or disease issues although spider mites may be a problem.

Hardiness—Zones 7 to 10

Seasonal Color—Evergreen foliage

Peak Season—Year-round

Mature Size (H x W)—40 to 70 ft. x 6 to 20 ft.

Water Needs—Medium. Water regularly to get trees off to a good start; once established, water deeply every other week.

DAWN REDWOOD
Metasequoia glyptostroboides

Why It's Special—If you have a large space for a tree, dawn redwood makes an attention-getting specimen for your landscape. This China native features soft, feathery foliage that's green during spring and summer and bronzy red in fall. There are small cones and reddish brown to gray shedding bark. It's deciduous so drops its needles and stems in fall. As a tree matures, the trunk becomes quite impressive. It is fast-growing, reaching up to 100 feet. 'Gold Rush' and 'Ogon' feature yellow-gold foliage; the latter grows just 15 to 18 feet tall and is hardy to zone 3.

How to Plant & Grow—In spring or fall, plant in full sun in moist, well-drained soil. See page 200 for detailed planting instructions.

Care & Problems—Refer to the section on "Fertilizing and Watering" for information. Dawn redwoods have minimal problems; spider mites can be bothersome in drier conditions.

Hardiness—Zones 4 to 8

Seasonal Color—Green in spring and summer, bronze-red in fall

Peak Season—Year-round

Mature Size (H x W)—70 to 100 ft. x 15 to 25 ft.

Water Needs—Medium to high. Water regularly.

DEODAR CEDAR
Cedrus deodara and hybrids

Why It's Special—Deodar, or Himalayan, cedar is native to the Himalayas where it can grow 150 feet. In the Northwest it's much shorter. This evergreen tree features wide, horizontal branches with a gracefully arching habit. It can be grown as a specimen, pruned as a hedge, or used as a windbreak. Sterling Frost™ 'Grester' has blue-green needles and grows 40 to 70 feet. 'Aurea' has golden yellow needles and can reach 35 feet. Dwarfs include 'Divinely Blue' (6 feet) and 'Snow Sprite' (4 feet), with silver-green needles and cream-colored tips. 'Electra Blue' has a dense habit, is hardy to zone 5, and grows to 8 feet in 10 years.

How to Plant & Grow—In spring or fall, plant in full sun, in acidic soil that is moist but well drained.

Care & Problems—"Fertilizing and Watering" section has more information. It develops both drought and heat tolerance. Trees have minimal insect or disease problems.

Hardiness—Zones 7 to 9

Seasonal Color—Evergreen foliage

Peak Season—Year-round

Mature Size (H x W)—Varies by cultivar

Water Needs—Medium. Water regularly while trees establish.

DOGWOOD
Cornus spp. and hybrids

Why It's Special—Dogwoods are coveted for their long-lasting, four-petaled flowers. They have red fruits prized by birds and red to purple fall foliage. The two most popular species are Kousa (*Cornus kousa*) and flowering (*C. florida*). Kousa is more cold hardy and drought tolerant than flowering dogwood, and more resistant to dogwood anthracnose. Kousa cultivars include white, floriferous 'Milky Way', red-pink 'Beni Fuji', variegated 'Wolf Eyes', and 'Gold Star', with gold-splashed foliage and white blossoms. Flowering dogwood cultivars include red-flowered 'Cherokee Brave', white 'Cloud 9', and pink 'Rubra'.

How to Plant & Grow—In spring, plant in full sun to part shade in average, well-drained soil. Do *not* fertilize at planting. Mulch around roots to retain soil moisture. Refer to "Planting a Tree" for detailed instructions.

Care & Problems—The "Fertilizing and Watering" section has additional information. Choose Kousa dogwood if anthracnose is prevalent in your area.

Hardiness—Zones 5 to 9

Seasonal Color—White, pink

Peak Season—April to June

Mature Size (H x W)—15 to 30 ft. x 15 to 30 ft.

Water Needs—Medium. Water regularly.

DOUGLAS FIR
Pseudotsuga menziesii

Why It's Special—Douglas fir is native to Alaska and western Canada, south to California, and east to the Rockies. The branches are covered in soft, densely growing aromatic needles. Often grown as a Christmas tree, it tolerates windy settings. 'Fastigiata' has a columnar growth habit, gray-green needles, and grows up to 40 feet. 'Graceful Grace' is a weeping form that reaches 40 feet and should be grown in full sun. Rocky Mountain Douglas fir 'Glauca' is cold hardy to zone 3.

How to Plant & Grow—In spring or fall, plant in all light conditions and in average soil; good drainage is a *must*. "Planting a Tree" has specific planting instructions.

Care & Problems—Refer to the section "Fertilizing and Watering" for information. It does not have any serious insect or disease problems.

Hardiness—Zones 4 to 9

Seasonal Color—Evergreen needles

Peak Season—Year-round

Mature Size (H x W)—40 to 80 ft. x 12 to 20 ft.

Water Needs—Medium. Water regularly to get trees off to a good start. Douglas fir prefers moist soil, but is drought tolerant once established.

DOVE TREE
Davidia involucrata

Why It's Special—In spring, dove tree is an attention-getter with unusual dangling white flowers that look like doves sitting on the branches. It's also known as handkerchief tree since they look like dangling hankies. Its dense branches are covered with bright green leaves and the tree bears brown fruits from summer into winter. Fall color is orange to red. Plant as a specimen in front of darker-foliaged trees or shrubs so it stands out. Both 'Sonoma' and variegated-leaved 'Lady Sunshine' bloom at an earlier age. While most dove trees are grown in zones 6 to 8, 'Vilmoriniana' is hardy to zone 5.

How to Plant & Grow—In spring or fall, choose an area sheltered from wind. Plant in full sun to part shade, in well-drained soil. Refer to "Planting a Tree," page 200 for detailed instructions.

Care & Problems—The "Fertilizing and Watering" section has more information. Trees have minimal problems.

Hardiness—Zones 6 to 8

Seasonal Color—White

Peak Season—April to May

Mature Size (H x W)—20 to 40 ft. x 20 to 40 ft.

Water Needs—Medium. Water regularly.

EASTERN RED CEDAR
Juniperus virginiana

Why It's Special—Native to central and eastern North America, Eastern red cedar has a pyramidal growth habit with horizontal branches and evergreen foliage composed of blue-green scales. It has exfoliating red to brown bark and blue, berrylike cones that attract birds. They like to roost and nest within the dense branches. Grow as a specimen, in groups for privacy screens or windbreaks, or for erosion control. 'Emerald Sentinel' features dark green foliage; 20 feet. 'Manhattan Blue' has intense blue-green foliage; 12 feet. 'Hillspire' features deep green foliage year-round; up to 30 feet.

How to Plant & Grow—In spring or fall, plant in full sun in average, well-drained soil. Refer to "Planting a Tree" section for detailed instructions.

Care & Problems—Refer to the section on "Fertilizing and Watering" for information. They have minimal pest or disease problems and are deer resistant.

Hardiness—Zones 2 to 9

Seasonal Color—Evergreen foliage

Peak Season—Year-round

Mature Size (H x W)—15 to 65 ft. x 8 to 25 ft.

Water Needs—Low to medium. Water regularly at first; established trees become very drought tolerant.

FALSE CYPRESS
Chamaecyparis spp.

Why It's Special—Native to Japan, false cypress has a pyramidal growth habit. The foliage is composed of deep green scales with white markings underneath. It has peeling, reddish brown bark. Grow as a specimen or plant multiples for impact. While Hinoki false cypress (*Chamaecyparis obtusa*) reaches up to 75 feet in height, many cultivars are more manageable. 'Gracilis' grows from 8 to 12 feet, and 'Nana Gracilis' is 6 to 8 feet. Hardy to zone 5, Lawson false cypress (*C. lawsoniana*) has blue-gray foliage and is 6 to 10 feet.

How to Plant & Grow—For best results, plant in full sun although it tolerates partial shade. Soil should be moist but well drained. Plant in spring or fall; refer to "Planting a Tree" for detailed instructions.

Care & Problems—Refer to "Fertilizing and Watering" for information. False cypress needs minimal care.

Hardiness—Zones 4 to 8

Seasonal Color—Evergreen foliage

Peak Season—Year-round

Mature Size (H x W)—6 to 75 ft. x 15 to 25 ft.

Water Needs—Medium. Water weekly or more often in the heat of summer.

FIR
Abies spp.

Why It's Special—Firs are evergreens commonly sold as Christmas trees. They have fragrant, lush growth, upright cones, and an erect growth habit. Korean fir (*Abies koreana*) is slow-growing and prefers cooler climates; it grows to 60 feet. 'Aurea' has golden needles while 'Horstman's Silberlocke' features twisted needles that reveal white undersides; both grow to 20 feet. The needles of subalpine fir (*A. lasiocarpa*) have white lines running lengthwise and purple immature cones; it grows to 20 feet and tolerates occasional dry conditions. 'Arizonica' features beautiful blue needles and grows to 40 feet. Noble fir (*A. procera*) has inch-long, blue-green needles along the upper surface of each branch and grows to 100 feet.

How to Plant & Grow—In spring or fall, plant in full sun to part shade in moist, well-drained soil. See page 200 for planting tips.

Care & Problems—Read more in "Fertilizing and Watering." Needle diseases, aphids, and woolly adelgids can be problems.

Hardiness—Zones 5 to 8

Seasonal Color—Evergreen needles

Peak Season—Year-round

Mature Size (H x W)—Up to 70 ft. x 30 ft.

Water Needs—Medium. Water regularly.

FLOWERING CHERRY
Prunus serrulata and hybrids

Why It's Special—Flowering cherries are a delightful sight in spring. They have an attractive vase shape; lush single, semidouble, or double flowers; and red fall foliage. Most cultivars are non-fruiting. Grow as a specimen where you can easily admire it. 'Kwanzan' features clusters of double pink blossoms and grows to 25 feet. 'Mt. Fuji' has fragrant, single white flowers and reaches 20 feet. 'Snow Fountains' has a weeping growth habit, showy white flowers, and a height of 12 feet. 'Amanogawa' features white, semidouble blossoms and will grow to 25 feet.

How to Plant & Grow—In spring or fall, plant in full sun where the soil drains quickly. Refer to "Planting a Tree" for detailed instructions.

Care & Problems—Refer to "Fertilizing and Watering" for details. This tree needs minimal pruning but it's susceptible to insects and diseases including aphids, scale, tent caterpillars, leaf spot, root rot, and powdery mildew.

Hardiness—Zones 5 to 8

Seasonal Color—Pink, white

Peak Season—April

Mature Size (H x W)—12 to 25 ft. x 15 to 25 ft.

Water Needs—Medium. Water regularly.

GINKGO
Ginkgo biloba and hybrids

Why It's Special—Native to China, ginkgo, also called maidenhair tree, is grown primarily for its unusual, fan-shaped leaves. This ancient species is a deciduous, slow-growing conifer with brilliant gold fall foliage. It averages a foot of growth annually. Grow as a specimen, or as a shade or street tree. Because female trees produce messy, smelly fruit, nurseries typically only sell males. Goldspire™ has a pyramidal shape, golden leaves in fall, and grows to 15 feet. 'Autumn Gold' has a rounded habit and grows to 40 feet. 'Pendula' features a weeping habit and tops out at 8 feet.

How to Plant & Grow—In spring or fall, plant in full sun in average, well-drained soil. Follow "Planting a Tree" advice on page 200.

Care & Problems—Ginkgoes are low maintenance and have minimal insect or disease problems. It is deer resistant.

Hardiness—Zones 3 to 9

Seasonal Color—Yellow fall foliage

Peak Season—Fall

Mature Size (H x W)—To 40 ft. x 30 or more ft.

Water Needs—Medium. Water regularly to get trees off to a good start; established trees are drought tolerant.

GOLDEN CHAIN TREE

Laburnum anagyroides

Why It's Special—Golden chain tree puts forth an amazing display of long chains of yellow, pea-like flowers each spring. It is also known as common laburnum and *Cytisus laburnum*. It's best grown as a specimen. Since *all parts are poisonous*, it is important to explain this danger to children who are likely to be active in the area. The hybrid *Laburnum × watereri* 'Vossi' produces less of the poisonous, pea-like seedpods.

How to Plant & Grow—Grow in full sun or part shade in regions with hot summers. The soil should be moist and have excellent drainage. Add compost to the planting area. Refer to "Planting a Tree" section for detailed instructions.

Care & Problems—Refer to the section on "Fertilizing and Watering" for information. Wear gloves when removing the seedpods or doing other gardening tasks. Prune suckers at the base of trees as they appear. Aphids and mealybugs can be problematic.

Hardiness—Zones 5 to 7

Seasonal Color—Yellow

Peak Season—May to June

Mature Size (H x W)—15 to 25 ft. x 15 to 25 ft.

Water Needs—Medium. Water regularly.

HEMLOCK

Tsuga spp.

Why It's Special—Hemlock is an evergreen having short needles on densely growing branches and small cones. The needles have white bands on the undersides. Canadian or eastern hemlock (*Tsuga canadensis*) is native to eastern North America and has pendulous branches; it grows 40 to 70 feet tall. 'Albospica' features dark green needles with white tips, 8 to 25 feet. 'Aurea Compacta' is a slow-growing dwarf with golden needles. Western hemlock (*T. heterophylla*) has branches with drooping tips and is native to western North America, up to 150 feet. Dwarf 'Thorsen' will reach 5 feet when staked.

How to Plant & Grow—Hemlocks grow in all light conditions in moist, well-drained soil. In spring or fall, select an area sheltered from wind. Refer to "Planting a Tree" on page 200 for detailed instructions.

Care & Problems— See "Fertilizing and Watering" for specifics. Hemlocks are susceptible to hemlock woolly adelgid.

Hardiness—Zones 3 to 7

Seasonal Color—Evergreen needles

Peak Season—Year-round

Mature Size (H x W)—Up to 125 ft. x up to 35 ft.

Water Needs—Medium. Water regularly until trees establish.

JAPANESE MAPLE

Acer palmatum

Why It's Special—Native to Japan and Korea, Japanese maples are prized for their airy branching habit, attractive palmate leaves, and stunning fall colors. They add an elegant look to woodland plantings, Japanese gardens, along fences or walls, in lawns, and even in containers. Cultivars grow more slowly than the species. Its insignificant flowers bloom in spring. 'Bloodgood' has rosy leaves that turn red in autumn. 'Butterfly' features green-and-white variegated foliage. 'Crimson Queen' has a weeping habit and stunning red leaves. 'Shaina' is a dwarf cultivar with burgundy leaves; up to 6 feet.

How to Plant & Grow—In spring, plant in full sun to part shade, with light shade ideal in inland regions with hot summers. Soil should be moist and well drained. See "Planting a Tree" on page 200 for detailed instructions.

Care & Problems—See more at "Fertilizing and Watering" on page 201. Trees are susceptible to leaf scorch and aphids.

Hardiness—Zones 5 to 8

Seasonal Color—Colorful fall foliage

Peak Season—Season-long

Mature Size (H x W)—6 to 25 ft. x 3 to 25 ft.

Water Needs—Medium. Water regularly.

JAPANESE PAGODA TREE
Sophora japonica

Why It's Special—When Japanese pagoda tree is in bloom, it's a traffic-stopper. Native to China and Korea, it is covered with 6- to 12-inch-long, ivory to yellow flower clusters. It later develops green pods that turn brown in fall. The tree is usually as wide as it is tall, although branches let enough dappled light through so lawns grow well underneath. It's also referred to as scholar tree and *Styphnolobium japonicum*. 'Columnaris' ('Fastigiata') grows more erectly to 40 feet tall and 20 feet wide. 'Regent' flowers at an earlier age and reaches 50 feet.

How to Plant & Grow—This tree grows best in full sun but tolerates part shade. It adapts to all well-draining soils. "Planting a Tree" has detailed planting instructions.

Care & Problems—See page 201, "Fertilizing and Watering," for information. Trees drop flowers, pods, and leaves but have minimal problems.

Hardiness—Zones 5 to 8

Seasonal Color—Yellow to white blossoms

Peak Season—July to August

Mature Size (H x W)—40 to 60 ft. x 40 to 60 ft.

Water Needs—Medium. See "Care & Problems."

KATSURA
Cercidiphyllum japonicum

Why It's Special—Katsura is a stunning specimen for its heart-shaped green leaves during spring and summer, followed by a spectacular display of yellow to apricot foliage. It has small, reddish green flowers in spring but they are inconsequential compared to the foliage. Native to China and Japan, this deciduous tree has an attractive, rounded habit that's ideal for use as a shade tree. 'Heronswood Globe' has a globular habit and grows to 15 feet, making it ideal for smaller gardens. 'Pendula' has a weeping habit; up to 25 feet.

How to Plant & Grow—In spring or fall, plant in full sun to part shade in an area sheltered from wind. It prefers moist, well-drained soil. For planting tips, see "Planting a Tree" in the introduction.

Care & Problems—"Fertilizing and Watering" has more information. It does not have any serious problems.

Hardiness—Zones 4 to 8

Seasonal Color—Yellow to apricot fall foliage

Peak Season—Fall

Mature Size (H x W)—40 to 60 ft. x 20 to 30 ft.

Water Needs—Medium. Water regularly; katsura doesn't tolerate drought.

MAGNOLIA
Magnolia spp.

Why It's Special—Magnolias are often associated with the South, but there are hardy varieties for the Northwest as well. They are most prized for their showy blossoms that appear in spring before the leaves sprout. Saucer magnolia or tulip tree (*Magnolia × soulangeana*) has large, luscious flowers; 30 feet. Bigleaf magnolia (*M. macrophylla*) is most notable for its huge leaves and fragrant, ivory blossoms; 40 feet. Both are hardy to zone 5. Star magnolia (*M. stellata*) can be trained as a small tree, has fragrant blossoms with straplike petals, and is hardy to zone 4; 8 feet.

How to Plant & Grow—In spring, plant in all types of light and in moist, acidic soil. Refer to "Planting a Tree" section for detailed instructions.

Care & Problems—Refer to section on "Fertilizing and Watering" for information. A late frost can burn the flowers but otherwise magnolias have minimal pest or disease issues.

Hardiness—Varies by species

Seasonal Color—Pink, rose, white, or yellow flowers

Peak Season—Early spring

Mature Size (H x W)—15 to 40 ft. x 30 ft.

Water Needs—Medium. Water regularly.

MAPLE
Acer spp. and hybrids

Why It's Special—Maples are popular for their stunning fall colors. Rocky Mountain maple (*Acer glabrum*) is native to the western half of North America, features orange, red, and yellow fall foliage, and is hardy to zone 6, 30 feet. Bigleaf maple (*A. macrophyllum*) is native to the West Coast from Alaska to northern California, has golden fall foliage, and is hardy to zone 5, 90 feet. Striped maple (*A. pensylvanicum*) has yellow foliage, is hardy to zone 3, and grows best in partial shade, 20 feet.

How to Plant & Grow—In spring or fall, plant in full sun to part shade although fall colors are better in sunny sites. Maples prefer moist, slightly acidic soil but are adaptable. "Planting a Tree" on page 200 has detailed instructions.

Care & Problems—See page 201 for fertilizing and watering information. Maples are susceptible to aphids, powdery mildew, and leaf scorch.

Hardiness—Varies by species

Seasonal Color—Red or yellow flowers; yellow, orange, or red fall foliage

Peak Season—Fall

Mature Size (H x W)—Up to 75 ft. x 40 ft.

Water Needs—Medium. Water regularly.

NEEDLE PALM
Rhapidophyllum hystrix

Why It's Special—Native to the coastal regions of the southeastern U.S., needle palm is the hardiest palm you can grow. The lush leaves are fan-shaped; within the leaf sheaths are stiff, black spines that keep wildlife—and gardeners—at bay. In summer, there are yellow-brown flowers that are followed by brown, seed-bearing fruits called *drupes*. This palm has short, hairy trunks.

How to Plant & Grow—In spring, plant in full sun to part shade, although it grows best in partial shade and where it is protected from winter winds. It prefers rich, moist, and well-drained soil. Plant potted palms at the same level they were growing in their pots.

Care & Problems—Fertilize annually with palm fertilizer. Before winter, mulch around the base to protect the roots. Needle palm has minimal insect or disease problems.

Hardiness—Zones 6 to 10

Seasonal Color—Yellow-brown flowers

Peak Season—June to July

Mature Size (H x W)—3 to 6 ft. x 4 to 8 ft.

Water Needs—Medium. Water regularly to get it off to a good start; it's drought tolerant once established.

PINE
Pinus spp.

Why It's Special—Pines are tough evergreens that make attractive additions to the landscape. Ponderosa pine (*Pinus ponderosa*) is native to the western U.S. and has 5- to 10-inch-long needles; it grows to 100 feet in cultivation. Shore pine (*P. contorta*), also known as beach or lodgepole pine, has clusters of twisted needles, 45 feet. Rocky Mountain bristlecone pine (*P. aristata*) is native to the mountains of the Southwest and grows slowly; it has attractive, bushy needles with white resin dots, 20 feet.

How to Plant & Grow—In spring or fall, plant in full sun in well-drained acidic soil. See page 200 for planting tips.

Care & Problems—Refer to "Fertilizing and Watering" for information. To control height, remove new candles by up to 50 percent in June. Stressed trees are susceptible to pine bark beetle. Pines can have problems with western gall rust and pine needle scale.

Hardiness—Zones 3 to 9

Seasonal Color—Evergreen foliage

Peak Season—Year-round

Mature Size (H x W)—Up to 75 ft. x 40 ft.

Water Needs—Low to medium. Water regularly until trees are well established.

PISTACHE
Pistacia chinensis

Why It's Special—The deciduous pistache (also called Chinese pistache or pistachio tree) has attractive fall foliage in shades of orange and red. While it blooms in spring, the green panicles are inconsequential. The grayish bark is exfoliating, which exposes salmon bark underneath. Unlike *Pistacia vera*, this species produces inedible nuts. Since it has deep roots, it's ideal as a shade tree, a specimen, or street tree. If planted in a wildlife garden, seeds will be eaten by birds and squirrels. 'Keith Davey' is fruitless, 35 feet.

How to Plant & Grow—Plant in full sun in spring or fall; pistache tolerates part shade but performs best in a sunny location. The soil should be rich, moist and well drained. See "Planting a Tree" for detailed instructions.

Care & Problems—Refer to the section on "Fertilizing and Watering" for details. Minimal problems.

Hardiness—Zones 6 to 9

Seasonal Color—Colorful fall foliage

Peak Season—Fall

Mature Size (H x W)—30 to 35 ft. x 20 to 30 ft.

Water Needs—Low to medium. Water regularly but well-established trees are drought and heat tolerant.

PODOCARPUS
Podocarpus spp.

Why It's Special—Podocarpus is grown for its interesting foliage and adaptability to many garden settings. Grow as a specimen tree or prune as a shrub. Bigleaf podocarpus (*P. macrophyllus*) has long, leathery needles similar to yews. The foliage is aromatic and the tree produces edible fruits. It is also known as Buddhist pine or yew pine. 'Maki' grows more slowly, to about 8 feet in 10 years. Totara (*P. totara*) is native to New Zealand and grows up to 30 feet. It has dense, attractive foliage and is hardy in zones 9 to 11.

How to Plant & Grow—In spring or fall, plant in full sun to part shade. The soil must be well drained and slightly acidic for best results. "Planting a Tree" section has detailed instructions.

Care & Problems—Read more in "Fertilizing and Watering" on page 201. It does not have any serious pest or disease issues.

Hardiness—Zones 7 to 9

Seasonal Color—Evergreen foliage

Peak Season—Year-round

Mature Size (H x W)—20 to 40 ft. x 10 to 20 ft.

Water Needs—Medium. Water regularly.

REDBUD
Cercis canadensis

Why It's Special—Eastern redbud is a deciduous tree popular for its heart-shaped leaves, showy pea-like flowers, and golden fall foliage. In spring, young leaves are tinged in red, maturing to dark green. Its seedpods turn brown in fall. The tree works well as a specimen and in woodland areas, and is perfect for small gardens. 'Alba' has white flowers while 'Silver Cloud' has variegated leaves. Lavender Twist™ 'Covey' features a weeping habit and rosy pink blossoms. *Cercis canadensis* subsp. *texensis* 'Oklahoma' has reddish purple flowers; hardy to zone 6.

How to Plant & Grow—In spring or fall, plant in full sun to part shade; it tolerates full shade. Redbud prefers moist, well-drained soil but adapts to other soils. Refer to "Planting a Tree" for detailed instructions.

Care & Problems—Read more about fertilizing and watering on page 201. Keep trees healthy; redbud is susceptible to canker and insect pests.

Hardiness—Zones 5 to 9

Seasonal Color—Pink flowers; yellow fall foliage

Peak Season—Early spring

Mature Size (H x W)—Up to 30 ft. x 30 ft.

Water Needs—Medium. Water regularly.

SPRUCE

Picea spp. and hybrids

Why It's Special—Spruce is a fast-growing evergreen with handsome needles, pendulous branches, and large cones that grow at branch tips. They can be grown as specimens, windbreaks, or privacy screens. Norway spruce (*Picea abies*) has green needles. 'Cupressina' has a narrow, columnar habit. Colorado blue spruce (*P. pungens* 'Glauca') is prized for its blue-green needles that contrast well with other foliage colors. Serbian spruce (*P. omorika*) has narrow, spirelike growth, hardy to zone 4. Sitka spruce (*P. sitchensis*), native from California to Alaska, prefers coastal growing conditions, and is hardy to zone 6.

How to Plant & Grow—In spring or fall, plant in full sun where tree will have plenty of room to grow. It prefers average, well-drained soil. Refer to "Planting a Tree" section for detailed instructions.

Care & Problems—For more information see "Fertilizing and Watering." Spruce trees are susceptible to needle cast, rust, Cooley spruce gall adelgid, budworms, and aphids.

Hardiness—Zones 2 to 7

Seasonal Color—Evergreen foliage

Peak Season—Year-round

Mature Size (H x W)—40 to 60 ft. x 25 to 30 ft.

Water Needs—Medium. Water regularly.

SWEETGUM

Liquidambar styraciflua

Why It's Special—Sweetgum is a deciduous tree with shiny green, star-shaped leaves that change to yellow, red, and purple in fall. Small spring-blooming flowers mature into bristly, round gumballs. It makes an excellent shade tree. 'Moraine' is one of the hardiest cultivars available, has red fall foliage, and grows up to 60 feet. 'Rotundiloba' is generally non-fruiting and has leaves with rounded lobes while 'Variegata' features variegated leaves and grows 25 to 30 feet; both are hardy to zone 6.

How to Plant & Grow—In spring or fall, plant in full sun where it will have enough room to grow. Trees thrive in average, well-drained soil. Page 200, "Planting a Tree," has detailed instructions.

Care & Problems—Refer to section on "Fertilizing and Watering" for information. The gumball litter means sweetgum is not a good candidate for a street tree. They are susceptible to webworms, scale, and borers.

Hardiness—Zones 5 to 9

Seasonal Color—Yellow-green

Peak Season—April to May

Mature Size (H x W)—60 to 80 ft. x 40 to 60 ft.

Water Needs—Medium. Provide regular moisture.

TULIP TREE

Liriodendron tulipifera

Why It's Special—A member of the magnolia family, tulip tree is a fast-growing, deciduous tree also known as yellow poplar. In spring, tulip-shaped flowers with yellow, green, and orange petals appear. These are followed by cone-shaped fruits that persist into winter. The leaves are golden in fall. Most trees need several years before blooming. It's a showy specimen and great shade tree. 'Compactum' grows half the size of the species and 'Aureomarginatum' has variegated leaves.

How to Plant & Grow—For best results, plant in full sun; it tolerates light shade as well. The soil should be moist, rich, and well drained. Give it plenty of room to grow. Refer to "Planting a Tree" for detailed planting instructions.

Care & Problems—Refer to the section on "Fertilizing and Watering" for details. It is susceptible to aphids and the resulting sooty mold, also leaf spot and mildew.

Hardiness—Zones 4 to 9

Seasonal Color—Yellow

Peak Season—May to June

Mature Size (H x W)—60 to 90 ft. x 30 to 50 ft.

Water Needs—Medium. Water regularly to get trees off to a speedy start.

VINE MAPLE
Acer circinatum

Why It's Special—Vine maples are popular because of their red, orange, and yellow fall foliage. Native from British Columbia to California and along the east slope of the Cascades, they have a graceful habit and eye-catching reddish brown bark. They are ideal for native gardens or woodland areas; their colorful leaves contrast beautifully with conifers. 'Monroe' has deeply cut leaves and a height of 12 feet. 'Little Gem' grows 4 feet tall while 'Pacific Fire' features bright red stems and grows 6 to 8 feet.

How to Plant & Grow—In spring or fall, plant in full sun to part shade in moist, well-drained soil. In inland regions with hot summers, light shade is a must. Refer to the "Planting a Tree" section for detailed instructions.

Care & Problems—Prune trees to shape in late fall or early winter, if desired. Keep trees healthy to thwart serious pest or disease problems.

Hardiness—Zones 5 to 9

Seasonal Color—Red flowers, fall foliage

Peak Season—Spring to fall

Mature Size (H x W)—Up to 20 ft. x 20 ft.

Water Needs—Medium. Water regularly.

WESTERN RED CEDAR
Thuja plicata

Why It's Special—Western red cedar is an attractive conifer with lush, drooping branches and scale-covered, featherlike sprays. It develops small, cinnamon-brown seed cones. Native from Alaska to California and east to Montana. Grow as a specimen or trim as a shrub for privacy. 'Spring Grove' grows to 30 feet. 'Fastigiata' has a narrow, upright habit and grows to 50 feet while 'Canadian Gold' has year-round golden foliage and can reach 70 feet; both are hardy to zone 6.

How to Plant & Grow—In spring or fall, select a location where a tree has plenty of room to grow. Plant in full sun to part shade; in areas with hot summers, plant where it gets afternoon shade. Soil should be moist but well drained. See "Planting a Tree" for detailed instructions.

Care & Problems—Refer to the section on "Fertilizing and Watering." It has minimal problems.

Hardiness—Zones 5 to 7

Seasonal Color—Evergreen foliage

Peak Season—Year-round

Mature Size (H x W)—50 to 70 ft. x 15 to 25 ft.

Water Needs—Medium. Red cedar doesn't tolerate dry conditions; water regularly.

WINTERSWEET
Chimonanthus praecox

Why It's Special—A native of China, wintersweet can be grown as a small tree or large shrub. It has shiny, dark green leaves and produces attractive, fragrant yellow flowers from late fall to spring. The petals are quite waxy and its fragrance is rather spicy, so it's also known as Japanese allspice. Its flowering branches are used by the floral industry.

How to Plant & Grow—Plant in spring or fall. For best results, plant in full sun although it tolerates very light shade. The soil should be slightly acidic and moist but well drained. See "Planting a Tree" for detailed instructions.

Care & Problems—Refer to the section on "Fertilizing and Watering" for information. Once plants are well established, annually remove some of the oldest canes after plant finishes flowering. Avoid pruning any later or you'll remove the next winter's flower buds. Wintersweet can be susceptible to aphids and spider mites.

Hardiness—Zones 7 and above

Seasonal Color—Yellow flowers

Peak Season—November to March

Mature Size (H x W)—12 ft. x 9 ft.

Water Needs—Medium. See "Care & Problems."

JANUARY

- Throughout the region, plan your pruning schedule. Any broken branches damaged by winter storms will need to be trimmed back. Ornamental trees can be shaped. If you have a big project, contact an ISA-certified arborist now to get on their schedule.

- Be prepared to gently knock heavy, wet snow off tree branches to prevent or reduce the potential of broken branches. Tap the branches gently with a pole from the underside of the branch.

- Evergreens can be transplanted if they are not showing any new growth at the tips of their branches.

FEBRUARY

- In all but the coldest areas, pruning can begin this month. Use sharp bypass hand pruners and handsaws to do the work. Make sure ladders are on a stable footing before climbing.

- West of the Cascades, apply dormant oils to deciduous trees early in the month. Dormant oil will smother the overwintering larvae and eggs of a number of insects including aphids, scale, and mites and diseases such as powdery mildew. East of the Cascades wait until the end of the month. Be sure to apply them in both areas before the trees begin to break bud.

- In snowy areas, check lower trunks for rodent damage. The damage will appear as small scrapes at the base of the tree where they have gnawed on the bark. Remove snow from the base of the tree to discourage them from gnawing. Surround the trunk with a fine mesh wire set at or just below the soil surface. They can't chew through metal.

MARCH

- In all areas, finish applying dormant oils before the buds on deciduous trees begin to swell.

- Begin planting bare-root trees if your ground is thawed and workable. If your ground is still frozen, store packaged bare-root trees in a cool garage or shed until the ground thaws. Open a small hole in packages to check for moisture. Add water if needed. They can also be temporarily grouped together in moist potting soil or in peat moss in a large pot.

- West of the Cascades, fertilize trees early in the month before they put out their full leaf canopy. Eastside gardeners need to wait until April. Use a 10-10-10 fertilizer and work it in to the soil surface around the drip line of the tree. This is where the tree's feeder roots are located. Keep weed and feed fertilizers away from a tree's drip line as trees can be damaged by the chemicals picked up by their roots.

APRIL

- Visit local parks and arboretums to see some of the early trees that are in bloom that you might want to add to your garden. They might include flowering cherry (*Prunus* spp.), magnolia (*Magnolia* spp.), and several kinds of dogwood (*Cornus* spp.).

- The nurseries will be fully stocked with the best selection of trees now. Do some research and see what interesting trees you can add to the garden.

- Check trees that were planted last year and this year regularly for water especially if the spring is dry. Lay soaker hoses around trees and hook them to a timer to make things easy through the summer.

- Apply a fungicide to dogwoods to reduce the potential of anthracnose as the buds break. Reapply according to label directions until the leaves as fully open. Anthracnose first appears as spots that turn purple on the lower leaves followed by the appearance of small cankers on twigs. Cool, wet springs are conducive to the disease's appearance.

- Celebrate Arbor Day by attending your community's Arbor Day celebration. The dates will vary by community but are generally mid-April to early May (though depending on the location, it's usually in the fall in Canada).

MAY

- Fertilize trees that are showing signs of nutrient deficiency such as pale green leaves. Use a balanced, slow-release fertilizer. Use a rhododendron food on acid-loving trees like dogwood and evergreens.

- Continue planting container-grown trees and finish planting any bare-root trees. If you can't plant bare-root trees immediately, plant them in a holding bed and keep them watered. Plan on getting them in the ground within a week.

- If you want to include native trees in your landscaping, take a road trip to see wild trees in bloom and then talk to your local Master Gardener program, native plant society, or native plant nursery about sources of nursery-grown plants. Never dig a tree out of the wild. Not only is it illegal, trees dug from the wild rarely survive the transplant shock.

JUNE

- Begin a regular watering program for all year-old and newly planted trees. Don't count on your lawn sprinklers to get water deep into the soil. Use soaker hoses or a separate line on your sprinkler system. Water enough every week to ten days to get moisture 6 to 10 inches into the soil.

- Check for insects on small trees and hose them off with a hard stream of water or apply insecticidal soap. Large trees with insect issues may need a professional to spray the crown of the tree or apply a systemic insecticide.

- In hot, dry parts of the region, refrain from planting new trees after the middle of the month until the weather cools in August.

- Monitor trees for aphid infestations. Aphids can be hosed off small trees; be sure to get the underside of the leaves. Large trees will need to be treated by a professional. In general, aphids don't damage the trees, they just leave a sticky mess of honeydew on anything under them.

JULY

- As the weather warms and dries, many trees will drop small twigs and leaves that are superfluous to the tree. This is normal.

- Make sure young trees get 2 inches of water a week especially in hot, windy weather. Build a shallow moat around tree root areas to help hold the water and allow it to soak in.

- As the humidity starts dropping, two-spotted spider mites and their fine webs will appear on the underside of leaves and the needles of some evergreens. Hose the plants down regularly with a hard stream of water to knock them off and raise the humidity around the plants which helps reduce the number of pests.

AUGUST

- Begin watching for nursery sales on containerized trees late in the month. Add some new ones to the garden or replace poor performers.

- Keep up on your watering especially of newly planted trees. One afternoon of hot, dry wind can kill a newly planted tree that is short on water. If you haven't put down mulch or built a watering moat around your tree, do it now.

- Take some time to sit in the shade of one of your trees. There is no better way to enjoy a hot summer day.

SEPTEMBER

- Nurseries will begin their fall sales this month. Shop early to find good bargains. Plant the trees as soon as possible and water well. Dig a flat, dish-shaped hole three times the diameter of the rootball and no deeper than the depth of the root ball. Set the tree in the hole so the point where the trunk flares into the root system is at the soil surface. Backfill the hole with native soil and water well.

- Continue your watering program until the steady rains return.

- Prepare your compost area for the new crop of leaves.

OCTOBER

- Many conifers including fir and ponderosa pine will shed their needles this month. Small needles can be raked into planting beds as a mulch. Larger ponderosa pine needles can be shredded and used as a mulch for roses or in place of bark mulch. They do not acidify the soil.

- Shred deciduous leaves with the lawn mower as you mow the lawn or run them through a shredder. Add them to the compost pile.

- If you live in deer, elk, and/or moose country, wrap young trees with 7-to 8-foot high deer fencing to keep the critters from browsing your trees. Bucks can damage small trunks by rubbing their antlers on them and damaging the bark or breaking branches.

- Surround the lower trunks of young trees with fine wire mesh to keep mice, voles, and other rodents from gnawing on bark over the winter. Pull mulch away from trunks to remove hiding places.

NOVEMBER

- Transplant conifers this month. They are dormant and will move easily. Wrap tall, floppy evergreens with twine to prevent their branches from bending under a heavy snow. Loosely tie a strong cord around the trunk at its base and then spiral wrap the tree to hold in floppy branches. Damage caused by snow is often permanent.

- If you are planning on having a living Christmas tree, dig the hole now and store the soil in a frost-free place.

DECEMBER

- Catch up on your journal entries and make notes about what you want to do next year.

- Living Christmas trees should not remain inside the house more than five to seven days to prevent them from breaking bud. Plant them immediately in your pre-dug hole, backfill with the stored, moistened soil. If the ground is thawed, water well.

- After the first few winter storms, check stakes and ties on newly planted trees and adjust accordingly.

VINES
for the Northwest

Vines can benefit a landscape in many ways. They add height to garden spaces as they ramble up and over fences, arbors, old stumps, trees, and retaining walls. Vigorous vines can hide ugly garden features and soften entrances to create a welcoming atmosphere. Vines trained onto stout pergolas provide shade on hot summer afternoons. Lastly, their varied leaf and flower color and fragrance add visual and sensory interest throughout the year.

RIGHT VINE, RIGHT PLACE

Bringing all this beauty and benefit to the garden does come with some major trade-offs, however. Many vines are vigorous growers and can quickly cover large expanses of space. As a result, they often require a lot of regular pruning and support to keep them from swallowing up nearby plants and structures.

Understanding how vines climb and support themselves will help determine what kind of support structure they will need. Most vines climb using one of three methods: twining, tendrils, or specialized roots. Twining climbers use thin stems to wrap themselves around thin support stakes, wires, string, or other plant stems as they climb. These thinner climbing supports will need to be anchored to a stout arbor or trellis. Vines that use twining to climb include Akebia (*Akebia quinata*), honeysuckle (*Lonicera* spp.), wisteria (*Wisteria* spp.), and clematis (*Clematis* spp.). Vines that climb using tendrils wrap coiled stem extensions around thin supports or other stems to climb and hold the vine in place. Tendril vines include grape (*Vitis* spp.) and scarlet runner bean (*Phaseolus coccineus*). The last group of vines use specialized roots or holdfasts to climb. The tiny suction cups or hooks at the end of the holdfasts attach to the rough surfaces of wood, concrete, brick, and masonry and hold the plant in place. Examples of vines in this group include climbing hydrangea (*Hydrangea anomala* subsp. *petiolaris*), trumpet vines (*Campsis* spp.), and wintercreeper (*Euonymus fortunei*).

Some vines lack any means of attaching themselves to a structure and will sprawl out or

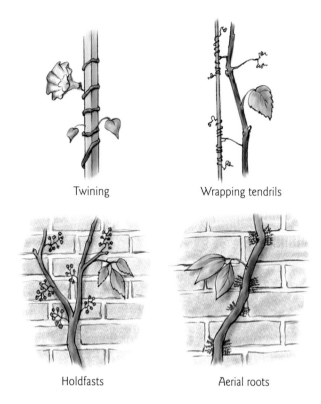

Twining   Wrapping tendrils

Holdfasts   Aerial roots

Vines cling to supports in one of three ways: wrapping tendrils, twining around, or clinging with holdfasts or aerial roots. Be sure you know what type of method a vine needs before you bring it home from the nursery.

wander through other plants for support. Left to their own rambling, they can overwhelm their host plant or create an unmanageable sprawl. This group is best trained onto a sturdy wood or wire trellis when young to ensure sturdy support and easy maintenance. Climbing roses (*Rosa* spp.) are the most familiar plant in this group.

The best way to balance these benefits and challenges is to select the right vine for the right place in the very beginning. Smaller spaces will require smaller, less vigorous vines, while larger spaces will be able to handle more robust vines that can cover a lot of space quickly. Robust vines can be very heavy when they mature and will require sturdy support to hold them up and keep them from crushing other plants. Support structures should be made of stout timber or metal uprights securely anchored in the ground and/or to a wall or frame. Wood structures should be made of rot-resistant woods like cedar, redwood, or pressure-treated lumber to reduce maintenance and increase the longevity of the structure. In snowy areas, plan for the weight of heavy, wet snow in addition to the weight of the vine when you design your structure.

For vines trained up a wall, consider how you will maintain the underlying wall over time. Vines climbing up brick, wood, concrete, and masonry—either on trellises or directly with aerial roots—can damage the wall surface by holding moisture close to the surface, which induces rot or by compromising the integrity of the surface. Plan ahead for the inevitable repairs to reduce potential problems and expense later.

HOW TO GROW AND CARE FOR VINES

Most vines need six to eight hours of direct sun per day to stay bushy and flower heavily. Their long stems will often climb to great heights to reach the sun. Vines that do not get enough sun will become leggy and bare at the base while their flowers and leaves fill out high overhead where you can't see or appreciate them.

Most vines should be planted in the spring when soil moisture is high, temperatures are moderate, and there is a good selection in the nurseries. Most vines except clematis (*Clematis* spp.) should be planted with the top of the rootball at the soil surface. Clematis rootballs should be planted 2 to 4 inches deep to reduce the effect of clematis wilt that damages aboveground stems. All clematis are susceptible to the disease, but the large-flowered varieties like *Clematis* 'Jackmanii' can be particularly susceptible. Burying the rootball deep provides a reservoir of healthy stem buds to regenerate the plant.

Amend the soil in the planting hole with a good-quality compost and mulch with two to three inches of medium-textured bark or pine needles. Water plants regularly for the first two to three years to support their rapid growth. Fertilize lightly, if at all. Too much nitrogen can overstimulate fast-growing vines and make them unmanageable.

Smaller, less vigorous vines are easy to grow in large containers. Clematis (*Clematis* spp.), beautyberry (*Callicarpa* spp.), and most annual vines can be planted in deep, 24-inch-diameter containers filled with good potting mix, then trained up a trellis. East of the Cascades, most containerized perennial vines will need to be heavily mulched or stored in a protected area in the winter.

PRUNING VINES

Most vines will need regular pruning to keep them within bounds and stimulate new growth and flowers. Late winter is often the best time to thin and head back most dormant deciduous vines because it's easy to see the branch structure. Check the plant profiles for the best methods for your particular vines.

Clematis can be broken into three groups for pruning depending on whether they produce flowers on old or new wood. Group 1 plants bloom on wood that grew during the previous season. They generally bloom in March and April and should be headed back and shaped right after flowering to stimulate new wood for next year's blooms. Plants in this group include *C. montana* cultivars and evergreen *C. armandii*. Group 2 plants are the large-flowered varieties that bloom in early to midsummer on new stems that arise from last year's wood. These should be pruned in late winter to early spring as the buds on the old wood begin to swell. New growth will sprout from the buds and bloom in June and July. Prune back to a pair of healthy buds on the stem, removing about one-third of the plant's growth each year. Plants in this group include *C.* 'Nelly Moser' and other large-flowered cultivars. Group 3 plants bloom late in the growing season on the current season's growth. These should be pruned in late winter to early spring to form a framework of well-spaced stems 6 to 12 inches tall. Clematis in this group include *C.* 'Jackmanii,' *C. viticella,* and *C. texensis* cultivars.

Vines are not only beautiful and fragrant, they are the gardener's best friend when it comes to providing shade and covering otherwise unsightly walls, views, and compost piles. In a small or narrow garden they can climb up walls and fences to create a vertical garden. Experiment with them in your garden—what ways can you use them?

AKEBIA VINE
Akebia quinata

Why It's Special—Akebia vine has showy, fragrant flowers and, in some areas, produces 2- to 4-inch-long, sausage-shaped fruits. Native to Japan, China, and Korea, it is deciduous in zones 4 to 6 and evergreen in warmer zones. The leaves are composed of five leaflets and do not change color in the fall. Also referred to as chocolate vine, plants are frequently used on slopes for erosion control and as large groundcovers. Cultivars include 'Alba' (white), 'Rosea' (reddish purple flowers), 'Variegata' (variegated foliage), and the more compact 'Purple Bouquet'.

How to Plant & Grow—In spring, choose a location with well-drained, sandy loam soil. Vines prefer full sun but grow in part to full shade. Provide plants with strong supports such as a trellis or fence to grow on.

Care & Problems—Vines grow quickly and can become invasive. Fertilizing is unnecessary. Prune after flowering or as needed to shape the plant. Plants are deer resistant.

Hardiness—Zones 4 to 8

Seasonal Color—Purple-brown

Peak Season—March to April

Mature Length—20 to 40 ft.

Water Needs—Medium. Water regularly.

BLACK-EYED SUSAN VINE
Thunbergia alata

Why It's Special—Native to East Africa, black-eyed Susan vine features attractive flowers and heart-shaped leaves. A fast grower, it is often planted in containers or along a trellis, arbor, or fence. The flowers are 1½ inches in diameter with five brightly colored petals surrounding a dark center. Suggested varieties are 'Superstar Orange', 'Susie Mix' (white, yellow, and orange), 'Bright Eyes' (white), 'Blushing Susie' (red, cream, and apricot), and 'Spanish Eyes' (apricot, cream, salmon, and rose).

How to Plant & Grow—Sow seeds indoors six to eight weeks before last frost date or sow seeds and purchased seedlings directly in the garden after danger of frost is past. Plant in full sun to part shade in well-drained soil.

Care & Problems—Apply slow-release fertilizer once in spring and again in two months to keep the blooms coming. Deadheading is unnecessary. Plants have minimal insect or disease problems

Hardiness—Annual

Seasonal Color—Orange, yellow, white, red, salmon, rose

Peak Season—Summer to fall

Mature Length—3 to 8 ft.

Water Needs—Medium. Water regularly throughout the season.

CLEMATIS
Clematis spp.

Why It's Special—Clematis add the perfect touch to English-style gardens with their breathtaking flowers. There are over 300 species available: early-flowering species like *Clematis alpina* and *C. montana*; midseason, large-flowering species and cultivars such as 'Nelly Moser' and 'Duchess of Edinburgh'; and late-flowering species including *C. ternifolia*, *C. texensis*, and *C. paniculata*. They grow on vertical supports, saving space in the garden.

How to Plant & Grow—Clematis require full sun or dappled shade and cool roots; use mulch to accomplish this. In spring, dig a large hole, set the top of the rootball 2 inches below the soil surface, and backfill. Provide support with a trellis or arbor.

Care & Problems—Feed monthly with a balanced fertilizer throughout the growing season. Pruning is important in order to be rewarded with a maximum bloom; refer to "Pruning Vines" in this chapter for correct timing. Young, large-flowered hybrids are susceptible to clematis wilt.

Hardiness—Zones 4 to 8

Seasonal Color—White, pink, red, purple, blue

Peak Season—May to October

Mature Length—5 to 18 ft. long

Water Needs—Medium. Water regularly.

CLIMBING HYDRANGEA
Hydrangea anomala subsp. *petiolaris*

Why It's Special—Climbing hydrangeas are one of the best vines for the Northwest. In summer, the plants are covered with clusters of fragrant, lacecap flowers. The leaves are heart-shaped and the exfoliating, reddish brown bark provides winter interest. Plants require two years to become established and three to five years to begin blooming. Vines grow vigorously and climb via rootlike holdfasts. Grow them near brick or stone walls, or as a groundcover to disguise rock piles or stabilize slopes. They will grow in heavy shade, are drought-tolerant, and rabbit resistant. The flowers are stunning whether fresh-cut or dried. Suggested cultivars are 'Firefly', 'Skyland Giant', and variegated 'Miranda'.

How to Plant & Grow—In spring or fall, select a location with rich, well-drained soil. Provide sturdy support if growing vertically.

Care & Problems—Prune after flowering as desired. No fertilizing is necessary. It has minimal insect or disease problems.

Hardiness—Zones 4 to 7

Seasonal Color—White blooms; yellow fall color

Peak Season—June or early July blooms

Mature Length—40 to 80 ft. long

Water Needs—Medium. Do not let soil dry out.

CUP AND SAUCER VINE
Cobaea scandens

Why It's Special—Cup and saucer vine is so-named due to its bell-shaped, fragrant flowers that sit atop a green calyx base. The blossoms have long, eye-catching stamens and attract hummingbirds. These fast-growing vines use tendrils to climb. Since plants are only hardy to zone 9, gardeners in most regions grow them as an annual. Recommended varieties are 'Purple', 'Royal Plum', 'Key Lime' (pale green), or 'Alba' (white).

How to Plant & Grow—Soak seeds in warm water before starting them indoors eight weeks before the last frost. Plant in full sun in average, well-drained soil once the danger of frost is past; in areas with hot summers, provide afternoon shade. Give vines a strong structure to climb.

Care & Problems—Feed a low-nitrogen liquid fertilizer once monthly during summer. This low-maintenance vine has minimal insect or disease problems.

Hardiness—Annual

Seasonal Color—Green, turning purple or white

Peak Season—Seasonal

Mature Length—10 to 20 ft.

Water Needs—Medium. Water regularly but do not overwater.

HONEYSUCKLE VINE
Lonicera spp.

Why It's Special—Honeysuckle vine is a profuse bloomer with tubular flowers that attract hummingbirds and butterflies. Birds are drawn to its red berries in the fall. The vines climb by twining around their supports. Trumpet honeysuckle (*Lonicera sempervirens*) has orange-red and yellow flowers. Look for 'Superba', coral 'Crimson Cascade', or scarlet-red 'Major Wheeler'. American honeysuckle (*L. americana*) is actually a European hybrid that is hardy to zones 7 to 9; blossoms are pink and yellow. Japanese honeysuckle (*L. japonica*) grows vigorously and can be quite invasive.

How to Plant & Grow—Honeysuckle adapts to all soil types and grows in full sun or part shade, although it blooms more if grown in a sunny spot. Plant in spring and provide vines with vertical support.

Care & Problems—Feed a balanced fertilizer each spring. Honeysuckle blooms on old wood so prune as needed after flowering. There are minimal insect or disease problems. It is deer resistant.

Hardiness—Zones 4 to 9

Seasonal Color—Orange, pink, yellow, red blooms

Peak Season—June through October

Mature Length—12 ft. long

Water Needs—Medium. Water regularly.

HYACINTH BEAN
Dolichos lablab

Why It's Special—Hyacinth bean is an attractive, twining vine with purple stems, deep green leaves, and purple pea-like flowers and pods. They are grown as annuals in the Northwest. These showy vines look beautiful when grown over arbors, pergolas, trellises, or next to a porch. 'Ruby Moon' has dark purple flowers while 'Alba' has white blossoms. 'Bronze Leaf' features pink flowers and bronze leaves and pods.

How to Plant & Grow—Select a sunny location with average, well-drained soil. Sow seeds directly in the garden after all danger of frost is past. Either soak seeds for twenty-four hours before planting or nick the seed coating to improve germination rates. Space 12 inches apart. Provide plants with a vertical support to grow on.

Care & Problems—Feed every two weeks with a high-phosphorus fertilizer until vines start flowering. Aphids and pod borers can be troublesome. *Note: The seeds and pods are poisonous.*

Hardiness—Annual

Seasonal Color—Purple, pink, or white flowers; purple fruit

Peak Season—Summer through fall

Mature Length—10 to 20 ft. long

Water Needs—Medium. Water plants regularly.

KIWI VINE
Actinidia spp.

Why It's Special—This appealing vine has heart-shaped leaves and produces fruit, provided you have male and female plants. One male plant will pollinate up to nine females. The vines provide season-long interest and are fire resistant. Hardy kiwifruit (*Actinidia arguta*), which grows in zones 5 to 9, produces small, hairless kiwi-style fruits. A native of Russia, ornamental kiwi (*A. kolomitka*), also known as Arctic Beauty, grows in zones 3 to 8 and features green leaves with pink or white splotches.

How to Plant & Grow—Choose a sunny location for *A. arguta* or part shade for *A. kolomitka*. Before planting in spring, incorporate compost into bed. Plant vines 10 feet apart; place a thick mulch on top of soil. Provide plants with sturdy supports.

Care & Problems—Feed each spring with balanced fertilizer. Prune twice during the growing season and once during dormancy. They have no serious pest or disease problems but are susceptible to late-season frosts.

Hardiness—Zones 3 to 9

Seasonal Color—White flowers

Peak Season—Season-long

Mature Length—20 ft. long

Water Needs—Medium. Don't let roots dry out.

PASSION FLOWER
Passiflora spp.

Why It's Special—To add a tropical look to your garden, plant passion flower. The exotic, purple-and-white flowers attract butterflies. Vines use tendrils to climb their supports. There are more than 500 species of passion flower. While purple passion flower (*Passiflora incarnata*) is the hardiest species, it isn't consistently hardy in zone 5 gardens. Blue passion flower (*P. caerulea*) grows in zones 7 to 9 and has lightly fragrant, 3-inch-diameter flowers. Both species produce edible fruits that ripen in fall. Vines are frequently grown as annuals in outdoor containers.

How to Plant & Grow—Plant passion flower in spring in all light conditions but protect from winds. It can be grown from seeds or nursery plants.

Care & Problems—Since vines flower on new growth, prune while dormant. Pinch buds to promote new growth. Feed low-nitrogen fertilizer during the growing season. Spider mites, whiteflies, and caterpillars can be troublesome.

Hardiness—Zones 5 to 9

Seasonal Color—White and purple blooms

Peak Season—Midsummer to fall

Mature Length—6 to 8 ft. long

Water Needs—Medium. Water regularly.

PORCELAIN BERRY
Ampelopsis brevipedunculata

Why It's Special—The key feature of this fast-growing vine is its showy berries. They are pastel-colored initially, maturing to deeper blue and purple shades. The berries attract birds to the garden. This deciduous vine uses tendrils to climb supports. To grow one as an accent in the landscape, try 'Elegans' with its variegated foliage.

How to Plant & Grow—Porcelain berry is easy to grow from seeds or container-grown nursery plants. Plant in spring in full sun to part shade, although vines produce more flowers and berries in sunny locations. They prefer well-drained soil. Provide support with arbors, trellises, or fences, or grow along a wall.

Care & Problems—Prune vines as needed while they are dormant since they flower on new wood. They are low maintenance and have minimal insect or disease problems but can be rather invasive.

Hardiness—Zones 4 to 8

Seasonal Color—Green flowers; blue fruits

Peak Season—July to August

Mature Length—15 to 20 ft. long

Water Needs—Medium. Established plants are drought-tolerant.

PURPLE-LEAF GRAPE

Vitis vinifera 'Purpurea'

Why It's Special—Purple-leaf grape is highly prized for its wonderful fall foliage. During spring and summer, the leaves are purple, but come fall, they put on a show by changing to burgundy-red. While related to wine grapes, this vine only produces small, bitter-tasting grapes in fall. The fruit and dense foliage attract birds to the garden. Consider planting along a fence, over an arbor, or up through an old tree.

How to Plant & Grow—Select a sunny location with well-drained soil. Plant purple-leaf grape in spring or fall. Cover the soil with a thick layer of mulch to protect the roots, impede weed growth, and conserve moisture.

Care & Problems—Feed with all-purpose fertilizer each spring. If vines require it, prune while they are dormant. Plants are susceptible to mildew, mealybugs, and scale.

Hardiness—Zones 5 to 9

Seasonal Color—Red leaves in fall

Peak Season—Fall

Mature Length—Up to 20 ft. long

Water Needs—Medium. Water regularly the first year; it's drought-tolerant once established.

SILVER LACE VINE

Polygonum aubertii

Why It's Special—Silver lace vine is a fast-growing deciduous plant that is covered in fragrant white flowers from midsummer to fall. It has shiny, heart-shaped leaves that are deer and rabbit resistant. The vine spreads by rhizomes and twines to climb its support. They are also used to prevent erosion by stabilizing slopes. 'Lemon Lace' is less vigorous than the species and has golden leaves. Silver lace vine is also known as silver fleece vine, *Polygonum baldschuanica*, or *Fallopia baldschuanica*.

How to Plant & Grow—The vine will grow in all light conditions, including heavy shade. It is adaptable to all soil types. Plant in early spring or fall from container-grown plants.

Care & Problems—Feed lightly with all-purpose fertilizer each spring. Silver lace vine can become weedy and invasive so prune back drastically when dormant or trim the height as needed anytime. Plants have minimal insect or disease problems.

Hardiness—Zones 4 to 7

Seasonal Color—White

Peak Season—July to frost

Mature Length—Up to 25 ft. long

Water Needs—Medium. Drought-tolerant once established.

TRUMPET VINE
Campsis spp.

Why It's Special—Trumpet vine has a stunning red or orange tubular flowers that attract hummingbirds. After blooming, long seedpods develop. Vines cling to their supports with aerial rootlets. Plants are deer resistant and thrive in hot, dry conditions. Look for trumpet creeper (*Campsis radicans*) 'Crimson Trumpet' (red), 'Flava' (yellow or orange), or 'Variegata' (variegated leaves and orange flowers). *C.* × *tagliabuana* 'Madame Galen' has salmon-colored flowers. Hardy in zones 6 to 9, Chinese trumpet creeper (*C. grandiflora*) 'Morning Calm' has peach-colored blossoms.

How to Plant & Grow—Plant in spring or fall in full sun and average, well-drained soil. Provide sturdy support such as a wall, fence, or arbor and stand back.

Care & Problems—It blooms on new wood so prune in late winter or early spring. It is *very* aggressive, sending up suckers from its roots, and self-seeds easily. There are no serious pest or disease issues.

Hardiness—Zones 4 to 10

Seasonal Color—Orange and yellow flowers

Peak Season—July

Mature Length—40 ft. or more in length

Water Needs—Medium. Trumpet vine becomes drought-tolerant once established.

WINTERCREEPER
Euonymus fortunei

Why It's Special—Wintercreeper grows as an evergreen to semi-evergreen vine in the Northwest. A native of China, the plant's stems root if they are in contact with the ground. 'Coloratus' is a trailing groundcover. 'Emerald Gaiety' has variegated leaves and, while it has a more compact habit, it will climb if given support. 'Harlequin' has frosty-looking, variegated leaves.

How to Plant & Grow—Plant in full sun to part shade in spring or fall. Wintercreeper adapts to most soils. The plants can be used as vines to climb the walls of structures and supports, or as groundcovers to stabilize areas with erosion problems.

Care & Problems—Do not plant near lawns as vines can take over. Do not fertilize. Prune in early spring to shape plants as needed. It's easily propagated by cuttings. Plants are susceptible to scale and can become invasive.

Hardiness—Zones 4 to 9

Seasonal Color—Inconspicuous white flowers

Peak Season—April

Mature Length—6 to 9 in. x 12 to 36 in.

Water Needs—Medium. Water regularly but do not overwater.

WISTERIA
Wisteria spp.

Why It's Special—Wisteria is known for its beautiful springtime display of cascading purple or white flower clusters. These deciduous vines have attractive, lacy foliage and hefty trunks and branches. Japanese wisteria (*Wisteria floribunda*) has more fragrant flowers than other species; consider 'Longissima Alba', with 3-foot-long white racemes, or pale blue 'Geisha'. Popular varieties of Chinese wisteria (*W. sinensis*) include 'Cooke's Special' and 'Prolific'.

How to Plant & Grow—Grow Japanese wisteria in full sun and Chinese wisteria in sun or part shade. Well-drained soil is a must and plants need plenty of room. For best results, purchase grafted or cutting-grown plants from a nursery because they'll bloom within a couple of years. Seedlings can take several years to flower. Provide extremely sturdy supports or structures to grow on.

Care & Problems—Fertilize young plants with balanced fertilizer once annually. Prune only after blooming.

Hardiness—Zones 4 to 9

Seasonal Color—Purple, violet, or white flowers

Peak Season—Late spring or early summer

Mature Length—30 ft. long

Water Needs—Medium to high. Water plants regularly.

JANUARY

- Review your garden notes on what worked and what didn't, and make a spring to-do list.

- If heavy, wet snows occur, gently knock the snow off vines to keep them from breaking or bringing down supports. Use a long bamboo pole or bow rake to gently bump the stems from the underside to release the load.

- Trim back any long stems that are being whipped around by the wind. If the weather is favorable, now is a good time to begin removing dense growth from mature vines. The leaves are off the plant and you can see the stems more easily.

FEBRUARY

- West of the Cascades, check on vine supports that need maintenance and make the repairs before the leaves grow back and make it difficult.

- Check out the catalogs and nursery racks for annual vine seeds while the selection is good.

- Gardeners west of the Cascades can begin pruning Japanese wisterias (*Wisteria floribunda*) and purple leaf grape (*Vitis vinifera*). Cut stems back to three to four buds near the main trunks to encourage flowering.

- Check on the soil in containerized tender vines you have in storage for moisture, and water if it's dry.

MARCH

- Transplant woody vines this month when the ground has thawed and dried out enough to work. If you are planting against a wall, plant rootballs away from roof overhangs so the plants can get rain.

- Gardeners east of the Cascades can begin pruning Japanese wisteria and purple leaf grape this month.

- Sow annual vines under lights indoors three to four weeks before the last frost date in your area.

- Late this month, prune back Group 3 late-season blooming clematis to several well-spaced stems 6 to 8 inches above the ground. Clematis in this group include *Clematis* 'Jackmanii,' *C. viticella*, and *C. texensis* cultivars. Trim back stems of Group 2 plants to a pair of healthy buds on the main stem. Plants in this group include *C.* 'Nelly Moser' and other large-flowered cultivars. Group 1 clematis should be trimmed and shaped right after they finish blooming in March and April. Plants in this group include *C. montana* cultivars and evergreen *C. armandii*.

APRIL

- If powdery mildew or insects were a problem last year, thin out vines to improve air circulation.

- Apply mulch to the base of vines to control weeds and retain moisture during dry weather.

- Evergreen clematis (*Clematis armandii*) can be headed back after it finishes flowering to remove spent flowers and clean up leggy stems.

- Resist the urge to fertilize vines unless there is weak growth or yellowing leaves. High nitrogen levels stimulate growth that will be difficult to control later.

MAY

- After the last frost date, annual vines like scarlet runner bean (*Phaseolus coccineus*), black-eyed Susan (*Thunbergia alata*), morning glory (*Ipomoea* spp.), and canary creeper (*Tropaeolum pereginum*) can be planted outdoors or direct-seeded. Keep frost protection handy.

- Prune back spring-flowering vines after they finish to keep them full at the bottom and within bounds.

- Begin pruning wisteria monthly to keep its vigorous stems in check. Regular trimming makes the task much easier in the long run.

JUNE

- Finish planting out annual vines early in the month. Fertilize all containerized and annual vines with a slow-release 10-10-10 fertilizer once a month from May through the growing season.

- If powdery mildew was an issue on certain vines last year, begin a weekly application of baking soda mixed with water. Mix 4 teaspoons of baking soda with 2½ tablespoons of Neem oil in a gallon of water.

- Repair vine supports and ties. Tie up new growth as it spreads to keep the vines in bounds and well-shaped. Use soft materials like heavy twine and plastic-coated wire ties to prevent damage to stems.

- Begin watching for signs of clematis wilt as large-flowering early-summer clematis start blooming. Remove infected stems down to the ground and dispose of them and any fallen leaves in the trash.

JULY

- Begin a regular watering program for vines. Remove other plants that are blocking sprinkler heads. Check that plants close to roof eave drip lines are getting adequate water.

- Stay on top of pruning wisteria and trumpet vine to keep them in bounds.

- If your vines are growing well but producing few flowers, cut back on fertilizer to nearby plants. Too much nitrogen encourages vine growth at the expense of flower production.

- To protect healthy plants from powdery mildew, apply copper sulfate, potassium bicarbonate, or homemade sodium bicarbonate solution (see the formula in June) to plants before the mildew appears.

- Hose aphids off vines with a hard stream of water and watch for beneficial insects before applying an insecticidal soap.

AUGUST

- Irrigation is a must this month. In hot, windy weather, leaves lose moisture faster than the roots can supply it, so water deeply. Reapply mulch to bare areas.

- Check the nurseries for end-of-season bargains. Heel in your finds in a shady holding bed and keep them moist until the weather is cool enough for planting.

- Keep trimming back the wisteria. You may be getting tired, but the vines aren't.

- Hold off fertilizing annual and container vines until the weather begins to cool at the end of the month.

SEPTEMBER

- East of the Cascades, begin to harden off the tender vines you want to bring indoors by reducing watering by half. Clean up the plants by removing dead leaves and tie up stems so they are easy to move indoors at the first hint of a frost.

- Continue to check for nursery bargains, but plan on getting all your finds planted before the end of the month.

- Visit local public gardens to observe the fall colors of vines. Some of them can be quite spectacular in bright yellows, reds, and oranges.

- Vines that took a beating in the hot summer weather could use a clean-up and trim to remove crispy leaves and heat damaged twigs. Give all plants a deep soaking.

OCTOBER

- Early in the month, make sure tender containerized vines are stored in a protected, frost-free place. Deep basement window wells with a cover will borrow heat from the house to keep them warm.

- Do a final trimming on wisteria and other fast growers to reduce the potential of long stems whipping around in the winter winds.

- Apply mulch to new plantings to prevent frost heaving.

NOVEMBER

- If it has been a dry fall, give all newly planted vines one last drink before you shut off the water.

- Mulch root areas with 2 to 3 inches of mulch to prevent winter weeds from popping up and to prevent frost heaving.

DECEMBER

- Do some early pruning. Wind long stems together from your pruning to make decorative holiday wreaths.

- Review your garden notes while they are fresh on your mind. Note any projects you want to focus on next year.

- Save evergreen boughs from Christmas trees and conifer prunings to cover new vine plantings to give them a little more protection from snow and cold and prevent frost heaving.

CARE OF YOUR VEGETABLE GARDEN

THINNING

Seeds, especially tiny ones, are usually sown thicker than is needed with the assumption that not all will germinate. The result is that most crops will need to be thinned out after the seeds have germinated. Removing some plants in a row to make room for others to grow is not always an easy task for gardeners, since you're getting rid of growing plants, but it is important. Plants grown too closely together will not mature properly and your harvest will be greatly reduced.

Thinning can be done with your fingers or you can use tweezers or small scissors. These tiny seedlings can often be replanted into another area of the garden, if you have the room. If you are going to do this, you will need to gently pull the seedlings to retain the roots. If you are not going to replant the seedlings, it is better to just cut them off at ground level so the roots of the remaining plants are not disturbed. You can toss the rootless thinnings from lettuces, onions, radishes, and carrots into a salad or soup and make use of them.

MULCHING

Mulching goes a long way toward controlling weeds in the vegetable garden and it improves the soil as it breaks down. It also helps keep plant foliage clean. Good material for mulch includes partially decomposed compost or leaves, weed-free straw, or dried grass clippings. Be sure to put it on thick enough to smother weeds, at least 3 or 4 inches but preferably 5 or 6. Keep it a few inches away from the stems of the crops.

Timing is important with mulching. You can mulch cool-season crops soon after planting, but warm-season crops should not be mulched until the soil has thoroughly warmed. If you lay the

Thinning is easier and the root disturbance is less if the soil is moist. Water several hours before thinning if the soil is dry.

mulch down on a weed-free soil, you should not have to weed your vegetable garden again all summer. Plants that you want to overwinter should have a winter mulch applied to them after the ground freezes.

FERTILIZING

Most vegetables will need regular fertilizing through the growing season. Generally, a good organic 10-10-10- liquid or granular fertilizer will do the trick. Granular fertilizers should be added to the soil at planting time and then added as a side-dressing through the season. Simply sprinkle a band of fertilizer along a row or around large plants and lightly work it into the soil, then water well. Foliar fertilizers can be sprayed on the leaves of the plants and are absorbed directly into the leaves. Foliar sprays will generally get more nutrition to the plant than granular ones. Check page 94 for a list of vegetable fertilizer needs.

WATERING

It is very important to maintain a consistent and even supply of water to your vegetables. Most vegetables require 1 inch of water a week. Many crops will suffer greatly if the soil is allowed to dry out. Tomatoes often develop blossom-end rot when they are exposed to a very dry period after a wet period. And peppers will drop their blossoms if the soil is too dry.

If your garden is small and reachable with a garden hose, you can use a sprinkler or watering wand. Just be sure to water deeply so the plants will develop deep root systems. Frequent shallow watering encourages shallow root systems that are unable to survive even the smallest dry period. Larger gardens will benefit from soaker hoses or a drip irrigation system. But make sure your system allows you to cultivate around the plants as needed and then remove the equipment in fall so you can turn the garden. These systems have the advantage of wetting the soil rather than the foliage.

Water in the morning so plants have a chance to dry off before the cooler evening temperatures

Apply a sidedressing of compost, manure, or granular fertilizer to give vegetables a midseason boost.

set in. Moist foliage and cool temperatures set the stage for disease development.

SUPPORTING YOUR PLANTS

Some vegetables will require some type of support to grow and produce at their best. Tomatoes are usually staked or caged, while pole beans and pea vines require some type of trellis or support system. Supports can also be used to grow vines and save space in smaller gardens. Stakes should always be put into the ground before seeding or transplanting to avoid root damage to half-grown plants. Heavy fruits such as melons require support for each individual fruit. You can use mesh bags or cloth slings that you tie to the trellis.

USING FLOATING ROW COVERS

Floating row covers are made of spun polyester fabric and are permeable to light, air, and water. These covers have a variety of uses in the vegetable garden. They can be used to shield young plants from strong drying winds. They warm the air around plants in spring and fall, offering between 2 and 10 degrees of added warmth. They can also be used to provide shade for plants that need a break from full sun conditions in midsummer.

Floating row covers provide a barrier against insect pests such as flea beetles, radish maggots, cucumber beetles, and more. But they must be removed as flowers start to set on insect-pollinated crops such as cucumbers, squashes, and melons, or the bees won't be able to get to the flowers. They are light enough that you can place them directly on the plants without damaging them. They should be spread with plenty of slack so they don't hinder plant growth. And the edges need to be secured so they don't blow away.

CLEAN UP

Always remove all dead plants and anything you won't be overwintering. Insects and diseases often overwinter in garden debris, so get it off your garden and into the compost bin. Turn the soil so that weed seeds are exposed to the elements. In spring, turn the soil again as soon as it is dry enough to be worked.

HARVEST

Harvest time is the reward for your efforts. You and your family get to enjoy the juicy tomatoes and freshly dug potatoes. And any extra produce you can't eat can be shared with friends or donated to a local food bank.

It can be tricky knowing when is the best time to harvest some crops to get the greatest payoff for your hard work. As a general rule, crops grown for their leaves, stems, stalks, and roots should be harvested when they are still young and tender, but most are still quite edible after they reach larger sizes. Fruit crops, including beans, cucumbers, eggplants, and summer squashes, taste better when picked slightly immature. Tomatoes should be left on the vine until they are fully ripe for maximum flavor but they will continue to ripen if picked before they have full color.

You should pick ripe fruits even if you aren't able to eat them or give them away. Overripe fruits

Leafy crops like lettuces and spinach should be cut rather than pulled to avoid uprooting plants, which will continue to produce fresh leaves for future use.

attract insect and disease problems and overripening reduces the plant's ability to produce more fruits. Regular cutting of leafy crops such as lettuces and spinach helps delay flowering and keeps them producing new leaves.

Try to harvest all vegetables when the plants are dry to reduce chances of spreading diseases. Use sharp shears or a knife to cut broccoli and cabbage heads and fruiting crops, including a small portion of the stem to extend storage life. Avoid bruising or puncturing tender skins. Harvest in the morning when the sugar content of most vegetables is higher.

STORAGE

Your homegrown produce will taste best right out of the garden, but we can't always eat everything we pick right away. Most produce will keep for several days or more in the refrigerator, and some vegetables can be stored for months.

Directions for storage vary with each crop, but there are a few general rules to follow. Most crops should be cooled as soon as possible after harvest to prolong storage life. However, if your produce isn't quite ripe, leave it at room temperature. Wash only the produce you plan to use immediately. Remove the tops from root crops to prevent them from drying out.

Some crops need to be cured before they can be stored for more than a few weeks. These include garlic, onions, potatoes, pumpkins, sweet potatoes, and winter squashes. Cure these crops by subjecting them to warm temperatures and dry conditions for ten days to two weeks after harvest. If the weather cooperates, this can be done right in the garden. After curing, they can be stored in a cool dry place (40 to 50 degrees Fahrenheit) for several months.

GROWING CULINARY HERBS

Herbs are the perfect complement to all the great vegetables you will be growing. There are many culinary herbs, but the best-known and easiest to grow are basil, dill, chives, parsley, thyme, oregano, rosemary, cilantro, and sage. Some are annual,

some biennial, and some perennial. They can be incorporated into the vegetable garden or grown in their own space, where they provide an interesting variety of shapes, textures, leaf colors, and in some cases, flowers.

Growing herbs is similar to growing leafy vegetables, but there are some differences. They all like lots of sun and well-drained soil. They do very well in raised beds, where they benefit from the improved drainage. Most grow best in a leaner soil than most vegetables. Rich soil produces lots of foliage but leaves have reduced oil content and less flavor and fragrance. Most do very well in containers, which you can place right outside your kitchen door or use to decorate your patio or deck.

Herbs benefit from regular harvesting, which encourages more leafy growth and delays flowering. Even if you don't have a use for your herbs in the kitchen, you should give them a good trimming about once a month during the growing season to encourage new leaf growth. Herbs can be harvested throughout the growing season but have their best flavor when picked just before they bloom. If you plan to dry herbs for winter use, this is the time to pick the stems.

OUT TO DRY

Herbs for drying should be picked when their leaves are dry. You can dry picked herbs by hanging them in bunches or by spreading them on drying screens. Place them in a dry, well-ventilated place out of the sun. Herbs will take a few days to a couple weeks to dry. You can tell when they are dry by rubbing a leaf between your fingers. A completely dry herb will crack and crumble.

If you are drying herbs for their seeds (dill, coriander), be sure that the seeds are ripe when you pick the plants. On most herbs the seeds turn from green to tan or light brown when ripe. Place a paper bag over the hanging bunches to catch the seeds as they ripen and fall.

When the herbs are completely dried, strip the leaves from the stems and pack them in clean jars with tight-fitting lids. Store the jars away from heat and light. They should last about a year—until next year's harvest!

GARDEN VEGETABLE PLANTING GUIDE

Crop	Days to maturity (range)	Seeds/plants per 100 ft. row	Planting depth (inches)	Spacing in row (inches)
VERY HARDY TO HARDY[1]				
Asparagus	Perennial	65 plants	10	18
Beet	60–65	1 oz.	1	2–3
Cabbage	60–70	50 plants		20–24
Carrot	65–70	½ oz.	½	2–3
Chard, Swiss	50	½ oz.	1	12
Chives	Perennial			12–18
Endive	65	½ oz.	½	8
Horseradish	Perennial			18
Jerusalem Artichoke	Perennial	65 plants	2–3	18
Kale	50–55	¼ oz.	½	18
Lettuce, Head	70–80	¼ oz.	½	12
Lettuce, Leaf	40–45	¼ oz.	½	3–6
Onion, Bulb	100	300 transplants		4
Onion, Bunching	60–80	½ oz.		1
Parsnip	85–120	½ oz.	½	3–4
Peas (fresh)	50–65	½ oz.	1½	2
Rhubarb	Perennial	30 plants		30
Rutabaga	90	¼ oz.	½	6
Turnip	50–60	½ oz.	½	3
HALF HARDY[2]				
Broccoli	70	50 plants		18
Brussels Sprouts	90–100	50 plants		18–24
Cabbage, Chinese	70	¼ oz.	¾	10–12
Cauliflower	50–55	50 plants		18
Celery	85–100	200 plants		4–8
Kohlrabi	55	½ oz.	1	4–6
Parsley	70	½ oz.	¾	6
Potato	80–120	12 lbs.	4	10–20
Radish	20–30	1 oz.	½	1

Spacing between rows (inches)	Average yield per 10 ft. row*	Germination temperature	
		Minimum °F	Optimum °F
40–48	6 plants		
18	4 lb. greens 10 lb. roots	40	50–85
30	8 lb.	Transplants	
18	10 lb.	40	45–85
24–30	10 plants	40	50–85
8–10	10 plants	Plant division	
18	8 heads	35	40–80
18	varies	Plant division	
24	varies	Plant tubers	
24	7 lbs.	40	45–85
18	10 heads	45	40–80
12–18	5 lbs.	35	40–80
18	10 lbs.	Sets or plants	
12	10 lbs.	Plants	
18	7 lbs.	35	50–70
18–30	2 lbs.	40	40–75
40–48	4 plants	Crown division	
18	15 lbs.	40	55–80
18	5 lb. roots	40	60–105
30	7 lbs.	Transplants	
24–30	5 lbs.	Transplants	
24–36	6 heads	Transplants	
30	8 lbs.	Transplants	
30–36	10 plants	Transplants	
18	5 lbs.	40	45–85
18	varies	40	50–84
36–40	varies	Seed pieces from tubers	
12–18	10 bunches	40	45–90

GARDEN VEGETABLE PLANTING GUIDE

Crop	Days to maturity (range)	Seeds/plants per 100 ft. row	Planting depth (inches)	Spacing in row (inches)
WARM SEASON[3]				
Beans, Bush	45–50	½ lb.	2	4
Beans, Pole	60–65	½ lb.	2	4
Corn, Sweet	65–80	¼ lb.	2	12–36
Cucumber	50–100	½ oz.	¾	36–48
Eggplant	60–80	65 plants	½	18
Muskmelon or Cantaloupe	85–120	½ oz.	1–2	3–6
Okra	55–65	¼ oz.	½	12–15
Pepper	70–80	80 plants		15
Pumpkin	100	1 oz.	½	48
Squash, Summer	55–65	1 oz.	1	40–50
Squash, Winter	55–105	1 oz.	1	40–50
Tomato	60–85	40 plants	1	30
Watermelon	100–130	¾ oz.	1–2	72–96

[1] These vegetables survive hard frosts and can be planted 2 to 3 weeks before the average date of the last 32-degree temperature in spring.

[2] These vegetables withstand light frosts and their seeds germinate at low soil temperatures. Plant them 2 weeks before the average date of the last 32-degree temperature in spring.

[3] These vegetables do not withstand frost and their seeds will not germinate in cold soil. Plant them at about the average date of the last 32-degree temperature.

* Yields will vary with local conditions.

Spacing between rows (inches)	Average yield per 10 ft. row*	Germination temperature	
		Minimum °F	Optimum °F
18–24	8 lbs.	60	60–85
18–24	15 lbs.	60	60–85
36	10 ears	50	50–95
40–48	12 lbs.	60	60–95
25	7 lbs.	Transplants	
48–84	10 fruits	60	75–95
38	varies	60	70–95
24	5 lbs.	Transplants	
48–60	25 lbs.	60	70–95
48–60	20 lbs.	60	70–95
48–72	15 lbs.	60	70–95
36–40	15 lbs.	Transplants	
72–96	7 fruits	60	70–95

WILDFIRE-RESISTANT, BENEFICIAL INSECT PLANTS

These plants are resistant to wildfire.

GROUNDCOVERS

Carpet bugleweed	*Ajuga reptans*
Creeping phlox	*Phlox subulata*
Creeping thyme	*Thymus praecox*
Dead nettle	*Lamium* spp.
Garden carnation or pinks	*Dianthus* spp.
Hens and chicks	*Sempervivum* spp.
Japanese pachysandra	*Pachysandra terminalis*
Kinnikinnick	*Arctostaphylos uva-ursi*
Mahala mat	*Ceanothus prostrates*
Pink pussy	*Antennaria rosea*
Purple iceplant	*Delosperma cooperi*
Rock cress	*Aubrieta deltoidea*
Sedum and stonecrops	*Sedum* spp.
Snow-in-summer	*Cerastium tomentosum*
Speedwell	*Veronica* spp.
Wild strawberry	*Fragaria* spp.
Yellow iceplant	*Delosperma nubigenum*

PERENNIALS

Basket-of-gold	*Aurinia saxatilis*
Blanket flower	*Gaillardia* hybrids
Chives	*Allium schoenoprasum*
Columbine	*Aquilegia* spp.
Coneflower	*Echinacea purpurea*
Coralbells	*Heuchera sanguinea*
Coreopsis or tickseed	*Coreopsis* spp.
Daylily	*Hemerocallis* spp
Delphinium	*Delphinium* hybrids
Evening primrose	*Oenothera* spp.
Fireweed	*Epilobium angustifolium*
Flax, blue	*Linum perenne*
Grayleaf cranesbill	*Geranium cinereum*
Heartleaf bergenia	*Bergenia cordifolia*
Honeysuckle	*Lonicera* spp.
Hosta lily	*Hosta* spp.
Iris, tall bearded	*Iris* hybrids
Lamb's ear	*Stachys byzantine*
Lavender	*Lavandula* spp.
Lupine	*Lupinus* spp.
Oriental poppy	*Papaver orientale*
Penstemon or beardtongue	*Penstemon* spp.
Prairie coneflower	*Ratibida columnifera*
Salvia or sage	*Salvia* spp.
Sea thrift	*Armeria maritima*
Sedges	*Carex* spp.
Sun rose	*Helianthemum nummularium*
Torch lily or red-hot poker	*Kniphofia uvaria*
Trumpet vine	*Campsis radicans*
Yarrow	*Achillea* spp.
Yucca	*Yucca* spp.

SHRUBS

Broadleaf Evergreens

Carol Mackie daphne	*Daphne × burkwoodii* var. 'Carol Mackie'
Cranberry cotoneaster	*Cotoneaster apiculatus*
Creeping Oregon grape	*Mahonia repens*
Orchid rockrose	*Cistus purpureus*
Oregon boxwood	*Paxistima myrtifolia*
Oregon grape	*Mahonia aquifolium*
Point Reyes ceanothus	*Ceanothus gloriosus*
Rhododendron	*Rhododendron* spp.
Salal	*Gaultheria shallon*

Deciduous Shrubs and Small Trees

American cranberry	*Viburnum trilobum* 'Compactum'
Blue-mist spirea	*Caryopteris × clandonensis*
Bumald spirea	*Spiraea × bumalda*
Dwarf burning bush	*Euonymus alatus* 'Compactus'
Fernleaf buckthorn	*Rhamnus frangula* 'Asplenifolia'
Flowering currant	*Ribes* species
Hardy shrub rose	*Rosa* species
Lilac	*Syringa* species
Mockorange	*Philadelphus* spp.
Oceanspray	*Holodiscus discolor*
Red osier dogwood	*Cornus sericea*
Rocky Mountain maple	*Acer glabrum*
Russian sage	*Perovskia atriplicifolia*
Serviceberry	*Amelanchier* spp.
Snowberry	*Symphoricarpos albus*
Sumac	*Rhus* species
Tallhedge buckthorn	*Rhamnus frangula* 'Columnaris'

Viburnum or Compact

Vine maple	*Acer circinatum*
Western azalea	*Rhododendron occidentale*
Western sandcherry	*Prunus besseyi*
Western spirea	*Spiraea douglasii*
Willow	*Salix* spp.
Wood's rose	*Rosa woodsii*

CONIFERS

Ponderosa pine	*Pinus ponderosa*
Western larch	*Larix occidentalis*

DECIDUOUS TREES

American sweetgum	*Liquidambar styraciflua*
Amur maple	*Acer ginnala*
Bigleaf maple	*Acer macrophyllum*
Birch	*Betula* species
California sycamore	*Platanus racemosa*
Canada red chokecherry	*Prunus virginiana* 'Schubert'
Chokecherry	*Prunus virginiana*
Common hackberry	*Celtis occidentalis*
Crabapple	*Malus* species
Eastern redbud	*Cercis canadensis*
European beech	*Fagus sylvatica*
Flowering dogwood	*Cornus florida*
Green ash	*Fraxinus pennsylvanica*
Hawthorn	*Crataegus* species
Horse chestnut	*Aesculus hippocastanum*
Kentucky coffee tree	*Gymnocladus diocius*
Mountain alder	*Alnus tenuifolia*
Mountain ash	*Sorbus aucuparia*
Oregon white oak	*Quercus garryana*
Pin oak	*Quercus palustris*
Purple Robe locust	*Robinia pseudoacacia* 'Purple Robe'
Quaking aspen	*Populus tremuloides*
Red alder	*Alnus rubra*
Red maple	*Acer rubrum*
Red oak	*Quercus rubra*
Thornless honeylocust	*Gleditsia triacanthos* var. *inermis* cvs.
Walnut	*Juglans* species
Western catalpa	*Catalpa speciosa*
Western or white ash	*Fraxinus americana*

These plants attract beneficial and pollinator insects.

PERENNIALS

Ajuga	*Ajuga reptans*
Basket of gold	*Aurina saxatalis*
Bearberry or kinnikinnick	*Arctostaphylos uva-ursi*
Caucasica sage	*Artemisia caucasica*
Creeping phylox	*Phxlox subdulata*
Creeping thyme	*Thymus praecox*
Giant flowered soapwort	*Saponaria* × *lempergii*
Green mat penstemon	*Penstemon davidsonii*
Groundcover rose	*Rosa* hybrids
Hardy ice plant	*Delosperma* spp.
Hens and chicks	*Eschevria* spp.
Japanese pachysandra	*Pachysandra terminalis*
Lamb's ear	*Stachys byzantine*
Lily-of-the-valley	*Convallaria majalis*
Mat penstemon	*Penstemon caespitosus*
Mother of thyme	*Thymus serphyllum*
Poppy mallow	*Callirhoe involucrata*
Pussytoes	*Antennaria* spp.
Rock soapwort	*Saponaria ocymoides*
Rockcress	*Arabis* spp.
Silver-edged horehound	*Marrubium rotundifolium*
Snow in summer	*Cerastium tomentosum*
Speedwell	*Veronica* spp.

VINES

Chocolate vine	*Akebia quinata*
Clematis	*Clematis* spp.
Climbing hydrangea	*Hydrangea anomala petiolaris*
Grapes	*Vitis* spp.
Honeysuckle	*Lonicera* spp. and hybrids
Hops vine	*Humulus lupulus*
Kiwi vine	*Actinidia kolmikta*
Matrimony vine	*Lycium barbarum*
Silver lace vine	*Polygonum aubertii*
Sweet autumn clematis	*Clematis terniflora*
Sweet pea	*Lathyrus latifolius*
Trumpet honeysuckle	*Lonicera sempervirens*
Trumpet vine	*Campsis redicans*
Virginia creeper	*Parthenocissus quinquefolia*
Wisteria	*Wisteria* spp.

SHRUBS AND TREES

Aspen	*Populus termuloides*
Birch	*Betula* spp.
Buckthorn	*Rhamnus* spp.
Buffalo berry	*Sheperdia* spp.
Currant	*Ribes* spp.
Lilac	*Syringa vulgaris*
Maple	*Acer* spp.
Mountain mahogany	*Cercis ledifolius*
Serviceberry	*Amelanchier* spp.
Skunkbush sumac	*Rhus tribolata*
Snowberry	*Symphoricarpos* spp.
Western sandcherry	*Prunus basseyi*
Willow	*Salix* spp.

NORTHWEST SEED & NATIVE PLANT COMPANIES

WASHINGTON

Burnt Ridge Nursery
432 Burnt Ridge
Onalaska, WA 98570
(360) 985-2873, FAX (360) 985-0882
www.burntridgenursery.com
Fruit trees including nuts, apples, native fruits, some ornamental trees and shrubs, fruiting groundcovers.

Cloud Mountain Farm Center
6906 Goodwin Road
Everson, WA 98247
(360) 966-5859
www.cloudmountainfarmcenter.org
Fruit trees including cider apples, caneberries, blueberries, grapes, huckleberries, currants, and gooseberries. Rootstock and scion wood.

Ed Hume Seeds
P.O. Box 73160
Puyallup, WA 98373
(253) 435-4414
www.humeseeds.com
Safe Seed Pledge
Carries hundreds of vegetable and flower varieties, all non-GMO, some organic. Selected for short-season and cool-climate areas. Suitable for early or late planting in milder climates.

Filaree Farm
182 Conconully Hwy
Okanogan, WA 98840
(509) 422-6940 (Office)
www.filareefarm.com
Safe Seed Pledge
Seed Types: seed garlic and green manures.
No credit card or online orders.

Fungi Perfecti
P.O. Box 7634
Olympia, WA 98507
(800) 780-9126 (Toll-Free)
www.fungi.com
Gourmet and medicinal mushroom technologies.

Irish Eyes Garden Seeds
5043 Robinson Canyon Rd
Ellensburg, WA 98926
(509) 964-7000 (Office)
(800) 964-9210 (Toll-Free)
www.irisheyesgardenseeds.com
Certified organic
Heirloom seed potatoes, vegetable, flower, and garden seeds

Oregon Native Plant Nurseries (directory)
www.plantnative.org/nd_or.htm

Osborne Seed Company
2428 Old Hwy 99 South Road
Mount Vernon, WA 98273
(360) 424-SEED (7333)
www.osborneseed.com
Safe Seed Pledge
Vegetables, herbs, and flowers. Organic, untreated and pelletized seed available. All varieties are test grown on-site and are available in bulk quantities.

Plants of the Wild
123 Stateline Rd.
Tekoa, WA 99003
(509) 284-2848
www.plantsofthewild.com
Specializes in plants that are native to the Pacific Northwest, including grasses, forbs, shrubs, and trees.

Raintree Nursery
391 Butts Road
Morton, WA 98356
(800) 391-8892
www.raintreenursery.com/home.php
Unusual and Northwest-adapted fruit tree varieties, cane and small bush berries, and ornamental edibles.

Uprising Seeds
2208 Iron St.
Bellingham, WA 98225
(360) 778-3749
www.uprisingorganics.com (no retail location)

Washington Native Plant Nurseries (directory)
www.plantnative.org/nd_wa.htm

CANADA

West Coast Seeds
Warehouse and Office Address
3925 64th Street, RR#1
Delta, British Columbia
Canada, V4K 3N2
(888) 804-8820
www.westcoastseed.com
Safe Seed Pledge
Over 800 varieties of untreated, non-GMO, open-pollinated, certified organic, and hybrid seeds. Sells into the U.S.

OREGON

Abundant Life Seeds
P.O. Box 279
Cottage Grove, OR 97424-0010
(541) 767-9606
www.abundantlifeseeds.com
As of 2013, being offered through Territorial Seed—see listing.

Green Journey Seeds
P.O. Box 38
Veneta, OR 97487
www.poppyswap.com/shop/greenjourneyseeds
Safe Seed Pledge
Medicinal herbs, favorite flowers, and unusual edibles.

Nichols Garden Nursery
1190 No. Pacific Hwy. NE
Albany, OR 97321
(877) 229-8487
www.nicholsgardennursery.com
Safe Seed Pledge
A wide range of unusual herbs and vegetable seeds regionally adapted to the Northwest.

One Green World
W6469 SE 134th Ave
Portland, OR 97236
(877) 353-4028
www.onegreenworld.com
Unusual fruit and nut trees, berries, and fruiting ornamentals.

Territorial Seed Company
P.O. Box 158
Cottage Grove, OR 97424
(800) 626-0866 (Orders)
www.territorialseed.com
Safe Seed Pledge
Produces a wide range of conventional and organic short- and cool-season vegetable, herb, and flower seeds tested in their Oregon test farms. Also hosts Abundant Life Seeds in their catalog.

Victory Seed Co.
P.O. Box 192
Molalla, OR 97038
(503) 829-3126 (Office)
www.victoryseeds.com
Safe Seed Pledge
Rare, open pollinated and heirloom vegetables, herbs, and flower seeds.

*NOTE: The Safe Seed Pledge noted in some entries refers to a group of seed companies that have agreed to the following pledge concerning genetically modified seed:

"Agriculture and seeds provide the basis upon which our lives depend. We must protect this foundation as a safe and genetically stable source for future generations. For the benefit of all farmers, gardeners and consumers who want an alternative, we pledge that we do not knowingly buy or sell genetically engineered seeds or plants. The mechanical transfer of genetic material outside of natural reproductive methods and between genera, families or kingdoms poses great biological risks, as well as economic, political and cultural threats. We feel that genetically-engineered varieties have been insufficiently tested prior to public release. More research and testing are necessary to further assess the potential risks of genetically-engineered seeds. Further, we wish to support agricultural progress that leads to healthier soils, genetically-diverse agricultural ecosystems and ultimately healthy people and communities."

INTERNET RESOURCES

PLANT INFORMATION

Plants for Pollinators in Oregon
ftp://ftp-fc.sc.egov.usda.gov/OR/Technical_Notes/Plant%20
    Materials/PMC13.pdf

USDA Plants Database
www.plants.usda.gov
Good source of natives of some of the plants listed in the Featured
    Plants list.

PLANT DISEASES

Pacific Northwest Plant Disease Management Handbook
www.pnwhandbooks.org/plantdisease

Washington State University Hortsense
www.pep.wsu.edu/hortsense
Home gardener factsheets for managing plant problems with
    Integrated Pest Management (IPM).

INSECTS

Attracting Beneficial Insects to Your Garden
www.grinningplanet.com/2005/04-26/beneficial-insect-natural-
    pest-control-article.htm

Bug Guide
www.bugguide.net/node/view/15740
Online community of naturalists who enjoy learning about
    and sharing our observations of insects, spiders, and other
    related creatures.

Plants for Pollinators in Oregon
ftp://ftp-fc.sc.egov.usda.gov/OR/Technical_Notes/Plant%20
    Materials/PMC13.pdf

A Pocket Guide to Common Pests of Crops and Gardens in the
    Pacific Northwest
www.ipmnet.org/Posters_and_Presentations/Pocket_Guide_
    Natural_Enemies.pdf

WSU Pestsense
pep.wsu.edu/pestsense
Factsheets for managing common indoor pest problems with IPM.

Insect Pest Management Ministry of Agriculture
www.agf.gov.bc.ca/cropprot/entomology.htm
Factsheets on common pests and IPM.

WEEDS

Oregon State Noxious Weed List
www.oregon.gov/ODA/plant/weeds/Pages/statelist2.aspx

PNW Weed Management Handbook
www.pnwhandbooks.org/weed

Washington State Noxious Weed Control Board
www.nwcb.wa.gov

Washington State Noxious Weed List
www.nwcb.wa.gov/nwcb_nox.htm

British Columbia Noxious Weed List
www.agf.gov.bc.ca/cropprot/noxious.htm

EXTENSION AND MASTER GARDENER PROGRAMS

Master Gardener Association of British Columbia
www.mgabc.org

Oregon State University Extension, Master Gardener Program
www.extension.oregonstate.edu

Washington State University Master Gardeners
www.mastergardener.wsu.edu

University of California Cooperative Extension Master
    Gardener Program
www.camastergardeners.ucanr.edu

ORGANIZATIONS

Hardy Plant Society of Oregon
www.hardyplantsociety.org

Hardy Plant Society of Washington
www.hardyplantsocietywa.org

Perennial Plant Association
www.perennialplant.org

Trees Are Good International Society of Arboriculture
www.treesaregood.com

Native Plant Society of British Columbia
www.npsbc.ca

North American Native Plant Societies
www.nanps.org/index.php/resources/native-plant-societies

GARDEN BLOGS

Garden Rant: Uprooting the Gardening World
www.gardenrant.com

North Coast Gardening
www.northcoastgardening.com

Rainy Side Gardeners
www.rainyside.com
Geared specifically toward gardening in the maritime Northwest.

Susan's In the Garden
www.susansinthegarden.blogspot.com
Tips and information for all types of gardening; based in Spokane, WA.

BIBLIOGRAPHY

Alt, David D. and Donald W. Hyndmahn. *Roadside Geology of Oregon*. Mountain Press Publishing Co. (1978)

Alt, David D. and Donald W. Hyndmahn. *Roadside Geology of Washington*. Mountain Press Publishing Co. (1984)

Beck, Alison and Marianne Binetti. *Annuals for Washington and Oregon*. Lone Pine Publishing (2000)

Beck, Alison and Marianne Binetti. *Perennials for Washington and Oregon*. Lone Pine Publishing (2000)

Bennett, Jennifer. *Dryland Gardening*. Firefly Books (2005)

Binetti, Marianne and Don Williamson. *Best Garden Plants for Washington and Oregon*. Lone Pine Publishing (2005)

Brenzel, Kathleen. *Sunset Western Landscaping Book*. Sunset Publishing Corporation (2006)

Creasy, Rosalind. *Edible Landscaping*. Sierra Club Books (2010)

Creeser, Rosemary. *Wildlife-Friendly Plants: Make Your Garden a Haven for Beneficial Insects, Amphibians and Birds*. Firefly Books (2004)

Detweiler, Amy and Stephen Fitzgerald. *Fire-Resistant Plants for Home Landscapes*. Oregon State University, Washington State University, University of Idaho PNW 590 (2006)

DiSabato-Aust, Tracy, Martin Knapp, Stacey Renee Peters, and C. Colston Burrell. *The Well-Designed Mixed Garden: Building Beds and Borders with Trees, Shrubs, Perennials, Annuals, and Bulbs*. Timber Press, Incorporated (2003)

Druse, Ken. *The Natural Habitat Garden*. Timber Press, Incorporated (2004)

Editors of Sunset Books. *Western Garden Book of Edibles: The Complete A-Z Guide to Growing Your Own Vegetables, Herbs, and Fruits*. Oxmoor House (2010)

Editors of Sunset Magazine. *The New Western Garden Book: The Ultimate Gardening Guide*. Oxmoor House (2012)

Editors of Sunset Magazine. *Gardening in the Northwest*. Sunset Publishing Corporation (2003)

Fitzgerald, Tonie et. al. *Landscape Plants for the Inland Northwest*. WSU/Spokane County Extension (2001)

Fitzgerald, Tonie and Michael D. Terrell. *Landscaping with Native Plants for the Inland Northwest*. WSU/Spokane County Extension (2001)

Hill, Lewis and Nancy. *The Flower Gardener's Bible: A Complete Guide to Colorful Blooms All Season Long*. Storey Books (2003)

Hume, Ed. *Gardening With Ed Hume: Northwest Gardening Made Easy*. Sasquatch Books (2003)

Humenick, Muriel and Laura Peters. *Roses for Northern California*. Lone Pine Publishing (2007)

Jackson, Philip L. and Jon Kimerling, Ed. *Atlas of the Pacific Northwest*. Oregon State University Press (2003)

Jalbert, Brad and Laura Peters. *Roses for Washington and Oregon*. Lone Pine Publishing (2003)

James, David. *Beneficial Insects, Spiders, and Other Mini-Creatures in Your Garden: Who They Are and How to Get Them to Stay*. WSU Extension pulication EM067E (2014)

Kruckeberg, Arthur R. *Gardening with Native Plants of the Pacific Northwest*. University of Washington Press (1989)

Link, Russell. *Landscaping For Wildlife in the Pacific Northwest*. University of Washington Press (1999)

Link, Russell. *Living with Wildlife*. University of Washington Press (2004)

Lyons, C.P. *Trees & Shrubs of Washington*. Lone Pine Publishing (1999)

Mass, Cliff. *The Weather of the Pacific Northwest*. University of Washington Press (2008)

Maureen, Gilmer. *The Complete Guide to Northern California Gardening*. Taylor (1994)

Miles, Carol. *Home Vegetable Gardening in Washington*. Washington State University EM057E (2013)

Nichols McGee, Rose Marie and Maggie Stuckey. *McGee & Stuckey's Bountiful Container: Create Container Gardens of Vegetables, Herbs, Fruits, and Edible Flowers*. Workman Publishing Company (2002)

Ondra, Nancy J. and Saxon Holt. *Grasses*. Storey Books (2002)

Orr, Stephen. *Tomorrow's Garden*. Rodale Books (2011)

Prinzing, Debra and Mary Robson. *Washington & Oregon Gardener's Guide*. Cool Springs Press (2004)

Robson, Kathleen, Alice Richter and Marianne Filbert. *Encyclopedia of Northwest Native Plants for Gardens and Landscapes*. Timber Press (2008)

Robson, Mary. *Month-By-Month Gardening In Washington & Oregon*. Cool Springs Press (2005)

Rose, Nancy, Don Selinger, and John Whitman. *Growing Shrubs and Small Trees in Cold Climates*. McGraw-Hill (2000)

Roth, Sally. *The Gardener's Weather Bible: How to Predict and Prepare For Garden Success in Any Kind of Weather*. Rodale Books (2003)

Smith, Charles W.G. *The Weather-Resilient Garden: A Defensive Approach to Planning & Landscaping*. Storey Publishing, LLC (2004)

Smith, Edward C. *The Vegetable Gardener's Bible*. Storey Books (2000)

Tanem, Bob and Don Williamson. *Annuals for Northern California*. Lone Pine Publishing (2002)

Tanem, Bob and Don Williamson. *Gardening Month By Month in Northern California*. Lone Pine Publishing (2004)

Tanem, Bob and Don Williamson. *Perennials for Northern California*. Lone Pine Publishing (2002)

Tanem, Bob and Don Williamson. *Tree and Shrub Gardening For Northern California*. Lone Pine Publishing (2003)

Taylor's Guide to Shrubs. Houghton Mifflin/Chanticleer Press (1987)

Taylor's Guide to Perennials. Houghton Mifflin/Chanticleer Press (1961)

Wingate, Marty. *Big Ideas for Northwest Small Gardens*. Sasquatch Books (2003)

GLOSSARY

Acidic soil: On a soil pH scale of 0 to 14, acidic soil has a pH lower than 7.0. Most garden plants prefer a soil a bit on the acidic side.

Afternoon sun: A garden receiving afternoon sun typically has full sun from 1:00 to 5:00 p.m. daily, with more shade during the morning hours.

Alkaline soil: On a soil pH scale of 0 to 14, alkaline soil has a pH higher than 7.0. Many desert plants thrive in slightly alkaline soils.

Annual: A plant that germinates (sprouts), flowers, and dies within one year or season (spring, summer, winter, or fall) is an annual.

***Bacillus thuringiensis* (Bt):** Bt is an organic pest control based on naturally occurring soil bacteria, often used to control harmful caterpillars such as cutworms, leaf rollers, and webworms.

Balled and burlapped (B&B): This phrase describes plants that have been grown in field nursery rows, dug up with their soil intact, wrapped with burlap, and tied with twine. Most of the plants sold balled and burlapped are large evergreen plants and deciduous trees.

Bare root: Bare-root plants are those that are shipped dormant, without being planted in soil or having soil around their roots. Roses are often shipped bare root.

Beneficial insects: These insects perform valuable services such as pollination and pest control. Ladybugs, soldier beetles, and some bees are examples.

Biennial: A plant that blooms during its second year and then dies is a biennial.

Bolting: This is a process when a plant switches from leaf growth to producing flowers and seeds. Bolting often occurs quite suddenly and is usually undesirable, because the plant usually dies shortly after bolting.

Bow rake: This tool has a long handle and rigid tines at the bottom. It is great for moving a variety of garden debris, such as soil, mulch, leaves, and pebbles.

Branch collar: In trees, a branch collar is a ridged area that denotes the point where a branch connects to its parent branch or to the trunk.

Brown materials: A part of a well-balanced compost pile, brown materials include high-carbon materials such as brown leaves and grass, woody plant stems, dryer lint, and sawdust.

Bud: The bud is an undeveloped shoot nestled between the leaf and the stem that will eventually produce a flower or plant branch.

Bulb: A bulb is a plant with a large, rounded underground storage organ formed by the plant stem and leaves. Examples are tulips, daffodils, and hyacinths. Bulbs that flower in spring are typically planted in fall.

Bush: *See* shrub.

Cane: A stem on a fruit shrub; usually blackberry or raspberry stems are called canes, but blueberry stems can also be referred to as canes.

Central leader: The term for the center trunk of a tree.

Chilling hours: Hours when the air temperature is below 45° Fahrenheit; chilling hours are related to fruit production.

Common name: A name that is generally used to identify a plant in a particular region, as opposed to its botanical name, which is standard throughout the world; for example, the common name for Echinacea purpurea is "purple coneflower."

Contact herbicide: This type of herbicide kills only the part of the plant that it touches, such as the leaves or the stems.

Container: Any pot or vessel that is used for planting; containers can be ceramic, clay, steel, or plastic—or a teacup, bucket, or barrel.

Container garden: This describes a garden that is created primarily by growing plants in containers instead of in the ground.

Container grown: This describes a plant that is grown, sold, and shipped while in a pot.

Cool-season annual: This is a flowering plant, such as snapdragon or pansy, that thrives during cooler months.

Cool-season vegetable: This is a vegetable, such as spinach, broccoli, and peas, that thrives during cooler months.

Cover crop: These plants are grown specifically to enrich the soil, prevent erosion, suppress weeds, and control pests and diseases.

Cross-pollinate: This describes the transfer of pollen from one plant to another plant.

Dappled shade: This is bright shade created by high tree branches or tree foliage, where patches of sunlight and shade intermingle.

Day-neutral plant: A plant that flowers when it reaches a certain size, regardless of the day length, is a day-neutral plant.

Deadhead: To remove dead flowers in order to encourage further bloom and prevent the plant from going to seed is to deadhead.

Deciduous plant: A plant that loses its leaves seasonally, typically in fall or early winter, is deciduous.

Diatomaceous earth: A natural control for snails, slugs, flea beetles, and other garden pests, diatomaceous earth consists of ground-up fossilized remains of sea creatures.

Dibber: A tool consisting of a pointed wooden stick with a handle. Used for poking holes in the ground so seedlings, seeds, and small bulbs can be planted.

Divide: A technique consisting of digging up clumping perennials, separating the roots, and replanting. Dividing plants encourages vigorous growth and is typically performed in the spring or fall.

Dormancy: The period when plants stop growing in order to conserve energy, this happens naturally and seasonally, usually in winter.

Drip irrigation: Drip irrigation, also known as micro-irrigation, is an irrigation method that allows water to drip slowly to the roots of plants, either onto the soil surface or directly onto the root zone.

Drip line: The ground area under the outer circumference of tree branches, this is where most of the tree's roots that absorb water and nutrients are found.

Drought tolerance: Drought tolerance refers to the degree to which a plant is adapted to arid or drought conditions.

Dwarf: In the context of fruit gardening, a dwarf fruit tree is a tree that grows no taller than 10 feet tall and is usually a dwarf as a result of the rootstock of the tree.

East of the Cascade Mountains: Region to the east of the crest of the Cascades Mountains in Oregon and Washington.

Evergreen: A plant that keeps its leaves year-round instead of dropping them seasonally is evergreen.

Floating row covers: Lightweight fabric that can be used to protect plants from pests. Usually white in color.

Floricane: A second-year cane on a blackberry or raspberry plant that will produce fruit.

Flower stalk: The stem that supports the flower and elevates it so that insects can reach the flower and pollinate it is the flower stalk.

Four-inch pot: The 4-by-4-inch pots that many annuals and small perennials are sold in. Four-inch pots can also be sold in flats of eighteen or twenty.

Frost: Ice crystals that form when the temperature falls below freezing (32° Fahrenheit) create frost.

Full sun: Areas of the garden that receive direct sunlight for six to eight hours a day or more, with no shade, are in full sun.

Fungicide: This describes a chemical compound used to control fungal diseases.

Gallon container: A standard nursery-sized container for plants, a gallon container is roughly equivalent to a gallon container of milk.

Garden fork: A garden implement with a long handle and short tines; use a garden fork for loosening and turning soil.

Garden lime: This soil amendment lowers soil acidity and raises the pH.

Garden soil: The existing soil in a garden bed; it is generally evaluated by its nutrient content and texture. Garden soil is also sold as a bagged item at garden centers and home improvement stores.

Germination: This is the process by which a plant emerges from a seed or a spore.

Granular sulfur: Pure, granulated sulfur used as a soil amendment to lower the pH of soil. It makes the soil more acidic.

Grafted tree: This is a tree composed of two parts: the top, or scion, which bears fruit; and the bottom, or rootstock.

Graft union: This is the place on a fruit tree trunk where the rootstock and the scion have been joined.

Granular fertilizer: This type of fertilizer comes in a dry, pellet-like form rather than a liquid or powder.

Germinating mix: Typically a soilless blend of perlite, vermiculite, peat moss, and other ingredients, seed-starting mix is specifically formulated for growing plants from seed. Also called seed-starting mix.

Grass clippings: The parts of grass that are removed when mowing, clippings are a valuable source of nitrogen for the lawn or the compost pile.

Green materials: An essential element in composting that includes grass clippings, kitchen scraps, and manure and provides valuable nitrogen in the pile, green materials are high in nitrogen.

Hand pruners: An important hand tool that consists of two sharp blades that perform a scissoring motion, these are used for light pruning, clipping, and cutting.

Hardening off: This is the process of slowly acclimating seedlings and young plants grown in an indoor environment to the outdoors.

Hardiness zone map: This map lists average annual minimum temperature ranges of a particular area. This information is helpful in determining appropriate plants for the garden. North America is divided into eleven separate hardiness zones.

Hedging: This is the practice of trimming a line of plants to create a solid mass for privacy or garden definition.

Heirloom: A plant that was more commonly grown pre-World War II.

Hoe: A long-handled garden tool with a short, narrow, flat steel blade, it is used for breaking up hard soil and removing weeds.

Hose breaker: This device screws onto the end of a garden hose to disperse the flow of water from the hose.

Host plant: A plant grown to feed caterpillars that will eventually morph into butterflies is called a host plant.

Hybrid: Plants produced by crossing two genetically different plants, hybrids often have desirable characteristics such as disease resistance.

Inflorescence: A cluster of flowers that grows at the top of a stem; the flowers may or may not be attached by means of a short stem.

Insecticide: This substance is used for destroying or controlling insects that are harmful to plants. Insecticides are available in organic and synthetic forms.

Irrigation: A system of watering the landscape, irrigation can be an in-ground automatic system, soaker or drip hoses, drip, micro-spray heads or hand-held hoses with nozzles.

Jute twine: A natural-fiber twine, jute is used for gently staking plants or tying them to plant supports.

Kneeling pad: A padded, weather-resistant cushion used for protecting knees while performing garden tasks such as weeding and planting.

Landscape fabric: A porous synthetic material laid on the soil surface that allows water and air into the soil but blocks weed emergence.

Larva: The immature stage of an insect that goes through complete metamorphosis; caterpillars are butterfly or moth larvae.

Larvae: This is the plural of larva.

Leaf rake: A long-handled rake with flexible tines on the head, a leaf rake is used for easily and efficiently raking leaves into piles.

Liquid fertilizer: Plant fertilizer in a liquid form, some types need to be mixed with water, and some types are ready to use from the bottle.

Long-day plant: Plants that flower when the days are longer than their critical photoperiod, long-day plants typically flower in early summer, when the days are still getting longer.

Loppers: One of the largest manual gardening tools, use loppers for pruning branches of 1 to 3 inches in diameter with a scissoring motion.

Micro-spray systems: Micro-spray systems are low-output, adjustable sprayer systems with heads that emit a spray pattern that covers up to 10 feet wide.

Morning sun: Areas of the garden that have an eastern exposure and receive direct sun in the morning hours are in morning sun.

Mulch: Any type of material that is spread over the soil surface around the base of plants to suppress weeds and retain soil moisture is mulch.

Nematode: Microscopic, wormlike organisms that live in the soil, some nematodes are beneficial, while others are harmful.

Native plant: Native plants are plants that have been growing in a region prior to European settlement. In the Northwest, European/American settlement began in the early 1800s.

Naturalized: Plants that are introduced into an area, as opposed to being native to it, are said to be naturalized.

Nectar plant: Flowers that produce nectar that attract and feed butterflies and hummingbirds, encouraging a succession of blooms throughout the season.

New wood (new growth): The new growth on plants, it is characterized by a greener, more tender form than older, woodier growth.

Nozzle: A device that attaches to the end of a hose and disperses water through a number of small holes; the resulting spray covers a wider area.

Old wood: Old wood is growth that is more than one year old. Some fruit plants produce on old wood. If you prune these plants in spring before they flower and fruit, you will cut off the wood that will produce fruit.

Organic: This term describes products derived from naturally occurring materials instead of materials synthesized in a lab.

Part shade: Areas of the garden that receive three to six hours of sun a day are in part shade. Plants requiring part shade will often require protection from the more intense afternoon sun, either from tree leaves or from a building.

Part sun: Areas of the garden that receive three to six hours of sun a day are in part sun. Although the term is often used interchangeably with "part shade," a "part sun" designation places greater emphasis on the minimal sun requirements.

Perennial: A plant that lives for more than two years is a perennial. Examples include trees, shrubs, and some flowering plants.

Pesticide: A substance used for destroying or controlling insects that are harmful to plants. Pesticides are available in organic and synthetic forms.

pH: A figure designating the acidity or the alkalinity of garden soil, pH is measured on a scale of 1 to 14, with 7.0 being neutral.

Pinch: This is a method to remove unwanted plant growth with your fingers, promoting bushier growth and increased blooming.

Pitchfork: A hand tool with a long handle and sharp metal prongs, a pitchfork is typically used for moving loose material such as mulch or hay.

Plant label: This label or sticker on a plant container provides a description of the plant and information on its care and growth habits.

Pollination: The transfer of pollen for fertilization from the male pollen-bearing structure (stamen) to the female structure (pistil), usually by wind, bees, butterflies, moths, or hummingbirds; this process is required for fruit production.

Potting soil: A mixture used to grow flowers, herbs, and vegetables in containers, potting soil provides proper drainage and extra nutrients for healthy growth.

Powdery mildew: A fungal disease characterized by white powdery spots on plant leaves and stems, this disease is worse during times of drought or when plants have poor air circulation.

Pre-emergent herbicide: This weedkiller works by preventing weed seeds from sprouting.

Primocane: A first-year cane on a blackberry or raspberry plant, which doesn't produce fruit.

Pruning: This is a garden task in which a variety of hand tools are used to remove dead or overgrown branches to increase plant fullness and health.

Pruning saw: This hand tool for pruning smaller branches and limbs features a long, serrated blade with an elongated handle.

Push mower: A lawn mower that is propelled by the user rather than a motor, typically having between five to eight steel blades that turn and cut as the mower is pushed.

Rain shadow: A rain shadow is a dry area on the lee side of a mountainous area. The mountains block the passage of rain-producing weather systems and cast a "shadow" of dryness behind them.

Reel mower: A mower in which the blades spin vertically with a scissoring motion to cut grass blades.

Rhizome: An underground horizontal stem that grows side shoots, a rhizome is similar to a bulb.

Rootball: The network of roots and soil clinging to a plant when it is lifted out of the ground is the rootball.

Root flare: The point at which the trunk of a tree flares out to form the root system. Trees should be planted no deeper than this point.

Rootstock: The bottom part of a grafted fruit tree, rootstocks are often used to create dwarf fruit trees, impart pest or disease resistance, or make a plant more cold hardy.

Rotary spreader: A garden tool that distributes seed and herbicides in a pattern wider than the base of the spreader.

Runner: A stem sprouting from the center of a strawberry plant, a runner produces fruit in its second year.

Scaffold branch: This horizontal branch emerges almost perpendicular to the trunk.

Scientific name: This two-word identification system consists of the genus and species of a plant, such as *Acer circinatum*.

Scion: The top, fruit-bearing part of a grafted fruit tree is the scion.

Scissors: A two-bladed hand tool great for cutting cloth, paper, twine, and other lightweight materials, scissors are a basic garden tool.

Seed packet: The package in which vegetable and flower seeds are sold, it typically includes growing instructions, a planting chart, and harvesting information.

Self-fruitful A plant that does not require cross-pollination from another plant in order to produce fruit is self-fertile.

Semidwarf: A fruit tree grafted onto a rootstock that restricts growth of the tree to one-half to two-thirds of its natural size is semidwarf.

Shade: Garden shade is the absence of any direct sunlight in a given area, usually due to tree foliage or building shadows.

Short-day plant: Flowering when the length of day is shorter than its critical photoperiod, short-day plants typically bloom during fall, winter, or early spring.

Shovel: A handled tool with a broad, flat blade and slightly upturned sides, used for moving soil and other garden materials; a shovel is a basic garden tool.

Shredded hardwood mulch: A mulch consisting of shredded wood that interlocks, resisting washout, and suppressing weeds; hardwood mulch can change soil pH.

Shrub: This woody plant is distinguished from a tree by its multiple trunks and branches and its shorter height of less than 15 feet tall.

Shrub rake: This long-handled rake with a narrow head fits easily into tight spaces between plants.

Side-dress: To sprinkle slow-release fertilizer along the side of a plant row or plant stem is to side-dress.

Slow-release fertilizer: This form of fertilizer releases nutrients at a slower rate throughout the season, requiring less frequent applications.

Soaker hose: This is an efficient watering system in which a porous hose, usually made from recycled rubber, allows water to seep out around plant roots.

Soil knife: This garden knife with a sharp, serrated edge, is used for cutting twine, plant roots, turf, and other garden materials.

Soil test: An analysis of a soil sample, this determines the level of nutrients (to identify deficiencies) and detects pH.

Spur: This is a small, compressed, fruit-bearing branch on a fruit tree.

Standard: Describing a fruit tree grown on its own seedling rootstock or a nondwarfing rootstock, this is the largest of the three sizes of fruit trees.

Succulent: A type of plant that stores water in its leaves, stems, and roots and is acclimated for arid climates and soil conditions.

Sucker: The odd growth from the base of a tree or a woody plant, often caused by stress, this also refers to sprouts from below the graft of a rose or fruit tree. Suckers divert energy away from the desirable tree growth and should be removed.

Summer annual: Annuals that thrive during the warmer months of the growing season.

Systemic herbicide: This type of weedkiller is absorbed by the plant's roots and taken into the roots to destroy all parts of the plant.

Thinning: This is the practice of removing excess seedlings (usually vegetables) so the remaining plants have enough space to grow and develop. It also refers to the practice of removing fruits while still small from fruit trees so the remaining fruits can grow larger.

Top-dress: To spread fertilizer on top of the soil (usually around fruit trees or vegetables) is to top-dress.

Transplants: Plants that are grown in one location and then moved to and replanted in another; seeds started indoors and nursery plants are two examples.

Tree: This woody perennial plant typically consists of a single trunk with multiple lateral branches.

Tree canopy: This is the upper layer of growth, consisting of the tree's branches and leaves.

Tropical plant: This is a plant that is native to a tropical region of the world, and thus acclimated to a warm, humid climate and not hardy to frost.

Trowel: This shovel-like hand tool is used for digging or moving small amounts of soil.

Turf: Grass and the surface layer of soil that is held together by its roots.

Variegated: The appearance of differently colored areas on plant leaves, usually white, yellow, or a brighter green.

Vegetable: A plant or part of a plant that is used for food.

Warm-season vegetable: This is a vegetable that thrives during the warmer months. Examples are tomatoes, okra, and peppers. These vegetables do not tolerate frost.

Water sprout: This vertical shoot emerges from a scaffold branch. It is usually nonfruiting and undesirable.

Weed and feed: A product containing both a herbicide for weed control and a fertilizer for grass growth.

Weeping: A growth habit in plants that features drooping or downward curving branches.

West of the Cascade Mountains: Region to the west of the crest of the Cascades Mountains in Oregon and Washington.

Wheat straw: These dry stalks of wheat, which are used for mulch, retain soil moisture and suppress weeds.

Wood chips: Small pieces of wood made by cutting or chipping, wood chips are used as mulch in the garden.

CONVERSIONS

METRIC EQUIVALENT

Inches (in.)	1/64	1/32	1/25	1/16	1/8	1/4	3/8	2/5	1/2	5/8	3/4	7/8	1	2	3	4	5	6	7	8	9	10	11	12	36	39.4
Feet (ft.)																								1	3	3 1/12
Yards (yd.)																									1	1 1/12
Millimeters (mm)	0.40	0.79	1	1.59	3.18	6.35	9.53	10	12.7	15.9	19.1	22.2	25.4	50.8	76.2	101.6	127	152	178	203	229	254	279	305	914	1,000
Centimeters (cm)					0.95	1	1.27	1.59	1.91	2.22	2.54	5.08	7.62	10.16	12.7	15.2	17.8	20.3	22.9	25.4	27.9	30.5	91.4	100		
Meters (m)																						.30	.91	1.00		

CONVERTING MEASUREMENTS

TO CONVERT:	TO:	MULTIPLY BY:
Inches	Millimeters	25.4
Inches	Centimeters	2.54
Feet	Meters	0.305
Yards	Meters	0.914
Miles	Kilometers	1.609
Square inches	Square centimeters	6.45
Square feet	Square meters	0.093
Square yards	Square meters	0.836
Cubic inches	Cubic centimeters	16.4
Cubic feet	Cubic meters	0.0283
Cubic yards	Cubic meters	0.765
Pints (U.S.)	Liters	0.473 (Imp. 0.568)
Quarts (U.S.)	Liters	0.946 (Imp. 1.136)
Gallons (U.S.)	Liters	3.785 (Imp. 4.546)
Ounces	Grams	28.4
Pounds	Kilograms	0.454
Tons	Metric tons	0.907

TO CONVERT:	TO:	MULTIPLY BY:
Millimeters	Inches	0.039
Centimeters	Inches	0.394
Meters	Feet	3.28
Meters	Yards	1.09
Kilometers	Miles	0.621
Square centimeters	Square inches	0.155
Square meters	Square feet	10.8
Square meters	Square yards	1.2
Cubic centimeters	Cubic inches	0.061
Cubic meters	Cubic feet	35.3
Cubic meters	Cubic yards	1.31
Liters	Pints (U.S.)	2.114 (Imp. 1.76)
Liters	Quarts (U.S.)	1.057 (Imp. 0.88)
Liters	Gallons (U.S.)	0.264 (Imp. 0.22)
Grams	Ounces	0.035
Kilograms	Pounds	2.2
Metric tons	Tons	1.1

CONVERTING TEMPERATURES

Convert degrees Fahrenheit (F) to degrees Celsius (C) by following this simple formula: Subtract 32 from the Fahrenheit temperature reading. Then multiply that number by 5/9. For example, 77°F - 32 = 45. 45 × 5/9 = 25°C.

To convert degrees Celsius to degrees Fahrenheit, multiply the Celsius temperature reading by 9/5, then add 32. For example, 25°C × 9/5 = 45. 45 + 32 = 77°F.

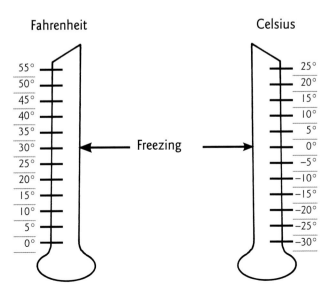

BOTANICAL INDEX

COMMON NAME INDEX

PHOTO CREDITS

NOTES

_____

_____

_____

_____

_____

_____

_____

_____

_____

_____

_____

_____

_____

_____

MEET PAT MUNTS & SUSAN MULVIHILL

Pat **Munts** of Spokane, Washington, is the small-farm and acreage coordinator for WSU Spokane County Extension and the Spokane Conservation District. Pat advises small-farm producers and landowners on how to manage their land, crops, animals, and businesses. She also serves as a regional director for the Garden Writers Association, a national organization of professional communicators in the lawn and garden industry. As a freelance garden writer, Pat has shared her gardening experiences and knowledge as a freelance columnist for the *Pacific Northwest Inlander*, *The Spokesman-Review* "Voices" section, and as the eastern Washington editor of Master Gardener magazine. On the national level, Pat has written for *GreenPrints* and *The American Gardener*. Pat and her husband, Steven, love to garden on their Spokane Valley property. This is Pat's first book.

Susan **Mulvihill,** also of Spokane, Washington, is a garden columnist for the Sunday edition of *The Spokesman-Review*, *Master Gardener* magazine, and author of the blog "Susan's in the Garden." She is also a garden photographer and member of the Garden Writers Association. In the late 1970s, she and her husband, Bill, moved from southern California to Spokane, where they live on five acres. While there's plenty of room to grow a wide variety of edibles, perennials, and other ornamentals, Susan's biggest challenge was learning what would grow in her new surroundings. Susan is known for her down-to-earth approach to teaching and writing that appeals to beginning and experienced gardeners alike. Her humor and enthusiasm for gardening have gained her a wide following over the years. This is Susan's first book, and her blog can be found at susansinthegarden.blogspot.com.